高 等 学 校 教 材

生物工程 生物技术 专业英语

大学英语专业阅读教材编委会组织编写

华东理工大学　邬行彦　储炬　宫衡　编

浙江大学　朱自强　主审

化 学 工 业 出 版 社

·北　京·

图书在版编目（CIP）数据

生物工程/生物技术专业英语/邬行彦等编. —北京：化学
工业出版社，1999（2024.1 重印）
高等学校教材
ISBN 978-7-5025-2631-3

Ⅰ．生… Ⅱ．邬… Ⅲ．①生物工程-英语-高等学校-教材
②生物技术-英语-高等学校-教材 Ⅳ．H31

中国版本图书馆 CIP 数据核字（1999）第 33557 号

责任编辑：赵玉清　徐世峰　　　　　　　　　装帧设计：田彦文
责任校对：蒋　宇

出版发行：化学工业出版社（北京市东城区青年湖南街 13 号　邮政编码 100011）
印　　装：大厂聚鑫印刷有限责任公司
787mm×1092mm　1/16　印张 19　字数 445 千字　2024 年 1 月北京第 1 版第 24 次印刷

购书咨询：010-64518888　　　　　　售后服务：010-64518899
网　　址：http://www.cip.com.cn
凡购买本书，如有缺损质量问题，本社销售中心负责调换。

定　　价：38.00 元

全国部分高校化工类及相关专业
大学英语专业阅读教材编审委员会

前　言

　　组织编审出版系列的专业英语教材，是许多院校多年来共同的愿望。在高等教育面向 21 世纪的改革中，学生基本素质和实际工作能力的培养受到了空前重视。对非英语专业的学生而言，英语水平和能力的培养不仅是文化素质的重要部分，在很大程度上也是能力的补充和延伸。在此背景下，教育部（原国家教委）几次组织会议研究加强外语教学问题，并制定有关规范，使外语教学更加受到重视。教材是教学的基本要素之一，与基础英语相比，专业英语教学的教材问题此时显得尤为突出。

　　国家主管部门的重视和广大院校的呼吁引起了化学工业出版社的关注，他们及时地与原化工部教育主管部门和全国化工类及相关专业教学指导委员会请示协商后，组织全国十余所院校成立了大学英语专业阅读教材编委会。在经过必要的调研后，根据学校需求，编委会优先从各校教学（交流）讲义中确定选题，同时组织力量开展编审工作。本套教材涉及的专业主要包括化学工程与工艺、石油化工、机械工程、信息工程、生产过程自动化、应用化学及精细化工、生物工程、环境工程、制药工程、材料科学与工程、化工商贸等。

　　专业英语是学生完成了两年基础英语学习后的一门后继课程。《大学英语专业阅读阶段教学基本要求（试行）》（1996）（以下简称《基本要求》）提出的目的是"通过指导学生阅读有关专业的英语书刊和文献，使他们进一步提高阅读和翻译英语科技资料的能力，并能以英语为工具获取专业所需的信息"。在科技领域，英语的重要性日益突出，生物工程领域尤为如此：重要的有关生物工程的期刊，都要求以英语发表；重要的国际会议都以英语为工作语言。

　　华东理工大学生化工程系在于接芸老师的领导和主持下，在 90 年代初即开始重视专业英语教材的建设，组织教师选编教材，注意内容广泛、系统覆盖整个专业，语言规范、体裁文笔多样，经过几次比较试用，选择了几本科普原版书籍，编写了词汇表和注释。学生反映较好，英语能力经调查也有较大提高。

　　1996 年化学工业出版社曾在几所高校中，对专业英语的编写工作进行过问卷调查。调查结果主要有三点：①编写教材的原则应有利于学生通过专业知识学英语；②教材内容不求新，但应有代表性，且覆盖面宽，以便于学生扩大专业词汇量；③课文难度应相当于科普读物，且略难于科普读物。我们觉得这三点意见提得正确、中肯，纠正了我们长期以来对专业外语教材的模糊认识。由于我们都是专业教师，很自然地看重于专业知识，而忽视语言知识。由此，我们对原教材作了较大修改，精简了一些有关近代生物工程的部分，但保留了专业的基本内容，使篇幅压缩在可允许的范围内，并重点加强了科技英语的语言基础和应用能力的培养，努力把英语与专业结合起来，以专业为背景，分析科技英语的各种表示方法。修改后的教材有如下特点。

1. 均选自原版英文科普书籍

（1）第1、3、4、5章选自J. E. Smith著"Biotechnology Principles"一书，1985年Van Nostrand Reinhold公司出版。该书属科普读物，英语规范，内容全面，涉及生物工程的主要内容。

（2）第2、6、7、8、9章选自J. D. Bu'Lock和B. Kristiansen主编"Basic Biotechnology"一书：1987年Academic Press出版，也是一本科普书，但内容比上一本稍深，各章由不同作者编写，文笔各异。第一本书没有生物化学方面的内容，检测仪表的叙述过于简单；第二本书的第2章和第7章补充了第一本的不足，并介绍了较新的动植物细胞培养的技术（第8、9章）。

2. 提高阅读理解能力

培养阅读理解能力是《基本要求》规定的目的之一，为此，本教材采取的措施有：①将难句作为英译中习题，并要求从文法上进行句子分析；②对难理解的关键词，作为习题要求给出英语解释；③介绍必要的专业背景知识。经验表明，学生对课文不能理解或理解不深，往往是缺乏有关专业背景的缘故。由于学生在第5学期还未接触到专业，为帮助理解课文，给出科普性质的注释（Notes）共32条。同时各章还附有理解题（Comprehension），题目内容覆盖整个章节，且难度适中，主要在于督促学生阅读，检查对专业内容理解的程度。

3. 包含了科技英语中主要的语法，句和词与词组的用法

所有语法及词的用法均在课文中出现时作出注释，或结合课文以习题的形式提出，达到提高语言基础的目的。这些内容汇总在附录3中，便于查找。

4. 重视词汇，书后附有详细的词汇表

全书课文约含10万字词，能在课堂上讲授的约6～7万（按每学时讲解800词，总学时数为72～90计算），即有约1/3的课文需学生在课外自学，而生物工程作为一门新兴学科，是几门学科的交叉，词汇范围广，分布在各类字典。为帮助学生自学查阅，文后附有详尽的词汇表，并注有音标和相应的页码和行次。对意义易混淆生词，除附英语解释外，还适当附同义词，以扩大词汇，但不包括大学英语大纲1～4级词汇。书末附有总词汇表，共计约1200个条目，符合《基本要求》的规定。为帮助学生记忆生词，了解前缀、后缀和构词成分，附录1和附录2分别列举书中遇到的常用前、后缀和化学、化工、生物方面的前、后缀。

5. 重视写作能力的培养

写作能力的培养主要依赖于实践，本书的大量习题都选自专业文献，选择科技论文摘要、引言或写作中所需表达的一些实验操作、装置和讨论方式，且文字较规范的译成中文，要求学生重新译成英文。书末还附有一些中译英习题，可供教师选用。

　　本书承浙江大学朱自强教授在百忙中审校了全书，提出了宝贵的意见；华东理工大学外语系周志培教授审阅了有关语法方面的注释，并提出了一些修改意见；华东理工大学专业英语教学指导委员会前任主任朱思明教授对本书给予关注并提出了一些意见；对此，我们一并表示深切的谢意。

　　本书不仅得到化学工业出版社和华东理工大学教务处的大力支持，还得到大学英语阅读教材编审委员会主任委员华东理工大学朱炳辰教授和副主任委员华南理工大学钟理教授的关心和帮助，我们也表示诚挚的谢意。

　　本书可作为生物工程、生物技术专业英语的教材，内容涉及整个生物工程领域，相当于专业概论，也可作为生物工程技术人员学习英语或其他科技人员了解生物工程的入门参考书。

　　本书的编写工作历经数年，在结合多年的教学实践的基础上，参阅了大量科技英语和专业方面书刊，但由于生物工程领域宽，学科面广，以及限于作者水平，错误之处在所难免，还望读者指正，不胜感谢。

编　者
一九九九年五月

目　　录

Chapter 1 Introduction

1.1 The nature of biotechnology

Biotechnology is an area of applied bioscience and technology which involves the practical application of biological organisms, or their subcellular components to manufacturing and service industries and to environmental management[①]. Biotechnology utilizes bacteria, yeasts, fungi, algae, plant cells or cultured mammalian cells as constituents of industrial processes. Successful application of biotechnology will result only[②] from the integration of a multiplicity of scientific disciplines and technologies, including microbiology, biochemistry, genetics, molecular biology, chemistry and chemical and process engineering.

Biotechnological processes will normally involve the production of cells or biomass, and the achievement of desired chemical transformations. The latter may be further subdivided into:

(a) formation of a desired end product (e. g. enzymes, antibiotics, organic acids, steroids);

(b) decomposition of a given starting material (e. g. sewage disposal, destruction of industrial wastes or oil spillages).

The reactions of biotechnological processes can be catabolic, in which complex compounds are broken down to simpler ones (glucose to ethanol), or anabolic or biosynthetic, whereby simple molecules are built up into more complex ones (antibiotic synthesis). Catabolic reactions are usually exergonic whereas anabolic reactions are normally endergonic.

Biotechnology includes fermentation processes (ranging from beers and wines to bread, cheese, antibiotics and vaccines), water and waste treatment, parts of food technology, and an increasing range of novel applications ranging from biomedical to metal recovery from low grade ores. Because of its versatility, biotechnology will exert a major impact in many industrial processes and in theory almost all organic materials could be produced by biotechnological methods. Predictions of future worldwide market potential for biotechnological products in the year 2000 have been estimated at nearly US $ 65bn (Table 1. 1). However, it must also be appreciated that many important new bio-products will still be synthesized chemically from models derived from existing biological molecules, e. g. , new drugs based on the interferons[③]. Thus the interface between bioscience and chemistry and its relationship to biotechnology must be broadly interpreted.

A high proportion of the techniques used in biotechnology tend to be more economic ,

2

less energy demanding[④] and safer than current traditional industrial processes and for most processes the residues are biodegradable and non-toxic. In the long term biotechnology offers a means of solving some major world problems, in particular those related to medicine, food production, pollution control and the development of new energy sources.

Table 1. 1   Growth potential for worldwide biotechnological markets by the year 2000

Market sector	$ (million)
Energy	16 350
Foods	12 655
Chemicals	10 550
Health care(pharmaceuticals)	9080
Agriculture	8546
Metal recovery	4570
Pollution control	100
Other(i. e. unexpected developments)	3000
Total	64 851

From T. A. Sheets Co. (1983). *Biotechnology Bulletin* November.

1. 2   Historical evolution of biotechnology

Contrary to popular belief biotechnology is not a new pursuit but in reality dates far back into history. In practice, four major developmental phases can be identified in arriving at modern biotechnological systems.

Biotechnological production of foods and beverages   Activities such as baking, brewing and wine making are known to date back several millenia; the ancient Sumarians and Babylonians were drinking beer by 6000 B. C. , the Egyptians were baking leavened bread by 4000 B. C. while wine was known in the Near East by the time of the book of Genesis. The recognition that these processes were being affected by living organisms, yeasts, was not formulated until the 17th century, by Anton van Leeuwenhoek. Definitive proof of the fermentative abilities of these minute organisms came from the seminal studies of Pasteur between 1857 and 1876. Pasteur can justifiably be considered as the father of biotechnology.

Other microbially based processes such as the production of fermented milk products, e. g. cheeses and yogurts, and various oriental foods, e. g. soy sauce, tempeh etc. , can equally claim distant ancestry. Of more recent introduction is mushroom cultivation which probably dates back many hundreds of years for Japanese shii-ta-ke cultivation and about 300 years for the *Agaricus* mushroom now widely cultivated throughout the temperate world.

It cannot be ascertained whether these microbial processes arose by accidental observation or by intuitive experimentation but their further and continued development were early examples of man's abilities to use the vital activities of organisms for his own needs. In more recent times, just as these processes have become more reliant on advanced technology, their contribution to world economy has equally increased out of all proportion to their humble origins.

Biotechnological processes initially developed under non-sterile conditions Many important industrial compounds such as ethanol, acetic acid, organic acids, butanol and acetone were being produced by the end of the 19th century by microbial fermentation procedures that were open to the environment; the control of contaminating micro-organisms was achieved by careful manipulation of the ecological environment and *not* by complicated engineering practices. However, with the arrival of the petroleum age in which these compounds could be produced more cheaply from the by-products of petroleum production, most of these emerging industries were eclipsed. Escalation of oil prices in recent years has lead to a re-examination of the early fermentation procedures with a view to a return to commercial production. Together with the previously mentioned food fermentations these fermentation practices are relatively simple and can be run on a large scale.

Other outstanding examples of non-sterile biotechnology are waste water treatment and municipal composting of solid wastes. Microorganisms have long been exploited for purposes of decomposing and detoxifying human sewage and, to a lesser extent, in the treatment of industrial toxic wastes such as those from the chemicals industry. Biotechnological treatment of waste waters represents by far the largest (but least recognised) fermentation capacity practised throughout the world (Table 1.2)[5].

Table 1.2 Total UK fermentation capacity

Product	Total capacity (m³)
Waste water	2800000
Beer	128000
Baker's yeast	19000
Antibiotics	10000
Cheese	3000
Bread	700

From Dunnill (1981).

The introduction of sterility to biotechnological processes A new direction in biotechnology came in the 1940s with the introduction of complicated engineering techniques to the mass cultivation of micro-organisms to ensure that the particular biological process could proceed with the exclusion of contaminating microorganisms. Thus by prior sterilization of the medium and the bioreactor and with engineering provision for the exclusion of incoming contaminants only the chosen biocatalyst was present in the reactor. Examples of such products, which represent an increasing volume of biotechnological activity, include antibiotics, amino acids, organic acids, enzymes, steroids, polysaccharides and vaccines. Most of these processes are complicated, expensive and suitable only for high value products. Although many of the products are produced in relatively large quantities they are still dwarfed in volume and financial returns by the older systems used in food and beverage biotechnology (Table 1.3).

New dimensions and possibilities for biotechnological industries Within the last decade there have been outstanding developments in molecular biology and process control which have created new and exciting opportunities not only to create new dimensions but

Table 1. 3   UK fermentation industry sales

Industry	Sales ($£$m)
Brewing	3190
Spirits	1860
Cheese	415
Cider , wine	190
Bread	150
Antibiotics	100
Yogurt	65
Yeast	25
Citric acid	20

From Dunnill(1981).

also to improve greatly the efficiency and economics of the established biotechnological industries. It is largely from these discoveries and developments that there have been such euphoric statements about the future role of biotechnology to the world economy.

What then are these new innovations? (Table 1. 4).

Table 1. 4   Techniques stimulating the development of biotechnology

Recombinant DNA manipulation
Tissue culture
Protoplast fusion
Monoclonal antibody preparation
Protein structural modification('protein engineering')
Immobilized enzyme and cell catalysis
Sensing with the aid of biological molecules
Computer linkage of reactors and processes
New biocatalytic reactor design

(a) *Genetic engineering*. Manipulation of the genome of industrially important organisms by sexual recombination and/or by mutution have long been part of the innovative repertoire of the industrial geneticist. New recombinant DNA techniques involve breaking living cells gently, the extraction of DNA, its purification and subsequent selective fragmentation by highly specific enzymes; the sorting, analysis, selection and purification of a fragment containing a required gene; chemical bonding to the DNA of a carrier molecule and the introduction of the hybrid DNA into a selected cell for reproduction and cellular synthesis. Recombinant DNA technologies permit easier manipulation of a genome and can readily bypass interspecies and intergeneric incompatability. Unlimited possibilities exist and already human insulin and interferon genes have been transferred into and expressed by microbial cells. Protoplast fusion, monoclonal antibody preparation and the wide use of tissue culture techniques including the regeneration of plants from suspension culture cells have had a profound impact on the development of biotechnology. (Chapter 3).

(b) *Enzyme technology*. Isolated enzymes have long been a part of many biotechnol -

ogical processes and their catalytic properties are being further utilized with the development of suitable immobilization techniques allowing reuse of the biocatalyst. Of particular importance has been the development of high fructose syrups (annual production 3 million tonnes) using immobilized bacterial glucose isomerase. A further development is the immobilization of whole cells for biocatalytic purposes (Chapter 5).

    (c) *Biochemical engineering.* Bioreactors play a central role in biotechnological processes by providing a link between the starting materials or substrates and final products (Fig. 1.1; Chapter 4). Major advances have been made in bioreactor designs, in process monitoring techniques and in computer control of fermentation processes. However, the application of process control in biotechnological industries is many years behind that in operation in the chemical process industry. New approaches to the processing of the products of biotechnology (downstream processing) will improve the economics of all processes. There is an increasing need to design efficient recovery processes, in particular for high value products e. g. the ratio of recovery to fermentation costs for L-asparaginase is about 3.0 whereas for ethanol it is 0.16. However, downstream processing is still the Cinderella subject of biotechnology.

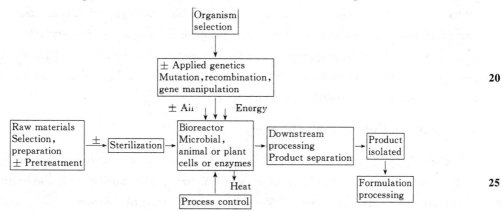

Fig. 1.1 Schematic overview of a biotechnological process

    (d) *Engineered products/systems*®. The ability to produce in quantity biological molecules such as antibodies or enzymes together with the techniques of protein and cell immobilization are allowing the development of radically new sensors that can be used for biodiagnostic, and biodetoxification, purposes. Such systems can be combined with micro-electronic devices and ultimately computers allowing sophisticated control programming in many biotechnological industries and services.

    Biotechnology has two characteristic features: its connection with practical applications, and interdisciplinary cooperation. The practitioners of biotechnology will employ techniques derived from chemistry, microbiology, genetics, biochemistry, chemical engineering and computer science , and their main mission will be the innovation, development and optimal operation of processes in which biochemical catalysis has a fundamental and irreplaceable role. Biotechnology does not constitute a new discipline but rather is an activity in which specialists from a wide range of disciplines can make their contributions.

A clear distinction must be drawn between bioscience and biotechnology. Bioscience refers to acquisition of biological knowledge whereas biotechnology refers to application of biological knowledge. Biotechnological processes will, in most cases[7], function at low temperatures, will consume little energy and rely in general on inexpensive raw materials as substrates.

Bioscientists and engineers of various specializations will make their individual contributions to biotechnology. The term *biotechnologist* has crept into our vocabulary as an all-embracing description of scientists or engineers engaged in applying their skills and knowledge to the *processing* of biological materials. However, the use of this term should be discontinued as it can only lead to confusion. In contrast a *biochemical engineer* is a process engineer whose role is to *transfer* the knowledge of the biological scientist into a practical operation. A biochemical engineer will have been trained in the scientific and engineering principles underlying the design and operation of biological operations[8].

A 'complete biotechnologist' will never exist, since no one can be expert in the skills of microbiology, biochemistry, molecular biology, chemical and process engineering, etc. However, for those who practise in this subject every effort must be made to understand the language of the other component subjects. The lack of a common language between specialists in different disciplines is undoubtedly the major obstacle in realising the full potential of biotechnology.

1. 3 Application of biotechnology

Biotechnological processes can be considered on the basis of volume and value. Thus, high volume, low value products or services include water purification and effluent and waste treatment and the production of methane, ethanol, biomass and animal feed; relatively high volume, intermediate value products include amino acids and organic acids, food products, baker's yeast, acetone, butanol and certain polymers, while low volume, high value products include antibiotics, interferons, vaccines, monoclonals, antibodies, enzymes and vitamins. Biotechnology can also be considered in terms of the levels of technology that will be necessary for product formation(Table 1. 5).

With reference to the scale of industrial development rather than the size of the individual production units, present and future biotechnology can also be conveniently divided into three areas.

(a) *Small scale biotechnology* is specifically concerned with biochemical products that can be produced economically only by biological means. This type of biotechnology has long existed and is rapidly developing, particularly in areas of new and novel products, but there exists fierce competition between industrial concerns to achieve market advances. Product examples include antibiotics, monoclonal antibodies and interferons.

Table 1.5 Biotechnology：based on technological level

Category	Input	Output
High level	High capital investment; sophisticated plant and processes often requiring strict containment; high maintenance costs；high operator skills.	High value-added products destined for health care and human food and food additives. Largescale continuous processes.
Intermediate level	Moderate capital investment and less complex operations.	Fermented foods and beverages. Animal feedstuffs. Biofertilizers and pesticides. Crude enzymes. Waste management processes which entail sophisticated operation and control.
Low level	Small capital investment and scale of operation, simple and usually indigenous equipment; labour intensive operations; often septic systems. Village level technology.	Low value products frequently related to alleviation of pollution, sanitation, fuel and food provision. Extensive use of naturally adapted mixed fermentations. Biogas；microbial protein from agricultural food and food wastes；traditional fermented foods and beverages；mushroom production.

From Bull *et al.* (1982).

(b) *Medium scale biotechnology* will compete with petroleum-based technology to produce current commodity chemicals and with agriculture to produce natural products including proteins and lipids.

(c) *Large scale biotechnology* will compete with petroleum and coal to supply the primary sources of organic compounds for fuels and high tonnage industrial products.

Although medium and large scale biotechnology currently have only a few truly economic successes there can be little doubt that within the next two decades there will be the establishment of large scale microbiological processes using vegetable materials as feedstock(Fig. 1.2). The market already exists for these products and the stimulus will be to develop economic biological alternatives.

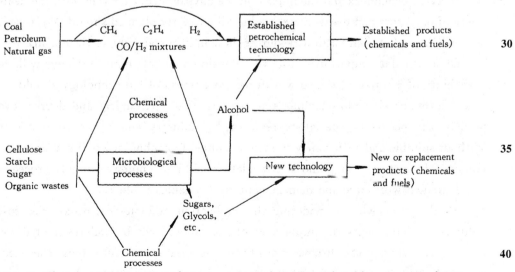

Fig. 1.2   The competitive routes to large tonnage products. Reproduced by permission from Atkinson and Sainter(1982),*Chemical Engineer November*：410-17

1.4 Growth in biotechnology

The continued successful growth of biotechnology will be dependent to a large extent on three premises, i. e. that there will be

(a) an expanding range of valuable products from both traditional and genetically engineered systems;

(b) the ability to obtain the raw materials from renewable resources[9];

5   (c) a growing awareness that biotechnological processes will in many cases become economical against the present chemical processing of vegetable materials.

A centrally important aspect of medium and large scale biotechnological developments will be the availability of suitable raw materials and substrates for processing. Substrate costs can amount to between 30 and 70% of the final product cost. Availability of substrates will be dependent on both technical and political factors. Thus gasohol production from various, organic substrates may not offer outstanding economic attraction but politically can present some bargaining power against escalating oil imports.

Renewable resources from agriculture, forestry and industrial organic wastes are gaining increasing importance since they offer, by biotechnological processing, a politically and strategically important base for food, feed, basic chemicals and energy production. However, to achieve this, wide ranging programmes not only in the component aspects of biotechnology but also in land management will be required.

1.5 Strategic planning in biotechnology

Each biotechnological scenario will require continuous assessment of the resources available, the economics and the impact on the environment, together with the health and safety of operators and users. Biotechnology if correctly planned should help to achieve a proper balance between natural resources, human needs and the environment.

Of particular importance for the development of biotechnology will be the availability of a suitably trained workforce. Awareness of biotechnology should begin at school level for all children while selective training at technical and degree level will produce the necessary specialists required by industry and by centres of research. Without suitable and sufficiently trained personnel biotechnology will not achieve its full potential. In particular high and intermediate level biotechnology can only proceed where a well trained workforce and management are available(Table 1.5).

Furthermore, when considering the application of biological discoveries to future industrial developments the importance of *time* should not be underestimated. Between the moment when a new discovery has been made and successful commercial production achieved, 5 to 20 years could have passed. Thus significant developments involving 'new' biotechnology must not be expected until the 1990s[10].

This short presentation will not attempt to describe or analyse the many and varied processes of current biotechnological practices. Rather it will attempt to identify the basic principles around which the core elements of biotechnology have developed.

1.6 Summary

Biotechnology can be considered to be the application of biological organisms and processes to manufacturing industries. Biotechnology encompasses a wide range of disciplines and subjects. Although present day activities are highly sophisticated and novel many of the processes have their roots in the dawn of history.

The specific processes are catalysed by microorganisms, plant or animal cells, or **5** products derived from them such as enzymes. The organisms of biotechnology can be harvested for biomass, can be used to perform chemical conversions and may be the source of biologically active molecules, including enzymes and monoclonal antibodies.

Gene manipulation techniques have brought a new dimension to applied genetics and have created the potential for completely novel industrial processes, for example human **10** interferon produced by bacterial cells. Significant developments are also occurring in process and control engineering and fermentation technology which will further advance the development of biologically-based industrial activity.

Biotechnology appears to be an area of expansion and opportunity involving many sectors of industry, including agriculture, food and feedstuffs, pharmaceutical, energy and **15** water industries. It will play a major role in the production of new drugs, hormones, vaccines and antibiotics, cheaper and more reliable supplies of energy and (in the longer term) chemical feedstuffs, improved environmental control and waste management. Biotechnology will be largely based on renewable and recyclable materials thus being better fitted to the needs of a world where energy will become increasingly more **20** expensive and in short supply.

Words and Expressions

page	line	
1	4	subcellular [ˌsʌb'seljulə] a. 亚细胞的

5 service industry 服务性工业 a diverse industrial sector that includes waste management, energy, service per se and some large activities (toxicity testing, biodeterioation and preservation).

6 bacteria [bæk'tiəriə] n. [复]细菌[bacterium 的复数]

yeast [ji:st] n. 酵母

fungi ['fʌŋgai] n. [复]真菌[fungus 的复数]

algae ['ældʒi:] n. [复]藻类[alga 的复数]

mammalian cell [mæ'meiljən sel] 哺乳动物细胞

9 genetics [dʒi'netiks] n. [复,用作单] 遗传学

molecular biology [məu'lekjulə bai'ɔlədʒi] 分子生物学

11 biomass ['baiəumæs] n. 生物体;菌体 mass of living matter

14 enzyme ['enzaim] n. 酶

page line

1   14 antibiotic [ˌæntibaiˈɔtik] n. 抗生素

     15 steroid [ˈsterɔid] n. 甾体;类固醇

     16 sewage [ˈsjuːidʒ] n. (阴沟等)污水

     17 spillage [ˈspilidʒ] n. 溢出 an act of spilling, causing a substance to run or fall out of a container, especially accidentally.

     18 catabolic [ˌkætəˈbɔlik] a. 分解代谢的

     19 glucose [ˈgluːkəus] n. 葡萄糖

           ethanol [ˈeθənɔl] n. 酒精;乙醇

           anabolic [ˌænəˈbɔlik] a. 合成代谢的

     20 whereby [hwɛəˈbai] ad. [关系副词] 靠那个 in accordance with or by means of which

     21 exergonic [ˌeksəˈgɔnik] a. 放能的 ex-向外;erg 能量

     22 endergonic [ˌendəˈgɔnik] 吸能的 end-[用在元音字母前]＝endo-表示吸入,在内

     24 cheese [tʃiːz] n. 乳酪;干酪

           vaccine [ˈvæksiːn] n. 疫苗

     26 versatility [ˌvəːsəˈtiliti] n. 多功能性 capability for many uses or applications

     30 bn.＝billion n. 十亿

           appreciate [əˈpriːʃieit] vt. 意识到 understand;be fully aware of

           interferon [ˌintəˈfiərɔn] n. 干扰素

           interface [ˈintəfeis] n. (两独立系统间互相衔接并互相影响的)接合部位,边缘区域 a place or area where different things meet and have an effect on each other

2   2 in the long term 从长远来说 from the point of view of long time

     19 pursuit [pəˈsjuːt] n. 事务;工作;职业 any activity to which one gives one's time, whether as work or for pleasure

           date back into(to) 始于… originate

     22 baking [ˈbeikiŋ] n. 烘,烤(面包)

           brewing [ˈbruːiŋ] n. 酿酒

     23 millenia[miˈleniə] n. [复]几千年[millennium 的复数]

           Sumerian [sjuːˈmiəriən] n. 苏美尔人[古代幼发拉底河下游的一个地区]

     24 Babylonian [bæbiˈləunjən] n. 巴比伦人[古代东方一个奴隶制国家]

           leaven [ˈlevən] vt. 加发酵剂,加曲

     26 Genesis [ˈdʒenisis] n. (基督教《圣经》中的)《创世纪》

     27 formulate [ˈfɔːmjuleit] vt. 系统地阐述 to express in systematic term or concept

     28 fermentative [fəˈmenteitiv] a. 发酵的

     29 seminal [ˈseminəl] a. 开创性的

           justifiably [ˈdʒʌstifaiəbli] ad. 可证明为合适地 qualifiedly

     32 yogurt [ˈjəugət] n. 酸乳酪

           soy sauce [sɔi sɔːs] n. 酱油

           tempeh [ˈtempei] n. 豆豉

page	line		
2	33	mushroom　['mʌʃruːm]　n. 蘑菇	
	40	reliant on　[ri'laiənt]　a. 依赖的　dependent	
	41	out of all proportion to　与……相比较大得不相称　too great as compared with	
3	1	sterile　['sterail]　a. 无菌的	
	2	acetic acid　[ə'siːtik 'æsid]　n. 醋酸	
		butanol　['bjuːtənəl]　n. 丁醇	
	3	acetone　['æsitəun]　n. 丙酮	
	5	ecological　[ˌiːkə'lɔdʒikəl]　a. 生态学的　pertaining to ecology, the science of the relationships between organisms and their environment	
	8	eclipse　[i'klips]　vt. (经比较)黯然失色　reduce in importance by comparison	
		escalation　[ˌeskə'leiʃən]　n. 逐步上升	
	10	with a view to　以……为目的　with the intention or hope of	
	14	composting　['kɔmpəstiŋ]　n. 堆肥　A mixture of decaying organic matter	
	23	baker's yeast　n. 面包酵母	
	35	polysaccharide　[ˌpɔli'sækəraid]　n. 多糖　poly-多，聚	
	39	dimension　[di'menʃən]　n. 方面，范围　an aspect	
4	4	spirits　['spiritz]　n. [复]烈性酒(如威士忌，白兰地等)	
	6	cider　['saidə]　n. 苹果酒	
	11	citric acid　['sitrik 'æsid]　n. 柠檬酸	
	15	euphoric　[juː'fɔrik]　a. 幸福愉快的　pertaining to a feeling of happiness and cheerful excitement	
	27	genetic engineering　[dʒi'netik ˌendʒi'niəriŋ]　n. 基因工程	
		genome　['dʒiːnəum]　n. 基因组　The complete, single-copy set of genetic instructions for an organism	
	28	sexual recombination　['seksjuəlˌriːkɔmbi'neiʃən]　n. 有性重组	
		mutation　[mjuː'teiʃən]　n. 突变　any heritable alternation of the genes or chromosones of an organism	
	29	repertoire　['repətwɑː]　n. 全部本领；一个剧团能演出的所有节目	
		geneticist　[dʒəne'tisist]　n. 遗传学家	
		recombinant DNA　[ˌriː'kɔmbiənt]　重组 DNA　DNA prepared by laboratory manipulation in which genes from one species are combined with those of another species	
	32	gene　[dʒiːn]　n. 基因　A hereditary unit located on a chromasome that determines a specific characteristic or function in the organism	
	33	hybrid　['haibrid]　n. 杂交物	
	35	intergeneric　[ˌintədʒə'nerik]　a. 属间的　inter-在……之间	
	36	incompatibility　[ˌinkəmˌpætə'biləti]　n. 不相容性	
		insulin　['insjulin]　n. 胰岛素	

page	line	
4	37	protoplast fusion ['prouteplæst 'fju:ʒən] n. 原生质体融合
		monoclonal antibody [,mɔnə'kləunəl 'æntibɔdi] n. 单克隆抗体
	38	tissue culture ['tisju:'kʌltʃə] n. 组织培养
5	3	high fructose syrup [hai'frʌktəus 'sirəp] n. 高果糖浆
	4	immobilize [i'məubilaiz] vt. 固定化
		glucose isomerase ['glu:kəus ai'sɔməreis] n. 葡萄糖异构酶
	12	downstream processing ['dəun'stri:m 'prɔsesiŋ] n. 下游(加工)过程
	15	asparaginase [,æspə'rædʒineis] n. 天冬酰氨酶
	16	cinderella [,sində'relə] n. 灰姑娘;被忽视的事物 A person or thing whose worth or beauty remains unrecognized
	25	formulation [fɔ:mju'leiʃən] n. 按(配)方配制 preparation according to a specific formula
	27	overview ['əuvəvju:] n. 概述 A broad, comprehensive view
	28	in quantity 大量地
	30	sensor [sensə] n. 传感器
	32	microelectronic ['maikəui'lektrɔnik] a. 微电子学的
6	7	substrate ['sʌbstreit] n. 基质,底物 the food on which a microorganism grows, or the substance on which an enzyme acts
	10	all-embracing [im'breisiŋ] a. 包括一切的
	12	in contrast 相反
	25	methane ['meθein] n. 甲烷
	26	amino acid ['æminəu'æsid] n. 氨基酸
	37	concern [kən'sə:n] n. 企业 a business establishment or enterprise
7	3	value-added a. 增值的,指商品在生产过程中的增值
		destine(for) ['destin] vt. 指定(供某种用途)
	4	containment [kən'teinmənt] n. 控制在一定范围 the action, keeping something within certain limits
	7	pesticide ['pestisaid] n. 杀虫剂
	8	entail [in'teil] vt. 使成为必要,需要 to impose, involve, or imply as a necessary accompaniment or result
	11	indigenous [in'didʒinəs] a. 本地的 native
		sanitation [sæni'teiʃən] n. 环境卫生,废水(物)处理 application of measures designed to protect public health
	13	septic ['septik] a. 感染的 infected ant. aseptic
	20	protein ['prəuti:n] n. 蛋白质
		lipid ['lipid] n. 脂质
	22	tonnage ['tʌnidʒ] n. 吨位 weight, measured in tons
	38	glycol ['glaikɔl] n. 乙二醇
8	1	premise ['premis] n. 前提 A proposition upon which an argument is based

page　line

　　　　　or from which a conclusion is drawn

　8　　11　gasohol　[ˈɡæzəhɔːl]　n. 酒精汽油　a motor fuel consisting of approximately
　　　　　　　90% gasoline and 10% alcohol

　　　14　forestry　[ˈfɔristri]　n. 林业

　　　21　scenario　[siˈnɑːriou]　n. 方案　an account or synopsis of a projected course of
　　　　　　　action or events

　9　　3　encompass　[inˈkʌmpəs]　vt. 包含　comprise，include

　　　4　dawn　[dɔːn]　n. 黎明，开端　a beginning

　　　16　hormone　[ˈhɔːməun]　n. 激素

Notes

① 本句为复合句，主语为 biotechnology，谓语为 is，an area of…and technology 是表语。定语从句由 which 引导，一般 which 应紧靠所修饰的词，但也有例外。在本句中 which 是修饰 area，而不是 applied bioscience and technology，这是因为：（1）从语法上来讲，从句中的谓语 involves 是单数第三人称，所以 which 替代的名词应是单数性的 area，而不是 of 后面的两个名词；（2）从意义上来说，理解为被修饰词是 area 更合适。注意，这个定语从句为限制性定语从句，故 which 前不加逗号。application 意为应用，应用于何处，一般用 to＋宾语来表示，如本句中的 to manufacturing … and to environmental management；如意义是在…领域中的应用，也可用 application in…。

　　本句可译为：生物工程是属于应用生物科学和技术的一个领域，它包含生物或其亚细胞组分在制造业、服务业和环境管理等方面的应用。

② will result 是一般将来时，但在本句中并不表示将来时，而是一种特殊用法，表示一种倾向或一种固有特性和规律。这在科技文献中很常见。又如：

Oil will float on water.　　油总是浮在水上面。

　　本句可译为：只有将微生物学、生物化学、遗传学、分子生物学、化学和化学工程等多种学科和技术结合起来，生物工程的应用才能获得成功。

③ 本句可译为：但也应理解，还会有很多重要的新的生物产品仍将以化学方法，按现有的生物分子模型进行合成，例如以干扰素为基础的新药。（这里的模型系指作用方式，例如参照干扰素作为药物的作用方式，设计并用化学方法合成新药）

④ energy demaning　名词与现在分词相结合的复合形容词，意为耗能的，有时中间加连字符，在科技文献中用得很多。如：time-cosuming 耗时的；rate limiting 限制速率的。

　　利用复合形容词能使文字简明扼要，故在科技文献中应用很广，共有下列八种类型：

（1）名词＋现在分词　这就是上面提到的形式

（2）形容词/副词＋现在分词

　　hard-working　工作努力的；good-looking　漂亮的

（3）名词＋过去分词

　　wind-driven　风力驱动的；enzyme-catalyzed（processes）　酶促（过程）；site-directed（mutagenesis）　定向（诱变作用）；purpose-designed（adsorbents）　专向设制的（吸附剂）

（4）副词＋过去分词

well-known 众所周知的；above-mentioned 上面提到的

如果副词以"-ly"结尾，则不加连字符，如：

microbially based processes 基于微生物的过程 recently developed (procedure) 新近开发的（操作）。如有另一副词修饰该复合形容词时，也不加连字符，如 very well studied (hypothesis) 非常仔细研究过的（假设）

(5) 形容词＋名词＋'ed'

old-fashioned (machine) 老式（机器）；three-storeyed (building) 三层（大厦）；medium-sized (machine) 中型（机器）

(6) 名词＋形容词

ice-cold 冰冷的；snow-white 雪白的；active center-specific (reagent) 对活性中心有特殊作用的（试剂）；cofactor-independent (enzyme) 不带辅因子的（酶）；time-dependent (reaction) 随时间而变的（反应）

(7) 形容词＋名词

first-order (reaction) 一级（反应）；large-scale (cultivation) 大规模（培养）；long-distance (call) 长途（电话）

(8) 副词＋形容词

above-average (results) 平均以上的（结果）；

ever-present (danger) 始终存在的（危险）

⑤ by far 与比较级或最高级连用，说明相差的程度，远比……得多，或（突出地）最……。如：
He is by far the best runner. 他突出地跑得最快（远比其他人快得多）。
本句可译为：在目前世界上实施的发酵过程中，用生物工程处理污水的规模最大（但对其了解则最肤浅）。

⑥ 工程化的产品和系统 这一节是讨论工业生产的控制和自动化，包括传感器和计算机的应用。

⑦ in most cases 意为在大多数场合，most 作大多数解，不是 many 或 much 的最高级。

⑧ 本句中 will have been trained 是被动语态的将来完成时，但并不表示将来时，参见 note②，而表示一种倾向或应遵循的规律，且含动作已完成之意。本句可译为：生化工程师应当在生物过程的设计和操作方面受过科学和工程原理的训练。

⑨ renewable resources 可再生资源 生物利用能量把周围物质（营养物）转变为生物体组织。转变时间的长短就是生物的寿命，例如植物纤维（如棉花）需要几个月；动物材料，如骨、皮需要几年，而木材需要几十年，和人的寿命相比，这些材料是可再生的。如果我们消耗这些资源的速度，不超过它们形成的速度，则这些资源是用之不尽的，称为可再生资源。地质过程所产生的材料需要百万年或几亿年，人们不能等候这么久，所以矿物资源称为非再生资源（nonrenewable resources）。

⑩ not…until… not 是一个否定项，until 可作介词或连词，词中有 un 词头也是一个否定项，所以本句是一种双重否定句，其意义为：不到……不…… 或 直到……才……。本句可译为：新的生物技术可望到 90 年代才能有较大的发展。

Comprehension

1. What is biotechnology? What are its characteristic points?

2. Name four developmental phases of biotechnology, denoting their chronological time, main products and techniques evolved.

3. As a student of biochemical engineering, could you give an exact definition thereof?

4. Why, according to the auther, will the term biotechnologist lead to confusion and why should a student of biochemical engineering learn the all-embracing knowledge of biotechnology?

5. What do you understand by the statement 'the stimulus will be to develop economic biological alternatives'? (7/27)❶

Word usage

1. Write sentences to bring out the difference between following pairs of words：
   e. g. (1/14), i. e. (8/1); practise(6/18), practice(2/20)
   utilize(1/6), use(5/30); personnel(8/30), personal.

2. Make sentences with each of the following phrases：
   of particular importance(8/26); with a view to(3/10); contrary to(2/19)

Grammar

1. Supply the missing words in the following sentence. Do not refer to the text until you have finished the exercise. Large scale biotechnology will compete … petroleum and coal … supply the primary sources of organic compounds … fuels and high tonnage industrial products. (7/21)

2. Put commas whenever they are needed in the following sentence. Do not refer to the text until you have finished the exercise.
   Thus high volume low value products or services include water purification and effluent and waste treatment and the production of methane ethanol biomass and animal feed. (6/23)

Sentence analysis and translation

First analyse the following sentences as in note①, and then translate them into Chinese：

  1. The reactions of biotechnological processes … into more complex ones(antibiotic synthesis). [1/(18~21)]

  2. Biotechnology appears to be an area of expansion … will become increasingly more expensive and in short supply. [9/(14~21)]

Writing

Translate the following sentences into English using compoundadjectives：

  1. 将 2g 左右的 OH⁻型抽干树脂放入 10×200mm 柱中（抽干—suction-dried）

  2. 硅元素进入植物体内和它的沉积部位是因植物种类而异的。（因种类而异的—species-specific；沉积—deposition）

---

❶ 括弧内数字表示页码和行次，如(7/72)表示第 7 页，第 27 行，后同。

Chapter 2　Biochemistry of Growth and Metabolism

2.1　Introduction

The purpose of a microorganism is to make another microorganism. In some cases the biotechnologist, who seeks to exploit the microorganism, may wish this to happen as
5　frequently and as quickly as possible. In other cases, where the product is not the organism itself, the biotechnologist must manipulate it in such a way that the primary goal of the microbe is diverted. As the microorganism then strives to overcome these restraints on its reproductive capacity, it produces the product which the biotechnologist desires. The growth of the organism and its various products are therefore intimately
10　linked by virtue of its metabolism.

Metabolism is a matrix of two closely interlinked but divergent activities. *Anabolic* processes are concerned with the building up of cell materials, not only the major cell constituents (proteins, nucleic acids, lipids, carbohydrates. etc.) but also their intermediate precursors—amino acids, purine and pyrimidines, fatty acids, various sugars
15　and sugar phosphates. Anabolic processes do not occur spontaneously: they must be driven by an energy flow that for most microorganisms is provided by a series of 'energy-yielding' *catabolic* processes. The degradation of carbohydrates to CO_2 and water is the most common of these catabolic processes, but a far wider range of reduced carbon compounds can be utilized by microorganisms in this way. The coupling of catabolic and
20　anabolic processes is the basis of all microbial biochemistry, and can be discussed either in terms of the overall balance or in terms of individual processes, as here.

In practice we can very usefully distinguish between organisms which carry out their metabolism *aerobically*, using oxygen from the air, and those that are able to do this *anaerobically*, that is, without oxygen. The overall reaction of reduced carbon compounds
25　with oxygen, to give water and CO_2, is a highly exothermic process; an aerobic organism can therefore balance a relatively smaller use of its substrates for catabolism to sustain a given level of anabolism, that is, of growth. Substrate transformations for anaerobic organisms are essentially *disproportionations*, with a relatively low 'energy yield', so that a larger proportion of the substrate has to be used catabolically to sustain a given
30　level of anabolism.

The difference is very clearly illustrated in an organism such as yeast, which is a *facultative* anaerobe—that is, it can exist either aerobically or anaerobically. Transforming sugar at the same rate, aerobic yeast gives CO_2, water, and a relatively high yield of new yeast, whereas yeast grown anaerobically has a relatively slow growth
35　which is now coupled to a high conversion of sugar into ethanol and CO_2.

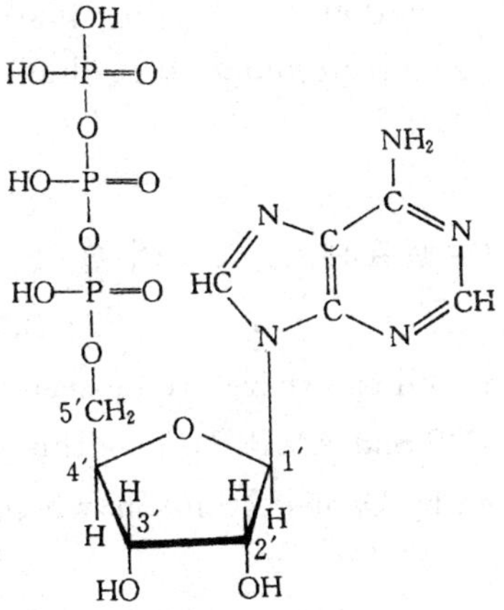

Fig. 2.1   Adenosine triphosphate(ATP)

2.2   Catabolism and energy

The necessary linkage between catabolism and anabolism depends upon making the varied catabolic processes 'drive' the synthesis of reactive reagents, few in number, which in turn are used to 'drive' the full range of anabolic reactions. These key intermediates, of which the most important is adenosine triphosphate, ATP(Fig. 2.1), have what biologists term a 'high-energy bond'; in ATP, the anhydride linkage in the pyrophosphate residue. Directly or indirectly the potential exergicity of the hydrolysis of this bond is used to overcome the endergicity of bond-forming steps in anabolic syntheses. Molecules such as ATP then provide the 'energy currency' of the cell. When ATP is used in a biosynthetic reaction it generates ADP (adenosine diphosphate) or occasionally AMP(adenosine monophosphate)as the hydrolysis product:

$$A+B+ATP \longrightarrow AB+ADP+P_i \; or \; A+B+ATP/AB+AMP+PP_i$$

(P_i=inorganic phosphate, and PP_i=inorganic pyrophosphate)

ADP, which still possesses a 'high-energy bond', can also be used to produce ATP by the adenylate kinase reaction:

$$ADP+ADP \longrightarrow ATP+AMP$$

Phosphorylation reactions, which are very common in living cells(see Figs 2.2, 2.4 to 2.6), usually occur through the mediation of ATP:

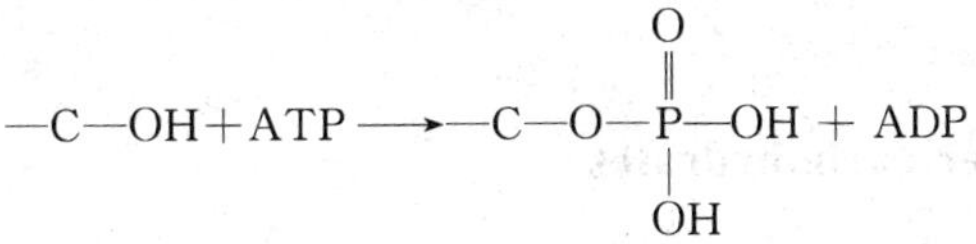

$$-C-OH+ATP \longrightarrow -C-O-\overset{\overset{\displaystyle O}{\displaystyle \|}}{\underset{\underset{\displaystyle OH}{\displaystyle |}}{P}}-OH + ADP$$

The phosphorylated product is usually more reactive (in one of several ways) than the original compound. Phosphorylation by inorganic phosphate does not occur because the equilibrium lies in the reverse direction due to the high concentration of water(55M) in the cell:

$$-C-OH + HO-\overset{\overset{O}{\|}}{\underset{\underset{OH}{|}}{P}}-OH \rightleftharpoons C-O-\overset{\overset{O}{\|}}{\underset{\underset{OH}{|}}{P}}-OH + H_2O$$

The 'energy status' of the cell can therefore be seen as a function of the prevailing relative proportions of ATP, ADP and AMP. To give this a numerical value, the concept of *energy charge* was introduced by Daniel Atkinson, who defined the energy charge of a cell as the ratio:

$$\frac{ATP + 0.5ADP}{ATP + ADP + AMP}$$

A 'fully charged' cell, wherein ATP was the only adenine nucleotide, gives an energy charge value of 1.0. When, say, there are equal amounts of the three nucleotides, ATP=ADP=AMP, then the energy charge of the cell would be 0.5[1].

Like all conventions, the concept of energy charge has limited usefulness. No one is very sure what it means if a cell is quoted as having an energy charge of 0.7 as opposed to 0.8 or 0.6. The concept does not take into account the *absolute* amounts of the nucleotides in a cell nor does it allow for quite striking differences in the response(see Section 2.8.1.5)of individual enzymes(to which the energy charge concept was initially applied)between ATP and its magnesium complex(the form in which ATP occurs in the cell). There are unexplained differences between energy charge values found typically in bacteria, yeasts and moulds. However, the concept is helpful in following energy changes, and corresponding changes in enzyme activity, within a given type of cell, for example during growth. When a cell is growing most rapidly[2], the energy charge value is at its lowest; ATP is used as rapidly as it can be resynthesized. As the growth rate begins to slow at the end of growth, the proportion of ATP rises relative to those of ADP and AMP; thus the energy charge begins to rise. The maximum energy charge will be reached when the cell has ceased to grow and all the ADP and AMP have been converted into ATP.

2.3 Catabolic pathways

Though microorganisms can use a wide variety of carbon compounds for growth, we shall consider mainly the metabolism of glucose and, in view of their increasing economic importance, that of ethanol(and other C_2 compounds), hydrocarbons and fatty acids, methane and methanol.

2.3.1 Glucose and other carbohydrates

In nearly all kinds of living cells, the two most important pathways of sugar metabolism are the hexose diphosphate and hexose monophosphate pathways ; they usually occur together, providing important links to anabolic processes, and their interactions are subject to key control mechanisms.

The *hexose diphosphate* pathway (often referred to as the *Embden-Meyerhof* or *glycolysis* pathway) is shown in Fig. 2. 2. It converts glucose into pyruvate without loss of carbon, reducing two molecules of NAD^+ coenzyme (see Fig. 2. 3(a)) to NADH (see Fig. 2. 3(b)) and generating two molecules of ATP. The pyruvate formed is a source of key anabolic precursors, and in aerobic organisms it is also a substrate for oxidation. In anaerobes the pyruvate or its transformation products must also act as a re-oxidizing agent for the NADH.

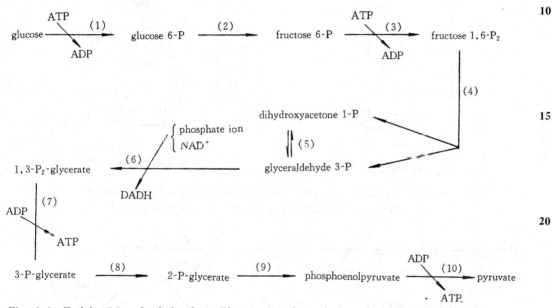

Fig. 2. 2 Embden-Meyerh of glycolysis. The reactions beyond glyceraldehyde 3-phosphate, steps 6-10, will involve 2 moles of reactants and products per mole glucose utilized, so the overall reaction is

$$glucose + 2NAD^+ + 2H_2PO_4^- \longrightarrow 2\ pyruvate + 2NADH + 2ATP$$

Successive enzymes are: (1) hexokinase, (2) glucose phosphate isomerase, (3) phosphofructokinase, (4) aldolase, (5) triose phosphate isomerase, (6) glyceraldehyde phosphate dehydrogenase, (7) 3-phosphoglycerate kinase, (8) phosphoglyceromutase, (9) phosphoenolpyruvate dehydratase, (10) pyruvate kinase. P represents a phosphate ester group

The *hexose monophosphate* pathway, also known as the *pentose phosphate* pathway, is shown in Fig. 2. 4. As an oxidative process it converts glucose into pentose and CO_2, reducing two molecules of $NADP^+$ [a coenzyme related to NAD^+, see Fig. 2. 3(a)] to NADPH. [NAD^+/NADH and $NADP^+$/NADPH both function by hydride transfer but have distinct roles; NADH mainly functions in energy-linked redox reactions while NADPH is mainly used for reductive steps in anabolic processes.]

Through the series of reversible interconversions shown in Fig. 2. 4 the pentose phosphate is freely equilibrated with other sugar phosphates having from three to seven carbons, with various metabolic roles which depend on overall circumstances. The triose phosphates are the same as those formed in glycolysis (Fig. 2. 2) and. by reversal of the cleavage step in that sequence , they can regenerate hexose as diphosphate ; the tetrose

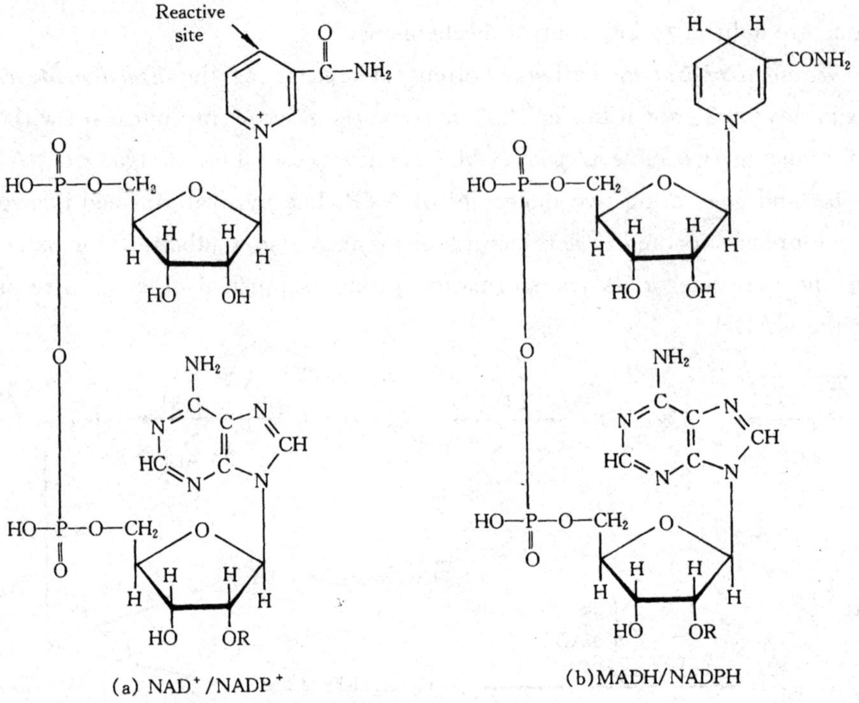

Reactive
site

O

CONH$_2$

H   H

CONH$_2$

HO—P—O—CH$_2$

H   H

H

HO   OH

NH$_2$

C

N

C   CH

HC   C   N

N

HO—P—O—CH$_2$ O

H   H

H   H

HO   OR

(a) NAD$^+$/NADP$^+$

HO—P—O—CH$_2$ O

H   H

H

HO   OH

NH$_2$

C   C—N

C   CH

HC   C   N

N

HO—P—O—CH$_2$ O

H   H

H   H

HO   OR

(b) MADH/NADPH

Fig. 2.3   (a) NAD$^+$/NADP$^+$(oxidized). (b) NADH/NADPH(reduced).
In NAD$^+$ and NADH, R＝H; in NADP$^+$ and NADPH, R＝PO$_3^{2-}$

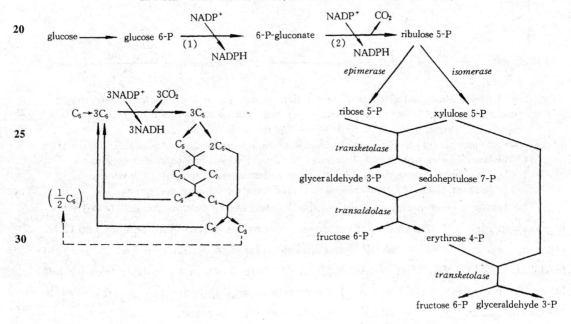

Fig. 2.4   The pentose phosphate cycle(hexose monophosphate shunt). The numbered enzymes are:
(1) glucose 6-phosphate dehydrogenase, (2) phosphogluconate dehydrogenase. Inset: summary
showing stoichiometry when fructose 6-phosphate is recycled to glucose 6-phosphate by an
isomerase; glyceraldehyde 3-phosphate can also be recycled by reverse glycolysis(Fig. 2.2).
With full recycling the pathway functions as a generator of NADPH, but the transaldolase
and transketolase reactions also permit sugar interconversions which are used in other ways

phosphate is important as an anabolic precursor for aromatic amino acids, and pentose phosphate is required for the synthesis of nucleic acids (see Fig. 2. 18).

In most organisms, between 66 and 80% of the glucose is metabolized via the Embden-Meyerhof pathway and the remainder by the pentose phosphate pathway. The point for controlling the proportion of carbon which flows down each pathway is normally found in the Embden-Meyerhof pathway at the phosphorylation of fructose 6-phosphate to fructose 1, 6-bisphosphate, catalysed by phosphofructokinase (PFK). The molecular constitution of this enzyme is such that its catalytic activity can be modulated according to the prevailing metabolic status of the cell: if more energy is required, activity of PFK is increased; if the cell has sufficient energy or sufficient amounts of C_3 metabolites then the activity of PFK is decreased.

This principle of enzyme control by modulation of the catalytic activity of key enzymes is widespread. Metabolic pathways must always be controlled, and for the cell to operate as efficiently as possible its whole activity must be coordinated. With respect to control of PFK this is achieved in two ways. Firstly, the enzyme is *activated*, i. e. the rate at which it can catalyse the reaction is increased, by the presence of AMP or ADP. Thus when the energy charge of the cell (see Section 2. 2) is low , PFK will operate at an increased rate. Secondly the enzyme is *inhibited* by an intermediate lower down the metabolic pathway, usually either phosphoenolpyruvate or citrate. Thus if one of these is not being effectively converted to other materials the cell will not need to continue their production.

Other points where glucose metabolism can be regulated vary from organism to organism but always in such a way that the catabolic process meets the anabolic demands as closely as possible.

The Embden-Meyerhof pathway and the pentose phosphate cycle are not the only pathways of glucose metabolism, though they are by far the most common. A major alternative to the Embden-Meyerhof pathway is the *Entner-Doudoroff pathway*, found in several species of *Pseudomonas* and related bacteria, shown in Fig. 2. 5. The enzymes of the pentose phosphate cycle are still required to produce the C_5 and C_4 sugars, but the flow is now reversed from the directions given in Fig. 2. 4.

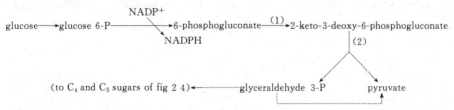

Fig. 2. 5　Entner-Doudoroff pathway. This sometimes replaces glycolysis (Fig. 2. 2). Numbered enzymes are: (1) phosphogluconate dehydratase. (2) a specific aldolase.

Another enzyme of some importance, perhaps more widespread than is generally recognized, is *phosphoketolase*. This type of enzyme (there may be more than one) acts on a C_5 or C_6 sugar phosphate to produce acetyl phosphate and either glyceraldehyde 3-phosphate or erythrose 4-phosphate (depending on whether the C_5 or the C_6 sugar is used) (see Fig. 2. 6). These enzymes were originally found in the heterofermentative lactobacilli(q. v. Section 2. 7. 2)and acetobacter where they function in place of the Embden-Meyerhof pathway. The resulting acetyl phosphate may be converted to acetate or ethanol. More recently phosphoketolase has been found to be an induced enzyme present in most yeasts when they are grown aerobically on xylose as sole carbon source.

Here, xylose is first metabolized via xylitol to xylulose and this then enters the scheme depicted in Fig. 2. 6 at the level of xylulose 5-phosphate. (In bacteria growing on xylose there is an isomerase which converts xylose directly to xylulose.) Under these circumstances, the C_5-phosphoketolase does not replace the Embden-Meyerhof pathway but merely provides an efficient route for the organism to convert a pentose into C_2 and C_3 units for further metabolism. The enzyme could therefore have a wide distribution in microorganisms, not just yeasts, when they are grown on xylose or other pentoses.

```
glucose ──→ glucose-6-P ─────→ 6-P-gluconate ─────────→ riblose 5-P
                  │                                          │
                  ↓                                          ↓
             fructose 6-P                                xylulose 5-P
               hexose                                      pentose
           phosphoketolase                             phosphoketolase
     ↙                   ↘                          ↙                  ↘
erythrose 4-P          acetyl -P ←──────────────                glyceraldehyde 3-P
     │                     │                                          │
     ↓                     ↓                                          ↓
(then as fig. 2.4)   (to AcOH or AcCoA)                        (to pyruvate)
```

Fig. 2. 6　Phosphoketolase pathways. These processes may be additional to those of Figs 2. 2 and 2. 4. of glucose metabolism by way of the pentose phosphoketolase pathway may replace glycolysis in some bacteria

2. 3. 2　Tricarboxylic acid cycle

The pathways so far discussed lead eventually to the production of specific C_3 or C_2 compounds, namely pyruvate or acetate, the latter as acetyl coenzyme A which is a thioester(Fig. 2. 7) with anhydride-type reactivity. The further aerobic metabolism of pyruvate and acetyl-CoA is via a cyclic process which serves two separate functions: it produces intermediates which are then used for biosynthetic reactions, and in the oxidation of compounds , eventually to CO_2 and water , it couples the oxidative reactions

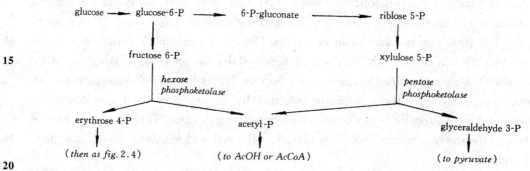

Fig. 2. 7　Coenzyme A(CoA)

to the transfer of energy. This cyclic process of acetyl-CoA oxidation, ubiquitous in all aerobic cells, is termed the *tricarboxylic acid cycle* (citric acid cycle, Krebs cycle).

In eukaryotic cells the reactions of the tricarboxylic acid cycle and of energy production are carried out in the mitochondria, while in bacteria the major energy-producing enzymes are associated with the cytoplasmic membrane. As the mitochondrial process begins with the transport of pyruvate into the mitochondrion, it is convenient to include the reactions linking pyruvate to the tricarboxylic acid cycle.

Pyruvate is converted to acetyl-CoA by a multi-enzyme complex, pyruvate dehydrogenase, which catalyses the overall reaction:

$$\text{pyruvate} + \text{CoA} + \text{NAD}^+ \longrightarrow \text{acetyl-CoA} + \text{CO}_2 + \text{NADH}$$

The subsequent metabolism of acetyl-CoA is through the reactions of the tricarboxylic acid cycle given in Fig. 2. 8.

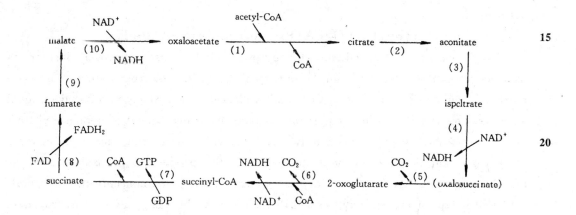

Fig. 2. 8   The tricarboxylic acid cycle. (ATP/ADP may replace GTP/GDP.) The overall reaction is:
  $$\text{acetyl-CoA} + 3\text{NAD}^+ + \text{FAD} + \text{GDP} \longrightarrow 2\text{CO}_2 + \text{coenzyme A} + 3\text{NADH} + \text{FADH}_2 + \text{GTP}$$
  The numbered steps are catalysed by: (1) citrate synthase, (2,3) aconitase, (4,5) isocitrate dehydrogenase, (6) 2-oxogluconate dehydrogenase, (7) succinate thiokinase, (8) succinate dehydrogenase, (9) fumarase, (10) malate dehydrogenase

The functions of this cycle are:

(i) to produce intermediates which can be used in other biosynthetic pathways (see Fig. 2. 18), for example:

```
2-oxoglutarate ──►glutamate──►proteins
                     │      ↘
                 glutamine   folic acid
  succinate ──►porphyrins ──►haems ──►cytochromes
      oxaloacetate──►aspartate──►proteins
                   ↙     │      ↘
            (lysine, methionine, threonine)
```

The reactions leading to aspartate and glutamate are particularly important as the main pathways by which cells assimilate ammonia.

(ii) to recover energy from the oxidative reactions. The enzymes isocitrate dehydrogenase , 2 - oxoglutarate dehydrogenase , succinate dehydrogenase , and malate dehydrogenase catalyse the progressive oxidation of the intermediate with the concomitant conversion of enzyme cofactor oxidants to reductants. The coenzymes are NAD^+ and FAD which become, respectively, NADH and $FADH_2$[cf. Fig. 2. 3(a)], these are then reoxidized to the original coenzymes by one process of *oxidative phosphorylation*

5 (see Section 2. 5)which produces 3 moles of ATP from each mole of NADH and 2 moles of ATP from the reoxidation of $FADH_2$. Energy is also recovered in the succinate thiokinase reaction(see Fig. 2. 8).

Although the cycle is apparently self-perpetuating, in that once primed by oxaloacetate it should keep working indefinitely, this cannot happen in practice. As

10 already noted, the cycle must also furnish intermediates for biosynthetic reactions, and when any such intermediate is removed from the cycle the synthesis of oxaloacetate and the regeneration of citrate cannot occur. It is therefore necessary that additional oxaloacetate can be formed independently, and this mainly occurs by the carboxylation of pyruvate:

15
$$pyruvate + CO_2 + ATP \longrightarrow oxaloacetate + ADP + P_i$$

This reaction is carried out by pyruvate carboxylase. However, insofar as oxaloacetate is also produced from the activity of the cycle, the carboxylation of pyruvate must be regulated so that acetyl-CoA and oxaloacetate are always produced in equal amounts. This is achieved by the pyruvate carboxylase being dependent upon acetyl-CoA

20 as a *positive effector*(see Section 2. 8. 1. 5), i. e one which increases its activity. The more acetyl-CoA that is present, the faster becomes the production of oxaloacetate. As oxaloacetate and acetyl-CoA are removed (to form citrate), the concentration of acetyl-CoA will fall; pyruvate carboxylase will then slow down but, as pyruvate dehydrogenase still operates as before, more acetyl-CoA will be produced. In this way not only will citric

25 acid synthesis always continue, but the two reactions leading to the precursors of citrate will always be balanced.

There are additional controls which can regulate the activity of the cycle. Some of its enzymes are inhibited by ATP and others depend on the presence of AMP for their activity. Therefore the cycle can be regulated by the prevailing ratio of ATP to AMP,

30 that is by the energy charge (see Section 2. 2)within the cell. These control mechanisms are not universal and they need to be ascertained for individual organisms, or groups of organisms; they will not be considered in further detail, but general principles of metabolic control, as discussed for the regulation of glycolysis, still apply.

35 **2. 3. 3 Glyoxylate by-pass**(growth on C_2 compounds)

If an organism grows on a C_2 compound or on a fatty acid or hydrocarbon that is degraded primarily into C_2 units (see Section 2. 3. 4), the tricarboxylic acid cycle is insufficient to account for its metabolism. As shown in the previous section, any compound which is used for synthesis, and so removed from the tricarboxylic acid cycle,

40 will , by its removal , effectively stop the regeneration of oxaloacetate . As C_2 compounds

cannot be converted to pyruvate (the pyruvate dehydrogenase reaction, is effectively irreversible)there is no way in which oxaloacetate, or indeed any such C_4 compound, can be produced from a C_2 compound by the reactions given so far.

Acetyl-CoA can be generated directly from acetate, if this is being used as carbon source, or from a C_2 compound more reduced than acetate, i. e. acetaldehyde or ethanol: **5**

$$C_2H_5OH \xrightarrow[\quad]{NAD^+ \quad NADH} CH_3CHO \xrightarrow[\quad]{NAD^+ \quad NADH} CH_3COO^- \xrightarrow[\quad CoA \quad]{ATP \quad ADP+P_i} Acetyl\text{-}CoA$$

The manner in which acetate units are converted to C_4 compounds is known as the glyoxylate by-pass (see Fig. 2. 9) for which two enzymes additional to those of the   **10** tricarboxylic acid cycle are needed: *isocitrate lyase* and *malate synthase*. Both enzymes are 'induced' (see Section 2. 8. 1. 3) when microorganisms are grown on C_2 compounds; the activity of the enzymes increases by some 20 to 50 times[3] under such growth conditions. The glyoxylate by-pass does not supplant the operation of the tricarboxylic acid cycle; for example 2-oxoglutarate will still have to be produced (from isocitrate) in order to   **15** supply glutamate for protein synthesis, etc. Succinate, the other product from isocitrate lyase, will be metabolized as before to yield malate, and thence oxaloacetate. Thus through the glyoxalate cycle, the C_4 compounds can now be produced from C_2 units, and are then available for synthesis of all cell metabolites (cf. Fig. 2. 18). Their conversion into sugars is detailed in Section 2. 4.   **20**

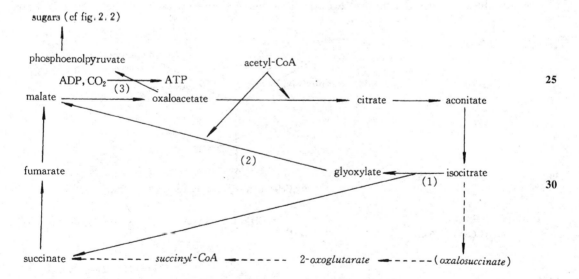

   25

   30

   35

Fig. 2. 9   The glyoxylate by-pass. The additional reactions, shown against the same background reactions as in Fig. 2. 8, are (1) isocitrate lyase, (2) malate synthase. The scheme also shows how the bypass functions to permit sugar formation from acetyl-CoA, with the added reaction (3) phosphoenolpyruvate carboxykinase, followed by reversed glycolysis (cf. Fig. 2. 2)

2. 3. 4   Fatty acids and hydrocarbons

The ability to grow on a hydrocarbon is not widespread but it is found amongst bacteria,   **40**

yeasts and moulds, while the ability to utilize fatty acids, or oils and fats containing them, is more common. Hydrocarbons are used as sole sources of carbon in the production of single cell protein in the USSR and can be used in other processes, e. g. for the production of citric acid. Fatty acids and vegetable oils are often added as
5 cosubstrates in the manufacture of antibiotics.

For the utilization of oils and fats(triglycerides), the organism must hydrolyse the ester linkage using a lipase(intracellular or extracellular). This yields free fatty acids(3 moles)plus glycerol(1 mole); the glycerol is utilized by the Embden-Meyerhof pathway. Many microorganisms can also utilize free fatty acids. However, whether such acids are
10 taken into the cell or actually formed there, they are extremely toxic (because of their surfactant properties) and must be converted immediately into their coenzyme A thioesters.

The thioester is suitably activated for degradation of the fatty acyl chain by the cyclic sequence of reactions depicted in Fig. 2.10. At each turn of the cycle, 1 mol of
15 acetyl-CoA is released and the fatty acyl-CoA ester, now two carbons shorter in chain length, recommences its oxidative cycle. The sequence, known as the *β-oxidation cycle* , continues until the substrate for the final reaction is the C_4 compound, acetoacetyl-CoA, which then gives 2 moles of the acetyl-CoA. If a fatty acid has an odd number of carbon atoms, the degradation proceeds until propionyl-CoA(C_3) is reached, which is converted
20 to pyruvate by the reverse of a sequence of reactions given in Section 2.7.3.

Microorganisms growing on *n*-alkanes usually commence with an initial attack on one of the two terminal methyl groups. The mechanism of attack by the enzyme, alkane

25

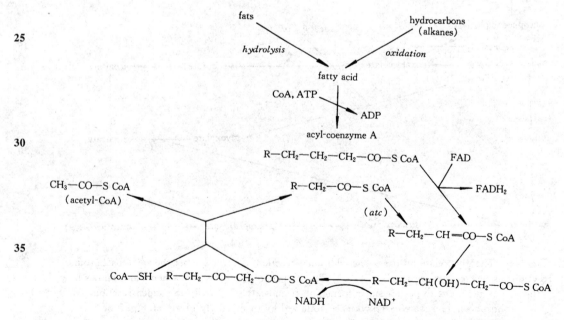

30

35

Fig. 2.10 *β*-Oxidation of fatty acids. With each 'turn'of the cycle acetyl-CoA is lost and a new fatty acyl-CoA with two carbon atoms fewer is formed, until the final products are
40 2 acetyl-CoA, or acetyl-CoA and propionyl-CoA, depending upon whether the original fatty acid has an even or an odd number of carbon atoms

hydroxylase, involves molecular oxygen and a re-oxidizable cofactor containing iron. The cofactor is also oxidized and regeneration of the reduced form is ultimately linked to a hydride carrier, either NADH or NADPH:

$$R.CH_3 \xrightarrow{O_2} \text{reduced cofactor} \quad FAD \quad NAD(P)H$$

$$\text{protein}$$

$$R.CH_2OH \xrightarrow{} \text{oxidized cofactor} \quad FADH_2 \quad NAD^+$$
$$H_2O$$

5

The fatty alcohol is then oxidized to the corresponding fatty acid in two dehydrogenase steps:

$$R.CH_2OH \xrightarrow{} R.CHO \xrightarrow{} R.COOH$$
$$NAD^+ \quad NADH \quad NAD^+ \quad NADH$$

10

Typically, all the enzymes associated with alkane degradation show broad substrate specificity and react readily with substrates from C_{10} to C_{18}. Several microorganisms can also attack either shorter or longer chains. In a few cases subterminal attack on alkanes has been reported with the production of a methyl ketone ($R.CO.CH_3$) which is eventually cleaved by further oxidation to give methyl formate and a fatty acid with two less carbon atoms than the original alkane.

15

Fatty acids arising from alkane degradation are usually degraded by the β-oxidation cycle (Fig. 2. 10) though in some organisms there is an ω-oxidation process which produces dicarboxylic acids. These are then degraded from one end by β-oxidation. The fatty acids are also used by the cell for the direct formation of its own lipids and thus the chain length of the alkane is reflected in the chain length of the fatty acids found in the cell.

20

Alkanes and some branched chain hydrocarbons may also be metabolized; they are not used on a commercial scale but may be present as minor components in the feedstock. Their oxidation invariably involves conversion to a fatty acid.

25

2. 3. 5　Methane and methanol

A small number of microorganisms (both bacteria and yeasts) which are termed *methyltrophs* can use methanol as sole source of carbon; the ability to utilize methane has so far been found only in a relatively small number of bacteria which are termed *methanotrophs*. A few microorganisms can use formate as carbon source. These three compounds are metabolically linked and can be oxidized ultimately to CO_2. The mechanism of their incorporation into cell material is different from that of autotrophic CO_2 fixation.

30

[Utilization of CO_2 as sole carbon source is the province of photosynthetic plants and microorganisms, and of a few *chemolithotrophic* bacteria which use reactions of inorganic compounds as energy source. These organisms currently have few applications in process biotechnology. The reader who would like to know more about the pathways

35

of autotrophic fixation of CO_2 should refer to almost any biochemistry textbook, but he should note that there are at least two distinct pathways: the Calvin cycle and a reductive carboxylic acid cycle.]

The mechanism of methane oxidation is stepwise:

$$CH_4 \longrightarrow CH_3OH \longrightarrow HCHO \longrightarrow HCOOH \longrightarrow CO_2$$

The first step is carried out by an oxygenase with NADH (or NADPH) as cofactor (compare oxidation of higher alkanes, above):

$$CH_4 + O_2 + NAD(P)H \longrightarrow CH_3OH + H_2O + NAD(P)^+$$

The enzyme (a complex of three proteins) will also oxidize a variety of other compounds including various alkanes and even methanol itself.

The second reaction in the sequence is catalysed by methanol dehydrogenase, using a newly-discovered pyrroloquinoline quinone (PQQ) as cofactor:

$$CH_3OH + PQQ \longrightarrow HCHO + PQQH_2$$

In some bacteria the further conversion of formaldehyde to formic acid is catalysed by the same enzyme; in others there may be a separate formaldehyde dehydrogenase with NAD as cofactor. The final step, conversion of formate to CO_2, is carried out by formate dehydrogenase and is again linked to NAD^+ reduction.

The assimilation of carbon from methane or methanol into cell material is at the level of formaldehyde, and by at least two independent routes: the *ribulose monophosphate cycle* (sometimes referred to as the Quayle cycle) and the *serine pathway*, shown in Figs 2. 11 and 2. 12, respectively.

HCHO

ribulose 5-phosphate ——— (1) ——→ 3-ketohexulose 6-phosphate

(2)

fructose 6-phosphate

Fig. 2. 11   Formaldehyde assimilation in bacteria: ribulose monophosphate cycle. Enzymes are (1) 3-ketohexulose 6-phosphate synthase, (2) phospho-3-hexulose isomerase. By the reactions of Fig. 2. 4, 5/6 of the fructose-6-phosphate is recycled to regenerate the acceptor, ribulose 5-phosphate

The ribulose monophosphate cycle (Fig. 2. 11) is similar to the Calvin cycle used for the autotrophic fixation of CO_2 in using the reactions of the pentose phosphate cycle (see Fig. 2. 4) to regenerate the acceptor for the incoming C_1 compound. Only two additional enzymes are needed: 3-hexulose phosphate synthase (A) and phospho-3-hexulose isomerase(B):

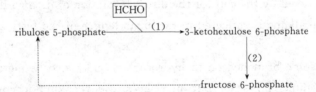

The key enzymes of the serine pathway (Fig. 2.12) are malyl-CoA lyase, which produces acetyl-CoA and glyoxylate, and serine transhydroxymethylase, a ubiquitous enzyme which uses tetrahydrofolate (a cofactor capable of forming the necessary activated C_1 intermediate, N^{10}-formyltetrahydrofolate). The glyoxylate by-pass (see Fig. 2.9) then operates to handle the acetyl-CoA, so that the cell is effectively growing on a C_2 substrate. Isocitrate lyase is de-repressed to ensure overall production of C_3 units.

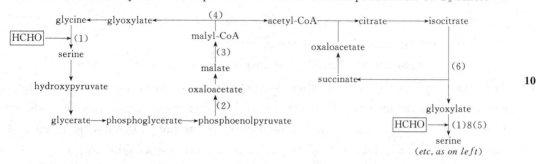

Fig. 2.12 Formaldehyde assimilation by the isocitrate lyase/serine pathway. The key
enzymes are (1) serine hydroxymethylase, for which tetrahydrofolate is the
formaldehyde-accepting cofactor, (2) phosphoenolpyruvate carboxylase (CO_2
assimilation), (3) malate thiokinase, (4) malyl-CoA lyase, (5) glyoxylate aminotr-
ansferase, (6) isocitrate lyase. For enzymes (4) and (6), compare Fig. 2.9. In certain
bacteria the reactions on the right-hand side of the diagram are replaced by a
set involving the homologous compounds homicitrate, glutarate, etc., again
converting the acetyl-CoA into formaldehyde-acceptor glyoxylate

In yeasts there is a further variation on the pentose phosphate cycle, by which formaldehyde reacts with xylulose 5-phosphate to produce glyceraldehyde 3-phosphate and dihydroxyacetone (see Fig. 2.13). This reaction is catalysed by a special type of transketolase enzyme (cf. Fig. 2.4). The only additional enzyme then needed to complete the cyclic assimilation of formaldehyde is a new kinase to convert dihydroxyacetone to dehydroxyacetone phosphate.

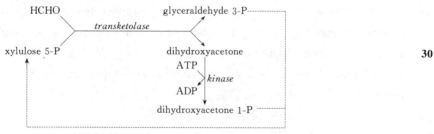

Fig. 2.13 Formaldehyde assimilation in methanol-using yeasts. The dotted line
shows regeneration of the acceptor, xylulose 5-phosphate, by the reactions of
Figs 2.2 and 2.4, which accounts for 5/6 of the triose phosphates formed

2.4 Gluconeogenesis

When an organism grows on a C_2 or C_3 compound, or a material whose metabolism will produce such compounds, at or below the metabolic level of pyruvate (for example aliphatic hydrocarbons, acetate, ethanol or lactate), it is necessary for the organism to synthesize various sugars to fulfil its metabolic needs. This is termed *gluconeogenesis*.

Though most of the reactions in the glycolytic pathways (see Figs 2.2 and 2.4) are reversible, those catalysed by pyruvate kinase and phosphofructokinase are not and it is necessary for the cell to circumvent these blockages.

In general, phosphoenolpyruvate cannot be formed from pyruvate, although in a few organisms there is an enzyme, phosphoenolpyruvate synthase, which can carry out the reaction:

$$pyruvate + ATP \longrightarrow phosphoenolpyruvate + AMP + P_i$$

More often, oxaloacetate is used as the precursor:

$$oxaloacetate + ATP \longrightarrow phosphoenolpyruvate + CO_2 + ADP$$

This reaction is catalysed by phosphoenolpyruvate carboxykinase which is the key enzyme of gluconeogenesis. The formation of oxaloacetate has already been discussed (Section 2.3.3). The irreversibility of phosphofructokinase (producing fructose 1,6-bisphosphate) is circumvented by the action of fructose bisphosphatase:

$$fructose\ 1,6\text{-bisphosphate} + H_2O \longrightarrow fructose\ 6\text{-phosphate} + P_i$$

From this point hexose sugars can be formed by the reversal of glycolysis and the C_5 and C_4 sugars can now be formed via the pentose phosphate pathway (Fig. 2.4). Glucose itself is not an end-product of 'gluconeogenesis' but glucose 6-phosphate is used for the synthesis of cell wall constituents and a large variety of extracellular and storage polysaccharides.

2.5 Energy metabolism in aerobic organisms

It has already been explained how, in the metabolism of glucose (Figs 2.2 and 2.4) and in the tricarboxylic acid cycle (Fig. 2.8), oxidation of the various metabolic intermediates is linked to reduction of a limited number of cofactors (NAD^+, $NADP^+$, FAD) to the corresponding reduced forms (NADH, NADPH and $FADH_2$). The reducing power of these products is released by a complex reaction sequence which in aerobic systems is linked eventually to reduction of atmospheric O_2. During this sequence, ATP is generated from ADP and inorganic phosphate (P_i) at two or more (usually three) specific points in the electron transport chain, depending on the nature of the orginal reductant. This is shown in Fig. 2.14.

The overall reactions may be written as:

$$NADPH + 3ADP + 3P_i + \frac{1}{2}O_2 \longrightarrow NADP^+ + 3ATP + H_2O$$

$$NADH + 3ADP + 3P_i + \frac{1}{2}O_2 \longrightarrow NAD^+ + 3ATP + H_2O$$

$$FADH + 2ADP + 2P_i + \frac{1}{2}O_2 \longrightarrow FAD + 2ATP + H_2O$$

The yields of ATP per mole of glucose metabolized by the Embden-Meyerhof pathway (Fig. 2.2) and from the resulting pyruvate, metabolized by the reactions of the tricarboxylic acid cycle (Fig. 2.8) are summarized in Table 2.1.

The production of biologically utilizable energy, in the form of ATP, occurs in membranes—either the membrane of the mitochondria in eukaryotic organisms or the

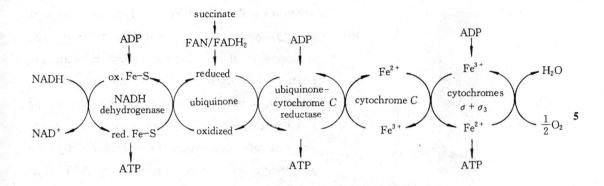

Fig. 2.14 Mitochondrial electron sequence. showing the sites which are coupled to
the phosphorylation of ADP to give ATP. Not all the electron carriers are shown; there
are at least 16 polypeptide chains involved, and there are minor modifications
to this sequence in bacteria[4]

Table 2 1   ATP yields for glucose metabolism

	Moles ATP produced per mole hexose
Glycolysis (glucose to pyruvate)	
Net yield of ATP = 2 mol	2*
NADH = 2 mol × 3	6
Pyruvate to acetyl-CoA	
NADH = 1 mol × 3 (× 2 for 2 pyruvate)	6
Tricarboxylic acid cycle	
NADH = 3 mol × 3 (× 2 for 2 acetyl-CoA)	18
FADH$_2$ = 1 mol × 2 (× 2 for 2 acetyl-CoA)	4
ATP = 1 mol (× 2 for 2 acetyl-CoA)	$\underline{2}$
	38

* Under anaerobic conditions all the NADH and pyruvate must be consumed without net oxidation
and these 2 moles of ATP represent the maximum attainable yield ('substrate-level phosphorylation').

cytoplasmic membrane in bacteria. Both processes are broadly similar, with differences
of detail between individual organisms. The main components of the electron transport
chain are flavoproteins, quinones and cytochromes (see Fig. 2.14) whose property is to
be able to become reduced (by acceptance of hydride ions or electrons) and then
oxidized, releasing electrons to the next carrier in a coupled and efficient manner. Each
carrier has a different redox potential, increasing stepwise from about -320mV for the
NADH/NAD$^+$ reaction to about $+800$mV for the final reaction: $\frac{1}{2}$O$_2$/H$_2$O. At certain
points in the chain the difference in redox potential between two adjacent carriers is
large enough to drive, in the direction of ATP synthesis, the reversible reaction: ADP +
P$_i$ $\rightleftharpoons$ ATP. This activity is associated with a complex, multisubunit, enzyme termed
ATPase.

32

There are two principal views as to how the ATPase is driven. In the chemiosmotic hypothesis, developed by Mitchell over the past twenty years, it is considered that the components of the electron transport chain are spatially arranged across the membrane. This generates a pH and electrical gradient due to the passage of protons from one side to the other. Protons returning across the membrane drive the ATPase reaction into synthesis of ATP. The ATPase is so oriented that protons have access to its catalytic site from one side only. This concept is shown in its simplest form in Fig. 2.15.

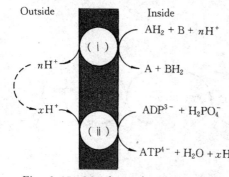

Outside   Inside

$AH_2 + B + nH^+$

$A + BH_2$

nH^+

xH^+

$ADP^{3-} + H_2PO_4^-$

$ATP^{4-} + H_2O + xH^+$

Fig. 2.15 Membrane function in coupling respiration, carried out by the electron transport carriers, with phosphorylation (energy production). Process (i) is a proton-translocating oxido-reduction, and transfers protons to the outside of the membrane; process (ii) uses the resulting proton gradient to drive the proton-translocating ATPase

The second explanation advanced to account for ATP synthesis envisages that carriers of the electron transport chain interact with hypothetical intermediate (s) which, on becoming activated, phosphorylate ADP. These intermediates are termed *coupling factors*.

Both theories have their strengths and weaknesses. Both can be adapted to account for the effect of 'uncouplers' of oxidative phosphorylation such as rotenone, amytal, antimycin A, etc. which have the effect of stopping ATP production.

2.6 Energy production in anaerobic organisms

The process of ATP production described in Section 2.5 depends on the provision of oxygen. Some organisms can substitute nitrate, others sulphate or ferric iron, for oxygen, and if these are supplied in quantity in the medium, the organism can still produce its ATP in the absence of air, using the electron transport carriers, and thus grow anaerobically. However, if no alternative electron acceptor is supplied, or if (like the majority of bacteria) the organism lacks this facility, then the organism deprived of oxygen will be unable to produce ATP in this way. Organisms growing anaerobically must therefore achieve ATP production by coupling the reaction directly to an energy-yielding reaction; this is termed *substrate level phosphorylation*. The number of reactions in which this can happen is very limited. The free energy change of the reaction must be sufficient to drive the phosphorylation of ATP (ATP $\longrightarrow$ ADP + P_i; $\Delta G^{0'}$ of $-31kJ$ mol^{-1}) and the most important reactions of this kind are summarized in Table 2.2.

Table 2. 2　Substrate-level phosphorylation reaction in anaerobes

Enzyme	Reaction catalysed	Occurrence
1. Phosphoglycerol kinase	1,3-bisphosphoglycerate+ADP $\longrightarrow$ 3-phosphoglycerate+ATP	widespread
2. Pyruvate kinase	phosphoenolpyruvate+ADP $\longrightarrow$ pyruvate+ATP	widespread
3. Acetate kinase	acetyl phosphate+ADP $\longrightarrow$ acetate+ATP	widespread
4. Butyrate kinase	butyryl phosphate+ADP $\longrightarrow$ butyrate+ATP	e. g. enterobacteria on allantoin
5. Carbamate kinase	carbamoyl phosphate+ADP $-\longrightarrow$ carbamate+ATP	e. g. clostridia on arginine
6. Formyl-tetrahydrofolate synthetase	N^{10}-formyl-H_4 folate+ADP+P_i $\longrightarrow$ formate+H_4 folate+ATP	e. g. clostridia on xanthine

Of these six reactions, the three last are only important in a few organisms; of the other three reactions in Table 2. 2, reactions 1 and 2 involve intermediates in glycolysis (see Fig. 2. 2). Reaction 3, involving acetyl phosphate, is also widespread amongst anaerobes. Acetyl phosphate is formed from acetyl-CoA by reaction with inorganic phosphate, and it is also generated by the action of phosphoketolases.

Acetyl-CoA can be produced by the degradation of acetoacetyl-CoA, or from pyruvate by one of three reactions: pyruvate dehydrogenase (NAD^+-linked); pyruvate formate lyase (which catalyses the reaction pyruvate+CoA $\longrightarrow$ acetyl-CoA +formate); or pyruvate: ferredoxin oxidoreductase, which gives the same reaction products as pyruvate dehydrogenase but involves an iron-sulphur protein, ferredoxin, rather than NAD^+ as oxidant (the reduced ferredoxin is oxidized back to ferredoxin by hydrogenase which releases H_2). Of these three enzymes, the latter two are sensitive to the presence of oxygen and quickly lose activity when the anaerobe containing them is exposed to air.

There is increasing evidence that electron transport phosphorylation can also occur through the mediation of fumarate reductase, which is probably important in several methane-producing bacteria, sulphate-reducing organisms, and hydrogen bacteria which ferment H_2 and CO_2. The reaction is: fumarate+$2H^-$+ADP $\longrightarrow$ succinate+ATP. The hydride ions may be supplied from a variety of cofactors, including NADH, and in some organisms such as *Escherichia coli* their generation may involve a sequence of electron carriers similar to, if not identical with, the components of the electron transport chain in aerobic organisms. Thus although O_2 is not involved the organism is able to couple various reactions so that ATP can be produced.

All anaerobes face two problems. First, lacking the coupling of NADH (or NADPH) reoxidation to ATP generation through oxidative phosphorylation, the yield of ATP per mole of substrate is much smaller than with aerobic metabolism. Second, the inability to couple the oxidation of NADH to the reduction of oxygen poses the problem of how to achieve this essential reaction, without which metabolism would rapidly come to a halt, as all the NAD^+ became irreversibly converted to NADH.

Anaerobes have adopted a variety of means to achieve the reoxidation of reduced cofactors. Essentially each scheme is of the kind:

$$AH_2 \quad NAD^+ \qquad BH_2$$
$$A \quad NADH \qquad B$$

Here, the step $AH_2 \longrightarrow A$ is part of the pathway by which substrate is being utilized by the anaerobe. Normally the substance B, required for the compensating reduction, will also be directly derived from the substrate; BH_2, once formed, need not be metabolized further. The essential metabolism of AH_2 is thus stoichiometrically linked to the compensating production of BH_2. Anaerobes must therefore accumulate reduced metabolites in order to carry out the degradation of any substrate. Moreover, since—as already noted—they derive relatively low ATP yields from substrate degradation, this accumulation of reduced metabolites is bound to be large relative to the amount of cell materials synthesized. Ways in which anaerobic metabolism is organized to achieve this are described in the following section.

2.7 Anaerobic metabolism

The choice of substrate with which to re-oxidize reductants such as NADH, NADPH, $FADH_2$, can be very wide and a corresponding variety of end-products will result. A description of pathways of anaerobic metabolism is therefore a description of what end-products are accumulated by individual organisms. Some of these, such as ethanol, have considerable commercial importance.

Even under anaerobic conditions glucose metabolism will still produce pyruvate, but only a small amount of pyruvate will be taken into the tricarboxylic acid cycle to produce intermediates for the biosynthesis of essential cell material. The tricarboxylic acid cycle reactions then function only to provide these intermediates and not to generate energy. Often the cycle is not fully operational and in particular 2-oxoglutarate dehydrogenase (see Fig. 2.8) may not operate. The 'cycle' is therefore a 'horseshoe' in which oxaloacetate is channelled to succinate and citrate is converted to 2-oxoglutarate.

2.7.1 Ethanol fermentation

In yeasts such as *Saccharomyces cerevisiae* the re-oxidant is acetaldehyde; most of the pyruvate generated from glucose is converted into ethanol:

$$\text{pyruvate} \longrightarrow \begin{array}{c} \text{2-hydroxyethyl-} \\ \text{thiamine} \\ \text{pyrophosphate} \end{array} \longrightarrow \text{acetaldehyde} \underset{NADH \quad NAD^+}{\longrightarrow} \text{ethanol}$$

As 2 moles of pyruvate are produced from 1 mole of glucose, the production of ethanol can re-oxidize both moles of NADH produced in the triose phosphate dehydrogenase reaction (see Fig. 2.2), and the overall stoichiometry is therefore:

$$\text{glucose} + 2ADP + P_i \longrightarrow 2\text{ethanol} + 2ATP$$

The net production of ATP provides energy for the yeast cells to grow but, as will be appreciated by comparison with Table 2.1, the yield per mole of glucose transformed is less than 5% of that which occurs under aerobic conditions.

Any glucose that is metabolized by the pentose phosphate pathway, to produce the essential C_5 and C_4 sugars, can produce no more than 1 mole of pyruvate from each mole of glucose, and only with the simultaneous generation of 2 moles of NADPH and 1 mole of NADH (see Fig. 2.4)[5]. These additional reducing equivalents (for the re-oxidation of which there is now insufficient pyruvate) must be re-oxidized by being coupled to other reactions. Prime amongst these other reactions is the formation of fatty acids, which are chemically reduced compounds whose synthesis demands a considerable input of reducing equivalents (cf. Fig. 2.18).

Ethanol is also produced by some bacteria (see Section 2.7.5), often in conjunction with other end-products, and by some moulds, and anaerobic conditions are generally needed for maximum ethanol production. If the producing organism is also capable of aerobic growth, as is *S. cerevisiae*, then when oxygen is introduced the accumulated ethanol will often be taken up by cells and utilized, by way of acetic acid, as a growth substrate.

2.7.2 Lactic acid fermentations

Fermentations producing lactic acid are second only to alcohol fermentations, both historically and in their importance to the food industry.

Heterofermentative lactic acid bacteria produce a variety of reduced compounds besides lactate, and do not have the key glycolytic enzyme, aldolase (see Fig. 2.2); instead they use phosphoketolase (p. 22) which produces acetyl phosphate. Under anaerobic conditions this is converted both into ethanol, which regenerates NAD^+, and into acetate by a reaction which can generate ATP (see Table 2.2). The other product of phosphoketolase is glyceraldehyde 3-phosphate, which is converted to pyruvate by the usual glycolytic sequence, and thence to lactate by the action of lactate dehydrogenase:

$$\text{pyruvate} + \text{NADH} \longrightarrow \text{lactate} + \text{NAD}^+$$

This reaction is also used by the homolactic acid bacteria; these organisms do not possess phosphoketolase and consequently lactate is virtually the sole end-product. Some lactobacilli produce D-lactate, others L-, and some a mixture of the two forms due to differences in the various lactate dehydrogenases.

2.7.3 Propionic acid fermentation

Propionibacteria, found for example in Gruyère cheese, convert pyruvate to propionate in a series of reactions with methylmalonyl-CoA as the key intermediate (Fig. 2.16). This is used as the immediate source of propionate in a unique transcarboxylation reaction:

The methylmalonyl-CoA is formed by an internal transcarboxylation from succinyl-

CoA, and can thus be regenerated from oxaloacetate (via malate, fumarate, and succinate) while 2 moles of NADH are oxidized to NAD^+. In some *Clostridium* species propionate is produced directly from pyruvate via lactate and acrylate; again, this conversion achieves the re-oxidation of 2 moles of NADH.

5

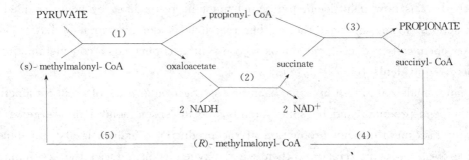

10

Fig. 2.16　Indirect reduction of pyruvate to propionate in propionobacteria. Enzymes are:
(1) transcarboxylase, (2) as in Fig. 2.8, through malate and fumarate,
(3) CoA transferase, (4) methylmalonyl-CoA mutase, (5) racemase

2.7.4　Butanediol fermentation

15 In *Aerobacter* (now *Klebsiella*) spp., *Serratia* and some *Bacillus* spp., 2 moles of pyruvate undergo condensation (again, the reactive intermediate is hydroxyethyl-TPP, see p. 34) and eventually produce 2,3-butanediol:

$$2 \text{ pyruvate} \longrightarrow \alpha\text{-acetolactate} + CO_2$$
$$\downarrow$$
$$\text{acetylmethylcarbinol} + CO_2$$
$$\downarrow$$
20
$$2,3\text{-butanediol}$$

Only the final step is linked to the oxidation of NADH, so that the yield of NAD^+ is only 0.5 mole per mole of pyruvate; these organisms also convert pyruvate to other products including lactate and formate (see below).

2.7.5　Formic acid fermentations

25 In various enterobacteria, pyruvate is converted partly to lactate and partly to acetyl-CoA+formate. The latter reaction is termed the *phosphoroclastic split*. The formate may accumulate in small amounts but is usually converted to CO_2 and H_2 by formate hydrogen lyase. The 'advantage' of this route from pyruvate to acetyl-CoA is that it does *not* produce NADH (compare pyruvate dehydrogenase) and so avoids the necessity
30 of a re-oxidation reaction. Acetyl-CoA can be converted to acetaldehyde by an aldehyde dehydrogenase:

$$\text{acetyl-CoA} + \text{NADH} \longrightarrow \text{acetaldehyde} + NAD^+$$

Reduction of the acetaldehyde to ethanol can occur with further oxidation of NADH. Note that this route to ethanol is not the same as that which occurs in yeast (Section 2.7.1).

2.7.6 Butyric acid fermentation

Historically, the production of butanol, acetone and propan-2-ol is the oldest of the 'deliberate' fermentation processes, i. e. ones developed from established principles using single strains of known organisms. This family of end-products from glucose metabolism are formed by members of the *Clostridium* group of bacteria, according to the   5
scheme shown in Fig. 2.17.

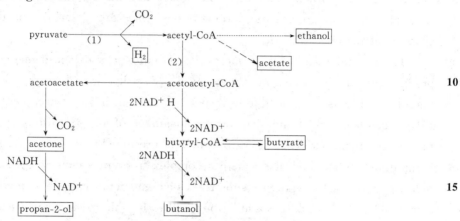

Fig. 2.17   Major end-products (boxed) from pyruvate in *Clostridium* species. Enzyme (1) is pyruvate-ferredoxin oxidoreductase plus hydrogenase; the latter enzyme also interconverts $(NAD^+ + H_2)$ and NADH. Enzyme (2) is thiolase; other CoA transfers are omitted. The relative amounts of acetone, propan-2-ol, butryrate and butanol   20 vary between strains and according to the total $NADH/NAD^+$ flux. Ethanol and acetate are normally minor products

There are a number of variations; some clostridia produce butyrate, acetate, CO_2 and H_2 whilst others produce mainly acetone rather than propan-2-ol. The proportions of the end-products varies according to the chosen species and strain and according to the   25
cultural conditions.

2.7.7 Miscellaneous

There are a number of other reduced products that may be produced by microorganisms growing anaerobically. including sugar alcohols, succinic acid and trimethylene glycol. Glycerol can be formed, and indeed was for a time produced commercially, by adding   30
bisulphite to yeast growing anaerobically. The bisulphite forms a complex with acetaldehyde, so that ethanol can no longer be produced, and the organism, seeking an alternative means to re-oxidize NADH, reduces triose phosphate to glycerol.

2.8 Biosynthesis and growth

The microbial cell is able to reproduce itself from the very simplest of nutrients. The   35
number of pathways which a cell must use to accomplish this is enormous; a bacterial cell probably contains well over 1000 different enzymes, and a eukaryotic cell may contain twice as many[6] . Cell macromolecules of all kinds (proteins , nucleic acids ,

polysaccharides, etc.) are built up from about 100 different monomer units. A general outline of the pathways of biosynthesis of these various monomers (amino acids, purines, pyrimidines, fatty acids, sugars, etc.) is given as Fig. 2. 18. Pathways of biosynthesis, as can be seen, are interrelated and all rely on the maintenance of 'pools'
5   of the necessary intermediates. Unfortunately it is not possible here to provide even outline particulars of these many pathways; their study is a major part of general biochemistry for which numerous textbooks exist. Insofar as particular pathways are especially relevant to specific fermentations, they are described in the appropriate chapters of the present book.

10   The cell carries out all its metabolic activities in a balanced manner so that end-products are neither over- nor under-produced; either would be disadvantageous. The microbial cell must also be able to respond to changes in its environment (temperature, pH, oxygen level, etc.) and also to take advantage of any gratuitous amounts of (say) preformed amino acids, purines or pyrimidines presented to it. This is frequently the case
15   in natural habitats, and also where a complex nutrient (such as corn steep liquor or molasses) is used as growth substrate; such nutrients contain a plethora of carbon compounds. It is therefore possible for a cell to be able to save both carbon and energy by ceasing the synthesis of any material of which it has sufficient, and to make further economies by ceasing to synthesize any redundant enzymes. Thus there are at least two
20   distinct ways—control of enzyme activity, and control of enzyme formation—by which a cell should be able to regulate synthesis of its various components. The same control mechanisms are also used to balance synthetic processes, even when no gratuitous materials are presented to the cell. Such general control mechanisms are described in this section.

25   ## 2. 8. 1 Control of metabolism

2. 8. 1. 1 *Nutrient uptake*
Control of cell metabolism begins by the cell regulating its uptake of nutrients. Most nutrients, apart from oxygen and a very few carbon compounds, are taken up by specific transport mechanisms so that they may be concentrated within the cell from dilute
30   solutions outside. Such 'active' transport[7] systems require an input of energy. The processes are controllable so that once the amount of nutrient taken into the cell has reached a given concentration, further unnecessary (or even detrimental) uptake can be stopped.

2. 8. 1. 2 *Compartmentalization*

35   The second form of metabolic control is by use of compartments, or organelles, within the cell wherein separate pools[8] of metabolites can be maintained. An obvious example is the mitochondrion of the eukaryotic cell which separates (amongst others) the

39

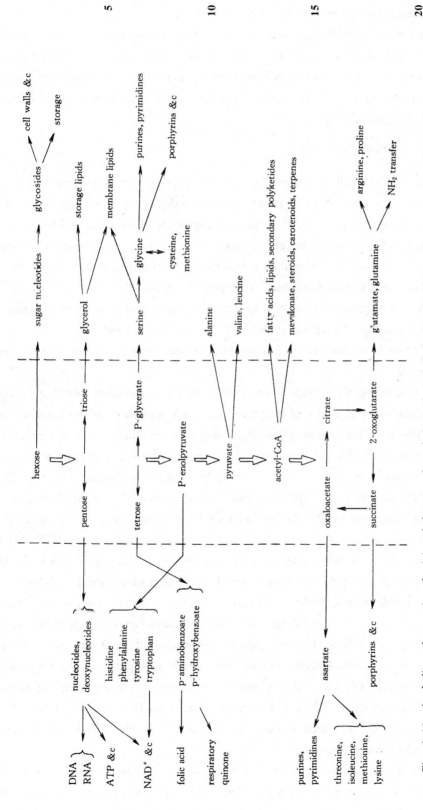

Fig. 2.18 Anabolic pathways (synthesis) and the central catabolic pathways. Only the main biosynthesis routes, and their main connections with catabolic pathways, are shown, all in highly simplified versions. Connections through 'energy' (ATP) and 'redox' (NAD⁺, NADP⁺) metabolism and through the metabolism of nitrogen, etc., are all omitted

tricarboxylic acid cycle reactions from reactions in the cytoplasm. Another, the peroxisome,contains enzymes for fatty acid degradation (see Fig. 2. 10),whereas the somewhat similar enzymes which carry out related reactions in the reverse direction, leading to the synthesis of fatty acids,are located in the cytoplasm. Separating the two
5 sets of enzymes prevents any common intermediates being recycled in a futile manner. Other organelles (vacuoles,the nucleus,chloroplast,etc.) are similarly used to control other reactions of the cell.

2. 8. 1. 3 Control of enzyme synthesis

10 Many enzymes within a cell are present constitutively;they are there under all growth conditions. Other enzymes only ' appear' when needed; e. g. isocitrate lyase of the glyoxylate by-pass (see Fig. 2. 9) when the cell grows on a C_2 substrate. This is termed *induction* of enzyme synthesis. Conversely enzymes can 'disappear' when they are no longer required; enzymes for histidine biosynthesis stop being produced if there is
15 sufficient gratuitous histidine available[⑨] to satisfy the needs of the cell. This is termed *repression*; when the gratuitous supply of the compound has gone, the enzymes for synthesis of the material 'reappear';their synthesis is *de-repressed*.

To understand how these controls operate it is necessary to outline the process of protein synthesis.

20 Proteins (including all enzymes) are synthesized by sequential addition of amino acid to amino acid by a complex of enzymes and RNA organized in the ribosome (see Fig. 2. 19). The code for ensuring the right sequence of amino acids is carried by a strand of messenger RNA,which in turn is synthesized by copying from a section of DNA in the chromosome (genome) of the cell;this process is brought about by DNA-
25 dependent RNA polymerases and is termed *transcription*. As is well known, the chromosome is composed of the double helix of DNA which is made up of a precise sequence of bases:adenine (A),cytosine (C),thymine (T) and guanine (G). The two chains are held together solely by hydrogen bonds between adjacent (A···T) and (C··· T) base pairs. As A always pairs with T and C with G,a new strand of DNA can be
30 made from one single strand of the molecule,and is then *complementary* to the original. In this way DNA can be replicated and the genetic message,or code,preserved;this is shown later (Fig. 2. 2). It is also from one of the strands of DNA that the messenger RNA is made (Fig. 2. 19). Except that the base uracil is substituted for thymine,the RNA complements the DNA strand and similarly carries the genetic code in the sequence
35 of its bases. Each messenger RNA is only made from a small part of the DNA,though many mRNAs can be produced by reading along the whole length of the DNA. Messenger RNAs remain single stranded.

Ribosomes become attached to the mRNA and,in the ribosome,the bases of the messenger RNA are 'read-off',that is *translated*,three at a time,to code for a particular
40 amino acid. The three bases are termed a *codon*. Thus,for example,the codon UCA codes

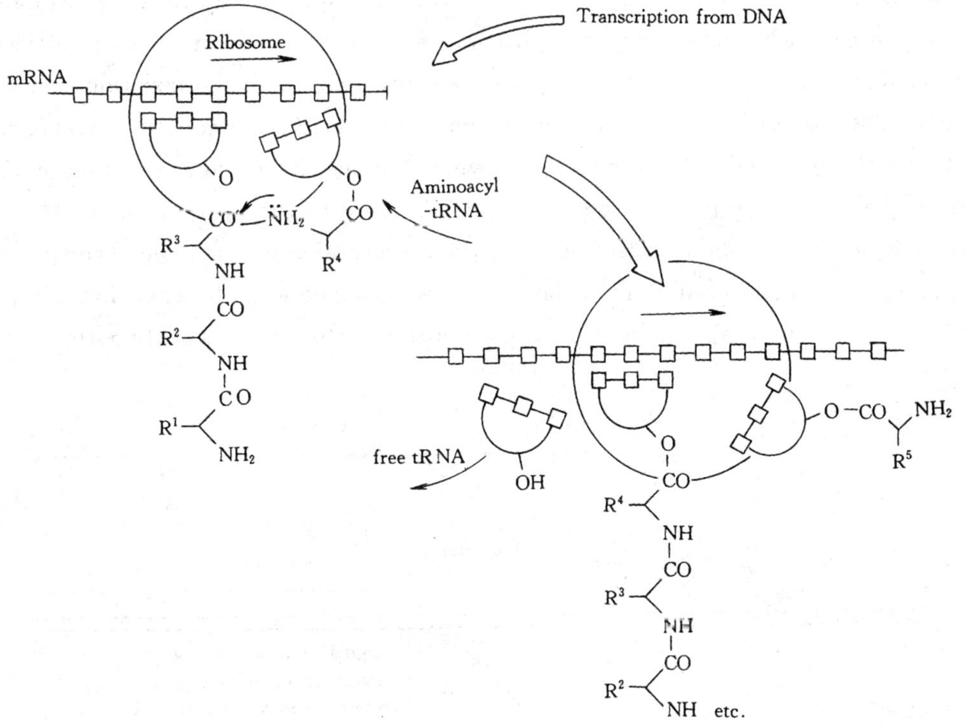

Fig. 2.19 Ribosome action (translation). Transfer RNA molecules (tRNA) complementary to successive base triplets in the messenger-RNA, and each carrying the corresponding aminoacid, transfer their aminoacyl residues in correct sequence to the growing peptide chain as the ribosome moves along the messenger RNA

specifically for serine and the codon CAG for glutamine; hence when the sequence UCACAG is encountered along the mRNA attached to the ribosome this will produce seryl-glutamine. Each amino acid is enabled to 'recognize' the three bases along the mRNA to which it corresponds to by being covalently linked to a specific transfer RNA (tRNA). The aminoacyl-tRNAs are the active units used by the ribosome to produce the growing peptide chain (see Fig. 2.19).

Each individual mRNA molecule thus codes for one protein and originates from one *gene* on the chromosome (more than one protein may be needed to make some functional enzymes, for example pyruvate dehydrogenase). Individual genes can be transcribed many times and there may be more than one copy of the gene on the chromosome. In either case, there is 'amplification' of the genetic information.

The regulation of protein synthesis through the overall mechanisms of transcription and translation is extremely complex; it differs, particularly in details, between prokaryotes and eukaryotes, and many aspects are still not elucidated. However the broad principles of the regulatory mechanisms can be illustrated from bacterial systems.

The machinery producing copies of mRNA from the DNA is controllable with respect to sections of the chromosome which code for *inducible* or *repressible* protein (see above). Such mechanisms are shown diagrammatically in Fig. 2. 20. Sections of DNA termed *regulatory genes* produce (by way of the corresponding mRNA) a regulatory *repressor protein* whose function is to become attached to another, usually adjacent, gene. Binding of the protein to this *operator gene* prevents further translation occurring

5 in the next section of DNA, that is in one or more *structural genes* which are responsible for the synthesis of mRNAs coding for enzyme proteins. If an inducer is present, this binds to the regulatory protein and prevents it binding to the operator gene. The free operator gene then permits transcription of the structural genes and the corresponding proteins can be synthesized. This is how a 'new' metabolic pathway is brought into

10 operation . As long as the inducer molecule is present the enzymes will continue to be

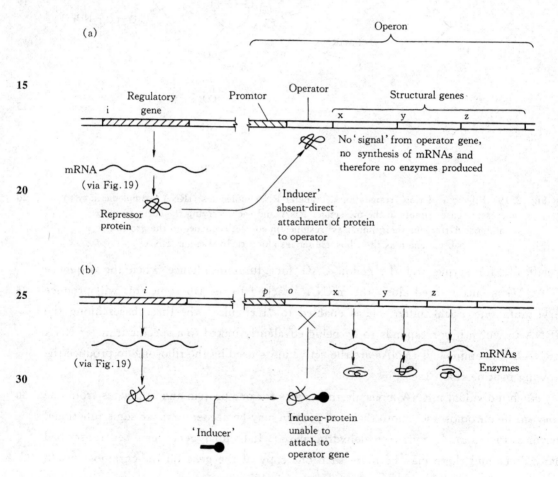

Fig. 2. 20 Induction. (a) In the absence of inducer (e. g. lactose), the product of the repressor gene
(*i*) combines with the operator gene (*o*) and this prevents transcription of the adjacent structural
genes (*x*, *y*, *z*).

(b) When the inducer substance is present, it combines with the repressor protein and prevents it
from binding to the *o* gene; transcription of the structural genes to messenger RNAs, and translation
of the mRNAs to enzymes now proceeds, and the enzymes are available for metabolism of the
inducer. *Note*. In other cases, the repressor protein will only bind to the operator gene when a
repressor substance is present ; the enzymes are only formed when the repressor substance is

removed (see text)

synthesized;if it is removed,or consumed (most frequently by the metabolic pathway it is inducing) then the enzymes will cease to be synthesized.

Repression (rather than induction) of enzyme synthesis occurs when a molecule, often the end-product of a pathway,interacts with the repressor proteins to produce a product which now blocks the operator gene. If the end-product is removed or consumed,the repressor proteins no longer bind with the operator gene,transcription of the structural genes takes place,and biosynthesis of the end-product can be resumed.

2. 8. 1. 4 Catabolite repression

This type of metabolic control is an extension of the ideas already set out with respect to enzyme induction and repression,being brought about by external nutrients added to the microbial culture. The term catabolite repression refers to several general phenomena, seen for example when a microorganism is able to select,from two or more different carbon sources simultaneously presented to it, that substrate which it 'prefers' to utilize. For example a microorganism presented with both glucose and lactose may 'ignore' the lactose until it has consumed all the glucose. Similar selection may occur for the choice of a nitrogen source if more than one is available. The advantage to the cell is that it can use the compound which involves it in the least expenditure of energy.

Detailed mechanisms of catabolite repression may well vary from organism to organism. The sequence of events shown in Fig. 2. 21 is for the process as described in the bacterium *E. coli*. The key to the sequence lies in the compound cyclic AMP (cAMP;its phosphate group is attached to both the 3' and 5' hydroxyl group of the ribose moiety forming a phosphodiester — see Fig. 2. 1). cAMP , formed from ATP by

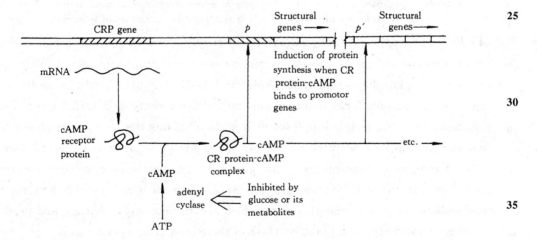

Fig. 2. 21   Catabolite repression. The mechanism shown is one mediated by cyclic AMP(cAMP) in *E. coli*. One or several operons (see Fig. 2. 20) are controlled simultaneously by their requirement for the product from cAMP and a catabolite repressor protein corresponding to an independent gene CRP. The eventual control in this mechanism is the effect of ATP and other nucleotides on the activities of enzymes producing or breaking-down the regulator molecule cAMP

5

10

15

20

25

30

35

40

adenyl cyclase, interacts with a specific receptor protein (CRP = Cyclic AMP Receptor Protein) which positively promotes transcription of an operon (cf. Fig. 2. 20).

Control of the pool size[⊛] of cAMP is crucial for this mechanism, and is achieved by regulating the relative activities of adenyl cyclase and of the phosphodiesterase which
5   converts cAMP to AMP. The level of cAMP relates closely to the 'energy charge' discussed in Section 2. 2. Various metabolites of glucose appear to be potent inhibitors of adenyl cyclase activity[see Section 2. 8. 1. 5(b)], and so long as these are present in the cell (indicating the continued availability of glucose) then the several operons under control of the cAMP-CRP complex will not be transcribed. Catabolite repression effects
10   are also important in controlling patterns of anabolic processes, particularly in the phenomena of 'secondary biosynthesis'.

2. 8. 1. 5   Modification of enzyme activity

Once an enzyme has been synthesized, its activity can be modulated by a variety of
15   means.

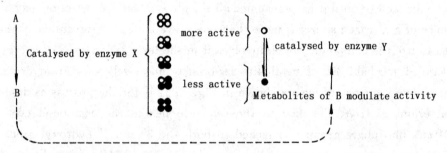

Fig. 2. 22   Enzyme control by a cascade mechanism. Metabolites derived from B affect (positively or negatively) the activity of enzyme Y, which interconverts more active and less
25   active subunits of enzyme X, which catalyses the formation of B from A

(a) Post-transcriptional modifications. Some enzymes can exist in an active and a less active form, which can be interconverted by the covalent attachment of some specific group (often phosphate, sometimes AMP or UMP). The attachment is mediated by a separate enzyme, which has no other function, whose activity is in turn regulated by the
30   presence of various metabolites (see next section). Thus the reaction catalysed by the first enzyme can be moderated by the prevailing metabolic status of the cell (see Fig. 2. 22). Examples of such processes are glutamine synthetase in E. coli (it is extremely important for the cell to regulate precisely the pool size[⊛] of the key metabolic intermediates glutamate and glutamine which are, respectively, substrate and product of
35   the enzyme) and glycogen phosphorylase in the mould Neurospora crassa.

(b) Action of effectors. Enzyme activity is very often slowed down by a build-up of the product of the reaction it is catalysing. The compound is then said to be an inhibitor, or negative effector, of the enzyme. This is a simple mechanism to understand: the reaction product blocks access of the substrate to the active site of enzyme, where both
40   are able to 'fit'. However, many enzymes, particularly those at the beginning of a

pathway, are similarly sensitive to the presence of compounds chemically unrelated to the reaction they are catalysing. The most common effect is known as *feedback inhibition*, in which the end-product of a pathway acts as a negative effector on the activity of an early enzyme in that pathway:

$$A \longrightarrow B \longrightarrow C \longrightarrow D \longrightarrow E$$

The effect of this inhibition is to ensure that once the end-product has been produced in sufficient quantity, no further carbon units will be channelled down the pathway; the product which is not needed is not produced. The same event will occur if the end-product is present in the growth medium taken up into the cell (see Section 2.8.1.1). Feedback inhibition often parallels repression of enzyme synthesis (see above), which is **10** also brought about by the presence of excess end-product; it can be thought of as *fine control* rapidly brought about and readily reversible, whereas enzyme repression provides a *coarse control* which takes longer to achieve.

The general mechanism of feedback inhibition is based upon binding of the effector molecule to the enzyme at a site which is different from the active site; the effector **15** modifies the conformation (shape) of the protein so that it is no longer so effective a catalyst for the reaction of its substrate. Such enzymes are said to be *allosterically controlled*. Examples can be found in most of the pathways of metabolism leading to the biosynthesis of amino acids, purines, pyrimidines and other monomers (see Fig. 2.18).

The process becomes more complicated where there is more than one product **20** derived from branches in a common pathway:

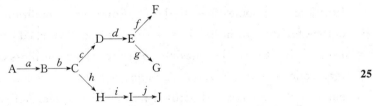

Here it is important that if one of the three end-products, F, G or J, reaches its optimum pool size[3], it should act to prevent more of itself being produced but at the same time not inhibit the synthesis of the other two end-products. Thus in the above diagram, assuming the three end-products were required in equal amounts, product F would be **30** expected to inhibit reaction *f* completely, reaction *c* by 50% and reaction *a* by 33%. Thus starting from A, first B and thence C would be formed at two-thirds the usual rate; C instead of producing twice as much D as H, would now produce equal amounts of these two compounds; all of D would now go to G, and H would go to J as before. **35**

The manner in which this partial inhibition of enzyme activity is achieved can vary from pathway to pathway and organism to organism. A common method is for the organism to use *isoenzymes*. That is, for reaction *a* above, there will be three distinct and independent enzymes each catalysing the reaction with equal efficiency. However one isoenzyme will be sensitive to feedback inhibition by F, the second by G, and the third by H. In this way, only one isoenzyme will be inhibited if one end-product reaches its optimum pool concentration. The reaction c may similarly be expected to be catalysed by two isoenzymes: one sensitive to feedback inhibition by F and the other by G.

Examples of this type of control occur in the biosynthesis of the three aromatic amino acids, phenylalanine, tyrosine and tryptophan, and in the biosynthesis of threonine, methionine and lysine (see Fig. 2.18).

Feedback effects are also involved in the regulation of transport processes (see Section 2.8.1.1). However, it may not be quite accurate to extend the concept to situations where metabolites such as ATP, ADP, AMP, NAD(P)$^+$ or NAD(P)H act as positive or negative effectors on a particular enzyme. For instance, several enzymes of the tricarboxylic acid (see Fig. 2.8), particularly citrate synthase, are inhibited by ATP, and as ATP is the 'end-product' of oxidative phosphorylation which is linked to the reaction of the cycle, this might be construed as a more indirect form of feedback inhibition. Irrespective of semantics, this type of control by different forms or general cofactors is quite widespread amongst the enzymes of the central pathways of metabolism.

2.8.1.6 Degradation of enzymes

Enzymes are not particularly stable molecules and may be quickly and irreversibly destroyed. The normal half-life is very variable; it may be as short as a few minutes, or as long as several days. Although the syntheses of enzymes can be regulated at the genetic level (see Section 2.8.1.3), once an enzyme has been synthesized it can remain functional for some time. If the environmental conditions change abruptly, it may not suffice for the synthesis of the enzyme to be 'switched off' i.e. repressed; the cell may need to inactivate the enzyme so as to avoid needless, or even perhaps deleterious, metabolic activity. Several examples are known where specific proteolytic enzymes, suitably activated, will destroy a particular enzyme. Activation is probably triggered by the presence (or absence) of a key metabolite.

2.8.2 Coordination of metabolism and growth

We have already considered how the cell is able to control the biosynthesis of its many constituent parts so that the correct amount of monomer is always synthesized as well as the appropriate number of different enzyme molecules. These control mechanisms are responses to the external environment of the cell. The cell always attempts to optimize its internal biochemistry so that it can make the most efficient use of preformed carbon and nitrogen compounds, maximizing the energy yield, minimizing energy expenditure, and growing as rapidly as it is able.

Under limiting environmental conditions, for example absence of any nitrogen source, the organism may not be able to reproduce. Under such conditions, end-products (some of which may well be desired by the biotechnologist) would be accumulated as the organism continued to metabolize the carbon available to it. The biosynthetic machinery of an organism does, and must, continue to work at all times; the only time the reactions of a cell come to equilibrium is when it is dead.

It is therefore essential for the organism to keep its cell biochemistry working and it can achieve this by a variety of means depending on the prevailing conditions: by de-repressing new anabolic enzymes it may channel the carbon substrate into any of a number of 'secondary' metabolites; it can produce large amounts of storage compounds such as poly-β-hydroxy-butyrate, lipid, glycogen and other polysaccharides. It may degrade these storage materials if placed in a 'starvation' situation where no external carbon is being supplied to the cell. What is produced is probably less important than that the cell keeps its pathways of metabolism operating.

Under 'normal' conditions, given a supply of all the essential nutrients, the organism grows[⑩]. In batch culture, the cells multiply in a closed system (there is no addition to, or subtraction from, the fermenter once it has been inoculated) until either some nutrient becomes exhausted or until some product accumulates to inhibit further growth, or the number of cells reaches such a level that there is no further space available for new ones to occupy. During the growth of the cells, the various components of the cell alter in relative amounts (Fig. 2. 23) and the cell even changes in size as it elongates before cell division. During the initial exponential growth period when the cells are growing at maximum rate, the RNA content of the cell increases rapidly due to the cells synthesizing more proteins on the ribosome (see Fig. 2. 19) The content of DNA may fall, as indicated in Fig. 2. 23 although the exact extent of this fall will depend upon the rate at which the cell is able to replicate its DNA (see Section 2. 8. 3).

The rate at which an organism can grow is expressed either as the doubling time (t_d), i. e. the time taken for one cell to become two, or as the specific growth rate (μ) which is the rate of synthesis of new cell material expressed per unit weight of existing cell material. These two values are related by the equations

$$\mu = \frac{1}{x} \cdot \frac{dx}{dt} = \frac{d(\ln x)}{dt} = \frac{\ln 2}{t_d}$$

(where $x=$ cell concentration, $t=$ time), from which $\mu = 0. 69/t_d$.

In batch culture the value of μ varies throughout, due to the continually decreasing concentration of nutrients; in many practical situations with aerobic organisms the rate of supply of oxygen eventually governs the rate of their growth. Only in continuous culture can the specific growth rate be held constant through the continuous introduction of fresh nutrients (and an ensured supply of oxygen). What governs the maximum growth rate that an organism can attain probably varies from organism to organism, and is quite unknown for most. It may be the ultimate rate at which DNA can be synthesized, or the

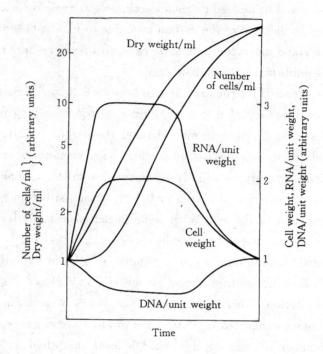

Fig. 2. 23   Idealized representation of the changes in cell size (i. e. cell weight),cell numbers,total dry weight and chemical composition during growth of bacteria in batch culture. Note that the scale on the left is logarithmic

rate at which a particular nutrient can be taken up into the cell,or the rate at which some part of the cell,such as the walls,can be assembled. Doubling times can range from about 10 minutes with *Benekea natriegens* through to several hours with yeasts and fungi. Most bacteria have doubling times of 30 minutes or more,and some have doubling times which extend to several days. Examples are listed in Table 2. 3.

Table 2. 3   Growth rates of various microorganisms under optimal conditions

Microorganism	Maximum specific growth rate, $\mu_m (h^{-1})$	Doubling time, $t_d(h)$ $(=0.693/\mu_m)$
Escherichia coli	2. 1	0. 33
Saccharomyces cerevisiae	0. 45	1. 5
Candida utilis	0. 40	1. 7
Schizosaccharomyces pombe	0. 17	4. 0
Penicillium chrysogenum	0. 28	2. 5
Geotrichum lactis	0. 35	2. 0
Fusarium graminearum	0. 28	2. 5
Chlorella pyrenoidosa	0. 08	8. 5

49

2. 8. 3   The cell cycle[①] and DNA replication

The processes of cell division are different in prokaryotes and eukaryotes, although both use essentially similar mechanisms for controlling the expression of genes and of regulating the activities of the gene products (enzyme proteins). In a rapidly growing bacterium DNA synthesis takes place more or less continuously, but in a eukaryotic cell **5** it forms only part of the cell cycle. The bacterial genome is but two molecules of DNA in the double helix conformation, linked head to tail to form a circular chromosome. The eukaryotic cell contains several physically separate chromosomes.

In the eukaryote, the cell cycle is divided into stages, each of variable duration depending on the growth conditions. The cycle culminates with the replication of all the **10** chromosomes which then divide between daughter and mother cell by a process known as *mitosis*. The process becomes more complex the higher one advances through the microbial kingdom when sexual reproduction, rather than the simple binary fission of bacteria or the budding of yeasts, may occur. The process of chromosomal division then occurs by *meiosis* in which chromosomes are distributed, after replication of the DNA, **15** into germ cells.

In all microorganisms the DNA probably replicates by similar mechanisms. The double-stranded DNA unwinds with each strand forming a new strand complementary to itself. This is shown in Fig. 2. 24. Each replication fork operates bidirectionally, that is unwinding and synthesis of the complementary DNA strand occurs at both ends of the **20** separation.

In bacteria, there can be more than one replication fork functioning at any one time so that the genome can be reproduced with great rapidity . This happens when the time

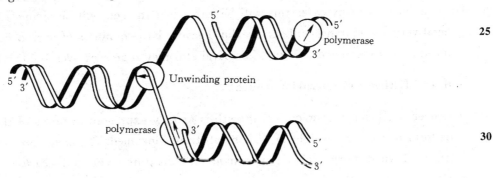

25

30

Fig. 2. 24   DNA replication. In the two complementary strands of DNA the phospho-3'-deoxyribotyl-5' 'backbone' runs in opposite directions. In replication, the complementary strands are first separated ('unwinding') so that additional **35** deoxyribonucleotides can complement the bases in each strand. On one strand DNA polymerase then acts directly to assemble the new DNA, but on the other it must act in short 'reverse' sections. The whole set of operations constitutes a 'replication fork'. In replication of the circular chromosome of bacteria, pairs of such forks are initiated and move in opposite directions around the chromosome **40**

for complete DNA replication is longer than the time for cell division, and under these conditions each cell will contain more than one copy of the replicated parts of the chromosome. Cell division is however synchronized to the complete replication of the chromosomes, so that each daughter cell receives its DNA before the dividing septum is formed. Apparently a 'termination protein' is synthesized when replication of DNA has been completed, and it is this protein which triggers septum formation and cell division.

Cell duplication in eukaryotic cells is complicated by the requirement for organelles also to divide during the course of the cell cycle. Mitochondria and chloroplasts (the photosynthetic apparatus of photosynthetic microorganisms and plants) have their own DNA and divide independently of the cell nucleus. In this way the number of mitochondria and chloroplasts can change according to the environmental conditions. For example, a yeast growing under anaerobic conditions does not rely on its mitochondria for provision of ATP (see Sections 2.5 and 2.6) and the number of mitochondria is minimal.

Although the genetic information carried by the DNA is accurately reproduced so that each daughter cell carries the same chromosomal programme as its parent, mistakes can be made. Such mistakes lead to the formation of a *mutant*. Mutants can arise both spontaneously, usually at a very low frequency (about 1 in every $10^8 \sim 10^{10}$ cell divisions), or can be induced by exposure of the organism to some DNA-damaging agent (mutagen). Mutants having altered capacities of enzyme activity can be of considerable benefit in increasing the productivity of a fermentation process. However, finding the one desired mutant amongst the many thousands of unwanted mutants can be a very long process.

In the vast majority of cases the mutants have an impaired capacity to carry out some activity; in many cases this will be lethal and the cell will be unable to grow. In general very few mutants will survive, but because large numbers of microorganisms are handled in an experiment a 0.001% survival still may represent over 10000 organisms.

2.8.4 Efficiency of microbial growth

The overall efficiency of microbial growth is usually expressed in terms of the yield of cells formed from unit weight of carbon substrate consumed. The *molar growth yield* Y_5 is the cell yield (dry weight) per mole of substrate, while the *carbon conversion coefficient*, which allows more meaningful comparisons between substrates of different molecular sizes, is the cell yield per gram of substrate carbon. Some typical values for both expressions are collected in Table 2.4; all are maximum values, because under certain conditions (in particular, at low growth rates; the use of substrates for cell growth becomes less than fully efficient.

A particular feature in Table 2.4 which can be readily understood by reference to previous discussions is the lower growth yields attained when facultative organisms are transferred from aerobic to anaerobic conditions, a phenomenon which is obviously

Table 2.4   Growth yields of microorganisms growing on different substrates

Substrate	Organism	Molar growth yield (g organism dry wt per g-mol substrate)	Carbon conversion coefficient (g organism dry wt per g substrate carbon)
Methane	*Methylomonas methanooxidans*	17.5	1.46
Methanol	*Methylomonas methanolica*	16.6	1.38
Ethanol	*Candida utilis*	31.2	1.30
Glycerol	*Klebsiella pneumoniae* (*Aerobacter aerogenes*)	50.4	1.40
Glucose	*Escherichia coli*:		
	aerobic	95.0	1.32
	anaerobic	25.8	0.36
	Saccharomyces cerevisiae:		
	aerobic	90	1.25
	anaerobic	21	0.29
	Penicillium chrysogenum	81	1.13
Sucrose	*Klebsiella pneumoniae* (*A. aerogenes*)	173	1.20
Xylose	*Klebsiella pneumoniae* (*A. aerogenes*)	52.2	0.87
Acetic acid	*Pseudomonas* sp.	23.5	0.98
	Candida utilis	21.6	0.90
Hexadecane	*Saccharomycopsis* (*Candida*)*lipolytica*	203	1.06
	Acinetobacter sp.	251	1.31

connected with the reduced energy flow, and lower yields of ATP, in anaerobic processes.

Empirically, the actual growth yield will depend on many factors:

(1) the nature of the carbon source.

(2) the pathways of substrate catabolism.

(3) any provision of complex substrates (obviating some anabolic pathways).

(4) energy requirements for assimilating other nutrients, especially nitrogen (less if amino acids are supplied than if NH_3 is used, and considerably more if nitrate ion is the nitrogen source).

(5) varying efficiencies of ATP-generating reactions.

(6) inhibiting substances, adverse ionic balance, or other medium components imposing extra demands on transport systems.

(7) the physiological state of the organism; nearly all microorganisms modify their development according to the external environment, often very considerably (e.g. spore formation), and the different development processes will entail different mass and energy balances.

In continuous culture systems, in which the growth rate and nutritional status of the cells are controlled, further factors can be identified:

 （8）the nature of the limiting substrate; carbon-limited growth is often more 'efficient' than, for example, nitrogen-limited growth, in which catabolism of excess carbon substrate may follow routes which are energetically 'wasteful' (however useful to the biotechnologist!).

 （9）the permitted growth rate.

As a final factor governing all aspects of microbial performances, one might usefully add:

 （10）"the inclinations of the microbe, and the competence of the microbiologist".

Words and Expressions

page   line

16   4   exploit ［ik'sploit］   vt. 利用   utilize

  7   divert ［dai'və:t］   vt. 转移,使转向   to turn aside from a usual course or direction; deflect

  11   matrix ［'meitriks］   n. 发源地   Origin

  divergent ［dai'və:dʒənt］   a. 分歧的   to move in different directions from a common point; differing

  13   nucleic acid ［nju:'kli:ik］   n. 核酸

  carbohydrate ［'kɑ:bəu'haidreit］   n. 碳水化合物;糖类

  14   purine ［'pjuəri:n］   n. 嘌呤

  pyrimidine ［pai'rimidi:n］   n. 嘧啶

  fatty acid ［'fæti］   n. 脂肪酸

  23   aerobic ［ɛə'rəubik］   a. 需氧的

  24   anaerobic ［ənei'rɔbik］   a. 厌氧的

  25   exothermic ［eksəu'θə:mik］   a. 放热的

  28   disproportionation ［disprəpɔ:ʃən'neiʃən］   n. 不匀称反应   a type of chemical reaction in which one molecule of reactant is reduced and another is oxidised.

  32   facultative ［'fækəltətiv］   a. 兼性的

17   16   adenosine triphosphate ［ə'denəsi:n trai'fɔsfeit］   n. 三磷酸腺苷

  17   term ［tə:m］   vt. 把……称为   name, call

  anhydride ［æn'haidraid］   n. 酐

  18   pyrophosphate ［paiərəu'fɔsfeit］   n. 焦磷酸盐

  exergicity   n. 放热

  19   endergicity   n. 吸热

  26   adenylate kinase ［ə'denileit 'kaineis］   n. 腺苷酸激酶

  28   phosphorylation ［fɔsfəri'leiʃən］   n. 磷酸化作用

18   7   prevailing ［pri'veiliŋ］   a. 优势的   prevalent

  9   energy charge   能荷

page	line		

18   13   adenine ['ædəniːn] n. 腺嘌呤

       16   convention [kən'venʃən] n. 惯用方法 a practice or procedure widely observed

       17   as opposed to 与……不同,与……相反 in contrast to

       19   striking ['straikiŋ] a. 显著的 making a powerful impression upon the mind

       23   mould [məuld] (=mold)霉菌

       33   in view of 鉴于,考虑到 taking into account

       34   hydrocarbon ['haidrəu'kɑːbən] 烃

       35   methanol ['meθənɔl] 甲醇

       38   hexose diphosphate pathway ['heksəus] 二磷酸己糖途径

            hexose monophosphate pathway 一磷酸己糖途径

19   2   be subject to 应服从的;受制于……的 owe obedience to

        4   glycolysis pathway [glai'kɔlisis] 糖酵解途径

            pyruvate ['paiəruveit] 丙酮酸盐(酯)

        5   NAD^+(=nicotinamide adenine dinucleotide) [nikə'tinəmaid 'ædəniːn dai'njuːkliətaid] 烟酰胺腺嘌呤二核甘酸,辅酶 I

            NADH 还原型烟酰胺腺嘌呤二核苷酸,还原型辅酶 I

        7   precursor [priː'kəːsə] 前体

       18   glycerate ['glisəreit] 甘油酸酯(盐)

            glyceraldchyde [glisə'rældihaid] 甘油醛

       22   phosphoenolpyruvate 磷酸烯醇丙酸

       27   hexokinase [heksəu'kaineis] 己糖激酶

            glucose phosphate isomerase [ai'sɔmereis] 磷酸葡萄糖异构酶

            phosphofructokinase 磷酸果糖激酶

       28   aldolase ['ældəleis] 醛缩酶

            triose phosphate isomerase ['traiəuz] 磷酸丙糖异构酶

            glyceraldehyde phosphate dehydrogenase 甘油醛磷酸脱氢酶

       29   phosphoglycerate kinase 磷酸甘油酸激酶

            phosphoglyceromutase ['mjuːteis] 磷酸甘油酸变位酶

       31   pentose ['pentəus] 戊糖

       33   $NADP^+$(=nicotinamide adenine dinucleotide phosphate) 烟酰胺腺嘌呤二核苷酸磷酸,辅酶 II

            NADPH 还原型烟酰胺腺嘌呤二核苷酸磷酸,还原型辅酶 II

            hydride ['haidraid] 氢化物

       34   redox reaction ['riːdɔks] 氧化还原反应

       40   tetrose ['tetrəus] 丁糖,四糖

20   20   gluconate ['gluːkəneit] 葡萄糖酸酯

            ribulose ['raibjuləus] 核酮糖

page	line		
20	22	epimerase [iˈpiməreis] 差向异构酶	

20 22 epimerase [iˈpiməreis] 差向异构酶

24 ribose [ˈraibəus] n. 核糖

    xylulose [ˈzailjuləus] n. 木酮糖

26 transketolase [trænsˈkiːtəleis] n. 转酮醇酶，酮醇基转移酶

28 sedohcptulose n. 景天庚酮糖

30 transaldolase [trænsˈældəleis] n. 转二羟丙酮基酶，转醛醇酶

31 erythrose [ˈeriθrəus] n. 赤藓糖

35 shunt [ʃʌnt] n. 旁路

36 phosphogluconate dehydrogenase n. 磷酸葡糖酸脱氢酶

    inset [ˈinset] n. 插图

21 8 modulate [ˈmɔdjuleit] vt. 调整 regulate

38 phosphoketolase [fɔsfəuˈkiːtəleis] n. 磷酸酮醇酶

39 acetyl phosphate [ˈæsitil ˈfɔsfeit] n. 乙酰磷酸

41 heterofermentative [hetərəfəˈmentətiv] a. 杂发酵的

22 1 lactobacilli [læktəubəˈsilai] n. 乳酸杆菌

    q. v. [拉] quod vide 参照 which see. Used to indicate a cross-reference

    acetobacter [əsiːtəuˈbæktə] n. 醋酸杆菌

4 xylose [ˈzailəus] n. 木糖

5 xylitol [ˈzailitɔl] n. 木糖醇

24 tricarboxylic acid cycle n. 三羧酸循环

27 thioester n. 硫酯

38 β-mercaptoethylamine [məkæptəeθiˈlæmin] n. β-巯基乙胺

    pantothenate [pænˈtəuθəneit] n. 泛酸(盐)

23 1 ubiquitous [juːˈbikwitəs] a. (同时)普遍存在的 Being or seeming to be everywhere at the same time; omnipresent

3 eukaryotic [juːkæriˈɔtik] a. 真核的

4 mitochondria [maitəˈkɔndriə] n. [复]线粒体

5 cytoplasmic membrane [saitəuˈplæzmik ˈmembrein] n. 细胞质膜

6 mitochondrion [maitəˈkɔndriɔn] n. 线粒体

15 malate [ˈmæleit] n. 苹果酸盐(酯)

    aconitate n. 乌头酸盐(酯)

18 fumarate [ˈfjuːməreit] n. 延胡索酸盐，反丁烯二酸盐

23 oxalosuccinate n. 草酰琥珀酸盐(酯)

    succinyl-CoA n. 琥珀酰辅酶 A

25 GTP(guanosine triphosphate) [ˈgwɑːnəsin] 三磷酸鸟苷

    GDP(guanosine diphosphate) 二磷酸鸟苷

26 FAD(flavin adenine dinucleotide) [ˈfleivin] n. 黄素腺嘌呤二核苷酸

    $FADH_2$ 还原型黄素腺嘌呤二核苷酸

27 citrate synthase [ˈsitrit ˈsinθeis] n. 柠檬酸合成酶

page line

| 23 | 27 | aconitase [ə'kɔniteis] n. 乌头酸酶 |

28 succinate thiokinase n. 琥珀酸硫激酶

29 fumarase ['fju:məreis] n. 延胡索酸酶

33 oxoglutarate ['ɔksəu'glu:təreit] n. 酮戊二酸

glutamate ['glu:təmeit] n. 谷氨酸盐

34 glutamine ['glu:təmi:n] n. 谷氨酰胺

folic acid ['fəulik 'æsid] n. 叶酸

35 succinate ['sʌksineit] n. 琥珀酸盐，丁二酸盐

porphyrin ['pɔ:firin] n. 卟啉

haem [hi:m] n. 血红素

cytochrome ['saitəkrəum] n. 细胞色素

36 oxaloacetate n. 草酰乙酸

aspartate [əs'pɑ:teit] n. 天门冬氨酸盐（酯）

37 lysine ['laisi:n] n. 赖氨酸

methionine [me'θaiəni:n] n. 甲硫氨酸

threonine ['θriəni:n] n. 苏氨酸

39 assimilate [ə'simileit] n. 同化

24   2 oxidant ['ɔksidənt] n. 氧化剂

reductant [ri'dʌktənt] n. 还原剂

4 oxidative phosphorylation n. 氧化磷酸化

8 perpetuate [pə'petjueit] vt. 使永久存在 to make to last for an indefinitely long time

prime vt. 起动 to start

13 carboxylation n. 羧化作用

16 carboxylase [kɑ:'bɔksileis] n. 羧化酶

20 positive effector n. 正效应物

35 glyoxylate n. 乙醛酸

25 11 lyase ['laieis] n. 裂解酶

14 supplant [sə'plɑ:nt] vt. 取代 replace

26   6 triglyceride [trai'glisəraid] n. 甘油三酯

hydrolyze ['haidrəlaiz] vt. 水解

7 lipase ['laipeis] 脂肪酶

13 acyl ['æsil] 酰基 RCO-

16 commence [kə'mens] vt. 开始 begin

23 alkane ['ælkein] n. (链)烷烃

27   1 hydroxylase [hai'drɔksileis] n. 羟化酶

3 hydride ['haidraid] n. 氢化物

14 ketone ['ki:təun] n. 酮

28 methyltroph n. 甲基营养菌

31 methanotroph n. 甲烷营养菌

35 province ['prɔvins] n. 范围 scope

36 chemolithotrophic a. 无机化能营养的

page	line			
35	31	propionibacteria	[ˌprəupiˌɔnibækˈtiəriə]	n. 丙酸细菌
		Gruyère	[ˈgruːjeə]	n. 格鲁耶尔, 瑞士地名
	32	methylmalonyl-CoA	[ˈmælənil]	n. 甲基丙二酰辅酶 A
36	13	mutase	[ˈmjuːteis]	n. 变位酶
		racemase	[ˈreisimeis]	消旋酶
	14	butanediol		n. 丁二醇
	18	acetolactate		n. 乙酰乳酸
	19	carbinol	[ˈkɑːbinəl]	n. 甲醇
	25	entero-	[构词成分]	肠
	26	phosphoroclastic split		n. 磷酸裂解反应
37	19	thiolase	[ˈθaiəleis]	n. 硫解酶, 乙酰辅酶 A 转乙酰酶
	29	trimethylene glycol		n. 1,3-丙二醇
38	13	gratuitous	[grəˈtjuːitəs]	a. 无偿的, 天生的 received without cost
	17	a plethora of	[ˈpleθərə]	过多 an excess
	28	apart from		除……外 with the exception of, besides
	30	active transport		主动传送
	34	compartmentalization	[kəmpɑːtmentəriˈzeiʃən]	n. 分隔成区域
39	2	nucleotide	[ˈnjuːkliətaid]	n. 核苷酸
		glycoside	[ˈglaikəsaid]	n. 糖苷
	5	histidine	[ˈhistidiːn]	n. 组氨酸
	6	phenylalanine	[feniˈlæləniːn]	n. 苯丙氨酸
	7	purine	[ˈpjuəriːn]	n. 嘌呤
		pyrimidine	[paiˈrimidiːn]	n. 嘧啶
		tyrosine	[ˈtaiərəsiːn]	n. 酪氨酸
	8	tryptophan	[ˈtriptəfæn]	n. 色氨酸
	9	cysteine	[sisˈtiːin]	n. 半胱氨酸
	10	methionine	[meˈθaiəniːn]	n. 甲硫氨酸
	11	alanine	[ˈæləniːn]	n. 丙氨酸
	13	valine	[ˈvæliːn]	n. 缬氨酸
		leucine	[ˈljuːsiːn]	n. 亮氨酸
	14	polyketide		n. 聚酮化合物
	15	mevalonate	[meˈvæləneit]	n. 甲羟戊酸
		carotenoid	[kəˈrɔtinɔid]	n. 类胡罗卜素
		terpene	[ˈtəːpiːn]	n. 萜
	18	arginine	[ˈɑːdʒiniːn]	n. 精氨酸
		proline	[ˈprəuliːn]	n. 脯氨酸
40	2	peroxisome	[pəˈrɔksisəum]	n. 过氧化物酶体
	5	futile	[ˈfjuːtail]	a. 无效的 completely ineffective
	6	vacuole	[ˈvækjuəul]	n. 空泡

page	line				
44	27	interconvert	[intə:kɔn'və:t]	vt. 互相转换	muturally convert
	28	UMP＝Uridine monophosphate	['juəridi:n]	n. 尿苷酸	
	35	glycogen	['glaikəudʒen]	n. 糖原	
	36	effector	[i'fektə]	n. 效应物	
		build-up		n. 积累	accumulation
45	2	feedback inhibition		n. 反馈抑制	
	17	allosterically	[æləu'sterikəli]	ad. 变构地	
	38	isoenzyme	[aisəu'enzaim]	n. 同功酶	
46	15	construe	[kən'stru:]	vt. 解释	explain, interpret
	16	semantics	[si'mæntiks]	n. 语义学	
	26	deleterious	[deli'tiəriəs]	a. 有害的	injurious
	27	proteolytic enzyme	[prəutiə'litik]	n. 蛋白(水解)酶	
	28	trigger	['trigə]	vt. 引发	initiate
49	1	cell cycle		n. 细胞周期	
	10	culminate	['kʌlmineit]	vi. 达到高潮	
	12	mitosis	[mai'təusis]	n. 有丝分裂	
	15	meiosis	[mai'əusis]	n. 减数分裂	
	16	germ cell	[dʒə:m]	n. 生殖细胞	
	19	replication fork		n. 复制叉	
50	3	synchronize	['siŋkrənaiz]	vt. 使同步,同时发生	to cause to operate with exact coincidence in time or rate
	4	septum	['septəm]	n. 隔膜	
	7	duplication	[dju:pli'keiʃən]	n. 成倍	
	17	mutant	['mju:tənt]	n. 突变体	
	20	mutagen	['mju:tədʒən]	n. 诱变剂	
	25	lethal	['li:θəl]	a. 致死的	
	30	molar growth yield		n. 摩尔生长率	
	31	carbon conversion coefficient		n. 碳转化系数	
51	41	adverse	['ædvə:s]	a. 不利的	unfavorable
	45	entail	[in'teil]	vt. 必需	to impose, involve or imply as a necessary accompaniment
52	10	inclination	[inkli'neiʃən]	n. 倾向(于某事,某种状态)	an attitude or disposition towards something; tendency
		competence	['kɔmpitəns]	n. 能力	ability

Notes

① 句中的 would be 不是表示虚拟态,也不是表示过去时,而是表示按某种判断"应当会……"之意,而且语气比较婉转。同样,would＋原形动词常用来表示行为按照规律应产生的结果,这种用法在科技文献中很常见。如:Thus starting from A, first B and thence C would be formed at two-thirds the usual rate. (45/32~33).

本句可译为：如果三种核苷酸的量相等，即 ATP＝ADP＝AMP，则细胞的能荷为 0.5。

② 在 most 前无定冠词"the"，或者有不定冠词"a"，就不含最高级意义而是和"very"相当。这里 most rapidly 即"很快"之意。注意这里 most 是副词，而在 ch.1，Note⑦ 中，则是形容词。又如：

A most amusing experience. (一段非常有趣的经历)

Some proteins are most prone to denaturation at their isoelectric point. (某些蛋白质在等电点时很易变性。)

③ increase by some 20 to 50 times. 增加到 20~50 倍左右。因为增加倍数的表示法，很容易理解错误，现作较详细的说明。

增加倍数表示法

英语中增加几倍的说法，与汉语稍有不同。汉语有两种方式，一种包括基数，如 A 为 B 的 3 倍；另一种不包括基数，如 A 比 B 多 2 倍。而英语中仅有一种表示方法，即包括基数的表示方法。下面举例来说明：

1. The oxygen atom is nearly 16 times as heavy as the hydrogen atom. 氧原子的重量差不多是氢原子的 16 倍。

2. The atomic weight of helium is 4 times heavier than that of hydrogen. 氦的原子量是氢原子量的 4 倍。(注意这里尽管用了比较级，但仍为 4 倍。如照汉语理解，重 4 倍，则为 5 倍，是错误的。)

3. Sound travels nearly 3 times faster in copper than in lead. 声音在铜中的传播速度几乎比在铅中快 2 倍。

4. Production in this way has increased 3 times over that of the previous method. 用这种方法生产的产量比前法增加 2 倍。(如在 increased 后加"to"或"by"其意义不变，即...has increased to 3 times... 或...has increased by 3 times...)；句中 over 也可以省，其意义不变。

5. The output of the factory in 1993 increased(to/by)3-fold more than that in 1983. 这家工厂 1993 年的产量为 1983 年的 3 倍。(比 1983 年增加 2 倍)。

6. The output of the factory in 1993 went up by a factor of 3 as much as that in 1983. 意义和 No.5 相同。

7. The output of the factory in 1993 trebled that in 1983. 意义和 No.5 相同。

8. C produces twice as much D as H. C 产生 D 的量为 H 的两倍。

9. The maximum speed exceeds the average speed by a factor of 2. 最大速度为平均速度的 2 倍。

如果用百分数来表示倍数，则英汉语习惯一致都表示净数。如 No.5 或 No.6 两句可写成：

10. The output of the factory in 1993 was(by)200% more than(over)that in 1983.

11. The output of the factory in 1993 increased(by)200% more than that in 1983.

附：减少分数的表示法

汉语中没有"减少几倍"的说法，只能说"减少百分之几"或"减少几分之几"，"减少到几分之几"。而英语中讲到减少,和增加一样,也常用"time",也包括基数,翻译时最好不要用减少几倍,而要按中文习惯译成减少几分之几。如:

1. The output of the factory in 1991 decreased to 4 times as compared with that of 1990.

2. The output of the factory in 1991 was 4 times less than that of 1990.

3. The output of the factory in 1991 decreased(by) 4 times less than that of 1990.

4. The output of the factory in 1991 decreased(by) 4 times as much as that of 1990.

以上 4 句的译文都为:该工厂 1991 年的产量降低到 1990 年的 1/4(或比 1990 年减少 3/4)。

No.3 句中用比较级实际意义为与 1990 年相比,意义不变,与增加倍数时相同。

如果不用"time",而用分数或百分数来表示,则有:

5. The output of the factory in 1991 was 1/4(25%)(of)that of 1990.

6. The output of the factory in 1991 was three fourths(75%)less than that of 1990.

7. The output of the factory in 1991 decreased(by)three fourths(75%)as compared with that in 1990.

8. The output of the factory in 1991 decreased to 1/4(25%)(of) that of 1990.

④ Fig. 2.14 中 Ox. Fe-S 代表氧化态铁、硫蛋白,red. Fe-S 代表还原态铁、硫蛋白。Cytochrome $a+a_3$ 代表细胞色素 a 和 a_3。

⑤ no more than+数字表示的是确数,带有否定感情色彩,说话人认为少。如 There are no more than five books on the desk. 桌上的书只有 5 本。

本句可译为:任何葡萄糖由磷酸戊糖途径进行代谢主要产生 C_3 和 C_4 糖时,1 摩尔葡萄糖仅能产生 1 摩尔丙酮酸,同时产生 2 摩尔 NADPH 和 1 摩尔 NADH。

与此相对应,no less than+数字也表示确数,不过与 no more 相反,no less 带有肯定感情色彩,说话人认为多。如 There are no less than five books on the desk. 桌上的书竟有 5 本之多。

注意与含 not 的类似句型相区别,如:

There are not more than five books on the desk. 桌上的书不超过 5 本(5 本是约数,或许少于 5 本;无感情色彩,只表示事实)。There are not less than five books on the desk. 桌上的书不少于 5 本(5 本是约数,或许大于 5 本;无感情色彩,只表示事实)。

⑥ a eukaryotic cell may contain twice as many. 是一个省略句,全句应为:a eukaryotic cell may contain twice as many enzymes as a bacterial cell.

⑦ active transport 主动传递 溶质在生物膜中沿着浓度梯度相反方向的传递称为主动传递,而按浓度梯度方向进行的则称为被动传递 passive transport。主动传递需依靠代谢能(如 ATP)或一种特殊的载体蛋白或脂蛋白。

⑧ pool 本章中多次出现 pool 或 pool size 如 38/4,44/3,44/33,45/28 等多处。pool 原意为(水)池,如 swimming pool 游泳池。但在生化中指一种物质或处于平衡状态的一组类似物质的总量,它们未被共价结合而参与稳定状态下的合成代谢或分解代谢反应。pool 此处可译为"库",而 pool size 可译为"库量"或"库容量"。

⑨ available 作为形容词可置于所修饰的名词 histidine 之后,除以-able 接尾的形容词外,尚有以-ible 接尾的形容词,这两种形容词均可以后置。如:

Engine revolution should not exceed the maximum permissible.

⑩ 句中 given 原来是 give 的过去分词,这里已转化为形容词,表示"假定"、"设想"的意思,相当于 if given。它后面可以跟名词、代名词或词组,也可以跟 that 从句,通常置于句首。

本句可译为:在"正常"情况下,如果所有的必需养分都能供应,则微生物能生长。

又如:Given good health,I hope to finish this work this year. 假如健康情况良好,我希望今年完成这项工作。

Given that he is innocent,he must be set free. 假如他是无罪的,就应将他释放。

given 的另一个意义是:如果考虑到……,鉴于……。如:

Given that catalysis cuts across so many scientific disciplines, this meeting was particularly important. 考虑到催化作用和这么多的学科有关,这次会议就显得特别重要。

除 given 外,尚有 granted 和 assuming 等,他们的用法与 given 相似。参见朗文当代英汉双解词典,第一版,1988。

⑪ cell cycle 细胞周期　真核细胞两次有丝分裂间所经历的变化一般可分为四个阶段:有丝分裂期(M),DNA 合成期(S)和两个间隔期(G),即各阶段的次序为 M,G_1,S,G_2,G_2 期后便进入另一次有丝分裂期。

Comprehension

1. What does the term"energy charge"mean?(p. 18)Explain its role in EMP pathway(p. 21), tricarboxylic cycle(p. 24)and catabolite repression(p. 44).

2. What are the two main pathways of sugar metabolism? Describe their relation to anabolic processes and how their interactions are controlled.

3. By which means a cell could produce acetyl-CoA and oxaloacetate in equal amounts in order to keep tricarboxylic acid cycle operating? (p. 24)

4. Give the reason for the number of moles ATP produced per mole hexose during each step of glucose metabolism stated in table 2. 1. (p. 31)

5. Compare the term "Oxidative phosphorylation" with that "substrate level phosphorylation". (p. 30,p. 32)

6. Fig. 2. 18 (p. 39) summarizes catabolic and anabolic pathways described in this chapter. Please find out as many as possible places in the text where the related changes have been referred to.

7. Which means does a cell use of to carry out metabolic reactions in a balanced manner? (p. 38)

8. Differentiate two kinds of RNA:mRNA(messenger RNA)and tRNA(transfer RNA)in regard to their functions. (p. 40～42).

9. A chromosone may be constituted from many sections,such as regulatory gene,promotor, operator and structural genes(the last three together are termed operon). What are the functions of these genes? Give a brief account explaining how an inducible enzyme is repressed or de-repressed. (p. 41～43)

10. Define the terms"effector","feed back inhibition"and"allosteric enzyme"and discuss their interrelationship. (p. 44～45)

11. What characteristics does the genome of a bacterial cell posses in comparison with that of

a eukaryotic cell? (p. 49)

12. Explain the formation of a mutant, its frequency and the method for raising the frequency. (p. 50)

13. How can the values of molar growth yield and carbon conversion coefficient be interchanged? (refer to the last two columns of table 2. 4 on page 51)

Vocabulary

Give another word or phrase to replace these words or phrases as they are used in the text:

mediation(17/30;33/26);coordinate(21/14);depict(22/6);effectively(25/1);

subterminal(27/13);would like(27/38);facility(32/31);deprive(32/31);

is composed of(40/26);moiety(43/23);crucial(44/13);throughout(47/31).

Word usage

1. Write sentences to bring out the difference between the following pairs of words:

exploit(16/4),use;successive(19/27),continuous;proportion(21/5),ratio;

principle(21/12),principal(32/1);whole(21/14),total;apparently(24/8),obviously;

sole(22/4),unique;capable(29/3),able(33/33);effect(32/24),affect(44/23);

adopt(33/40),adapt.

2. Make sentences with the following words or phrases:

in turn(17/15,40/23);be subject to(19/2);

ascertain(24/31);in conjunction with(35/9);

entail(51/45);account for(explain the cause of)(24/38);

account for(constitute the proportion of)(29/37).

Patterns

1. Abbreviated form of relative clauses by using"when,if,as,once,while,althrough/though, unless,etc. +past participle"   Examples appearing in the text:

   a. Other enzymes only 'appear' when needed. (40/11)

      (If written in full,the sentence would be:Other enzymes only 'appear' when they are needed.)

   b. It may degrade these storage materials if placed in a 'starvation' situation.

   c. As already noted,the cycle must also... (24/10)

      but general principles of metabolic control,as discussed for the regulation of glycolysis, still apply(24/33).

      As shown in the previous section,any compound... (24/38)

   d. BH₂,once formed,need not be metabolized further. (34/5)

      Notice that some linkers can also be used with an adjective:when necessary;if possible; once fall;while still hot;though fine in principle.

      Exercises

      Make sentences in abbreviated form as described above with the following linkers: While,Although/though,unless.

2. It is+adjective+to   This pattern is an essential feature of the scientific style. By using this type of introduction to a sentence,we avoid using the personal form.

Example in the text:

Unfortunately it is not possible here to provide even outline particulars of these pathways. (38/5)

Exercises

Change these statements into the pattern shown above:

a. We prefer to simplify the process of protein purification by using affinity chromatography at an earlier stage as possible.

b. There is some advantage in working with low agitation speed during cell cultivation. Sentence analysis and translation.

First analyse the following sentences as in Ch. 1, Note ①, and then translate into Chinese:

    1. Section 2.7 Anaerobic metabolism(34/13 to 34/25)

    2. The third paragraph of page 45(45/20~35)

Writing

Translate the following sentences relating to quantity multiplication or diminution into English:

1. 经过 3 次循环操作后,高峰浓度达到进料浓度的 2.3 倍。

2. 实验 3 中溶液浓度比实验 1 增加 1 倍以上,此时 K_D 值约增加 7%。

3. 盐酸的离解能力为二氯醋酸(dichloroacetic acid)的 1/3。

4. 溶剂的改变可使反应速度改变一百万倍(million-fold)。

5. 在红细胞(erythrocyte)中,水扩散经过膜的速度为尿素的 100 倍,而当膜不存在时,水的扩散速度要比尿素高出 10^4 或 10^5 倍。

Chapter 3　Applied Genetics

The initial step in developing a biotechnological process is generally a search for a suitable organism. Such organisms will be expected to create a product or service that will generate a financial return to that industry. In practice, the geneticist has to select an organism that produces the desired product. Once a suitable organism is found, conventional breeding and mutagenesis methods are used where possible to induce genetic changes that may produce even more of the desired product. Selection of improved organisms is tedious and time demanding and most of the methods available to the geneticists up until recently have involved trial and error. However, new genetic technologies, i. e. protoplast fusion and the use of recombinant DNA techniques, are allowing new approaches by which useful genetic traits can be inserted directly into the chosen organism. Thus, totally new capabilities can be engineered and microorganisms in particular and plant and animal cells to a lesser extent may be made to produce substances beyond their naturally endowed genetic capabilities.

Increased productivity is not the only goal of the applied geneticist when manipulating a potential industrial organism. Thus, resistance to viral infection and increased genetic stability may be incorporated into organisms that lack them, the formation of harmful by-products can be reduced or eliminated and objectionable odours, colours or slime products can be removed.

A successful industrial culture should ultimately exhibit most or all of the following characteristics; it should be a pure culture; be genetically stable; be easily propagated; exhibit rapid growth characteristics; have good rate of product formation; be free of toxic byproducts; and be amenable to genetic manipulation.

Cultures that are used industrially generally have arisen in three stages; (1) as a research culture——studied to seek a useful product; (2) as a development culture——a research culture which has gained a measure of importance; and (3) as a production culture——a research culture that is now actually used for industrial production.

The final culture may be the same as the original research culture but more often it will have been subjected[①] to an array of treatments to maximize productivity. This final industrial organism will have been genetically programmed to perform a metabolic function far in excess of that of the wild type. This will only be achieved by maximum control of the growth of the organism during production. The development of the industrial organism from a wild type will have required changes in its genetic information that eliminate undesirable properties or even introduce entirely new ones.

Finding the desired organism and improving its capabilities is now a fundamental aspect of most biotechnological processes (Fig. 3. 1)

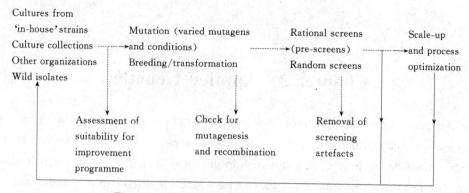

Fig. 3. 1   Flow diagram for strain improvement

3. 1   Selection and screening

In all aspects of biotechnology major efforts are directed to screening programmes to generate new organisms, either from some natural source or from established cultures by way of mutation or by hybridization programmes, including genetic engineering. These organisms must be screened for useful products and grown up on a large enough scale to produce and extract the desired product and then to subject the product to critical evaluation. Screening can be defined as the use of highly selective procedures to allow the detection and isolation of only those microorganisms or metabolites of interest from a large population. The further advancement of an isolate will involve improvement and preservation of the culture. However, a major hindrance to the full exploitation of this capacity is the availability of suitable screening procedures which can identify the necessary product, especially in the presence of culture medium constituents.

The major group of organisms presently used in biotechnology are microorganisms. The screening methodologies to be described will concentrate largely on this group.

In the search for new microorganisms from the environment for biotechnological processes there are normally three types of option available; these involve the choice of habitat for sampling, the physical separation procedures for separating out the desired microorganism and the choice of method to achieve selection which in most cases involved enrichment cultures (Table 3. 1).

Although many new producer microorganisms are wild-types and have been isolated from natural environmenrs, major efforts are also directed to generating new genomes from existing genomes by laboratory manipulation. Organisms can be modified by mutation, recombination, transformation, transduction and gene cloning either by single processes or in combinations (Table 3. 1).

With natural selection and, more particularly, with genetic manipulation, all industrially important microorganisms will have been subjected to some form of screening. The design of the screening programme is of major importance to achieve maximum recognition of new genotypes. Screens can be divided into two basic forms:

Table 3.1 Generation of producer microorganisms (Adapted from Nisbet,L.J.1982)

Ecological approach	Genetic approach
Strategy	*Strategy*
Set up isolate library of known species	Generate biosynthetic mutants suitable for precursor feeding
Enrich isolate library in rare species	Prepare hybrid strains to produce antibiotics
Explore unusual habitats and develop isolation techniques for new species	Use gene cloning to redirect biosyntheses
Dispersal Techniques	*Techniques*
Soil dilution	Mutation and selection
Flotation	Recombination by
Particle sedimentation	Conjugation
and air sampling	Protoplast fusion
Microhabitat outgrowth	Fungal,sexual and parasexual cycles
Selection and enrichment techniques	Transformation and transduction
Selective substrates,e.g. chitin	(enhance by using protoplasts)
	Gene cloning by
Selective inhibitors,e.g. cycloheximide, rifampicin	Target-directed cloning of specific genes
Physical environment,e.g. temperature, pH,Eh	Random shotgun cloning to generate a gene library

(1) *non-selective random screens with* all the isolates being tested individually for the desired qualities;and

(2) *rational screens* in which there is some aspect of preselection.

Random screening can be very time-consuming because each isolate must be studied in detail. In studies of antibiotic production thousands of shake-flask cultures of single spore isolates are regularly used. Agar disc techniques have accelerated the process but this method is best used as a primary screen before using the shake flasks. Large numbers of isolates or mutants can now be plated out,exposed to a wide range of environmental conditions and the responses recorded automatically over any time period using television monitoring and computer control.

In contrast,rational screens make more use of the knowledge of the biochemistry of specific product formation,setting up a selection process that uses a characteristic of the desirable genotype which is not the particular one of interest but which can be more readily scored or assayed. At its best the rational screen should selectively kill all undesirable genotypes thus permitting much higher numbers of isolates to be tested routinely. Thus antibiotic production in *Cephalosporium acremonium* has recently been shown to correlate with proteolytic activity suggesting a possible basis for a screen.

After screening procedures have been employed and potentially worthwhile microorganisms isolated the final proof of efficiency will come under production conditions. Product optimization from new and existing microorganisms also involves selection of the best method of cultivation, solid or liquid, batch or continuous. The type of medium used to propagate the organism can have a major influence on phenotypic expression

5 of product formation. Thus medium composition can influence biomass concentration, specific rate of product formation, duration of product formation, rate of decomposition of the product and stability of the producer organism. However, the production environment cannot remain static and successful production may well also require modification to the medium and the environmental control parameters.

10 Strain degeneration is a regular problem encountered in biotechnology. Stability is genetically controlled and can be modified by specific control of environmental factors such as medium or by the inhibition of the genetic events that lead to instability.

3. 2 Culture maintenance

15 Having generated a novel microorganism either by natural selection or by genetic manipulation, the new organism must be stored or preserved with minimum degeneration of its genetic capabilities. Maintenance, preparation and propagation of the organism must achieve specific standards of reproducibility. The maintenance process of an industrial microorganism is an intergral feature of the infrastructure of biotechnology. There are no

20 methods common to all industries. Specific maintenance techniques for industrial microorganisms are usually well kept industrial secrets. In practice most industrial microorganisms will be preserved by any one of the following procedures:

(1) *on agar medium* with regular subculturing;

(2) *by reduced metabolism*-mineral oil coverage, refrigeration, or storage in a deep

25 freeze;

(3) *drying*-dry sand, silica gel, soil or filter paper;

(4) *freeze drying*-widely practised because of convenience and gives greater stability than previous methods;

(5) *cryopreservation at ultra low temperatures* ($-70\,℃$ to $-196\,℃$——a more costly

30 method but suitable for a wide range of organisms and one that gives high survival rates).

Culture collections throughout the world are playing an increasingly important role in biotechnology in providing a comprehensive range of pure, verified organisms that are of past, present or potential interest. Important operating strains must be retained in a

35 viable and productive condition. In particular, many new genetically manipulated organisms exhibit some degree of instability and preservation must aim at achieving minimal strain drift.

The remaining part of this chapter will examine in some detail the various techniques that are now available to the applied geneticist for modifying the genome of industrially important organisms.

3.3 Mutagenesis

Once a useful organism has been isolated by preliminary screening several options are available for improving productivity,which include modifications to the medium and fermentation conditions (Chapter 4),mutation (spontaneous or induced) and hybridization. Since mutation is the ultimate source of all genetic variation it has become a topic of **5** fundamental importance in industrial microbiology. Furthermore,many of the important microorganisms used industrially (*Penicillium chrysogenum*,*Aspergillus oryzae*) do not exhibit normal sexuality and therefore do not lend themselves easily to hybridization. For this reason there has been considerable use of various mutagenesis techniques to produce many of the currently used production strains. Indeed,for many industrial **10** processes,mutagenesis programmes represent the main approach to increased productivity. Mutagen-induced improvements in productivity or titre have long been practised for antibiotic production in *Penicillium*,*Cephalosporium* and *Streptomyces*,for organic acid production and enzyme production with *Aspergillus* species,amino acid production by various bacterial strains and for numerous other industrial microorganisms. **15** Mutagenesis cannot yet be routinely supplanted by the newer techniques of genetic engineering.

It is now recognized that the most effective method for increasing the yield of a fermentation product is by use of induced mutations followed by selection of the improved strains. The main difficulty is that mutations occur at low frequencies and have to be se- **20** lected from large non-mutant populations.

There are many examples of major mutational changes leading to improved industrial strains producing more efficacious products. Tetracycline producing strains of *Streptomyces* have been particularly significant in this area. A mutant strain of *S. aureofaciens* S-604 was found to synthesize 6-demethyltetracycline which was not synthesized by the **25** parent production strain. This mutant is now one of the main commercial producers.

However,minor mutations have normally been the main approach to strain improvement. Such mutations normally lead to small improvements in product formation ($5\% \sim 10\%$) without any phenotypic manifestations. Successive use of small mutational changes can lead to an increase in the concentration of the hereditary factors responsible **30** for the productivity of the original genotype. The cephalosporin-producing organisms have been of special interest here together with the penicillin producing *Penicillium chrysogenum* strains.

Selection of mutagens   Although mutagens can be classified into physical (radiation) and chemical sources,this is not of much relevance to the industrial geneticist. The main **35** reason for choice will be the ability of the chosen technique to generate as wide a spectrum of mutants as possible for purposes of selection. Many induced mutations are not directly the result of the type of damage caused to the DNA but rather the result of the cellular DNA repair processes acting on the damage to make it into a fixed alteration in the base sequence. Mutagens which induce this phenomenon include UV, ionizing radiation, thymine starvation and certain chemical mutagens such as mitomycin C, 5-bromouracil, methylmethane sulphonate, nitrogen mustard and the nitrofurans.

5 Knowledge about the molecular basis of mutagen specificity is incomplete, but it is substantially dependent on mutagenic repair processes. In practice, producer strains can become refractory to a particular mutagen and it is advisable to alternate between several mutagens which function through different repair pathways. Furthermore, correct choice of mutagen dose can considerably increase the frequency of the desired type of mutant in the mutagenized population and in this way increase the chances of identification when
10 the whole population is screened.

Mutation rate in an organism is genetically controlled and can be changed by mutator or antimutator genes. These genes are able to affect spontaneous or induced mutability or both. In screening programmes mutator strains are important since some will give a high frequency of mutants per survivor after mutagenesis and this will provide a most ef-
15 fective input.

The environment immediately after mutagenesis can affect the overall mutation frequency and specificity. Thus growth on a complete medium rather than a minimal medium following mutagenesis may increase the yield of mutants.

Most living organisms have a mechanism for exchanging nuclear material with other
20 similar but genetically different individuals resulting in the formation of offspring with genotypes different from either of the parents. This process is known as hybridization and is essentially a method of promoting recombination of the available genetic material. Whereas mutation alters an organism's genes, recombination or hybridization rearranges genes or parts of genes and brings together in an individual organism genetic in-
25 formation from two or more organisms. Hybridization has long been practised in plant and animal breeding and in more recent times has been used to develop improved microorganisms for many biotechnological processes. In principle, hybridization can be expressed in two ways; these are sexual hybridization with eukaryotic organisms and parasexual hybridization for prokaryotes, certain eukaryotes that do not exhibit true sexuali-
30 ty and for most eukaryotic tissue cultures. In the context of biotechnology, fungi and bacteria have been the main subjects of hybridization programmes.

3. 4 Sexual hybridization

In sexual hybridization haploid nuclei from opposite mating types are brought
35 together in one cell (karyogamy); the nuclei will ultimately fuse to form the diploid nucleus and will then undergo meiosis. During the meiotic divisions there will be a rearrangement and reorganisation of the chromosomes resulting in recombination of the genetic elements (Fig. 3. 2). This homologous recombination is very effective in producing new genotypes. Thus if two organisms differ in n genes, recombination between their sets of genes will generate 2^n genotypes . If the two strains differ only in a dozen base

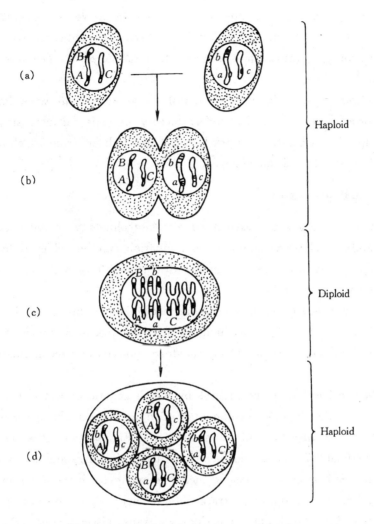

(a)

(b)

Haploid

(c)

Diploid

(d)

Haploid

Fig. 3. 2   Meiosis in eukaryotes. Recombination in eukaryotes involves crossing-over between
parts of chromosomes and the reassortment of chromosomes. A typical yeast is haploid during   **5**
most of its life cycle, with a single set of 15 or more chromosomes; only two are shown
here. Two cells of opposite mating types can fuse (a), then their nuclei fuse (b) to form a
diploid nucleus with two complete sets of chromosomes. During meiosis (a phase of sexual reproduction) the chromosomes become double structures consisting of two chromatids (c).
Homologous chromosomes pair and exchange parts of their chromatids by crossing-over. Then   **10**
four haploid sexual spores are formed (d). Each spore can have a new combination of genes
that were different (black and barred) in parent cells; genes on the same chromosome (A,a;
B,b) recombine by crossing-over and genes on different chromosomes are shuffled as members of chromosome pairs reassort[2]

pairs scattered among many millions of base pairs this would generate 2^{12} or 4096 new   **15**
genotypes.

Sexual hybridization can be complicated in many organisms by the existence of
breeding systems which regulate the outbreeding of a population by impeding inbreeding
through self - fertilization . In this way breeding systems encourage a continuous mixing

of suitable genetic material. Breeding systems have been well-documented for many higher Ascomycetes and Basidiomycetes, and have been exploited extensively in the commercial production of various mushrooms: *Agaricus bisporus*, *Lentinus edodes* and *Volvariella volvacea*.

Sexual hybridization of different strains of the yeast *Saccharomyces* has been used for the rapid production of bread by modern factory methods, for increasing the alcohol content of liquors for distillation and for brewing special beers from which nearly all the soluble carbohydrates have been removed.

3. 5 Parasexual processes

Few of the important organisms used in current biotechnology exhibit overt sexual recombination abilities. However, limited recombination can be achieved by parasexual mechanisms. Parasexual processes encompass all non-meiotic, genetic recombination processes in vegetative cells.

Parasexual processes utilize many cellular mechanisms to bring together genetic material from different sources. The mechanisms that have practical application to biotechnology include conjugation, transduction, transformation, mitotic recombination and protoplast fusion.

Conjugation in bacteria is the process by which genetic information is transferred from one cell to another by cell-to-cell contact. Conjugation can also occur in eukaryotes when haploid gametes fuse to form a diploid zygote [Fig. 3. 3(a)]. It is one of the most adaptable methods of transfer and has been most useful for intra-and interspecies genetic transfer. In bacteria it is usually plasmid-mediated and, even in the exceptional cases involving Hfr and related strains, an extra genetic element which was once a plasmid has become integrated into the chromosome. Conjugal transfer accompanies DNA replication and can result in the integration of the transferred DNA into the genome of the recipient. Although conjugation has been characterized in Gram-negative bacteria it has also been demonstrated in Gram-positive bacteria. The first bacterial conjugation system to be discovered involves cell-to-cell contact of two different strains of *Escherichia coli* and the transfer of genetic material via a sex pillus or tube which is formed by one of the two mating types . The cell forming the pillus contains an extra genetic element , the *F* -

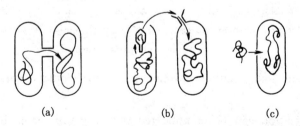

(a)   (b)   (c)

Fig 3. 3   Mechanisms of parasexual processes
(a)conjugation, (b)transduction, (c)transformation

factor[3] or plasmid, which is responsible for the cleavage of the circular bacterial DNA and its movement to the other bacterial cell where recombination occurs between the two genomes. The availability of broad host-range plasmids[4] has allowed the transfer of genes among a wide range of Gram-negative bacteria. Conjugation has found practical applications for strain improvements of *Streptomyces* and *Nocardia* for antibiotic produc-   **5** tion.

Transduction involves the transfer of genetic material from one cell to another by means of a viral vector and its subsequent incorporation by recombination [Fig. 3. 3 (b)]. Lysogenic bacteriophages[5] (bacterial viruses such as *lambda*) may integrate parts of the bacterial genome into their own genome, transfer this into another host cell and   **10** under suitable conditions this bacterial DNA may be expressed in the new cell. Transduction has been successfully used to improve the bacteria involved in the Pruteen process for the production of single cell protein (SCP) by Imperial Chemical Industries in the UK. With animal cells the *Simian virus* 40 (*SV* 40) and the mouse virus polyoma are gaining in interest while for plant cells one type of viral transfer agent has   **15** been of particular interest. This is the cauliflower mosaic virus (CMV), a double-stranded DNA molecule which is restricted in host range to the Cruciferae. It is not anticipated that this viral system will have major use in plant biotechnology.

Transformation, or the unidirectional transfer of genetic material in which DNA originating from one cell is taken up and stably maintained by another, has been widely   **20** used with bacteria [Fig. 3. 3(c)]. It is being developed extensively and rapidly with yeast and *Streptomyces* but so far with only limited success in filamentous fungi and plant and animal cells. The transforming DNA can be subjected to *in vitro* treatments or manipulation including mutagenesis before introduction into cells. The main disadvantage of transformation is that for most bacteria only a small proportion of cells in a population   **25** will be transformed (about 0.1% with *E. coli*, 10 to 100 times higher with *B. subtilis*). It has been shown with *E. coli* that large plasmid DNA molecules ($>$20 kb) transform relatively inefficiently compared to smaller molecules. Transformation has become the main method of genetic engineering using plasmids as transport vehicles and is discussed later in this chapter.   **30**

Mitotic recombination has been of particular interest with filamentous fungi. With certain fungi where the vegetative phase is haploid small numbers of the nuclei can fuse to form diploids. This diploid phase in the asexual cycle of the fungus results from the fusion of vegetative nuclei which are in the heterozygous condition. The process consists of the following stages: heterokaryon (two or more different nuclei with a single cyto-   **35** plasm) formation between two haploid mycelia; nuclear fusion by a small number of the opposite nuclei (frequency of 10^{-6}); mitotic crossing over within the diploid nucleus (frequency about 10^{-2} per nuclear division) giving interchromosomal exchange; and haploidization where the diploid nuclei are reduced to the haploid condition at a frequency of about 10^{-3} per nuclear division (Fig. 3. 4) . This mitotic recombination makes possible genetic analysis and controlled breeding in organisms with no sexual cycle. With respect to efficiency of recombination mitotic recombination is very much less effective than sexual recombination. This form of parasexual hybridization is known to occur in many industrial fungi including *Penicillium chrysogenum*, *Aspergillus oryzae* and *Cephalosporium acremonium*. It is difficult to know how widely this system has been used in industrial practice due to the requirements of industrial secrecy. However, there is little doubt that it has been successfully used with citric acid and penicillin producing organisms. Mitotic recombinations have also been recorded for some higher plants and animal tissue cultures.

The primary necessity for achieving parasexual hybridization is the fusion of the desired cells. Many barriers exist due to homogenic and heterogenic incompatibility. However, these incompatibility or species barriers can now be overridden in many cases by specific laboratory procedures which permit protoplasts from cells to fuse

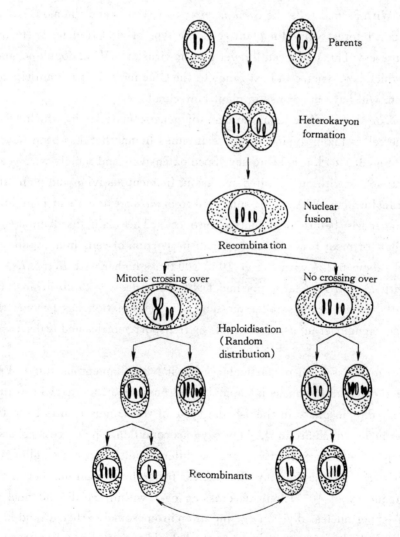

Fig. 3. 4   Scheme of mitotic recombination

directly or to be infected with isolated DNA by way of transformation.

Protoplast fusion   The main natural barrier to recombination between dissimilar organisms is usually the cell wall. If this barrier is removed by preparing protoplasts and recognizing that cell membranes have relatively similar compositions, it is feasible that protoplasts of different species could be induced to fuse and form a hybrid cell, in this way   5
allowing their genes to recombine. The field of induced fusion of microbial protoplasts is one of great expansion and there has been a rapid accumulation of data in both basic and applied areas. The present success in protoplast fusion and regeneration technology with bacteria, fungi and plant and animal cells owes much to the many earlier studies establishing the basic techniques of protoplast release and cell regeneration. Protoplasts can   10
now be routinely formed from most microbial cells.

Although mechanical and other non-enzymic methods for protoplast release have been reported, the main directions of study have favoured use of lytic enzymes for protoplast isolation. The principal components of this lytic digestion are the enzymes, the osmotic stabilizer and the organism.   15

Yeast protoplasts can be produced using commercial preparations of snail digestive juice which is available as helicase or sulphatase. In general, most commercial lytic preparations have not been very effective for preparation of protoplasts from filamentous fungi. However, many other organisms, in particular *Streptomyces* spp. and certain filamentous fungi, can produce highly effective mycolytic activity. In most cases the synthesis   20
sis of the wall digesting enzyme complex by the producer organism requires the presence of inducer substrates in the growth medium. A novel approach to the production of wall digesting enzymes is to grow the producer organism in a medium low in normal carbohydrate source such as glucose or sucrose but containing relatively purified cell walls of the subject organism. Successful growth of the producer organism will require appropriate   25
production of wall digesting enzymes in order to generate essential low molecular weight energy sources.

In general, exponential phase cells produce protoplasts more readily than stationary phase cells, suggesting that wall chemistry changes during the growth cycle.

Chemical stabilizers are also essential to provide osmotic support to the protoplasts   30
after the removal of the cell wall. Inorganic salts, sugars and sugar alcohols have been successfully used for retaining the integrity of the released protoplasts. Without osmotic stabilizers, released protoplasts will rapidly burst.

A high proportion of protoplasts can generate a new cell wall and subsequently a full reversion to a normal growth can be achieved. Thus if mitotic recombination can be   35
achieved between isolated fused protoplasts, the ensuing reversion could lead to a genetically altered and viable organism.

Fusion between natural protoplasts of similar or dissimilar strains occurs at a very low frequency. However, with the introduction of polyethylene glycol (PEG) as a fusogenic agent, the frequency of fusion has been enhanced at least 1000-fold[6]. Methodological studies on PEG-induced fungal protoplast fusion has shown that PEG preparations with molecular weights of 4000 or 6000 were optimal in fusion induction in the concentration range 25 to 40%. The presence of Ca^{2+} ions is critical for the attainment of high-frequency fusion. In practice fusion events start with agglutination of the protoplasts

5   caused by extensive dehydration and formation of various aggregates. Protoplasts then shrink and become highly distorted. Translocation of intramembrane protein particles occurs at the sites of close contact, and is followed by their aggregation. Lipid-lipid interaction occurs between adjacent protein-denuded membranes[7] and there is certain reorganization of the lipid molecules assisted by calcium ions. This results in fusion of small ar-

10 eas of membranes in contact; small cytoplasmic bridges are formed which enlarge until finally the two protoplasts fuse.

    A novel electrofusion method for protoplast fusion has recently been developed. Electric field fusion is a rapid and gentle process used to fuse like cells into giant cells, unrelated cells into hybrids and to encapsulate substances within cells. Cells are ex-

15 posed to low-level, non-homogenous, high frequency electric fields which orientate the cells into chains. A direct current is then applied which opens micropores in adjoining cell membranes, allowing intermixing of the cellular contents and cell fusion. This process can also alter the permeability of the outer cell membrane to permit substances the size of genes to be encapsulated.

20   When two protoplasts derived from different strains fuse, the resultant cell is heterokaryotic since it will contain nuclei from different genetic sources. In the heterokaryon, nuclear fusion or diploidization can take place between haploid nuclei of different genotypes as well as between nuclei of the same type. The former results in a heterozygous diploid nucleus while in the latter a homozygous diploid nucleus will be

25 formed. The fused protoplasts with their mixed complement of haploid and diploid nuclei can then be made to regenerate into a growing organism with normal means of propagation.

    During this growing out phase the diploid nuclei may undergo division with occasional mitotic crossing-over. As a result new combinations and linkages will occur and

30 these recombinations give the organism some of the advantages of normal sexuality.

    By way of this parasexual process new diploid strains of previously haploid organisms can be formed. However, more often haploidization of the diploid colonies will occur. Some of the new haploid strains will be genotypically different from either parent because of mitotic recombinations producing new linkage groups. In filamentous fungi

35 haploidization more often shows up in conidia formation where individual conidia are uninucleate and haploid.

    When protoplast fusion is to be used to improve industrial strains three events must occur:

    (a) the generation of viable protoplasts,

    (b) high fusion frequency,

(c) regeneration of the fused protoplasts to growing colonies in which diploidization and haploidization can be realized.

Fusion of protoplasts seems to be the most promising method for strain improvements of *Streptomyces* and other known producers of antibiotics. This could well lead to the generation of new antibiotic structures and to the increase in the pool of yield-enhancing genes. Recently two different types of yeast have been fused and the regenerated cells propagated for use in sherry production. For this system cell fusion techniques are more promising than recombinant DNA techniques since there are large numbers of genes involved in such improvements. Protoplast fusion in filamentous fungi together with inter-specific protoplast fusions has produced successful strain improvements. Protoplast fusion seems to be the only means of obtaining interspecific heterokaryons and recombinants in filamentous fungi that do not have a demonstrable sexual cycle.

Protoplasts can be prepared from most plant species but only a limited number can regenerate cell walls, divide and ultimately differentiate into normal plants. Many important crop plants are in the latter category. The production of novel somatic hybrids by fusion of isolated plant protoplasts is recognized as an important technological advancement in the plant sciences.

In practice, following induced fusion, protoplasts in liquid culture regenerate cell walls and undergo mitosis, creating a mixed population consisting of parental cells, homokaryotic fusion products and heterokaryotic fusion products or somatic hybrids. Somatic hybrids can be identified and recovered generally through expression of genetic markers, physiological growth requirements or alternatively by micromanipulation. Protoplast fusion between divergent species can sometimes produce hybrids but these are invariably sterile, precluding integration into a breeding programme. A role for somatic hybrids in crop improvement can only be realized if the hybrids can be integrated into conventional breeding programmes. As yet no new varieties have been established in agricultural practice by protoplast fusion technology. However, this will undoubtedly occur in the near future and will open up a new dimension of creative and beneficial agricultural advancement.

Protoplast fusion is also possible with animal cells but there is no opportunity to have complete organism development. However, both with plant and animal tissue propagation, protoplast fusion can be a valuable means of changing the genetic complement.

Unusual examples of intergenetic and inter-kingdom protoplast fusions have occurred, e. g. yeast protoplasts with hen erythrocytes, animal-fungal heterokaryons, and bacteria with yeast. However, there have so far been no immediately worthwhile genetic consequence resulting from these experiments, but they do suggest that the future may offer some potential for fusing taxonomically quite distant cells with the possibility of specific transfer of genetic elements.

Cell fusion   Direct cell fusion has formed the basis of monoclonal antibody formation—

one of the most active and successful areas of new biotechnology. Monoclonal antibodies are antibodies derived from a single source or clone® of cells which recognize only one kind of antigen.

    A longstanding area of health care has been the preparation of vaccines to combat
5 disease. Vaccines allow the body to build up resistance, i. e. to build up an adequate level of antibody and a primed population of cells that will grow and produce antibodies when the pathogen occurs in a virulent form. Vaccines are complex entities made up of a mixture of antibodies too complex to be synthesized chemically.

    When a foreign substance or microorganism (antigen) is introduced into a verte-
10 brate animal the immune response reacts by forming plasma cells (derived from B-lymphocytes) which secrete antibodies that recognize, neutralize and eliminate the antigen with great specificity. In practice the antibody response to a particular antigen is highly heterogeneous. It is practically impossible to separate these antibodies and so conventional antisera contain mixtures of antibodies. However, each antibody is now recognized
15 to be made from a different line of B-lymphocytes and their derived plasma cells. Thus if one cell line could be cloned it would be possible to produce only one antibody. Unfortunately, plasma cells cannot be cultured. In 1975 Kohler and Milstein in their now famous experiment demonstrated that antibody producing lymphocytes could be fused with malignant, rapidly proliferating myeloma cells and the hybrid-myeloma
20 cells or hybridomas could express both the lymphocyte-specific antibody production and the myeloma property of continuous proliferation. Thus was born the monoclonal antibody.

    Monoclonal antibody formation is carried out by injecting a mouse or rabbit with the antigen, removing the spleen and then allowing fusion of spleen cells with myeloma
25 cells (Fig. 3. 5). About 1% of the spleen cells are antibody secreting plasma cells and 10% of the final hybridomas consist of antibody secreting cells. Each hybridoma cell is capable of producing only one antibody and selection techniques can be developed to identify them and then to carry out further propagation or cloning®. Clones derived from monoclonal antibody hybridomas may be kept frozen, injected into an animal or grown in
30 culture where the clone produces the antibody in large amounts. Many of these clones are genetically unstable and lose chromosomes to become more stable, but more often the chromosomes lost are those which encode for the desired antibody.

    Monoclonal antibodies have a wide range of uses as very precise and sensitive analytical reagents for various pharmaceutical products such as peptides, proteins and hor-
35 mones. They are also important as diagnostic reagents for a number of medical and therapeutic purposes, including screening for the presence of undesirable agents in blood samples used for transfusions. A combination of genetic manipulation and monoclonal antibody techniques might well give rise to new approaches to efficient production of viral, bacterial and parasitic antibodies. Other important uses will include tissue typing, *in vivo* tumour location , clinical diagnosis and therapy including targeting of

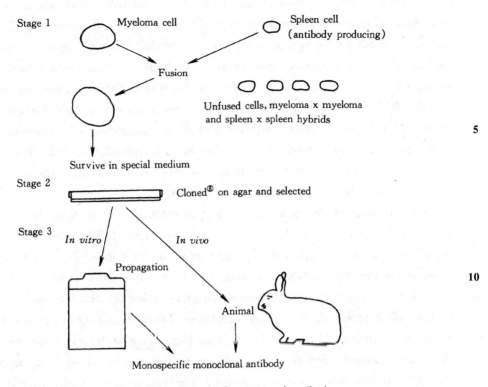

Fig. 3. 5 Diagram illustrating the formation of antibody-
producing hybridomas by fusion techniques

chemotherapeutic agents.

There is now little doubt that fusion technologies will contribute substantially to
the biotechnological utilization not only of prokaryotes and simple eukaryotes like yeast
and filamentous fungi but also for higher plants and animal tissue cultures where specific
products are being sought.

3. 6 Recombinant DNA technology

The analysis and manipulation of genetic material has been revolutionized by the development of *in vitro* gene cloning[®] techniques which have allowed the isolation, purification
and selective amplification in suitable biological systems of almost any discrete segment
of DNA from almost any organism. Due to deletion of DNA not containing relevant
genes, gene cloning enables the methods employed for analysis and manipulation to be
targeted primarily on the gene region of interest, thus vastly increasing the efficiency of
the method used and simplifying the identification and characterization of the new modified derivatives. In contrast to protoplast fusion where large parts or entire genomes are
mixed and the characteristics of interest are controlled generally by a large number of
genes (for example, antibiotics), recombinant DNA technology is primarily concerned
with small numbers of individual genes controlling known gene products (for example,
proteins, peptides, etc.).

The 1978 Genetic Manipulation Regulations defined genetic manipulation as 'the formation of new combinations of heritable material by the isolation of nucleic acid molecules, produced by whatever means outside the cell, into any virus, bacterial plasmid, or other vector system so as to allow their incorporation into a host organism in
5   which they do not naturally occur but in which they are capable of continued propagation'. Genetic manipulation thus defined does not include, for example, monoclonal antibody work, strain improvement of microorganisms by conventional genetic techniques, and *in vitro* fertilization or cloning techniques for animal use. Genetic manipulation techniques have so far made only a small contribution, although an important
10   one, to biotechnological research and applications.

Over the last ten years several important discoveries were made in molecular biology which led to the rapid development of recombinant DNA technology. Of particular significance were the isolation of a mutant strain of *Escherichia coli* unable to break down or restrict foreign DNA introduced into the cell, and the identification and charac-
15   terization of restriction endonucleases—enzymes which are able to cleave double-stranded (ds) DNA at specific sites. In general, such DNA fragments are unable to transform or replicate efficiently in host cells. This problem has been largely overcome by inserting the DNA fragments into vectors which can be inserted into host cells and which allow the relevant information to be expressed. The vectors are usually bacterial plasmids,
20   phage or yeast 2μ DNA. Covalent bonding of the DNA fragments into the vector is achieved with the enzyme DNA ligase. The newly synthesized vectors or chimeric DNA molecules are introduced by transformation into host organisms such as *E. coli*, *Bacillus subtilis* or *Saccharomyces cerevisiae* and as the host cells grow and multiply (cloning)[®] so also will the vectors replicate and amplify the foreign DNA. It is possible to clone[®] an
25   entire genome, thus creating a large collection or library of independent DNA molecules. A genomic library will contain all the sequences of the organism genome and in principle it should be possible to isolate any gene provided that a specific probe for detecting it can be obtained. If the average size of a cloned[®] sequence is 20 kilobases, approximately 700000 individual clones would be required for a complete library of the hu-
30   man genome.

Genetic manipulation techniques offer revolutionary abilities because they are rapid, universally applicable, allow a high degree of control over the manipulation process and above all generate the formation of new genetic combinations which have never before been selected by laboratory methods. Recombinant DNA technology has been one of the
35   most rapidly developing aspects of bioscience.

Central to this new technology is the concept of cloning which has been defined by Timmis (1981) as 'the separation and individual propagation of a single element that is capable of reproduction from a mixture of similar elements'. In practice, cloning has long been used to propagate pure cultures of viruses, microorganisms and plants by vegetative means thus ensuring exact continuation of the organism's genome (Table. 3. 2) .

Table 3.2 Cloning

Origin of genes	Typical habitat	Separation	Growth medium	Amplification	Requirements
Bacteria	Soil	Physical, by dilution on solid medium	Nutrient agar plate	Of individual bacteria to form colonies	Nutrient medium
Viruses	Sewage	Physical and biological, by dilution, infection of sensitive host cells by individual virus particles	Pure culture of host bacteria; nutrient agar plate	Of individual viruses to form plaques in growing lawn of host cells	Host bacteria; nutrient medium
Plasmids	Bacterial lysate	Physical and biological, by dilution, transformation of competent cells by individual molecules	Pure culture of host bacteria; nutrient agar plate containing agent selective for a plasmid-encoded property	Of individual plasmid molecules in individual bacteria that form colonies	Host bacteria; nutrient and selective medium
Genes*	Chromosomes	Biochemical or physical; by breakage into gene-sized fragments and ligation into plasmid molecules and subsequent transformation of competent cells	Pure culture of host bacteria; nutrient agar plate containing agent selective for a plasmid-encoded property	Of individual plasmid molecules in individual bacteria that form colonies	Cloning vector; appropriate DNA fragmentation procedure; DNA ligase; host bacteria; nutrient and selective medium

* This entry refers to the *in vitro* cloning of genes. From Timmis (1982).

Nowadays, the term also encompasses the isolation and maintenance of individual autonomous genetic elements such as plasmids and cryptic virus genomes. Cloning[®] of cellular organisms needs only a nutrient medium; cloning[®] of viruses and plasmids will involve a specific host cell together with a nutrient medium, while cloning[®] of genes will

5　require a vector replicon, a specific host cell and a nutrient medium. All types of cloning have important roles in biotechnology; thus all microorganisms, plant and animal cells to be used in biotechnological processes need to be maintained and propagated in a pure and constant state, while viruses and plasmid propagation or amplification, in particular, have become identified as powerful tools in the new biotechnology.

10　　　The principles of gene cloning or recombinant DNA technology will be briefly discussed using mainly the example of the *Escherichia coli* K-12 plasmid vector system. Although gene cloning techniques using viral vectors differ in detail, the principles involved are similar.

　　　The basic requirements for *in vitro* transfer and expression of foreign DNA in a host

15　bacterial cell are outlined in Figs 3. 6 and 3. 7 and can be summarized as follows:

　　　(1) The isolation of circular plasmid DNA molecules which must contain one site where the integration of foreign DNA will not destroy essential functions.

　　　(2) The generation of DNA fragments that are suitable for cloning by way of restriction endonucleases. The insert may be a chromosomal fragment from an-

20　　　　other microorganism (prokaryote or eukaryote), from an animal or plant, or from a chemically-synthesized DNA sequence.

　　　(3) A method of splicing the foreign DNA into the vector.

　　　(4) Incorporation of the hybrid DNA recombinants into the host cell.

　　　(5) Expression of the transformants which have the recombinant plasmids.

25　　　Thus a major feature of this new genetic technique is that it allows considerable control over the DNA segment to be cloned[®] and can be used essentially for any DNA fragment from any organism.

Plasmids.　　Fundamental to this new technology are plasmids. Plasmids are basically molecules which can be stably inherited without being linked to the chromosome. They

30　are important in medicine and agriculture since they confer antibiotic resistance to pathogens of man and animals and can code for toxins and other proteins which may increase the virulence of such pathogens. They are also important since some may be involved in nitrogen fixation in *Rhizobium sp.* while others can code for a wide range of metabolic activities that allow certain bacteria to degrade compounds that could become

35　environmental pollutants. Plasmids are molecules of double-stranded DNA which exist as covalently closed circular molecules (CCC) in their host cells. The molecular weight of plasmids ranges from about 1×10^6 to 200×10^6. Conjugative plasmids can transfer copies of themselves from one bacterium to another and can pass pieces of chromosomal DNA between bacteria. Insertion sequences and transposons can also be carried on plasmids. Plasmids can be used as vectors to clone DNA.

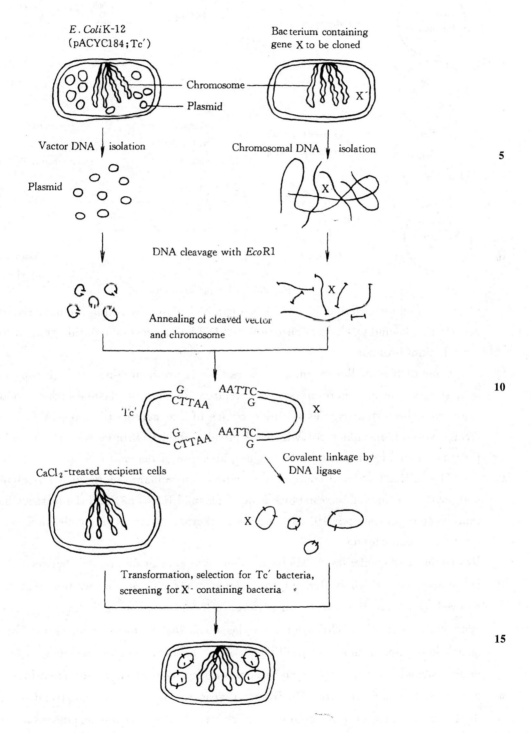

Fig. 3.6   The gene cloning procedure.

Plasmids carrying antibiotic resistance genes are termed resistance (R) plasmids and certain of the *E. coli* R plasmids have been used as plasmid vectors. One of the most frequently used plasmids for cloning *E. coli* genes is pBR322 which confers resistance to

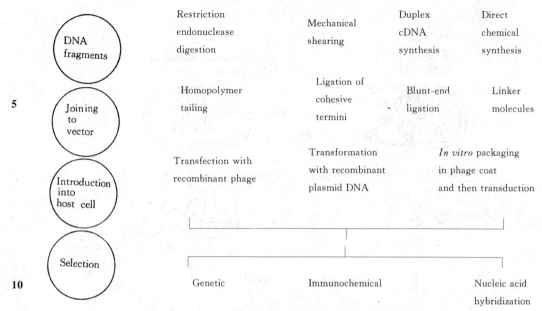

DNA fragments	Restriction endonuclease digestion	Mechanical shearing	Duplex cDNA synthesis	Direct chemical synthesis
Joining to vector	Homopolymer tailing	Ligation of cohesive termini	Blunt-end ligation	Linker molecules
Introduction into host cell	Transfection with recombinant phage	Transformation with recombinant plasmid DNA	*In vitro* packaging in phage coat and then transduction	
Selection	Genetic	Immunochemical	Nucleic acid hybridization	

Fig. 3. 7   Cloning strategies

ampicillin and tetracycline. Plasmid DNA can be isolated by lysing the bacterial cells and separating plasmid DNA from chromosomal DNA in a caesium chloride gradient containing ethidium bromide.

Some of the smaller plasmids such as Col E1 are maintained at high copy numbers in host cells and can therefore synthesize large amounts of plasmid-coded products because each bacterium carries multiple copies of the genes of interest. When cells are treated with chloramphenicol, which selectively inhibits chromosomal DNA replication, there is a further substantial selective amplification of plasmid DNA.

The pBR322 plasmid contains replication determinants of the Col E1-related plasmid pMB1, the ampicillin resistance gene of plasmid R1 (Tn3) and the tetracycline resistance gene of plasmid pSC101 as selection markers. It contains single cleavage sites for at least ten endonucleases.

Restriction endonucleases.   Microorganisms are able to distinguish between their own DNA and that which is derived from some other source. The system that has been evolved to achieve the distinction between self and non-self relies on two types of enzyme within the cell: modification methylases and restriction endonucleases. The methylases add methyl groups in a specific fashion to various nucleotide residues in the nascent double-stranded DNA chain. Such recognition sequences are normally from four to seven base pairs in length and are palindromic, that is, the sequence in one strand of the DNA duplex is the same as in the complementary strand. Most organisms possess a number of different modification methylases. The restriction endonucleases identify the same sequences as the modifying enzyme but, instead of methylating, cut the DNA at the sequence. However, the endonuclease will not cut 'self' sequences but will degrade 'foreign' DNA. This property of recognition and cleavage of specific sequences of double -

stranded DNA has become the basis for excising DNA fragments from most types of organisms.

Different types of restriction endonucleases occur, namely types Ⅰ, Ⅱ, Ⅲ and Ⅳ. Only type Ⅱ is of importance to the new DNA technology.

Type Ⅱ restriction endonucleases have special importance because they are sequence specific and can create double-stranded breaks at exact locations in double-stranded DNA. In this way they break up long foreign DNA molecules into smaller segments as well as make a single break in the plasmid vector at the site at which DNA fragments can be inserted. With some of these enzymes, the breaks produce single-stranded ends and the base sequence of these termini will be identical for all fragments produced by a given restriction nuclease. In this manner any fragment generated by a specific endonuclease can base-pair with any other fragment cleaved by the same endonuclease and anneal thus creating a hybrid molecule. Since many restriction endonucleases are now available from a range of bacteria a standard terminology has been adopted. The genus and species name of the host organism is identified with the first letter of the genus and the first two letters of the species to form a three letter abbreviation in italics, e.g. E. coli, Eco. Strain or type identification is given in non-italicized symbols (EcoR) and the number of the endonuclease in Roman numerals—EcoR Ⅱ.

Different endonucleases can be used to generate different sizes of DNA fragments with different 3'-or 5'-tetranucleotide single-stranded extensions. The DNA fragments can then be purified electrophoretically.

Hydrolysis of the single target site of pBR322 by EcoR Ⅰ, or by any of the other restriction endonucleases for which there is a single target site, converts the circular plasmid to a linear DNA molecule.

The sites recognized by most type Ⅱ restriction endonucleases have a two-fold axis of symmetry; they can be tetra-, penta- or hexa-nucleotide sequences. Enzymic cleavage of DNA can create either *blunt ends* or *sticky*, 'cohesive ends' in which a few unpaired nucleotides terminating in either 3'-hydroxyl or a 5'-monophosphate group project from the ends. Many of the most useful restriction endonucleases recognize tetra- or hexa-nucleotide palindromic sites. Thus the enzyme *Hinc* Ⅱ which cleaves in the middle of a six base pair sequence [Fig. 3. 8(a)] will result in the formation of 'blunt ended' DNA molecules which can only be joined at low efficiency by DNA ligase. EcoR Ⅰ cleaves the recognition site away from the centre [Fig. 3. 8(b)] and because of the palindromic nature of the enzyme recognition site causes the formation of double-stranded DNA fragments with single stranded termini or 'sticky ends'. When mixtures of these fragments are mixed hydrogen bonding occurs between complementary bases on the single stranded sequences and the ends become associated.

A particular hexanucleotide sequence should occur on average every 4096 (4^6) base pairs. Fragments generated by an endonuclease recognizing a tetranucleotide sequence would have[a] an average length of 256 base pairs; note that the amount of DNA required

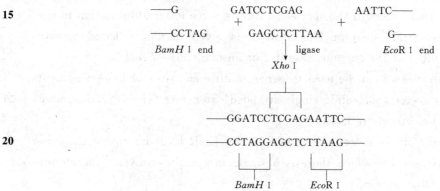

(a) Blunt end cleavage and ligation

(b) Sticky end cleavage and ligation

(c) Joining non-complementary ends using a linker

Fig. 3.8   Mode of action of restriction and ligase enzymes

to code for a typical protein of molecule mass 35 000 would be about 1000 nucleotides long.

DNA fragments for cloning may also be obtained other than by using restriction endonucleases: these include mechanical shearing, sonication, chemical synthesis, or by using the enzyme reverse transcriptase to synthesize 'copy DNA' (c DNA) from a eukaryotic messenger RNA template. This last method overcomes the problem of *introns or intervening sequences* which are characteristic of most genes in higher eukaryotes. Such introns cannot be removed during transcription of eukaryotic DNA in bacteria whereas in eukaryotic expression they are removed by *splicing* the primary RNA transcript of the gene.

Joining to vectors.   The insertion and linking of DNA fragments into plasmid vectors can be achieved by several methods.

Treatment of mixtures of DNA fragments with *E. coli* or bacteriophage T4 DNA ligase will generate covalent linkages between the cloning vector and the DNA molecules. Covalent phosphodiester bonds will be formed between the fragments which have annealed to each other by their cohesive ends.

A much less efficient method of ligation is 'blunt end' or 'flush-end' ligation [Fig. 3. 8(a)]. In this case the DNA molecules do not have projections of single-stranded DNA and require high concentrations of DNA ends and enzymes for effective liga- **5** tion. However, this method does allow a much wider range of endonucleases to be used increasing the range of DNA under study. When such a hybrid has been formed it cannot be cleaved by either of the endonucleases which were used to generate the original DNA fragments.

This potential disadvantage can be overcome by using *linkers*, i. e. short synthetic **10** polynucleotides containing one or more endonuclease recognition sequences. Many linkers are now available which allow easy modification of DNA fragment termini. The use of linker sequences permits blunt-end ligation of the linker to the DNA fragment followed by the cleavage of the linker by the appropriate endonuclease to form the specific termini necessary [Fig. 3. 8(c)]. In this way the cloned fragment can be reisolated easily **15** from the recombinant plasmid by digestion with the correct endonuclease.

A less used method involves adding a tail of several deoxyguanosine residues to the 3'-ends of the vector and deoxycytosine residues to the 3'-ends of the insert thus creating complemenary single-stranded extensions of insert and vector. Linkage occurs by complementary base pairing. **20**

The new product of a plasmid plus inserted DNA fragment is termed a plasmid chimera.

Transformation. The techniques for introduction of DNA into bacteria have long been appreciated and can involve chromosomal or plasmid DNA. Transfection occurs when bacteriophage DNA is involved. **25**

In a typical plasmid transformation experiment there will be an extremely heterogeneous mixture of DNA molecules with only a small number consisting of a single vector molecule linked to a single DNA fragment. When *E. coli* is used for transformation the DNA molecules are mixed with the bacterial cells that have been made competent or permeable by being exposed to a cold solution of calcium chloride (0.1M). The cells are **30** then warmed to 37℃ for 5 minutes to allow the DNA to be taken up. The cells are then transferred to broth and after a short incubation period are able to express the functions of the newly acquired chimeric DNA. The bacteria carrying hybrid molecules are identified by a specific screening procedure and purified; their hybrid plasmids are isolated and characterized, or the new products are isolated and studied. Transformation efficiencies **35** are about 10^6 transformants per μg cloning mixture DNA.

Plasmid vectors are being developed for other bacteria while phage vectors and cosmids (which consist of a normal plasmid containing the cohesive ends of phage λ) can also be employed.

Gram-negative bacteria, in particular *E. coli*, have been widely used for recombinant

DNA work. Special plasmid vectors have had to be developed for Gram-positive bacteria, in particular for *Bacillus subtilis* and *Streptomyces* strains.

Extensive studies are in progress to transfer this new genetic engineering technology to eukaryotic systems. Yeasts are strong candidates as hosts for eukaryotic cloning and bifunctional plasmids using the 2μ DNA from yeast and the pBR322 plasmid from *E. coli* have been developed and used successfully. Cloning in animal cells can be achieved using the genomes of special animal viruses, for example, the Simian virus SV 40. In plant cells cloning is not so well established; the Ti plasmids of *Agrobacterium tumefaciens* are proving useful.

In higher plants recombinant DNA technology is being viewed with increasing importance for its potential in breeding, allowing the direct genetic modification of useful plants to improve their productivity. The functional expression of a novel gene in a genetically engineered plant has yet to be reported. A major reason for this is the limited understanding of the molecular basis of gene expression in plants. Furthermore, the genes for most important plant characteristics have yet to be identified. Whereas populations of engineered cells are the useful product in microbial genetic engineering, engineered plant cells are of little value if they cannot be regenerated into whole plants. Unfortunately, relatively few agronomically significant crop plants can yet be regenerated from cell cultures. The potential for the improvement of crop plants through genetic engineering is undoubtedly vast but more basic research is required in almost all areas of plant molecular biology before it can be realized.

Identification of transformants.   In most cloning experiments the major part of the programme will be concerned with the identification of the transformed recombinant clones. Normally the quantity of transforming DNA incorporated into the recipient host will be very much less than the host chromosomal DNA, so identification of product expressed from the transforming fragment will be extremely difficult. However, various methods have been developed to identify clones that carry desired DNA sequences.

(*a*) *Complementation*   Some in-coming genes are able to complement defective copies of the same gene on the chromosome of the recipient; that is, they code for a normal, active product for which the recipient is deficient. For example, the *lacz*$^+$ gene (coding for β-galactosidase) will complement a *lacz*, β-galactosidase-deficient host to yield lac$^+$ recipients which can be selected as red colonies on MacConkey's Agar.

(*b*) *Antibiotic resistance genes*   These genes confer resistance to an antibiotic in normally susceptible cells. This can be exemplified with plasmid pBR322 which carries genes for tetracycline and ampicillin resistance and transformants can be selected on media containing one of these antibiotics; the foreign DNA is usually cloned into the gene coding for resistance to the other, unselected antibiotic.

(*c*) *Hybridization*   A widely used method of analysing a collection of recombinant DNA molecules or cloned cells is by colony or plaque hybridization. Cells containing recombinant DNA are transferred to a nitrocellulose filter and lysed. Purified, complementary radioactive nucleic acids are then hybridized to the DNA in the nitrocellulose-bound cells. Complementary DNA will hybridize and it can be detected by autoradiography. The extent of hybridization will reflect the amount of complementarity. Copy DNA synthesized from an mRNA template can also be used to screen for recombinant DNA bound to a nitrocellulose filter in a similar way.   5

(*d*) *Restriction endonuclease analysis*   This method can be used to determine whether the cloned DNA produces the same size of fragments as a standard DNA molecule. Restriction endonuclease analysis provides mapped fragments which are often a prerequisite to sequence analysis.

(*e*) *Immunological methods*   Immunological methods are finding increasing use and   10 depend largely on the development of antibodies, primarily against protein products.

Identification of recombinant DNA is a highly secretive aspect of industrial cloning programmes and the results of most of the studies will remain privileged information. This is an inevitable but regrettable aspect of the commercial importance of these new technologies.   15

Genetic engineering must be properly seen as the capstone of the massive framework of applied genetics which has been developed so successfully over the past three decades. Notwithstanding, it is certainly the most exciting and potentially the most creative technique available to the industrial geneticist.

The scientific and economic applications of recombinant DNA technology are limit-   20 less and will include:

(i) Increasing the yield of a particular gene product.

(ii) Improving the rate of synthesis of a particular end product by cloning additional enzymes into the organism or by specifically altering a cloned enzyme by site-directed mutation (e.g. cloning energy-conserving nitrogen pathway from   25 *E. coli* into ICI single cell protein organism *Methylophilus methylotrophus*).

(iii) 'Tailoring' an organism by transferring a particular activity to a more desirable host organism.

Recombinant DNA technology will have a major impact on pharmaceutical products in the very near future. It is now possible to introduce genes from mammalian sources in-   30 to bacteria and obtain the production on a commercial scale of the products encoded by these mammalian genes. Compounds of particular importance include insulin, human growth hormone, enzymes, antibodies, interferon and vaccines. The time scale for development and commercial application hopefully will permit many of these products to be available later this decade. In the veterinary field new animal vaccines derived by genetic   35 engineering will soon be available. Although cloning of foreign genes is now routinely performed with *E. coli*, a major problem is that this organism secretes very few proteins. Secreted proteins are characterized by signal sequences which consist mainly of hydrophobic amino acid residues which determine the export of the protein across the cell membrane . During the export process the signal peptide is cleaved off to yield the

protein or hormone. In part this problem with *E. coli* can be overcome by fusing the gene for the desired product with another foreign gene whose gene product is exported; another approach would be to make the cell more 'leaky'. However, other bacteria such as *Bacillus subtilis*, which is becoming increasingly used in genetic engineering and can ex-
5 crete over 50 proteins, will undoubtedly find greater use in industrial application of foreign gene cloning.

In the long term the greatest potential for recombinant DNA techniques should be in agriculture. The possibility of transferring the nitrogen fixation genes from bacteria into important crop plants other than legumes is being actively studied. Similarly the
10 possibility of transferring the structural genes of legumes controlling nitrogen-fixing association with *Rhizobium* is also being studied.

In the future many other areas of biotechnology including energy and chemical feedstocks and waste treatment will benefit from the ability of applied geneticists to produce the 'ideal' organism for a desired purpose.
15 Although there are now many genetic manipulations that can be carried out with organisms it is worth noticing that the following important technical limitations presently restrict wide industrial applications.

(1) There is inadequate information about (or concerning) the chromosome location of desired genes for most industrially useful organisms, e. g. *Penicillium chryso-*
20 *genum*, *Aspergillus oryzae*.

(2) The availability of useful vectors for most industrially important organisms is at an early stage of development.

(3) Physiological patterns and, in particular, enzymic steps catalysing important conversions are not well understood for many important processes.
25 (4) Processes that require multiple gene involvement present formidable problems.

(5) Chimeric plasmids will only be useful in host cells if they are stably retained within the cell. The danger is not that the plasmid will be broken up but that after a few generations in continuous culture it may simply be lost. The additional 'genetic load' of a chimeric plasmid may affect the growth rate and
30 chimeric plasmid-free cells may outgrow and replace the other cells. However, many studies are now showing that instability amongst plasmids can be overcome either by novel changes or insertions in the chimeric plasmid or by careful control of fermentation parameters.

3. 7 Regulation and control of recombinant DNA experimentation

35 The ability of recombinant DNA technology to produce hybrid molecules of DNA never before seen in nature has caused concern within society (Table 3. 3). In an industrial context genetic manipulations by the new techniques have proceeded rapidly and are now widespread. Advances in this technology can be translated into economic power and its marketability may obscure the profound ecological and ethical implications of genetic

Table 3. 3   Major events in the commercialization of new biotechnology

1973	First gene cloned
1974	First expression of a gene cloned from a different species in bacteria.
	Recombinant DNA (rDNA) experiments first discussed in a public forum (Gordon conference).
1975	US guidelines for rDNA research outlined (Asilomar conference).
1976	First firm to exploit rDNA technology founded in the United States (Genetech).
	Genetic Manipulation Advisory Group (UK) started in the United Kingdom.
1980	Diamond v. Chakrabarty-US Supreme Court rules that microorganisms can be patented under existing law. Cohen/Boyer patent issued on the technique for the construction of rDNA.
	United Kingdom targets biotechnology (Spinks' report).
	Federal Republic of Germany targets biotechnology (Leistungsplan).
	Initial public offering by Genetech sets Wall street record for fastest price per share increase ($ 35 to $ 89 in 20 minutes).
1981	First monoclonal antibody diagnostic kits approved for use in the United States.
	First automated gene synthesizer marketed.
	Japan targets biotechnology (Ministry of International Trade and Technology declares 1981 'The Year of Biotechnology').
	France targets biotechnology (Pellsolo report).
	Hoesch/Massachusetts General Hospital agreement.
	Initial public offering by Cetus sets Wall street record for the largest amount of money raised in an initial public offering ($ 125 million).
	Industrial Biotechnology Association founded.
	Du Pont commits $ 120 million for life sciences R & D.
	Over 80 new biotechnology firms (NBFs) had been formed by the end of the year.
1982	First rDNA animal vaccine (for collbacillosis) approved for use in Europe.
	First rDNA pharmaceutical product (human insulin) approved for use in the United States and the United Kingdom.
	First R & D limited partnership formed for the funding of clinical trials.
1983	First plant gene expressed in a plant of a different species.
	$ 500 million raised in US public markets by NBFs.

Source : Office of Technology Assessment.

engineering.

The original guidelines set out by countries involved in genetic engineering were initially very restrictive but have now been relaxed to the point where they afford little protection. Although the early fears about the risks involved in genetic manipulation were exaggerated, constant vigilance should be maintained.

Producing new strains of organisms for biotechnological processes can be extremely costly and for this reason most industrial concerns keep a high security level around important producer strains. Although living organisms can now be patented in many countries there is considerable doubt that patents can offer worthwhile protection . *The*

Budapest Treaty on the International Recognition of the Deposit of Microorganisms for the Purpose of Patent Procedure (1978) legitimizes existing national practices of countries that have signed the Convention and allows for international recognition, through the issue of a patent, of a microorganism which has been transmitted to the depository. How successful this treaty will be has yet to be shown.

3.8 Summary

Applied genetics is concerned with deriving new and improved strains of organisms that can be utilized for the benefit of mankind. In biotechnology this will involve the selection of organisms from natural sources, from culture collections and other organizations, or by further exploitation of 'in house' strains. A wide variety of techniques is available to modify, delete or add to the genetic complement of organisms. Selection and screening activities occupy a major part of biotechnological programmes. Screening is the use of procedures to allow the detection and isolation of only those organisms or metabolites of interest among a large population. Screens may be non-selective random screens in which all the isolates are treated as individuals for the requisite qualities or they may be rational screens involving some aspect of preselection.

Producer organisms must be preserved with minimum degeneration of genetic capabilities. Preservation can be on agar medium, by reduced metabolism, drying, freeze drying or by ultra-low temperature.

Organism genomes can be modified by mutagenesis or by various forms of hybridization. Mutational programmes are primarily aimed at strain improvement and mutagens available include UV and ionizing radiation, thymine starvation and a wide selection of chemical mutagens. The mutation rate in an organism is genetically controlled and can be altered by mutator or anti-mutator genes.

Hybridization is essentially a method that facilitates the recombination of genetic material between organisms and can be expressed by sexual or parasexual mechanisms. Sexual hybridization occurs between haploid nuclei and will involve karyogamy, nuclear fusion and finally meiosis. Recombination of the genetic characteristics will arise because of rearrangement and reorganization of the chromosomes.

Parasexual processes use various cellular mechanisms to bring together genetic material from different genetic sources. The main methods practised industrially involve conjugation, transduction, transformation and mitotic recombination.

Protoplast fusion techniques are widely practised with many microbial cells as well as with plant and animal cells. Fusion rates have been greatly increased by means of the fusogen polyethylglycol.

Recombinant DNA technologies allow the isolation, purification and selective amplification in specific host cells of discrete DNA fragments or genes from almost any organism. The basic requirements of this technology are restriction endonuclease enzymes which can cleave double-stranded DNA at specific sites generating DNA fragments of defined sizes. These fragments can then be inserted into carrier vehicles such as plasmids or phage and be covalently bonded by DNA ligase enzymes. Transformation is the main method used for the insertion of these chimeric DNA molecules into host cells. The types of host cell are typically but not exclusively specific mutant cells of *E. coli*, *B. subtilis* or *S. cerevisiae*. Transformed cells are identified by several means including complementation and resistance markers, hybridization, immunological methods and restriction endonuclease analysis.

5

Words and Expressions

page   line

65   1   genetics [dʒi'netiks] （复）（用作单） n. 遗传学

6   breeding [b'riːdiŋ] n. 育种
    mutagenesis [mjuːtə'dʒenisis] n. 诱变作用，引起突变

8   tedious ['tiːdjəs] a. 乏味的，单调的   boring, monotonous, tiresome

9   up until （时间上）一直到

10   protoplast fusion ['prəutəplæst 'fjuːʃən] n. 原生质体融合

11   trait [treit] n. 特征   character, a distinguishing quality

12   engineer [endʒi'niə] vt. 设计，建造，利用精巧技术进行设计或加工   to plan, construct and manage as an engineer

14   endow [in'dau] 赋予 vt.   to equip with talent or quality

16   viral ['vaiərəl] a. 病毒的

18   objectionable [əb'dʒekʃənəbl] a. 令人不愉快的   unpleasant
    slime [slaim] n. 粘质物   a mucous substance

23   amenable [ə'miːnəbl] a. 顺从的   tractable, able to be guided

29   an array of [ə'rei] 大量   a multitude of

66   2   in-house a. 机构内部的   being or coming from within an organization
    strain [strein] n. （菌）株
    screen, screening n. 筛选

4   transformation [trænsfə'meiʃən] n. 转化

8   artefact ['aːtifækt] n. 赝物

14   hybridization [haibridai'zeiʃən] n. 杂交

20   hindrance ['hindrəns] n. 障碍   obstacle, obstruction

24   methodology [meθə'dɔlədʒi] n. （学科的）一套方法   the system of principles, practices, and procedures applied to any specific branch of knowledge

28   habitat ['hæbitæt] n. 栖息地   The area in which an organism normally lives or occurs.

34   transduction [trænz'dʌkʃən] n. （基因）转导   以病毒为载体（对细菌而言便是噬菌体）把遗传物质从一种细胞转移到另一种细胞的过程。
    gene cloning 基因克隆（=Recombinant DNA technology）

39   genotype ['dʒenətaip] n. 基因型   一个个体的全部基因组成。

page line

67 10 dispersal [dis'pə:səl] n. 分散 the act or process of dispersing

12 flotation [flou'teiʃən] n. 浮选

13 conjugation [kɔndʒu'geiʃən] n. 接合

15 outgrowth ['autgrəuθ] n. 长出物

sexual cycle ['seksjuəl] n. 有性循环

parasexual cycle n. 准性循环

17 chitin ['kaitin] n. 甲壳素

19 cycloheximide [saikləu'heksimaid] n. 放线菌酮

20 rifampicin ['rifəmpin] n. 利福平

21 shotgun cloning n. 鸟枪法克隆 将一种生物的基因组任意切割成碎片,进行克隆(建立基因或克隆文库)

22 gene library n. 基因文库 一种重组 DNA 分子的集合,代表整个基因组

Eh 氧化还原电位

27 shake-flask culture n. 摇瓶培养

28 spore [spɔ:] n. 孢子

68 4 phenotypic a. 表型的

phenotype ['fi:nətaip] n. 表型 在合适的外界环境条件下,特定遗传型的个体通过新陈代谢和生长发育所表现出来的外观和性状,称为该生物的表型

10 degeneration [di,dʒenə'reiʃən] n. 退化

13 culture maintenance n. 菌种保藏

19 integral ['intigrəl] a. 构成整体所必需的 necessary to the whole

infrastructure ['infrə,strʌktʃə] n. 基础结构 an underlying base

23 subculturing n. 移种;接种

27 freeze drying n. 冷冻干燥

29 cryo- [构词成分] 表示"寒冷"、"冰冻"

69 16 supplant [sə'plɑ:nt] vt. 取代 replace,supersede

23 efficacious [,efi'keiʃəs] a. 有效验的 capable of producing the desired effect, effective,efficient.

29 manifestation [mæni'festeiʃən] n. 表现 demonstration

70 2 mitomycin [,maitəu'maisin] n. 丝裂霉素

5-bromouracil [,brəuməu'juərəsil] n. 5-溴尿嘧啶

3 methylmethane sulfonate n. 甲基甲烷磺酸酯

nitrogen mustard [mʌ'stəd] n. 氮芥子气

nitrofuran [naitrəu'fjuəræn] n. 硝基呋喃

6 refractory [ri'fræktəri] a. 难驾驭的 not responsive to treatment. obstinate, unmanageable.

11 mutator gene n. 增变基因 能使其他基因突变率增加的基因

12 antimutator gene n. 减变基因 能使其他基因突变率降低的基因

13 mutator strain n. 增变(菌)株 含增变基因的菌株

page	line	

70　**17**　complete medium　n. 完全培养基　在基础培养基上,增加酵母膏、酪蛋白水解物等成分,以便使营养缺陷型细菌也能生长

minimal medium　n. 基本培养基,最低培养基　一种合成培养基,仅能供野生型微生物生长,不能供营养缺陷型生长。含无机化合物,有机物则只含碳源,如糖。

　　20　offspring　['ɔːfspriŋ]　n. 后代

　　30　context　['kɔntekst]　n. 背景,环境　the circumstances in which a particular event occurs.

　　32　sexual hybridization　n. 有性杂交

　　34　haploid　['hæplɔid]　n. 单倍体　一个个体或细胞只具有单套同源染色体

　　35　karyogamy　[ˌkæri'ɔgəmi]　n. 核配　在有性繁殖中,两个配子的核的融合

　　　　diploid　二倍体

　　36　meiosis　[mai'əusis]　n. 减数分裂

　　38　homologous recombination　[hɔ'mɔləgəs]　n. 同源重组　具有相同或近于相同的碱基次序的 DNA 分子间的交换

71　**4**　crossing-over　n. 交换　同源染色体间遗传物质的交换,产生基因重组

　　5　assortment　[ə'sɔːtmənt]　n. 分组

　　6　life cycle　n. 生命周期　一个生物从开始产生到死亡的各个阶段

　　9　chromatid　['krəumətid]　n. 染色单体　双股染色体中的一股

　　13　shuffle　['ʃʌfl]　vt. 把……移来移去,洗牌

　　18　breeding system　n. 繁殖系统

　　　　outbreeding　n. 远交,远系繁殖　The crossing of individuals of the same species that are not closely related

　　　　inbreeding　n. 近交,同系交配　The mating of closely related individuals

　　9　self-fertilization　n. 自体受精　同一个体的雌雄配子的结合

72　**1**　document　['dɔkjumənt]　vt. 用文件(或文献等)证明　To support an assertion or claim with evidence or decisive information.

　　2　Ascomycetes　[ˌæskəumai'siːtiːz]　n. 子囊菌纲

　　　　Basidiomycetes　[bəˌsidiəumai'siːtiːz]　n. 担子菌纲

　　10　overt　['ouvəːt]　a. 明显的　open and observable

　　12　encompass　[in'kʌmpəs]　vt. 包含　comprise,include

　　13　vegetative cell　['vedʒitətiv]　n. 营养细胞　正在快速生长的细胞

　　19　gamete　['gæmiːt]　n. 配子

　　　　zygote　['zaigəut]　n. 合子　由雌雄配子结合产生的细胞

　　22　Hfr strain＝High frequency of recombination strain　高频率重组株　一种细菌株,其染色体有 F 因子并入,因而具有高频率重组能力

　　28　sex pillus　['pailəs]　n. 性纤毛　具 2.5nm 的中空结构,正好通过 DNA 分子.

73　**1**　cleavage　['kliːvidʒ]　n. 开裂　The act of splitting or cleaving

　　8　vector　['vektə]　n. 载体

　　9　lysogenic　[laisə'dʒenik]　a. 溶源性的

page　line

73　14　simian virus　n. 猿猴病毒

15　polyoma　[ˌpɔli'əumə]　n. 多瘤

16　cauliflower　['kɔliflauə]　n. 花（椰）菜

mosaic　[məu'zeiik]　n. 花斑病

17　Cruciferae　n. 十字花科

27　kb　kilobase　千个碱基

34　heterozygous　[ˌhetərə'zaigəs]　a. 杂合的

35　heterokaryon　[ˌhetərə'kæriɔn]　n. 异核体

74　11　homogenic　[ˌhɔməu'dʒenik]　a. 同种的,同基因的

heterogenic　[ˌheterəu'dʒenik]　a. 异种的,异基因的

incompatibility　['inkəmˌpætəbiliti]　n. 不相容

12　override　[ˌəuvə'raid]　vt. 使无效　set aside;胜过　prevail over

75　17　helicase　n. 蜗牛酶

sulphatase　['sʌlfəteis]　n. 硫酸酯酶

20　mycolytic　a. 溶真菌的

35　reversion　[ri'və:ʃən]　n. 回复　a return to a former condition

40　fusogenic agent　n. 促融剂

76　4　agglutination　[əˌglu:ti'neiʃən]　n. 凝集　adhesion of dintinct parts

6　translocation　[ˌtransləu'keiʃən]　n. 移位　a change in location

8　denude　[di'nju:d]　vt. 使裸露　make bare

14　encapsulate　[in'kæpsəleit]　vt. 用囊状物包,封装　to encase in or as if in a capsule.

35　show up　出现　to be clearly or ultimately visible

conidia　[kəu'nidiə]　n. 分生孢子

uninucleate　[ˌju:ni'nju:klieit]　a. 单核的

77　7　sherry　['ʃeri]　n. 雪利酒,一种葡萄酒

10　inter-specific　a. 种间的

15　differentiate　[ˌdifə'renʃiet]　v.　分化

16　somatic　[səu'mætik]　a. 体细胞的(与生殖细胞相区别)

25　sterile　['sterail]　a. 不生育的

preclude　[pri'klu:d]　vt. 防止　prevent

33　complement　n. 一套染色体

35　erythrocyte　[i'riθrəusait]　n. 红细胞

38　taxonomical　[ˌtæksəu'nɔmikəl]　a. 分类学的

78　6　prime　vt. 使准备好　to prepare for operation

7　virulent　['virjulent]　a. 有毒力的　extremely harmful or pathogenic

9　vertebrate animal　['və:tibrit]　脊椎动物

10　plasma cell　浆细胞　由 B 淋巴细胞产生的能分泌抗体的细胞

lymphocyte　['limfəsait]　n. 淋巴细胞　在淋巴组织、脾脏和血液中存在的一种

page　line

　　　　细胞,其特点是具有一个大而圆的核,在免疫反应中起主要作用,能产生抗体,
　　　　识别抗原,可分为 B 细胞和 T 细胞

78　14　antisera　n. 抗血清　含抗体的血清

　　19　malignant　[mə'lignənt]　a. 恶性的(指肿瘤)

　　　　proliferate　[prə'lifəreit]　vt. 增殖　to reproduce rapidly

　　　　myeloma　[ˌmaiə'ləumə]　n. 骨髓瘤

　　20　hybridoma　[ˌhaibri'dɔːmə]　n. 杂交瘤

　　37　transfusion　[træns'fjuːʒən]　n. 输血

　　39　parasitic　[ˌpærə'sitik]　a. 寄生虫的

　　　　tissue typing　组织定型　对一种组织的抗原进行表征的过程,该组织能引起同
　　　　　种的其他动物产生抗体

79　10　propagation　[ˌprɔpə'geiʃn]　n. 繁殖　increase or spread,as by natural repro-
　　　　　duction

　　23　amplification　[ˌæmplifi'keiʃən]　n. 扩大　enlargement

　　　　discrete　[dis'kriːt]　a. 各别的,分离的　individual,distinct

　　24　deletion　[di'liːʃən]　ɴ 删除,(部分染色体)丢失　omission

80　2　heritable　['heritəbl]　a. 可遗传的　capable of being inherited

　　8　fertilization　[ˌfəːtilai'zeiʃan]　n.　受精

　　15　restriction endonuclease　[ˌendəu'njuːklieis]　n. 限制性核酸内切酶

　　19　express　vt. 表达　名词形式为 expression　以得到的或遗传的基因信息为基础
　　　　　而合成某一蛋白质的过程称为表达。在分子生物学中,如果由载体所插入的一
　　　　　个重组基因合成了所编码的蛋白质,那么就称这一重组基因已被表达

　　21　DNA ligase　['laigeis]　DNA 连结酶

　　　　chimeric DNA　[kai'miərik]　嵌合 DNA　重组 DNA 分子,含不同来源的基因

　　27　probe　[prəub]　n. 探针　一种物质,通常用同位素标记,以鉴别和分离一种基
　　　　　因,基因产物或蛋白质

81　8　plaque　[plɑːk]　n. 噬菌斑,空斑

　　14　competent cell　['kɔmpitənt]　感受态细胞　细胞能进行转化的生理状态

82　1　encompass　[in'kʌmpəs]　vt. 包含

　　　　autonomous　['ɔːtəunəməs]　a. 自发的,自主的　existing and functioning inde-
　　　　　pendently

　　2　cryptic　['kriptic]　a. 隐性的　除复制和转移外,不具其他功能

　　5　replicon　['replikɔn]　n. 复制子　复制时的独立遗传单位,相当于转录时的操
　　　　　纵因子由起始基因和复制基因构成

　　22　splice　[splais]　vt. 拼接　不同来源的 DNA 片段共价结合成重组 DNA 分子
　　　　　的过程

　　24　transformant　[træns'fɔːmənt]　n. 转化体　进行转化后的细胞

　　30　confer　[kɔn'fəː]　vt. 赋予　bestow

　　32　virulence　['virjuləns]　n. 毒性

page   line

82   39   transposon [træns'pouzən] n. 转位子,转座子　是一类附加的 DNA 分子,是染色体片段,与染色体其他区域的不同点在于它能转座到染色体的其他部位,或转座到质粒、病毒或不同的染色体上,转座因子的移动不是经常发生但却是随时可能发生的,是由该因子编码的酶来中介的。有些还编码另一些酶,如赋予抗药性的酶。也可用作比插入序列(insertion sequences)更复杂的 DNA 片段的同义词

83   8   annealing [ə'niːliŋ] n. 退火　一种核酸杂交的过程。将变性的核酸混合物,缓慢冷却,使不同来源的双股核酸分子形成杂交分子。由限制性内切酶作用产生的 DNA 上的粘性末端可通过退火而粘合

84   3   digestion [di'dʒestʃən] n.(酶切)消化

        5   homopolymer tailing n. 同聚物加尾

            cohesive [kou'hiːsiv] a. 粘性的　cohesive end　粘性末端

            blunt end [blʌnt] n. 钝端,平头

            linker n. 接头

        7   transfection n. 转染　以噬菌体 DNA 进行转化的过程。由于没有蛋白质的衣壳,必须先使细菌宿主对 DNA 有良好通透性

      12   ampicillin [ˌæmpi'silin] n. 氨苄青霉素

            tetracycline [ˌtetrə'saiklain] n. 四环素

      13   caesium chloride ['siːzjəm] n. 氯化铯　CsCl

      14   ethidium bromide [i'θidiəm 'brəumaid] n. 溴化乙锭　一种荧光染料使 DNA 片段显色

      18   chloramphenicol [ˌklɔːræm'fenikɔl] n. 氯霉素

      20   replication determinants　复制功能基因组　(在免疫学中,抗原上能与抗体结合的活性部位称为抗原决定簇 antigenic determinant)

      27   modification methylase n. 修饰性甲基化酶　一种酶,它催化 DNA 某些碱基的甲基化反应,从而使其限制性内切酶不能识别,保护了该 DNA

      30   palindromic sequence [ˌpælin'drəumik] n. 回文序列　在对称结构的 DNA 片段中,一股 DNA 的碱基次序(如按从 5′到 3′位置)与另一股 DNA 相同。如

                5′…GAATTC…3′

                3′…CTTAAG…5′

86   26   sonication [ˌsɔni'keiʃən] n. 声处理

      27   reverse transcriptase n. 逆转录酶

      28   intron n. 内含子　真核基因 DNA 中的中介序列,位于外显子(exon)之间,这种序列不被转录成 RNA,而被切除,不被转译,又称为 intervening sequences

87   3   flush end [flʌʃ] n. 平头

      17   deoxyguanosine [diːˌɔksi'gwɑːnəsin] n. 脱氧鸟苷

      18   deoxycytosine [diːˌɔksi'saitəsiːn] n. 脱氧胞嘧啶

      22   chimera [kai'mirə] n. 嵌合体

      37   cosmid n. 粘粒　由质粒和病毒入 DNA 的 cos 位点构建而成的载体

page	line		
88	18	agronomical [ˌægrə'nɔmikəl]	a. 农(艺)学的
	28	complementation [ˌkɔmplimən'teiʃən]	n. 互补
	31	β-galactosidase [gəˌlæktəu'saideis]	n. β-半乳糖苷酶
89	2	autoradiography [ˌɔːtəuˌreidi'ɔgrəfi]	n. 放射自显影术 所研究的对象用放射性同位素标记,放在暗室里使它与照相胶片或乳剂紧贴在一起,显出放射性辐射引起的图像,从而确定其位置。
	16	capstone ['kæpstəun]	n. 顶点 culmination
		framework ['freimwəːk]	n. 体系,结构 a basic system
	24	site-directed mutation	定点突变
	40	signal peptide	n. 信号肽
90	9	legume ['legjuːm]	n. 豆科植物
	12	feedstock ['fiːdstɔk]	n. 原料 raw material
	25	formidable ['fɔːmidəbl]	a. 可怕的,令人生畏的 causing fear
	39	obscure [əb'skjuə]	vt. 使变暗,遮蔽 to darken, overshadow
		ethical ['eθikəl]	a. 道德的,伦理的 moral
91	4	forum ['fɔːrəm]	n. 论坛,讨论会
	14	offering ['ɔfəriŋ]	n. 上市的股票
	27	colibacillosis [ˌkəulibæsi'ləusis]	n. 大肠杆菌病
	40	concern [kən'səːn]	n. 公司,企业 company, enterprise
92	15	requisite ['rekwizit]	a. 需要的,必不可少的 required, necessary
	22	thymine starvation	胸腺嘧啶饥饿(胸腺嘧啶不存在会导致 DNA 拆成单链)

Notes

① 这里以及本段其他地方应用的将来完成时和简单将来时一样(参见 Ch. 1, Note②和⑧)也并不表示将来时,但含有完成之意,表示一种推测或很可能发生之事,是一种委婉的说法。如 They will have arrived home by now. 他们可能已经到家了。[参见张道真:实用英语语法(第二次修订本),1979,p. 149]。

　　本句可译为:最后的培养物可以与原始的研究培养物相同,但更常见的是,将它经过一系列的处理,以提高产率。

② 本句可译为:在同一染色体上的基因(A,a;B.b)由于交换而重新组合;而在不同染色体上的基因则任意地重新分配组成染色体对。注意此处 reassort(重新分配)是子句的动词。

③ F-factor F 因子 在某些细菌中存在的质粒或附加体,能使细菌发生结合。

④ broad host-range plasmids 意为多种宿主的质粒。

⑤ lysogenic bacteriophage(溶源性噬菌体)也称为 temperate phage(温和噬菌体),其基因能整合于宿主的染色体中,但不会溶解宿主细菌细胞。此时的宿主细胞也称为 lysogenic bacterium(溶源性细菌)。

⑥ 1000-fold 加了连字符后,fold 后就不可加 s,即不能写成 1000-folds。连字符的一些用法如下:

（1）fold 接在数字后，需加连字符，如 25-fold。但接在名词后则不加连字符，如 fivefold，multifold。

（2）当一个数字加上单位作为形容词时，需加连字符，如 a 12-min exposure；a 20-ml aliquot；a 10-mg sample。例外有：a 37℃ water bath；a 0.1M NaOH Solution；a 0.1 mol·dm^{-3} solution。

（3）当几个复合形容词具有相同的基词，如：

20-to 50-mg samples；0.5-x 10-cm tube；first-and second-order reactions.

（4）当复合形容词含有数字时：

three-dimensional model；aqueous two-phase partitioning；three-neck flask；4-mm-thick layer.

（5）专有名词前的词首，需加连字符，如：

non-Gaussian；non-Newtonian.

⑦ protein-denuded membrane　（表面）去除蛋白质的膜。protein-denuded 为一复合形容词，参见 Ch. 1，Note④.

⑧ clone 和 cloning 都译作克隆，前者为名词，后者为动词的-ing 形式，在生物技术文献中经常出现，了解其意义，很重要。

clone　n.　　1. 遗传性能相同的细胞群，由同一细胞经无性繁殖得到。

　　　　　　　2. 由 DNA 重组技术得到的相同 DNA 序列的拷贝。

clone　vt.　　1. 将一个基因引入到宿主中复制成许多相同拷贝的过程。（和上述当名词用的第 2 种含义相对应）

　　　　　　　2. 从广义上说，指得到或大量得到克隆（名词）的过程。

⑨ would have…表示按某种判断"应当有…"之意，而且语气比较婉转，参见 Ch. 2，Note①。本句可译为：识别 4 核苷酸序列的内切酶所产生的片断，其平均长度应为 256 个（＝4^4）碱基对。

Comprehension

1. Define the two terms "selection" and "screening" . (p. 66, p. 92)

2. The author cited Nisbet that there are two methods for generating new strains of organisms: ecological and genetic. what are their respective prerequisites? (p. 66, Table 3.1)

3. The reason for mutation has not been fully understood. With this in mind, please give an account of its possible mechanism (section 3.3, p. 69~70)

4. Enumerate the main genetic methods to improve the productivity of an existing strain (in classified form) . (p. 66~67, p92~93)

5. Name the different stages of sexual hybridization. (p. 70~71)

6. How is the genetic material transferred from one cell to another by conjugation? (p. 72)

7. Name the different stages of mitotic recombination. (p. 73~74, Fig, 3.4) .

8. What are the constituents of an asmotic stabilizer and what is its function in protoplast making? (p. 75)

9. Why did the author consider protoplast fusion as the most promising method for strain improvement in antibiotic industry?

State briefly the usual conditions of fusing protoplast. (p. 75~77)

10. What is hybridoma and what are its characteristics? (p. 78)

11. Could you give some examples of application of monoclonal antibodies both in health care and in industry? (p. 78~79)

12. Outline the main steps of gene cloning. (Fig. 3. 6, p. 83)

13. What is the method commonly used in isolation and separation of plasmid in bacteria? (p. 84)

14. Why can a microorganism recognize and destroy foreign DNA but does not harm its own DNA? (p. 84)

15. Explain in brief the method of homopolymer tailing for DNA fragments joining to a vector. (p. 87)

16. What is transformation and what is meant by the term "competence"? State briefly a typical transformation process using E. coli as host cells. (p. 87)

17. What is a cosmid? (p. 87)

18. Why, in contrast to microorganism, has genetic engineering gained little success in plants? (p. 88)

19. Discuss briefly the identification methods of transformants. (p 88~89)

20. What is the main demerit of using E. coli as the host cell and the measures to overcome it? (p. 89~90)

Vocabulary

Give another word or phrase to replace these words or phrases as they are used in the text:

artefact (66/8); a wide range of (68/30); comprehensive (68/33);

lend themselves to (69/8); mutagen-induced (69/12); alternate (70/6);

by way of (75/1); owe much to (75/9); approach (75/22); subject (75/25);

wall chemistry (75/29); ensuring (75/36); as yet (77/27); entity (78/7); substantially (79/16); duplex (84/31); termini (85/10); project (85/28); blunt ended (85/31);

yet (88/13); yet (88/18); confer (88/33); susceptible (88/34);

reflect (89/3); privileged (89/13); translate (90/38) .

Word Usage

1. Write sentences to bring out the difference between the following pairs of words:

potential (65/16), potent; in contrast (67/33), on the contrary; use (82/26), employ (67/40); can (84/16), may (70/18); experimentation (90/34), experiment; efficacious (69/23), effective; among (73/4), between (75/36); compared to (73/28), compared with; born (78/21), borne (229/13); technical (90/16), technological (77/17); lose (78/31), loose; feedstock (90/12), feed; in contrast to (79/28), in contrast with; continuous (71/19), continual (47/31);

2. Make sentences with the following phrases:

be amenable to (65/23); a measure of (65/26); make use of (67/33); instead of (84/33); other than (86/25) .

Patterns

1. It is + adjective + that ···

   This is another common impersonal start to a statement (see p. 63) .

   Here is a typical sentence in the text：

   ···, it is feasible that protoplasts of different species could be induced to fuse and form a hybrid cell, ··· (75/4~5)

   Exercises

   Change these statements into the pattern shown above：

   a. Important operating strains must be retained in a viable and productive condition. (68/ 34~35)

   b. There is now little doubt that fusion technologies will contribute substantially to the biotechnological utilization of prokaryotes. (79/16~17)

2. ···so as to···

   This is a common way of expressing the purpose for which we do something, e. g.：

   ···the formation of new combinations of heritable material by the isolation of nucleic acid molecules, ···, into any virus, bacterial plasmid, or other vector system so as to allow their incorporation into a host organism··· (80/1~6)

3. ···too···to···

   This pattern is used to indicate consequence or result, e. g.：

   Vaccines are complex entities made up of a mixture of antibodies too complex to be synthesized chemically (78/7~8) .

   Exercises

   Change these statements into the patterns shown above：

   (a) The purpose of removing cell wall is to fuse protoplasts and form a hybrid cell.

   (b) Strain improvements of streptomyces and other known producers of antibiotics involve large numbers of genes and thereby recombinant DNA technology can hardly be used.

4. The final present participle phrase to express result.

   Examples

   However, this method does allow a much wider range of endonucleases to be used, increasing the range of DNA under study. (87/6)

   Frequently the words thus or thereby are added to emphasise the meaning, such as：

   In practice, cloning has long been used to propagate pure cultures of viruses, microorganisms and plants by vegetative means, thus ensuring exact continuation of the organism's genome. (80/38~40)

   Exercises

   Rewrite these statements, using thus or thereby and the present participle of the verb.

   (a) The rational screen could selectively kill all undesirable genotypes and permit much higher numbers of isolates to be tested routinely. (67/36)

   (b) In general, exponential phase cells produce protoplasts more readily than stationary phase cells. This suggests that wall chemistry changes during the growth cycle. (75/28~29)

Sentence analysis and translation

First analyse the following sentences as in Ch. 1，Note① and then translate into Chinese：

1. The second paragraph on page 70 (70/4~10).

2. The second paragraph on page 77 (77/3~13).

3. The first two paragraphs of section 3. 7 (90/35~91/38).

4. The last paragraph of section 3. 8 (92/36~93/7).

Writing

1. 此法的收率为 90%，纯度提高 120 倍。（倍数用 fold，注意连字符）。

2. 鉴于图 4 所示的特异性，我们可得出结论，反应是通过在活性位点（active site）上的结合作用而产生。（利用 Given 作为引导词，参见 Ch. 2，Note⑩）

3. 已知停留时间分布（residence time distribution）和一级反应的速度常数，则非理想流动反应器（non-ideal flow reactor）的特性就能准确地决定。（利用 Given 作为引导词，参见 Ch. 2，Note⑩）

4. 酶的等电点（isoelectric point）较高（pI 8.8），因此带正电，有利于吸附在带负电荷的基质（matrix）上。（利用现在分词，表示结果，参见 pattern 4）。

5. 该共聚物（copolymer）含有环氧基（epoxy group），与 9M 氨水在 40℃反应 3h，就转化为氨基树脂（amino resin）。（利用现在分词表示结果，参见 pattern 4）。

Chapter 4　Fermentation Technology

4.1　The nature of fermentation

The origins of fermentation technology were largely with the use of microorganisms for the production of foods and beverages such as cheeses, yoghurts, alcoholic beverages, vinegar, sauerkraut, fermented pickles and sausages, soya sauce and the products of
5　many other Oriental fermentations (Table4.1) The present-day large scale production processes of these products are essentially scaled up versions of former domestic arts. Paralleling this development of product formation was the recognition of the role microorganisms could play in removing unpleasant wastes and this has resulted in massive world-wide service industries involved in water purification, effluent treatment and
10　waste management. New dimensions in fermentation technology have made use of the ability of microorganisms (1) to overproduce specific essential primary metabolites such as glycerol, acetic acid, lactic acid, acetone, butyl alcohol, butane diol, organic acids, amino acids, vitamins, polysaccharides and xanthans; (2) to produce useful secondary metabolites (groups of metabolites that do not seem to play an immediate recognizable
15　role in the life of the microorganism producing them) such as penicillin, streptomycin, oxytetracycline, cephalosporin, giberellins, alkaloids, actinomycin; and (3) to produce enzymes as the desired industrial product such as the exocellular enzymes amylases, proteases, pectinases or intracellular enzymes such as invertase, asparaginase, uric oxidase, restriction endonucleases and DNA ligase. More recently, fermentation technology has
20　begun to use cells derived from higher plants and animals under conditions known as cell or tissue culture. Plant cell culture is mainly directed towards secondary product formation such as alkaloids, perfumes and flavours while animal cell culture has initially been mainly concerned with the formation of protein molecules such as interferons, monoclonal antibodies and many others.

25　　Future markets are largely assured for fementation products because, with limited exceptions, it is not possible to produce them economically by other chemical means. Furthermore economies in production will also occur by genetically engineering organisms to unique or higher productivities. The commercial market for products of fermentation technology is almost unlimited but will ultimately depend on economics and
30　safety considerations.

　　The processes of commercial fermentation are in essence very similar no matter what organism is selected, what medium is used and what product formed. In all cases, large numbers of cells with uniform characteristics are grown under defined, controlled conditions. The same apparatus with minor modifications can be used to produce an en-

Table 4. 1 Fermentation products according to industrial sectors

Sector	Activities	
Chemicals		
Organic (bulk)	Ethanol, acetone, butanol	
	Organic acids (citric, itaconic)	**5**
Organic (fine)	Enzymes	
	Perfumeries	
	Polymers (mainly polysaccharides)	
Inorganic	Metal beneficiation, bioaccumulation and leaching (Cu, U)	
Pharmaceuticals	Antibiotics	**10**
	Diagnostic agents (enzymes, monoclonal antibodies)	
	Enzyme inhibitors	
	Steroids	
	Vaccines	
Energy	Ethanol (gasohol)	**15**
	Methane (biogas)	
	Biomass	
Food	Dairy products (cheeses, yogurts, fish and meat products)	
	Beverages (alcoholic, tea and coffee)	
	Baker's yeast	**20**
	Food additives (antioxidants, colours, flavours, stabilizers)	
	Novel foods (soy sauce, tempeh, miso)	
	Mushroom products	
	Amino acids, vitamins	
	Starch products	**25**
	Glucose and high fructose syrups	
	Functional modifications of proteins, pectins	
Agriculture	Animal feedstuffs (SCP)	
	Veterinary vaccines	
	Ensilage and composting processes	**30**
	Microbial pesticides	
	Rhizobium and other N-fixing bacterial inoculants	
	Mycorrhizal inoculants	
	Plant cell and tissue culture (vegetative propagation, embryo	
	production, genetic improvement)	**35**

zyme, an antibiotic, an organic chemical or a single cell protein. In its simplest form fermentation processes can be just the mixing of microorganisms with a nutrient broth and allowing the components to react. More advanced and sophisticated large-scale processes require control of the entire environment so that the fermentaton process can proceed efficiently and, what is more important, can be exactly repeated with the same amounts of **40** raw materials, broth and cell inoculum producing precisely the same amount of product.

All biotechnological processes are carried out within a containment system or bioreactor. The physical form of most common bioreactors has not altered much over the past 30 years. Recently, however, many novel forms have been designed and they may play an increasingly active part in biotechnology. The main function of a bioreactor is to minim- **45** ize the cost of producing a product or service while the driving force behind the continued improvement in design and function has been the need to increase the rate of product formation and the quality of the product or service. Studies have considered better aseptic design and operation, better process control including computer involvement, and how to obtain a better understanding of the rate-limiting steps of a system, especially heat and mass transfer.

In biotechnology, processes can be broadly considered to be either conversion cost intensive or recovery cost intensive. With conversion cost intensive processes the volumetric productivity, Qp (kg of product m$^{-3} \cdot$h^{-1}), is of major importance while with recovery cost intensive processes the product concentration, P (kg$\cdot$m^{-3}), is the main criterion for the minimization of cost. Examples of the diverse product categories produced in bioreactors in the biochemical process industry are given in Table 4.2 while Table 4.3 identifies the various cultivation methods employed in biotechnology.

Table 4.2　Examples of products in different categories in biotechnological industries

Category	Example
Cell mass*	Baker's yeast, single cell protein
Cell components**	Intracellular proteins
Biosynthetic products**	Antibiotics, vitamins, amino and organic acids
Catabolic products*	Ethanol, methane, lactic acid
Bioconversion*	High-fructose corn syrup, 6-aminopenicillanic acid
Waste treatment	Activated sludge, anaerobic digestion

　　* Typically conversion of feedstock cost-intensive processes.
　　** Typically recovery cost-intesive process.

There are three main operating types of bioreactors for biotechnological processes together with two forms of biocatalysts. Bioreactors can be operated on a batch, semi-continuous (fed-batch) or continuous basis. Reactions can occur in static or agitated cultures, in the presence or absence of oxygen, and in aqueous or low moisture conditions (solid substrate fermentations). The biological catalysts can be free or can be attached to surfaces by immobilization or by natural adherence. The biocatalysts can be cells in a growing or non-growing state or isolated enzymes used as soluble or immobilized catalysts. In general, the reactions occurring in a bioreactor are conducted under moderate conditions of pH(near neutrality) and temperature (20 to 65℃). In most bioreactors the processes occur in an aqueous phase and product streams will be relatively dilute.

The optimization of a bioreactor process involves minimizing the use of raw materials (e. g. nutrients, precursors, acid/base, air) and energy(the cost of energy since 1978 has risen at an annual rate of 16%), and maximizing product purity and quality in the broth before recovery. Process optimization is achieved by manipulation of both the physical and chemical parameters associated with the process. The range of process variables that are important to process development are listed in Table 4.4 and are discussed later.

Table 4.3 Characteristics of cultivation methods

Type of culture	Operational characteristics	Application
Solid	Simple, cheap, selection of colonies from single cell possible; process control limited	Maintenance of strains, genetic studies; production of enzymes; composting
Film	Various types of bioreactors: trickling filter, rotating disc, packed bed, sponge reactor, rotating tube (see chapter 5)	Waste water treatment, monolayer culture (animal cells); bacterial leaching; vinegar production
Submerged homogeneous distribution of cells: batch	'Spontaneous' reaction, various types of reactor: continuous stirred tank reactor, air lift, loop, deep shaft, etc.; agitation by stirrers, air, liquid process control for physical parameters possible; less for chemical and biological parameters	Standard type of cultivation: antibiotics, solvents, acids, etc.
Fed-batch	Simple method for control of regulatory effects, e.g. glucose repression	Production of baker's yeast
Continuous one-stage homogeneous	Proper control of reaction; excellent tool for kinetic and regulatory studies; higher costs for experiment; problem of aseptic operation, the need for highly trained operators	Few cases of application in industrial scale; production of single cell protein; waste water treatment

Table 4.4 Process variables in fermentation processes

Temperature	pH	Respiratory quotient
Pressure	Oxidation reduction potential	Cell concentration
Agitation speed	Dissolved oxygen	Cellular composition:
Power input	Dissolved CO_2	protein (enzymes)
Air flow rate	Effluent oxygen	DNA
Feed rate of:	Effluent CO_2	RNA
nutrients	Dissolved concentations of:	lipid and carbohydrate
precursors	carbohydrate	Specific activity of
inducers	nitrogen	enzyme
Weight of broth	mineral ions	Specific rates of:
Volume of liquid	precursor	product formation
Viscosity (apparent)	inducer	growth
Cumulative amount of:	product	oxygen uptake
acid	metabolites	precursor utilization
base	Broth rheology	nutrient uptake
antifoam	Power characteristics	CO_2 production
	Energy balance	Oxygen transfer rate

Adapted from Ryu and Humphrey (1973) *Journal of Applied Chemistry and Biotechnology* 23, 283~295.

The remainder of this chapter will be concerned with the principles of organism growth in bioreactors and special attention is given to microbial cells used in product formation. The use of bioreactors for enzymic function either in soluble or immobilized form together with certain types of immobilized microbial cell systems will be considered in Chapter 5.

5   4. 2   Principles of microbial cultivation in aqueous systems

Growth of organisms may be considered as the increase of cell material expressed in terms of mass or cell number and is the result of a highly coordinated series of enzymically catalysed biological steps. Optimal expression of growth will be dependent on the transport of necessary nutrients to cell surfaces (mass transfer) and on environmental 10 parameters such as temperature and pH being optimally maintained.

The quantity of cell material (X) or biomass in a bioreactor can be determined gravimetrically (by dry weight, wet weight, DNA, or protein) or numerically (by number of cells). Doubling time (t_d) relates to the period of time required for the doubling in weight of biomass while generation time (g) relates to the period necessary for the doubling of 15 cell numbers. During balanced or exponential growth, when growth is controlled only by intrinsic cellular activities, $g = t_d$ provided every cell of the population is able to divide. Average doubling times increase with increasing cell size and complexity; the following range of values in hours has been achieved experimentally: bacteria 0. 25 to 1, yeast 1. 15 to 2, mould fungi 2 to 6. 9 and plant cells 20 to 40.

20   Under ideal conditions the biosynthetic potential of microorganisms can be very great with a biomass doubling time of only 15 minutes for certain types of bacteria. However, it is seldom that optimal growth conditions will prevail for any length of time and in practice growth will become dependent on a limiting factor, for example, an essential nutrient. As the concentration of this factor drops to zero, so also will the growth 25 potential of the organism decrease. The classical studies of Monod (1942) have allowed the development of mathematical equations describing the essential features of microbial growth in bioreactors. The original mathematical equation described the specific growth rate μ as a function of the concentration S:

$$\mu = \mu_{max} \frac{S}{K_s + S} \qquad (1)$$

30   In this case S is the concentration of a substrate in the medium which is in limiting concentration when compared with other essential nutrients, μ_{max} is the maximum specific growth rate of the organism while K_s represents a saturation constant. K_s is the substrate concentration at which $\mu = \mu_{max}/2$. Thus exponential growth can occur at specific growth rates having any value between zero and μ_{max} if the substrate concentration can 35 be held constant at the appropriate value (which will be of significance for continous culture). Identification of the nutrients essential for growth as well as the optimum conditions required for growth have been derived from batch and continuous bioreactor systems. The rate of increase of concentration of organisms (dx/dt) is the *growth rate* while

the *specific growth rate* is the rate of increase/unit of organism concentration $(1/x)(dx/dt)$. A simple relationship exists between growth and utilization of substrate. In simple systems growth rate is a constant fraction, Y, of the substrate utilization rate:

$$\frac{dx}{dt} = -Y\frac{ds}{dt} \tag{2}$$

Y is the *yield constant* and over any finite period of growth

$$Y = \frac{\text{weight of cells formed}}{\text{weight of substrate used}}$$

Knowing the values of the three growth constants μ_{max}, K_S and Y, equations (1) and (2) can give a complete quantitative description of the growth cycle of a batch culture.

In batch culture the inoculum and nutrients that will be required for growth will be brought together in a containment vessel under optimum environmental conditions of temperature, pH and mixing. This represents a closed system except for[①] aerobic organisms where a continuous supply of air will normally be supplied to the bioreactor.

In batch cultivation, the growth rate and specific growth rate will seldom be constant, reflecting the changing nutrient environment characteristic of the system. The complex nature of batch growth of microorganisms is shown in Fig. 4.1. The initial *lag phase* is a period of no observable growth but chemical analyses show much hidden metabolic turnover indicating that the cells are adapting to the new environment and that growth will begin in due course. The physiological condition of the inoculum is now considered not only to be a major influencing factor of the duration of the lag phase but also to influence the nature of future growth and product formation, e.g. antibiotic synthesis. There is a *transient acceleration phase* after inoculum outgrowth and before exponential growth occurs. This phase is not well understood physiologically or mathematically because the population of cells is heterogeneous in age structure and metabolism. In the *exponential phase* organism growth is unlimited with nutrients in excess and inhibitors absent. The specific growth rate will achieve its maximum, i.e. $\mu = \mu_{max}$. However, in most batch cultivations exponential growth is transitory. As nutrients are used up by the growing cell population unlimited growth will be replaced by limited growth and although the cell population is still increasing the specific growth rate at any particular point tends to become smaller and smaller, i.e. $< \mu_{max}$. This *deceleration phase* is then followed by a *stationary phase* in which overall growth can no longer be achieved due to nutrient exhaustion. Biomass balance arises because

rate of growth = rate of death.

Many important biotechnological products are optimally formed during this period of the growth cycle, e.g. antibiotics. The final phase of the cycle is the *death phase* when the specific growth rate is negative $(\mu < 0)$. Most biotechnological batch processes are stopped before this phase is reached, because of decreasing metabolism and cell lysis.

In practice, batch cultivation is used to optimize organism or biomass production and then to carry out specific chemical transformations such as end-product formation (an-

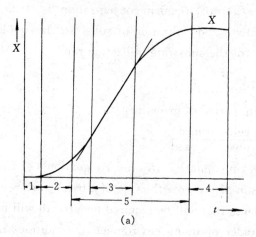
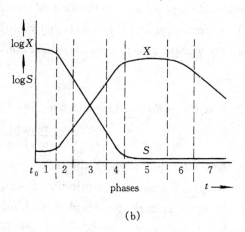

(a) (b)

Fig 4.1　Growth characteristics in a batch culture of a microorganism (a) Biomass concentration (or mass) X as a function of time; 1. Lag phase; synthesis of mRNA and enzymes, any production of biomass cancelled by destruction, zero net growth ($\mu=0$); 2. Exponential growth phase, $\mu=\mu_{max}$; 3. Centre part of decelerating phase; 4. Zero net growth, $\mu=0$. 5. Span of variable μ-values, $\mu_{max}\rightarrow<\mu_{max}\rightarrow0$. (b) Logarithm of concentration of mass of X (biomass) and S (substrate, e. g. glucose) vs. time, semilogarithmic plot (t scale linear); 1. Lag phase, $\mu=0$; 2. Accelerating phase; 3. Exponential phase, $\mu=\mu_{max}$; 4. Decelerating phase; 5. Stationary phase, $\mu=0$ [cf. 4 in Fig. 4.1(a)]; 6. Decline phase; 7. Death

tibiotics, organic acids) or decomposition of substances (sewage treatment). Many impor-

10　tant products are optimally formed during the stationary phase of the growth cycle in batch cultivation.

In contrast to batch culture, in continuous cultivation the addition of nutrients and the removal of an equal fraction of the total culture volume occur continuously. Continuous methods of cultivation will permit organisms to grow under steady state

15　conditions[2], that is, growth occurs at a constant rate and in a constant environment. Factors such as[3] pH and the concentrations of nutrients and metabolic products which inevitably change during the growth cycle of a batch culture can be held constant in a continuous culture. Indeed, these parameters can be independently controlled allowing the experimenter to obtain realistic information on the role of each to the growth of

20　the organism.

In a completely mixed continuous culture system sterile medium is fed into the bioreactor at a steady flow-rate (f) and culture broth emerges from it at the same rate keeping the volume of culture in the vessel (v) constant. With efficient mixing incoming medium should be rapidly and uniformly dispersed throughout the bioreactor. The char-

25　acteristics of all stirred continuous bioreactor systems can be described mathematically by setting up balanced equations for cells, substrates, products, etc. in which the overall rate of change in concentration of any component is given as the resultant of the rates of all the processes tending to increase or decrease it. In practice these can be (a) increase due to inflow to the bioreactor—equal to the inflow rate multiplied by the concentration of component in the inflow, (b) decrease due to outflow, (c) increase (of cells) due to growth, (d) decrease (of substrates) due to utilization, (e) increase in product formation and biomass.

Residence-time, in a continuous bioreactor, is determined not by the absolute values of the flow-rate and culture volume but by their ratio, the dilution rate D, where $D=f/v$, or the number of complete volume changes per hour. The mean residence time of a particle in the culture vessel is equal to $1/D$. Assuming complete and uniform mixing every cell in the bioreactor has an equal probability of leaving it or being washed out within a given time.

The net increase of organisms is given by the simple equation

$$\text{increase} = \text{growth} - \text{output}$$

$$\frac{\mathrm{d}x}{\mathrm{d}t} = \mu x - Dx$$

When $\mu > D$, $\mathrm{d}x/\mathrm{d}t$ is positive and cell concentration will increase; when $\mu < D$, $\mathrm{d}x/\mathrm{d}t$ is negative and cell wash-out will occur; when $\mu = D$, $\mathrm{d}x/\mathrm{d}t = 0$ and x is constant. In this case, the steady state has been achieved where the concentration of organisms will not change with time.

Dilution rate will also affect the concentration of substrates in the bioreactor. In the bioreactor substrate enters at a concentration s_R, is consumed by the organism and flows out at a concentration s. The net rate of change of substrate concentration is obtained by another balanced equation:

$$\text{increase} = \text{input} - \text{output} - \text{consumption}$$

$$= \text{input} - \text{output} - \frac{\text{growth}}{\text{yield constant}}$$

$$\frac{\mathrm{d}s}{\mathrm{d}t} = DS_R - Ds - \frac{\mu x}{Y}$$

When the dilution rate exceeds the μ_{max} value, wash-out of the organisms will occur.

When a continuous culture system is viewed as a production system (e. g. SCP process) its performance will be judged by two criteria: (1) the quantity of cells produced in unit time—*the output rate*; and (2) the quantity of cells produced from unit weight of substrate—*the effective yield* or 'yield coeflicient'. In the steady state condition the total output will be equal to the product of flow-rate and concentration of organisms. For maximum output of cells or biomass the dilution rate should be high but obviously it cannot exceed μ_{max}. In practice maximum production efficiency combining a high output with efficient utilization of substrate will be obtained with a flow-rate at or a little below the maximum output rate and the highest practicable substrate concentration. Such optimum conditions will only be relevant to biomass production. Although similar conditions would be used when the desired product, for example ethanol, is a fermentation product which is formed in proportion to the amount of substrate consumed, widely different conditions might be required for the production of complex metabolic products such as antibiotics.

Fed-batch culture(see below)is a form of cultivation which involves a continuous or sequential addition of medium or substrate to the initial batch without any withdrawal from the system. Product yield from such systems can well[④] exceed conventional batch culture. This approach is widely practised in industry—for example, in the production of
5   baker's yeast.

In practice, batch, fed-batch and continuous cultivation systems are used in industry for production of biomass or cellular products. For many reasons batch cultivation techniques represent the dominant form of industrial practice. For a fuller understanding of the kinetics of the various techniques of growing organisms, reference should be made to
10   Pirt (1975, Principles of Microbe and Cell Cultivation, Halsted Press, New York) and Fiechter (1981, Biotechnology, vol. 1 pp. 453~505, Verlag Chemie, Basel.).

4. 3   Bioreactor design

The bioreactor is the containment system for the biological reactions of a biotechnolog-ical process. It will provide the correct environment for optimization of organism growth
15   and metabolic activity; it should prevent contamination of the production culture from the environment while also preventing release of the culture into the environment, and it should have the associated instrumentation or probes to allow optimum process control (Table 4. 5).

Table 4. 5   Basic bioreactor design criteria

20	1.	Microbiological and biochemical characteristics of the cell systems(microbial, mammalian, plant)
	2.	Hydrodynamic characteristics of the bioreactor
	3.	Mass and heat characteristics of the bioreactor
	4.	Kinetics of cell growth and product formation
25	5.	Genetic stability characteristics of the cell system
	6.	Aseptic equipment design
	7.	Control of bioreactor environment (both macro-and micro-environments)
	8.	Implications of bioreactor design on downstream product separation(s)
	9.	Capital and operating costs of the bioreactor
30	10.	Potential for bioreactor scale-up

Many bioreactor systems will be required to operate under aseptic conditions. In most systems of industrial importance pure cultures of the producer organism will be used and the presence of foreign unwanted contaminating organisms can influence the process in several ways—for example, by interfering with the biological catalyst, de-
35   stroying the product, producing substances that can impair downstream processing, and introducing toxic molecules into the system.

To avoid these problems the medium, bioreactor and all ancillary pipework must be sterilized (usually with high pressure steam) and all incoming air must be passed through sterilized glass wool to remove contaminants. In batch fermentation medium is normally sterilized in the bioreactor whereas in continuous systems external sterilization is practised. In the fermentation industry there will be occasions when contaminating microorganisms do enter the bioreactor and cause damage. For this reason in the antibiotics industry bioreactors are seldom larger than 200 m^3 because of the considerable loss that will occur when contamination occurs. When continuous processes are used there is even greater need for stringent sterile operation. The anticipated greater use of genetically engineered microorganisms in industry will necessitate even more expensive exclusion techniques.

For aerobic processes the design must include a mechanism for incorporating air and mixing the contents and all systems must have provision for inoculation and sampling and for charging and discharging the vessel. Energy input from the stirring,aeration and metabolic oxidation processes will need to be removed by cooling mechanisms. Measurement of energy input will be necessary to determine the overall mixing and aeration rates.

The materials for construction should be non-toxic,able to withstand pressurized steam and to resist chemical and electrolytic corrosion. Industrial bioreactors are usually constructed from highly polished stainless steel. Bioreactors exist in many shapes and sizes and the ratio of height to diameter (the aspect ratio)is an important working parameter.

The size of industrial bioreactors will be affected by the required product concentration and whether batch or continuous operation is chosen. Although continuous culture techniques are widely used in research they have found only limited use in industry,for example,SCP and ethanol production processes and waste water treatment. Almost all other industrial processes use batch or fedbatch cultivation methods.

The dominance of batch and fed-batch culture techniques in industry is due to some or all of the following reasons:

(a) Products may be required in relatively small quantities at any given time.

(b) Market requirements can be intermittent.

(c) Shelf life of certain products is short.

(d) High product concentration is required in broth to optimize downstream processing.

(e) Certain products are produced only during stationary phase of the growth cycle.

(f) Instability of some production strains requires their regular renewal.

(g) Continuous processes still offer many technical difficulties.

Although there are numerous designs for industrial bioreactors,the long established continuous stirred tank reactor(CSTR) or vessel continues to be the most widely used [Fig. 4.2(a)]. In bioreactors without mechanical agitation,e.g. tower and loop bioreactors,agitation is achieved with very high gas throughputs [Fig. 4.2(b)]. In large scale bioreactors of these types with aqueous fermentation broths it is now accepted that such

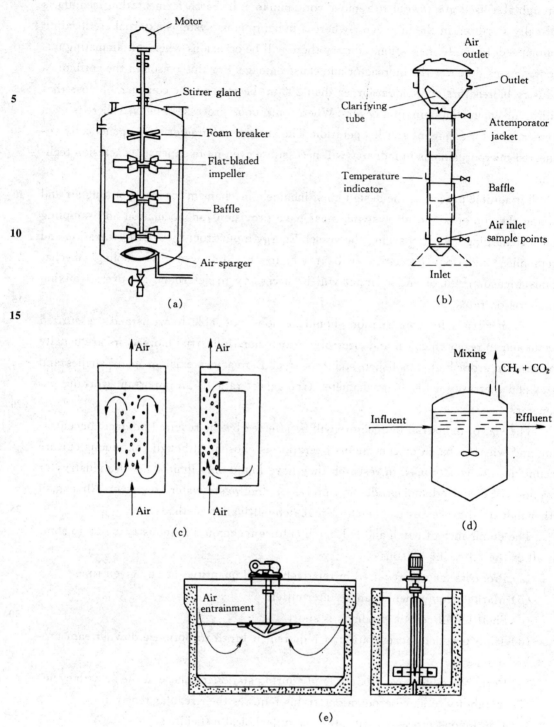

Fig. 4.2 Various forms of bioreactor (a) Continuous stirred tank reactor;
(b) Tower reactor; (c) Loop (recycle) bioreactor; (d) Anaerobic digester
or bioreactor; (e) Activated sludge bioreactor

designs can be economically competitive with mechanically agitated bioreactors,However-er,in all systems inceasing viscosity can create major problems with aeration as smaller bubbles tend to coalesce creating large bubbles with reduced interfacial areas.

In general,fermentation industries require a bioreactor which can meet a number of different running conditions including varying viscosity,aeration rate, intensity of agita- **5** tion and fermentation volume and in practice the CSTR has become widely accepted. A further consideration in determining choice is that many industries will need to process different products in the same plant;thus a flexible system that can be easily modified will be favoured.

The basic design of the CSTR was developed during the 1940s and 1950s with the **10** industrial production of penicillin. It is generally a fully baffled upright cylinder and the baffle width is 10% of the tank diameter[Fig. 4.2(a)].Sterile air is introduced at the base of the vessel by way of an open pipe or ring sparger. The vertical shaft with over-head drive will carry one or more impellers depending on the aspect ratio. The impellers are usually spaced at intervals equivalent to one tank diameter along the shaft to avoid a **15** swirling type of liquid movement. Flat-bladed(Rushton) turbines are used in the majori-ty of bioreactors and usually 3 to 5 are mounted to give good mixing and dispersion throughout the height of the system [Fig. 4.2(a)]. Such turbine systems require a high power input and numerous studies have been made to find more efficient designs. A typi-cal industrial CSTR is shown in Fig. 4.3. **20**

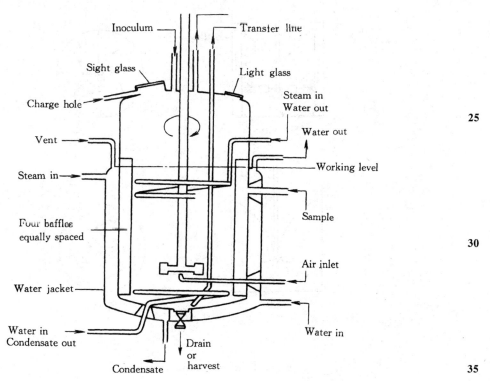

Fig. 4.3   An industrial continuous stirred tank reactor

The role of the impellers is to create agitation or mixing within the bioreactor and to facilitate aeration (Fig. 4. 4). Agitation and aeration account for a significant part of the CSTR operating costs. The primary function of agitation is to suspend the cells and nutrients evenly throughout the medium, to make the nutrients, including oxygen, available to the cells and to allow heat transfer. The majority of industrial organisms are aerobic and in most fermentations the organisms will exhibit a high oxygen demand. Since oxygen is a sparingly soluble gas in aqueous solution, fermentations can only be supported by vigorous aeration of the broth. The oxygen transfer coefficient (K_La)can be influenced in three ways by agitation: (1) the impeller can break up the air into smaller bubbles thus increasing the gas/liquid interfacial area, (2) agitation can delay the loss of air from the bioreactor, and (3) turbulent shear can reduce film thickness at the gas/liquid interface.

Tower bioreactors can be defined as elongated tubular vessels with an aspect ratio greater than 6 : 1[Fig. 4. 2(b)]. Tower bioreactors do not have mechanical agitation; air is introduced at the bottom of the tower and mixing occurs only by way of the rising bubbles. For this reason there is little shear effect on the organisms. Loop(recycle)bioreactors incorporate a forced, controlled liquid bulk flow in a specified direction[Fig. 4. 2 (c)]. This has been achieved by incorporating draft or baffle tubes to give an 'internal recirculation' of the fluid or by 'external recirculation' using a recirculation pipe.

Large amounts of organic wastewaters from domestic and industrial sources are

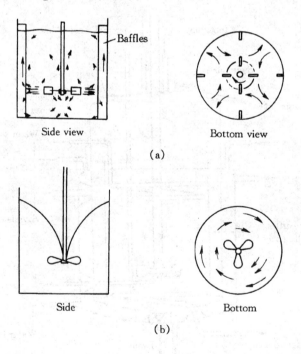

Fig. 4. 4   Mixing patterns in bioreactors
(a)Radial flow pattern in baffled bioreactor; (b)Unbaffled flow pattern

routinely treated by anaerobic and aerobic bioreactor systems. In the absence of free oxygen, certain specialized microorganisms are able to convert biodegradable organic material to methane, carbon dioxide and new microbial cells. Approximately 90% of the chemically bound energy in the original organic material is recovered as methane, 5% to 10% of the energy is used for formation of new microorganisms and about 3% wasted as heat. This is in sharp contrast to aerobic degradation processes where about 60% of the energy available is present in new cell growth and about 40% lost as process heat.

The most common type of anaerobic bioreactor or digester is the CSTR [Fig. 4.2 (d)] operated in a continuous or semi-continuous manner. With this system concentrated wastewaters—for example, sludge from municipal sewage treatment—are mixed with the anaerobic microoganisms at approximately 30℃ and the hydraulic retention time (the average time the water remains in the bioreactor) is selected to give efficient wastewater stabilization and high methane yield. For medium strength wastewaters from food and fermentation industries, techniques have been devised to retain the microbial biomass for longer periods in continuously operating systems. Thus solid retention time is uncoupled from the fluid retention time and high microbial concentrations can be obtained in the digesters thus giving high degradation rates. For very dilute wastewaters, for example, municipal sewage, very long solids retention time is required and this can only be achieved with fluidized bed processes (see Chapter 5).

The outstanding example of methane fermentation is the Chinese biogas programme where several million family size anaerobic biorectors have been built. Such bioreactors are used for treatment of manure, human excreta and straw, producing biogas for cooking and lighting, and the sanitization of the waste which then becomes an excellent fertilizer.

With volumetric loads up to 4 kg dry matter per day per m^3 of bioreactor and mean residence time as low as 10 days, full-scale methane bioreactors can be expected to produce routinely up to 1 m^3 gas per day per m^3 of bioreactor.

Activated sludge processes are widely used for the oxidative treatment of sewage and other industrial wastes. These processes use batch or continuous agitated bioreactor systems to increase the entrainment of air to optimize oxidative breakdown of the organic matter [Fig. 4.2(e)]. These bioreactors are very large and for optimum functioning will have several or many agitator units to facilitate mixing and oxygen uptake of most municipal sewage treatment plants. Because of their open nature there can, on occasion, be problems of smell.

Anaerobic biological treatment of industrial wastewaters is becoming more accepted because:

　　(1) no energy is needed for aeration;

　　(2) there is a high conversion of organic matter into biogas, which can be used as
　　　　fuel;

(3) there are no smell problems;

(4) little surplus sludge is produced;

(5) by manipulation of microbes, high value products can be formed.

4. 4　Media design

Media are designed to meet the nutritional demands of the producer organism, the objectives of the process and the scale of the operation. For most large scale biotechnological processes cost, availability and handling properties of the medium components are major factors in determining selection.

The basic nutritional requirements of heterotrophic microorganisms are an energy or carbon source, an available nitrogen source, inorganic elements and, for some microorganisms, growth factors. For most biotechnological processes carbon and nitrogen sources are more often derived from relatively complex mixtures of cheap natural products or byproducts (Table 4. 6), while trace metals are normally present in sufficient amounts in the tap water or in the main raw materials. Salts are often added as supplementary sources of nitrogen, phosphorus, sulphur or calcium. Growth factors when required may be supplied in pure form but for economic reasons would generally be added as a plant or animal extract. The main types of growth factors required are B-group vitamins or related compounds, certain amino acids and some fatty acids. Proper balance of carbon and nitrogen sources can be important to the pH pattern of processes if pH control is not applied. For most processes the nutrients have to be dissolved in water. In batch systems nutrients are normally all present in the initial volume. Fermentation reactions can be further regulated and controlled in batch cultures by feeding some of the nutrients on a specific rate basis (fed-batch culture). In this way essential inducer concentrations can be maintained. Nutrient availability will exert strong physiological control over fermentation reactions and product formation.

Table 4. 6　Sources of carbohydrate and nitrogen for industrial media

Sources of carbohydrate	Sources of nitrogen (%nitrogen by weight).
Glucose—Pure glucose mono hydrate, hydrolysed starch	Barley(1. 5~2. 0) Beet molasses(1. 5~2. 0)
Lactose —Pure lactose, whey powder	Corn-steep liquor(4. 5)
Starch　—Barley, groundnut meal, oat flour, rye flour, soya bean meal	Groundnut meal(8. 0) Oat flour(1. 5~2. 0) Pharmamedia(8. 0)
Sucrose —Beet molasses, cane molasses, crude brown sugar, pure white sugar	Rye flour(1. 5~2. 0) Soya bean meal(8. 0) Whey powder(4. 5)

Economy is of paramount consideration in medium formulation since raw material can account for 60% to 80% of the variable costs of fermentation processes. Raw material input to a fermentation will be largely dependent on the cost of the material at a particular time since commodity market prices fluctuate with seasonal and other variables. Choice of materials will also depend on handling and storage costs, ease of formulation and sterilization, while health and safety considerations must also be included.

Product optimization will be strongly influenced by medium formulation and specific nutrient availability during the fermentation. Thus, if biomass or a growth-associated product is the objective of the fermentation then the medium must permit maximum growth potential throughout. For a compound that is not growth limited, e. g. organic acids, antibiotics etc., a medium is developed which, after an initial growth phase, will become deficient in one or more nutrients. Depending on the nature of the process under study, particularly if a secondary metabolite is required, limitation of phosphorus, nitrogen, carbohydrates or trace metals have been successfully used. Some processes require the presence of an inducer in the medium while other processes may be repressed by a component of the medium. Catabolite repression is a particularly common problem with enzyme production and is manifested usually in media containing glucose. Repression can be avoided by replacing glucose by slowly fementable carbohydrates or partially hydrolysed starch. Incremental or continuous feeding of a concentrated component can also be used for specific fermentations.

The composition of an industrial medium is not only based on the requirements of the fermentation stage of the process but also on the subsequent purification steps[5]. The formulation of the medium should also aim to produce a final fermentation broth that is low in viscosity, has an easily separable cell mass, and is low in residual compounds that could affect final product specifications.

Sterilization methods for media must achieve maximum kill of contaminating microorganisms with minimum temperature damage to medium components or the precipitation of minerals. Bacterial endospores can constitute a serious problem in medium stabilization since they are only killed at temperatures in excess of 100℃. At these temperatures many media components are labile and could be destroyed. In such cases alternative sterilization methods involving filtration or radiation must be applied.

For most media batch-wise sterilization in the bioreactor is still the method of choice, although continuous methods are gaining wider acceptability. Continuous sterilization processes with short holding time at temperatures in excess of 120℃ can give an efficient spore kill without serious detrimental effects on medium nutrients. In practice continuous sterilization is obtained by passing the medium through a heat exchanger where it is raised to the required high temperature in a short time. The medium is then passed to a holding coil, maintained at this temperature for a predetermined time, and finally rapidly cooled by countercirculation in the exchanger against cool input medium and then cold water. High-temperature/short-time processes result in improved preservation of growth factors and less development of colour. Recovery of heat may be an additional advantage. Direct steam injection (<140℃) can also be used for rapid sterilization.

4.5 Instrumentation and process control in bioreactors

All living organisms are subject to a wide range of intracellular and extracellular regulatory factors,such as temperature,pH and O_2. The identification and role of each of these
5 factors has been derived from traditional physiological and biochemical investigations. In all biotechnological processes it is essential to optimize productivity. This can only be achieved by identifying and controlling the many factors that are known to regulate organism activity. The characteristic environmental parameters that control biological activity can be physical,chemical and biochemical and are not always easy to identify and measure(see Table 4.4).

10   Instrumentation of bioreactors has become increasingly important for measuring specific parameters,recording them,and then using this information to improve and optimize the process (Table 4.7). In practice,for process control a measurement is obtained by a *sensor* which can then be compared with a set point. A discrepancy between the two values is then used to alter the position of an *activator* that can manipulate the process,
15 thus ensuring that the measured value is brought closer to the set point. The physical device that allows the measurement to be compared with the set point is a *controller* and in this way a control loop,able to regulate a specific factor,will consist of a sensor,controller and an activator.

Table 4.7   Instrumentation currently associated with bioreactors

Parameter measured	Equipment used
Pressure	Pneumatic or strain gauge sensor
Fermenter contents magnitude:	
Volume	Differential pressure cells at top and bottom
Weight	Fermenter mounted on load cell
pH	Glass and reference electrodes
Stirrer speed	Tachometer
Air flow	Variable area flowmeter,orifice plate
Carbon dioxide production	Infrared analyser
Oxygen consumption	Zirconia analyser
Dissolved oxygen	Polarographic oxygen electrodes
Temperature	Thermocouple,resistance thermometer, thermistor,capillary

Bioreactor control measurements can be made in either an on-line or an off-line
manner. For on-line measurement the sensor is placed directly into the process stream
35 whereas for off - line measurement a sample is removed aseptically from the process stream and analysed. Ideally a sensor should be steam-sterilizable,give a reliable continuous signal and operate on-line. It should be easy to calibrate,be robust and should not

affect the process. The lack of efficient on-line sensors for measurement and control is a major bottleneck in the development of fermentation technology. The more common types of sensors for on-line measurement include those for temperature, pH, pressure, liquid and gas flow rates, CO_2 and O_2. Complete bioreactor processing is still severely limited by a lack of reliable instruments capable of on-line measurement of important **5** variables such as DNA, RNA, enzymes and biomass. Off-line analysis is still essential for these compounds and since the results of these analyses are not normally available until several hours after sampling, they cannot be used for immediate control purposes.

A few of the well proven on-line systems will be examined briefly together with some of the projected future types of on-line measurement techniques. **10**

4.6 Measurement techniques

Temperature.   Temperature can influence biological processes by kinetic effects on reaction rates and catalytic effects on the activity or stability of enzymes. There are many types of sensors available to monitor temperature in bioreactors which include thermocouples, resistance thermometers, thermistors and capillaries. They all function by pro- **15** ducing an output signal that can be used in a control loop. Large volume bioreactors need several temperature sensors to ensure reasonable temperature distribution throughout the fermentation volume.

pH.   Growth of most organisms is sensitive to pH changes, each group of organisms having specific optimum pH values. The optimum value of pH for product formation is **20** usually different from that for growth. pH is believed to exert its main effect on cell wall permeability and on the rates of reactions associated with the enzymes bound to the outer cell wall. pH sensors or ion-selective electrodes have been extensively used in bioreactors. A modern pH probe can withstand steam sterilization and some considerable degree of handling. **25**

Dissolved oxygen.   Most organisms used in bioreactors need a constant supply of oxygen. Dissolved oxygen(DO)probes measure the amount of oxygen dissolved in the process liquid. The relationship between organism activity and dissolved oxygen is often the major determinant for the eventual success of most biotechnological processes. There are two kinds of DO probes, galvanic and polarographic. They do not differ significantly in **30** design, each carrying two electrodes in a glass or stainless steel housing. The main problems with DO probes are that they have a slow response and are not very reliable at low DO concentration. There can also be considerable time drift and they do not stand up to repeated sterilizations.

The rate of oxygen uptake within a bioreactor can be obtained by measuring oxygen **35** concentrations in the inlet and outlet gas streams using a paramagnetic oxygen analyser or a mass spectrometer which is faster but much more expensive.

Dissolved carbon dioxide.   Determination of dissolved CO_2 levels in a fermentation broth provides considerable information about a process. Membranecovered electrodes are now available for dissolved CO_2 measurements but they are expensive and lack reliability. On-line measurement of gaseous CO_2 can be achieved with spectrophotometric, gas chromatographic or mass spectrometric methods.

Immobilized enzyme probes.   These new generations of probes are produced by immo-
5   bilizing enzymes near the surface of an electrochemical sensor, usually a DO or pH probe. The enzyme can react with a specific molecule producing a response which can be detected by the electrochemical sensor. Enzyme electrode prototypes have been reported for many compounds including glucose, sucrose, urea, pyruvate, penicillin, ethanol, lactate, methane, cholesterol and several amino acids. These electrodes are highly specific
10   and not affected by other compounds, are easy to calibrate and have high senstitivity. However, they have long response times, are not steam-sterilizable and are difficult as yet to use in on-line control loops. Yet, undoubtedly, their specificity and unlimited range of applications make enzyme probes an exciting area for future development in fermentation technology.

Biomass.   It is not yet possible to have automated on-line analysis of biomass at a real-
15   istic cost. Indirect methods have been considered based on material balances of gaseous oxygen and carbon dioxide. In practice, biomass determinations including protein, DNA and RNA must still be performed as a time consuming off-line activity.

Data processing.   The data gathered from various on-line and off-line measurements were originally stored in notebooks and recorder charts but now more often will be
20   stored in the memory of a computer or magnetically encoded on tapes or disks. In a computer, data for a particular biotechnological process will be stored in the form of files which in practice will cover medium formulation, the fermentation process and the intricacies of downstream processing. The storing and organization of historic data is now a major operation in most industrial fermentation processes. The computer has become a
25   valuable, indeed indispensible, means of understanding and controlling fermentation processes. Thus in one functional unit it is now possible to have process monitoring, sequence control, continuous control, calculation, data storage, data supply and reporting. Further applications of computers in biotechnology include nucleic acid and protein sequence analysis, restriction map generation, simulation of molecular processes and ex-
30   periment planning and debugging.

4.7   Mass and energy transfer

Growth and metabolism of organisms in bioreactor systems requires the continuous supply and uptake of essential nutrients together with the elimination of toxic waste metabolites. The exchange of materials between the surface of the organism and its ex-
35   ternal environment is known as mass transfer. Mass transfer and concomitant growth and biological activity of the organisms can only be achieved if certain forms of energy can be supplied to or removed from the whole bioreactor system. Thus heat energy is required for sterilization and process temperature control, and mechanical energy for stir-

ring and mixing of bioreactor contents : as a result of biological activity, metabolic energy will be generated.

Mass and energy transfer processes represent a major part of all fermentation processes and furtherance of their understanding will be of major importance to maximizing biotechnological processes. The principles governing mass and energy transfer are derived from chemical engineering practice.

Mass transfer. Central to all bioreactor processes will be the need to supply the correct amount of nutrient to meet organism or metabolic demand for optimum growth and/or product formation[6].

A nutrient component will need to cross through several resistances during passage from the source phase (e. g. oxygen sparger, nutrient feed inlet) into the organism phase. These phases may be continuous or dispersed. The continuous phase will normally be liquid (aqueous or non-aqueous) but can sometimes be gaseous, while the dispersed phase can be gaseous (air, CO_2, methane, etc), liquid (hydrocarbons) or solids (microbial pellets, flocs, immobilized cells or solid substrates), The locations of the mass transfer resistances are shown in Fig. 4. 5.

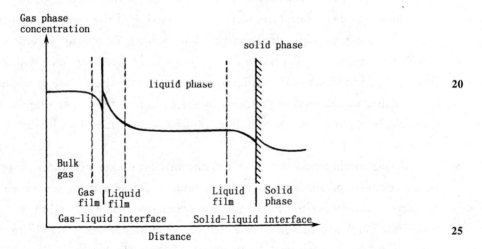

Fig. 4. 5   Mass transfer resistances in a system with gas, liquid, and solid phases

Most organisms used in biotechnology are aerobic and consequently oxygen mass transfer has always been an important consideration when designing bioreactor systems. The rates of mass transfer between gas and liquid phases will be strongly influenced by the solubility of the gaseous components in the liquid. Unfortunately oxygen is only sparingly soluble in water and this has meant developing oxygen dispersion techniques to maximize the availability of the oxygen to the organism in the bioreactor. Methods of monitoring dissolved oxygen in aqueous solution and in the gaseous phase have been well developed and are considered elsewhere. Measurement of $k_L a$ or dissolved oxygen concentrations are important for knowing the availability of oxygen to the organisms in a process.

Air or oxygen is introduced into a bioreactor system by way of an orifice producing bubbles and the size of the bubbles together with the velocity at which they rise in the fermentation liquid will determine the rate of oxygen transfer. In non-mechanical agitated systems, such as tower bioreactors, bubble diameter will determine the interfacial sur-
5   face area and bubble rise velocity. Conversely, in mechanically agitated vessels (CSTR) bubble size will depend on the level of bulk turbulence and the physical properties of the liquid rather than the orifice or sparger design. Excessive viscosity of the liquid will further adversely influence oxygen transfer.

Mass transfer across solid/liquid phase boundaries in fermentation systems are not
10   strongly influenced by the hydrodynamics of the whole system. All transfers will be by molecular diffusion and the rate of diffusion of nutrients (including oxygen) to the cells and of metabolites from the cells will limit the rate of biological activity. Diffusion will always be accompanied by reaction, i. e. either consumption or production of the diffusion molecules.

15   Aerobic fermentation can be seen as a gas/liquid mass transfer step, a liquid/solid mass transfer step and a chemical or biochemical reaction step. Mixing has a greater effect on the gas/liquid mass transfer step than on the liquid/solid step.

The complete and uniform dispersion or mixing of the medium components within a bioreactor becomes increasingly more complex with increasing volume of the bioreac-
20   tor. The mechanism of dispersion throughout the bioreactor volume will involve the bulk flow of liquid together with mixing by entrainment via the turbulent eddies that are generated either by mechanical agitation or the turbulent flow of the liquid. Mixing will be particularly important for the addition of air and of nutrients in fed-batch or continuous culture.

25   Mixing mechanisms should aim to optimize both axial and radial dispersion thus ensuring complete preservation of the fermentation components (medium and organism) in all parts of the bioreactor. Seldom is this completely achieved and in large-scale fermentation rapid and near uniform dispersion of added ingredients can only be achieved by using many ports of entry into the bioreactor. Indeed, the large ICI Pruteen bioreactor uti-
30   lizing methanol as substrate involves 2600 individual entry points. When broths are non-Newtonian and highly viscous there will always be parts of the bioreactor volume that are stagnant and not fully participating in the overall fermentation process. When axial dispersion is near zero and radial dispersion is infinite, the so-called plug flow bioreactor occurs.

35   Thorough mixing of fermentation broths will encourage good mass transfer rates and subsequent high biological productivity. In practice, in most industrial fermentations high productivity must be paralleled by low operating costs to maximize financial returns. The conventional CSTR design requires a high power input and in consequence many new bioreactor designs have attempted to lower the specific power uptake and to
40   optimize power input and productivity. Some of these new bioreactors provide high inter-

facial areas at low power inputs (bubble column,etc.)and can create a strong control of flow pattern independent of gas hold up by an inserted draft tube (loop reactors).

Energy transfer.   In bioreactor processes energy will be generated within the system from four main sources.

(1) *Mechanical agitation energy*:electrical power input or work to stirring mecha-   **5**
    nisms will be converted into kinetic energy of fluid motion which will be dissi-
    pated in various ways to appear eventually as heat.

(2) *Gassing and aeration energy*:some energy will be dissipated at the sparger holes
    and in creating turbulent eddies although most of this type of energy will rep-
    resent the work done by the gas as it expands when moving through the liquid   **10**
    static head[7].

(3) *Metabolic energy*:the organisms within the bioreactor oxidize organic molecules
    and some of the energy will be dissipated as heat.

(4) *Enthalpies*:heat can be generated in the bioreactor if the input streams are at a
    higher temperature than the bioreactor contents.   **15**

Build-up of heat in a bioreactor can result in the temperature of the fermentation broth exceeding the optimum temperature for productivity. Consequently heat may have to be removed from a bioreactor. Heat can be removed across solid boundaries to the surrounding air or to cooling water in internal coils, external jackets or external heat exchangers. Examples of cooling systems for bioreactors are shown in Fig. 4. 6. When   **20**
bioreactors are run at temperatures above ambient then, even allowing for the generation

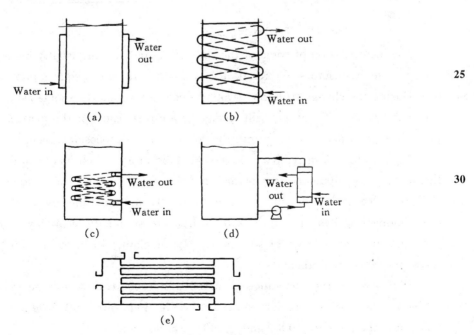

25

30

Fig. 4. 6   Methods of heat removal. (a) Jacketed vessel;(b) External half coils   **35**
(exaggerated dimensions);(c) Internal coil;(d) External heat exchanger;
(e) Shell and tube heat exchanger(schematic)

of heat by the above mechanisms, a source of heat may be required to maintain an optimum temperature.

4. 8 Scale-up

Most biotechnological processes will have been developed at laboratory scale and commercial success will largely depend on the ability to scale-up the process first to pilot plant level and then to commercial scale. The achievement of successful process scale-up must fit within a variety of physical and economic constraints. To date it has not been possible to establish a uniform design procedure or a simple method for process scale-up. For most products of commercial interest the producer organism (microbe, animal cell etc.) will optimize production under limitation of a nutrient or due to unfavourable environmental conditions. Microbial culture systems are usually heterogeneous and process problems will occur primarily from the transfer of nutrients and to a lesser extent from the transfer of products. (Fig. 4. 7).

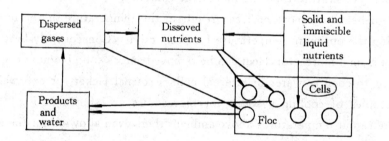

Fig. 4. 7 The heterogeneous nature of microbial culture systems

The identification of some of the controlling factors can usually be made with laboratory scale bioreactors (5 to 10 L) while others may require pilot scale bioreactors. During the change from one scale of operation to another some aspects will remain constant (Table 4. 8); others will change as a direct result of the increased scale (Table 4. 8) while yet others can be within the control of the process engineer.

A pilot plant is in reality a large-scale laboratory which has been designed to give flexibility for equipment accommodation (bioreactors, pumps, heat exchangers, storage facilities, electrical and piping services, etc.), and adaptability for process operation. Engineering design criteria will incorporate simplicity, economy of operation and containment of air and water wastes. Each pilot plant will have its own particular features and design requirements.

Pilot plant bioreactors range from 100 L to 10000 L total volume and the larger pilot bioreactors can on occasion be used as production units. Full scale industrial bioreactors can range between 40000 and 400000 L in volume.

When moving from the laboratory to the industrial scale major problems arise with heat removal, oxygen transfer and availability and insufficient diffusion of the components in the medium , for example nutrients , toxic metabolites and acids or bases . The management of scale-up problems requires high capital investment in mixing and aeration, in monitoring and control devices, and in stringent maintenance of sterility.

Table 4.8   Factors associated with scale-up

Items which remain constant	Items which change	Items which are in control of operator	
(a) Basic design of the bioreactor and pipework arrangements	Bioreactor dimensions will increase	Components in the medium might be changed in concentration and also obtained in cruder, commercial grades	**5** **10**
(b) Number of personnel required to operate the bioreactor	Mass of material and of equipment will increase	Overall pressure on the fermenter is often increased above atmospheric pressure	
(c) Species and strain of microorganism	Quantity of material to be handled before and after the culture process will increase	Energy input per unit mass will, if possible, be reduced	**15**
(d) Medium components and special nutrient limitations	Number of vessels to process a given quantity of materials will decrease	Impeller speeds will be reduced accompanied by increased fluid flow and velocities but perhaps by decreased turbulence	**20**
(e) Sterilizing and operating temperatures	Cost of infections and other failures in the process operation will increase	Circulation times and mixing times will be adjusted to maintain adequate blending of the additions to the culture	**25**
(f) Rheological properties of the culture	Overall sterilizing cycle will change due to increased heating and cooling times		**30**
(g) Bubble sizes in range 0.005 to 0.2 mm diameter	Area-to-volume ratio will decrease and wall effects will virtually disappear		
(h)	Surface aeration will decrease substantially		**35**

4.9   Solid substrate fermentation

Solid substrate fermentations are concerned with the growth of microorganisms on solid materials in the absence or near absence of free water (Table 4.9). The upper level of solid substrate fermentation (i.e. before free water becomes apparent) is a function of absorbancy and thus moisture content which will, in turn, be dependent upon type of substrate. Biological activity ceases when the moisture content of a substrate is about 12% and as this value is approached microbiological activity becomes increasingly retarded. Solid substrate fermentations are not concerned with the fermentation of slurries (i.e. liquids with high levels of insoluble solids) or with the fermentation of solid substrates in a liquid medium. The most common substrates used in solid substrate fermen-

Table 4. 9   Some examples of solid-substrate fermentations

Example	Substrate	Microorganism(s)involved
Mushroom production European and Oriental)	Straw,manure	*Agaricus bisporus* *Lentinus edodes* *Volvariella volvaceae*
Oriental fermentations	Wheat and soybeans	*Aspergillus oryzae*
Soy sauce	Soybeans	*Rhizopus* sp.
Tempeh	Peanut press cake	*Neurospora sitophila*
Ontjom		
Cheeses	Milk curd	*Penicillim roquefortii*
Leaching of metals	Low grade ores	*Thiobacillus* sp.
Organic acids	Cane sugar,molasses	*Aspergillus niger*
Enzymes	Wheat bran,etc	*Aspergillus niger*
Composting	Mixed organic material	Fungi,bacteria,actinomycetes
Sewage treatment	Components of sewage	Bacteria,fungi and protozoa

tations are cereal grains, legume seeds, wheat bran, lignocellulosic materials such as wood and straw, and a variety of other plant and animal matter. The compounds are invariably polymeric molecules, insoluble or sparingly soluble in water, but are cheap, easily obtainable and represent a concentrated source of nutrients.

Solid substrate fermentations have great antiquity, having been practised in the Orient for hundreds of years. Many oriental food fermentations such as soy sauce, miso, tempeh, etc. , have an essential solid substrate phase, while other solid substrate processes have been used to produce enzymes and chemicals such as citric acid. In the western hemisphere solid substrate fermentations have centred around composting of plant and animal wastes, ensiling, mushroom cultivation, and cheese manufacturing. Solid substrate fermentations of lignocellulose could well be a major industry of the future, producing biomass, ethanol, methane and many other commercially valuable products[⑧]. Most microbial-based biotechnological products could be produced by solid substrate fermentations. The determining factor for such practice will depend on the relative economics when compared with liquid fermentation processes.

The types of microorganisms that grow well under conditions of solid substrate fermentations are determined in large part by the water activity factor(a_w). The a_w of the substrate quantitatively expresses the water requirement for microbial activity.

$$\ln a_\mathrm{w} = \frac{-\nu m \phi^{④}}{55.5}$$

where ν=the number of ions formed, m=the molar concentration of solute, ϕ=the molar osmotic coefficient, and 55. 5=the molar concentration of an aqueous solution of pure water.

Pure water has an a_w=1. 00 and a_w will decrease with the addition of solutes. Bacteria are mainly found at the higher a_w values while certain filamentous fungi and a few yeasts can grow at values between 0. 6～0. 7. Organisms that can tolerate and propagate at low a_w levels are in general the main organisms that occur in solid substrate fermentations.

Microbial types. Solid substrate fermentations can occur in many different forms depending on whether the microorganisms utilized are indigenous, pure cultures or mixed cultures.

Fermentations that use indigenous microflora are primarily *ensiling* and *composting*. Ensiling is an anaerobic process involving agricultural vegetation and is carried out at $25\sim30°C$ for $1\sim2$ weeks. *Lactobacillus bulgaricus* becomes the dominant organism, producing lactic acid and subsequently inhibiting potential putrefactive bacteria, and because of the absence of oxygen aerobic mould fungi cannot grow. Moisture level is critical at $50\%\sim65\%$, thus ensuring that the osmotolerant lactobacilli are active and dominant. In contrast, composting involves a succession of microorganisms from mesophilic bacteria, yeasts and mould fungi, through to thermophilic actinomycetes and fungi. Heat generation by biological activity is a serious problem and the compost must be turned mechanically to avoid sterilization. Composting for mushroom production is one of the most successful means of creatively using lignocellulosic materials.

Solid substrate fermentations using pure fungal cultures are best illustrated with the ancient Koji process for the fermentation of grains and soya beans with the fungus *Aspergillus oryzae*. The cooked substrate is inoculated with a pure culture of *A. oryzae* and grown in shallow layers in trays or in special rotating bioreactors to produce amylases and proteases to break down polymeric materials in the substrate. The Koji process is the basis for other types of fermentations including commercial enzyme production, organic acids and ethanol. The Koji process is also finding novel uses for biomass production from starchy materials (Raimbault/Alazard process) and from cellulosic materials (Waterloo process).

Certain solid substrate fermentations deliberately use known mixed culture inoculations to achieve optimum end product formation. Thus straw can be more efficiently converted to fungal biomass using mixed cultures of *Chaetomium cellulolyticum* and *Candida lipolytica* than by using either fungus alone. Such fermentations are considered to have considerable potential for low technology conversion of lignocellulosic materials.

A feature characteristic of many solid substrate fermentations is the need to pretreat the substrate raw materials to enhance the availability of the nutrients, or to reduce the particle size to optimize the physical parameters of the fermentation. Polymeric molecules may need to be partially hydrolysed to facilitate organism growth while suitable particle size can be achieved by numerous forms of physical treatment, for example ball milling. Cost aspects of pretreatment must be balanced with product value.

The design of solid substrate fermentation processes will be further controlled by the need to establish good mass and heat transfer characteristics. Inter-particle mass transfer and intra-particle diffusion are the two main mass transfer steps limiting solid substrate fermentations.

Inter-particle mass transfer. In a solid substrate fermentation, particle size determines the amount of space within the substrate mass that can be occupied by air (the void space). Most fermentations involve aerobic microorganisms and transport of oxygen into the void space is a critical parameter controlling successful development of growth and product formation. Oxygen transfer into the void space is closely related to moisture level since high free moisture level effected by forcing air out will ensure low void space. In practice, satisfactory inter-particle transfer of oxygen can be achieved by careful mixing and aeration. Oxygen levels can be monitored within the substrate mass and when necessary intermittent mixing and aeration can be practised. It is also essential to avoid CO_2 build-up in the void spaces.

Intra-particle mass transfer. Intra-particle mass transfer is concerned with the transfer of nutrients and enzymes within the fermentation substrates. In solid substrate fermentations using filamentous fungi, hyphae will grow over the particle surface as well as penetrating into the substrate mass. The aerobic hyphae will require the diffusion of oxygen to support their continued growth. The kinetics of oxygen diffusion in these complex solid substrate matrices is far from being understood.

Intra-particle mass transfer is also concerned with the role of enzymes in hydrolysing the water-insoluble polymers into soluble substrates to be utilized by growing fungi. These hydrolytic enzymes therefore have a major role in the overall degradation or utilization of the substrates. Substrates with open, porous structures are more easily degraded than those with less porous surfaces. The enzymic hydrolysis of cellulosic materials has been extensively studied with solid substrate systems and has been shown to be dependent on the action of an enzyme complex, cellulase, which involves three types of enzymic reactions:

(1) endo-β-1,4-glucanase[①] which hydrolyses cellulose randomly producing glucose and cellobiose as end products;

(2) exo-β-1,4-glucanase which attacks the non-reducing end of a cellulose polymer chain and produces cellobiose;

(3) cellobiase or β-glucosidase which acts mainly on the cellobiose to form glucose.

Heat transfer. Because of the high substrate concentrations per unit volume, microbial heat generation is much greater per unit volume than for liquid fermentations. Also, the low moisture content of these fermentations creates difficult conditions for heat transfer, so the control of temperature is more difficult than for liquid fermentations. In particular, heat removal from large-scale operations is a major problem. Heat removal can be facilitated by increasing the aeration rate or the frequency of aeration for systems that are not continuously aerated. A corollary to this is that when a fermentation temperature is too low then reduced aeration can generally result in increasing the operating temperature without the need to add an external source of heat. In practice, metabolic heat generation can be regulated by several means including adjusting the temperature and relative humidity of the air, the aeration rate and the agitation speed.

Bioreactors. Solid substrate fermentations can be classified into fermentations wit-

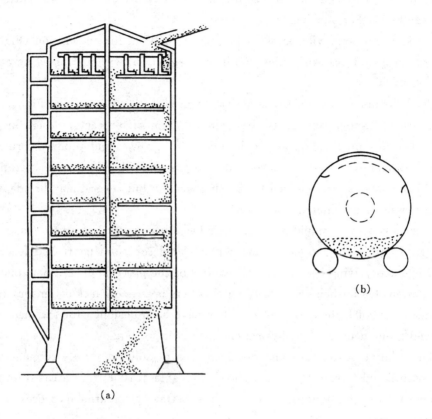

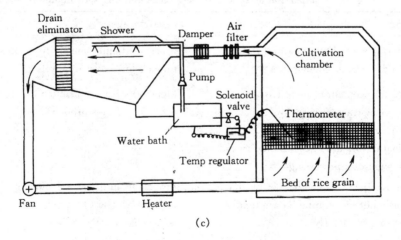

Fig. 4. 8   Bioreactor systems for solid substrate fermentations
(a) Earp-Thomas tower bioreactor；(b) Rotating drum bioreactor；(c) Japanese Koji bioreactor

132

hout agitation, fermentations with occasional agitation and fermentations with continuous agitation. Fermentations without aeration include ensiling and a limited range of composting processes and will not be further considered. The latter two types of fermentation can be further subdivided into:

5   (1) fermentations with occasional agitation, without forced aeration (Fig. 4. 8);

     (2) fermentations with slow continuous agitation, without forced aeration (Fig. 4. 8);

     (3) fermentations with occasional agitation with forced aeration (Fig. 4. 8).

Group (3) above represents the main direction of bioreactor design in Japan and
10 current systems provide a good environment for growth and product formation, controlled mechanical agitation, reasonable process control and sterile operation conditions. Most systems are designed for batch operation but several may be adapted for semi-continuous or continuous operation.

Process control in liquid fermentations has allowed increased monitoring of biologi-
15 cal activity within the bioreactor and sophisticated computer-controlled feedback loops can be operated, giving better dynamic control of the process. In contrast solid substrate fermentations lag far behind in this respect. There is an acute lack of sensors: most existing sensors are of little value because they have been designed for the measurement of dissolved components or for physical characteristics of liquids.

20 The relative advantages and disadvantages of solid substrate fermentations compared with liquid fermentations are shown in Table 4. 10. Future areas of improvement in solid substrate fermentations will be in substrate pretreatment, process control and fermenter design.

Table 4. 10 Comparison of solid substrate fermentations with liquid fermentations

Advantages	Disadvantages
Simple media with cheaper natural rather than costly synthetic components	Processes limited mainly to moulds that tolerate low moisture levels
Low moisture content of materials gives economy of bioreactor space, low liquid effluent treatment, less microbial contamination, often no need to sterilize, easier downstream processing	Metabolite heat production in large-scale operation creates problems
Aeration requirements can be met by simple gas diffusion or by aerating intermittently rather than continuously	Process monitoring, e. g. moisture levels, biomass, O_2 and CO_2 levels is difficult to achieve accurately
Yields of products can be as high	Bioreactor design not well developed
Low energy expenditure compared with stirred tank bioreactors	Product limitations
	Slower growth rates of microorganisms

4.10 Summary

Growth is the increase of cell material expressed in terms of mass or cell number. The doubling time of an organism population is the time required for the doubling in biomass while generation time relates to the period necessary for the doubling of cell numbers. Mathematical equations have been developed describing the essential features of **5** microbial growth in bioreactors. In batch cultivation, there is a continuously changing nutrient environment which is reflected in the physiological state of the culture. In contrast, in continuous culture, with controlled addition and removal of medium, a steady state of population characteristics can be achieved.

In fermentation technology, large numbers of cells are grown under defined, con- **10** trolled conditions for biomass or product formation. In general the processes are carried out in a containment system or bioreactor, the main function of which is to minimize the cost of producing a product or service. Processes can be considered as conversion cost-intensive or recovery cost-intensive. Bioreactors can operate on a batch, fed-batch or continuous basis. The biocatalysts (microorganisms, plant or animal cells or enzymes) can **15** function in a free form or be immobilized. Optimization of a bioreactor process will involve minimizing raw materials and energy use and maximizing product formation.

Bioreactor design will depend on the nature of the process. The continuous stirred tank system (CSTR) is the most widely used bioreactor and can be operated for aerobic processes as well as for anaerobic processes. Mixing in a CSTR bioreactor is achieved by **20** a mechanically operated central shaft equipped with blades or impellers. In contrast, tower bioreactors do not have mechanical agitation and mixing of contents is achieved by the rising air bubbles.

Medium is formulated to meet the nutritional demands of the producer organisms, the objectives of the process and the scale of the operation. Cost of medium is a critical **25** factor in determining the economics of a fermentation process, and for most industrial processes relatively complex mixtures of cheap natural products are used.

Instrumentation of bioreactors involves measuring specific parameters, recording them and then using this information to improve and optimize the process. Measurements can be made on-line or off-line. There is a lack of efficient on-line **30** sensors for bioreactor processes. Off-line determinations are slow and unsuitable for computer systems. There is an increasing involvement of computer control of fermentation processes.

Mass and energy transfer processes are a major part of all fermentation processes. Mixing mechanisms aim to optimize both axial and radial dispersion to ensure com- **35** plete dispersion of medium components throughout the bioreactor, thus encouraging good mass transfer rates and high biological productivity.

Solid substrate fermentations are concerned with the growth or microorganisms on solid materials in the absence or near absence of free water. These fermentations can use indigenous microorganisms, pure single cultures and pure mixed cultures. Inter-particle mass transfer and intra-particle diffusion are the two main conditions limiting solid substrate fermentations.

Words and Expressions

page	line		
104	3	beverage ['bevəridʒ] n. 饮料	
	4	sauerkraut ['sauəkraut] n. 泡菜	chopped cabbage that is salted and fermented in its own juice
		pickle ['pikl] n. 腌菜[常用复数]	vegetables in brine, vinegar or spicy solution to be preserved

13 xanthan ['zænθən] n. 黄原胶 一种胞外多糖,相对分子质量 $10^6 \sim 10^7$,由植物病原菌野油菜黄单孢菌产生

16 oxytetracycline [ˌɔksiˌtetrə'saiklain] n. 土霉素

cephalosporin [ˌsefələu'spɔːrin] n. 头孢菌素

giberellin [gibə'relin] n. 赤霉素

alkaloid ['ælkələid] n. 生物碱

actinomycin [ˌæktinəu'maisin] n. 放线菌素

17 amylase [ˌæmi'leis] n. 淀粉酶

protease ['prəutieis] n. 蛋白酶

18 pectinase ['pektineis] n. 果胶酶

invertase [in'vəːteis] n. 转化酶

asparaginase [ˌæspə'rædʒineis] n. 天冬酰胺酶

uric oxidase [ˌjuəri'kɔksaideis] n. 尿酸氧化酶

22 perfume ['pəːfjuːm] n. 香水

flavour ['fleivə] n. 调味品

105 5 itaconic acid [ˌitə'kɔnik] n. 衣康酸

7 perfumery [pə'fjuːməri] n. 香料(总称)

9 beneficiation ['beniˌfiʃi'eiʃən] n. 选矿,富集

22 miso ['misəu] n. 日本豆面酱

30 ensilage ['ensilidʒ] n. 饲料的青贮

32 rhizobium [rai'zəubiəm] n. 根瘤菌 一种真菌,其菌丝和某些植物的根共生

33 mycorrhizal [ˌmaikəu'raizəl] a. 菌根的

34 embryo ['embriəu] n. 胚

42 containment [kən'teinmənt] n. 容纳

106 5 rate-limiting step 速度控制步骤

107 7 trickle ['trikl] vi. 滴流 drip gently but steadily to flow or fall in drops. or in a thin, intermittent stream

20 fed-batch culture n. 半连续培养 在培养中底物分批加入的操作方式

page	line			
122	30	debug	[diːˈbʌɡ]	vt. 排除故障，调试
123	4	furtherance	[ˈfəːðərəns]	n. 促进　the act of furthering
	32	sparingly	[ˈspɛəriŋli]	a. 少量地，贫乏地　scantily,meagerly
124	21	turbulent	[ˈtəːbjulənt]	a. 湍流的
125	2	draft tube	[drɑːft]	n. 通流管
	6	dissipate	[ˈdisipeit]	vt. 消散　scatter,disperse,dispel
	11	static head		n. 静压头
	37	shell and tube heat exchanger		列管式(管壳式)换热器
	9	ontjom		n. 发酵花生饼
	10	milk curd	[kəːd]	n. 凝乳
128	16	wheat bran	[bræn]	n. 麦麸
		lignocellulosic	[ˈlignəuˌseljuˈlɔsik]	a. 木素纤维素的
	20	antiquity	[ænˈtikwiti]	n. 古代

129　2　indigenous　[inˈdidʒinəs]　a. 在当地生长的　occuring or living naturally in an area.

	4	microflora	[maikrəˈflɔːrə]	n. 微生物区系　生长于一定位置与环境中的微生物的总称
	5	vegetation	[ˌvedʒiˈteiʃən]	n. 植物(总称)
	7	putrefactive	[ˌpjuːtriˈfæktiv]	a. 引起腐烂的　corrupt
	10	mesophilic bacteria	[ˌmesəˈfilik]	n. 嗜温细菌
130	11	hyphae	[haifə]	n. 菌丝[复]，单数为 hypha　在真菌生长期形成的线状菌体
	21	cellulase	[ˈseljuleis]	n. 纤维素酶
	23	glucanase	[ˈgluːkəneis]	n. 葡聚糖酶
	24	cellobiose	[ˌseləuˈbaiəus]	n. 纤维二糖
	27	glucosidase	[ˌgluːˈkəusideis]	n. 葡糖苷酶
		cellobiase		n. 纤维二糖酶
131	1	drain eliminator		n. 液滴消除器
	2	damper	[ˈdæmpə]	n. (调节)风门
	6	solenoid valve	[ˈsəulinɔid]	n. 电磁阀

Notes

① 注意 except 与 except for 在意义上的差别。except 指的是从整体中除去某部分，而 except for 则表示对句子的主要部分所说明基本情况的补充和修正，通常是与主要部分相反的细节。例如：We all succeeded except him. 除了他，我们都成功了。
His composition is good except for some spelling mistakes. 他的作文很好，只有几处拼法错误。

② Continuous methods of cultivation will permit organisms to grow under steady state conditions. 本句用的是一般将来时，实际上是表示一种规律性、倾向性或习惯性的动作（参见 Ch.1，Note②），这在科技文章中很常见，在本书的其他地方也常出现，请读者留心。参

见，张道真：实用英语语法（第二次修订本），1979，商务印书馆，p. 126。

③ 当举例时，有时可以用 'as' 或 'like'，但最常用、最好的表示方法是用 'such as'。本章中其他例子可见 108/10，111/37 和 121/6。

④ well 置于句中助动词与动词之间时，可表示"有理由地、合理地、可能地、适当地"（with good reason, justice or likelihood; advisably）。这种用法在本书中也很常见，请读者注意。参见：牛津现代高级英汉双解辞典。

⑤ 句中有 not only…but also 连接两个并列成分，所强调的重点在后面的成分。not only…but…as well 表达的意义相同，都表示"不但…，而且…"，例如：

I not only heard it，but (also) saw it. 我不但听到，而且看见它。

另外 as well as 也是连接两个并列成分，但所强调的重点在前面的成分。所以翻译时，应先译 as well as 之后的词，然后再译它之前的词。如：

The child is lively as well as healthy. 这孩子既健康又活泼。

⑥ Central to all bioreactor processes…and/or product formation. 本句为倒装句。为强调表语而放在句首，便造成句子倒装。本句可译为：一切生物反应器过程的中心是供给适量的养分以满足微生物代谢的需要，达到最适生长和产物形成。

⑦ …as it expands when moving through the liquid static head. 分词短语前加上 when（或while），与不加 when 时相比较，这是强调分词短语的动作与谓语动词所表示的动作同时发生，但应注意主语必须相同。这个从句可译为：当气体向上运动，所受液体静压头减小而膨胀。

⑧ producing…起首的分词短语，作为定语，修饰前面的 industry，在意义上作为分词短语的主语。这种分词短语可以分为限制性（即不能省去的）和非限制性（即可以省去，省去后主要意义不受影响）两种。对于前者，不能用逗号和主句隔开；对于后者，应用逗号隔开。在本句中，为非限制性，故用逗号。以 which 引导的定语从句也是这样。

⑨ $\ln a_w = \dfrac{-\nu m\phi}{55.5}$ 此式是利用溶液的依数性质求取水的活度的公式，其推导可参阅

P. W. Atkins：Physical Chemistry，2nd ed. 1982，p. 343。式中 $55.5 = \dfrac{1000}{18}$ 为 1000g 水的摩尔数，即纯水的摩尔浓度

⑩ glucanase 源于 glucan，后者译为葡聚糖，而 dextran 亦译为葡聚糖，要注意两者之区别。两者都以葡萄糖为构成单元，dextran 系以 α-糖苷键相连，而 glucan 以 β-糖苷键相连，包括纤维素、淀粉、糖原、淡黄青霉多糖等。

Comprehension

1. What is the difference in meaning between the terms primary and secondary metabolites? (p. 104)

2. What, according to the author, do the research activities about bioreactor aim at? (p. 106)

3. Explain the reason why conversion-cost-intensive and recovery-cost-intensive processes do have different criteria in efficiency evaluation? (p. 106)

4. What are the three kinds of cultivation on the basis of the mode of operation? (p. 106)

5. Under what conditions does the doubling time equal generation time and why? (p. 108)

6. Write down the Monod equation and Michaelis—Menten equation for enzyme kinet-

ics. Could you give the reason for their formal similarity? (p. 108)

7. What is meant by the statement that "Thus exponential growth can occur at specific growth rates having any value between zero and μ_{max} if the substrate concentration can be held constant at the appropriate value"? (lines 33~35, page 108)

8. Examine the Fig. 4. 1 (a) and (b). Explain the various phases of a batch culture and find the phases missing in (b).

9. The balance equation for substrate in a continuous culture system is

$$\frac{ds}{dt} = DS_R - DS - \frac{\mu x}{Y}$$

State the meaning of each term thereof. (p. 111)

10. What is the feature characteristic of a fed-batch culture system? In which case should we consider to make use of this system? (p. 107, 112, 119)

11. Why have the continuous culture systems not been widely used in industry? (p. 113)

12. Enumerate the various functions of mixing in a fermentation system. (p. 116)

13. Explain the reason why in waste water treatment the anaerobic bioreactor is gaining predominance over aerobic bioreactor. (p. 117)

14. What are the main factors in choosing a medium for fermentation? (p. 118~119)

15. Continuous sterilization method are now gaining wider acceptability. Draw a scheme illustrating the process in accordance with that described on page 119.

16. Usually for process control each parameter is regulated by a control loop, consisting a sensor, controller and an activator. Describe their functions and the interrelationship between them through a schematic diagram, taking temperature control as an example. (p. 120~121)

17. State some new directions for developing on-line measuring techniques. (p. 121~122)

18. Oxygen mass transfer is of great importance in aerobic fermentations. Which, judging from Fig. 4. 5, are the main resistance steps in oxygen transfer and what measures should be taken to reduce the transfer resistance? (p. 123~124)

19. What do you understand by the word "dissipation", which frequently occurs in section Energy transfter (p. 125)?

20. What are the main problems associated with bioreactor scale up and what efforts should be done to overcome them? (p. 126)

21. How does the author define the term "solid substrate fermentation"? (p. 127)

22. What promising method has the author mentioned to utilize straw, abundant in our country? (p. 129)

23. What are the enzymes involved in a cellulase and how do they act on the cellulose? (p. 130)

24. Give a brief introduction to koji process. (p. 129; p. 131~132)

Vocabulary

Give another word or phrase to replace these words or phrases as they are used in the text:

version (104/6); paralleling (104/7); assure (104/25); in essence (104/31); defined (104/

33); provided (108/16); due (109/18); sequential (112/2); impair (112/35); implication (112/28); uncoupled (117/17); throughout (119/8); handling (121/25); can be seen as (124/15); on occasion(126/35); independent(125/2); a succession of(129/10); subdivide (132/4); critical(133/25).

Word usage

1. Write sentences to bring out the difference between the following pairs of words:
   basis (106/26), base; alternative (119/28), alternating; instrumentation (120/2), instrument; eventually(125/7), finally; yet(126/27), still.
2. Make sentences with the following phrases:
   method of choice(119/30); as yet(122/11); by way of(124/1);
   conversely(124/5); in consequence(124/38); in this respect(132/17).

Grammar

1. Supply a, an, and the where necessary in the spaces below. Do not refer to the text until you have finished the exercise:
   ··· optimization of ··· bioreactor process involves minimizing ··· use of ··· raw materials (e. g. nutrients, precursors, acid/base, air) and ···energy (···cost of···energy since 1978 has risen at···annual rate of 16%), and maximizing···product purity and quality in···broth before ··· recovery. ··· process optimization is achieved by··· manipulation of both··· physical and chemical parameters associated with the process. ···range of···process variables that are important to···process development are listed in Table 4.4 and are discussed later.
2. Rewrite the following sentence to avoid the dangling participle:
   Knowing the values of the three growth constants μ_{max}, K_S and Y, equations(1)and (2) can give a complete quantitative description of the growth cycle of a batch culture. (109/7~8)

Patterns

1. how, when, where, what, which, who, whether etc. + inf. This common construction is used as an abbreviated form for noun clause object.
   Examples:
   When you have completed the first part of the experiment you will be told what to do next. (the full noun clause object is: what you have to do next).
   In order to write a good report the writer must know where to begin. (the full noun clause object is: where he should begin).
   Exercises
   Rewrite the following abbreviated construction as a full clause:
   Studies have considered better aseptic design and operation···, and how to obtain a better understanding of the rate-limiting steps of a system. (106/3~5)
2. The final present participle phrase used in place of 'and'. It is a simple addition to the preceding statement. The subject of the second part is normally different from the subject of the first part, and must be stated.
   Example
   Growth of most organisms is sensitive to pH changes, each group of organisms having

specific optimum pH values. (121/19~20)

Exercises

Join these statements by using the final present participle clause as above:

1. In the exponential phase organism growth is unlimited with nutrients in excess and inhibitors absent. The specific growth rate will achieve its maximum, i. e. , $\mu = \mu_{max}$. (109/23~25)

2. Most microbial-based biotechnological products could be produced by solid substrate fermentations. The determining factor for such practice will depend on the relative economics when compared with liquid fermentation processes. (128/27~30)

Sentence analysis and translation

First analyse the following sentences as in ch. 1, Note① and then translate into Chinese:

1. The last paragraph on page 110(110/21~111/3)

2. The last paragraph on page 120(120/33~121/8)

3. The first paragraph on page 116(116/1~12)

4. The section Heat transfer(130/29~39)

Writing

1. 如发酵罐等主要设备进行设计时,工作量很大。

(such…as…,参见 Note③)

2. 不管遇到什么困难,他决心达到目的,决不动摇。

(no matter what…,参见 104/31~32)

3. 如何将酶固定在电化学传感器的表面上是制造酶电极的关键。(按 pattern 1)

4. 在生物工程中应用的微生物大多是需氧微生物,因而当设计生物反应器时,氧的传递是一个重要的应该考虑的问题。(按 pattern 2)

5. 在发酵中培养方式可以分为:分批培养、连续培养和半连续培养三种。(分类的表示法,参见 130/40)

Chapter 5   Enzyme and Immobilized Cell Technology

Microorganisms, in particular yeasts, have been used for several thousand years for the production of beers, wines and other fermented products. However, it was not until 1878[①] that the actual components of the yeast cells responsible for the fermentation were named as enzymes (derived from the Greek meaning *in yeast*). Less than two decades
5   later the inanimate nature of enzymes was clearly demonstrated with cell free extracts of yeast which were able to catalyse the conversion of glucose to ethanol. The final demonstration that enzymes were proteins came only in 1926 with the purification and crystallization of urease.

In the following years, with the evolution of the new scientific discipline of biochem-
10 istry, enzymes were demonstrated as being in all living organisms and utilized by living cells to catalyse specific chemical reactions. Subsequently, enzymes have been shown to be highly specific in their action, functioning at high conversion rates, and to operate under mild physiological conditions of low pressure and temperature and in aqueous solutions. Although the normal locus of enzyme action is in the interior of the living cell
15 there are numerous examples of cells being able to excrete enzymes (extracellular enzymes) into the environment to break down large organic molecules (proteins, fats, starches) which otherwise could not enter the cell. For some microorganisms extracellular enzyme production is of major importance for normal growth and it was from this source that enzymes were first commercially exploited.

20 ## 5.1   The commercial role of isolated enzymes

All products of commercial fermentation processes are the end result of enzyme activities within the producer organisms. Could isolated enzymes substitute for the producer organisms in specific fermentations? This question has often been asked but satisfactory results have seldom been realized in practice.
25   The use of whole organisms undoubtedly creates certain drawbacks in fermentation processes:
    (a) optimum conditions may differ for growth and product formation;
    (b) a high proportion of the substrates may be converted to biomass;
    (c) wasteful side reactions may occur;
30   (d) the conversion rate to the desired product may be slow;
    (e) separation of the desired product from the fermentation may be difficult.
    Thus by the use of isolated and purified enzymes most, if not all, of these limitations could be reduced or overcome. The most obvious advantages would be easier handling, greater predictability of activity and improved specificity in catalytic function. However,

for most fermentations the traditional use of whole organisms is likely to continue well into the future.

Although over 2000 enzymes have been isolated from microorganisms, plants and animals, fewer than 20 are used on a scale that can be considered significant to either the commercial producers or the user industry or service. At present the major output of commercial producers is concerned with relatively simple enzymes for use in crude form primarily in the food and related industries and with detergent manufacture (Fig. 5.1). The majority of the enzymes are hydrolases such as amylases, cellulases, pectinases, proteases, etc., and function mainly as additives or process aids in the baking, dairy, brewing and fruit juice industries. In contrast to the crude bulk enzymes there is a rapidly expanding market for certain highly purified enzymes such as glucose isomerase and glucose oxidase. These enzymes and many others are finding increasing applications in the pharmaceutical industry, in therapeutic applications and in clinical and chemical analyses.

5.2 Sources of enzymes

Commercially used enzymes are derived from plant and animal tissues and from selected microorganisms. Enzymes that have traditionally been obtained from plants include the proteases (papain , ficin and bromelain), amylases, lipoxygenases and certain specialized

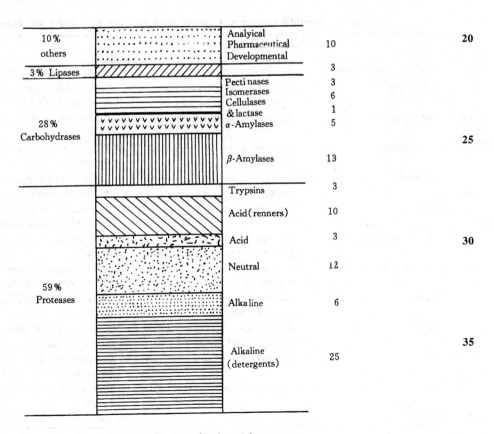

Fig. 5.1 Distribution of industrial enzymes

enzymes. From animal tissues the main enzymes are pancreatic trypsins and lipases and the rennets of cheese making. With both plant and animal sources there can be many supply problems; these include seasonal variations, low concentrations and high processing costs for plant enzymes while for animal enzymes derived from meat industry byproducts there can be limited supply and competition by other users. It is now apparent that many of these traditional sources are inadequate for present world enzyme demand and increasing recourse is being made to seeking out microbial sources for existing and new enzymes.

In practice, microbial enzymes are derived from a relatively limited range of microorganisms and, in particular, microorganisms with a long history of acceptability as food and beverage producers are preferred. It is particularly costly for a manufacturer to obtain approval from legislative authorities for the use of products derived from unproven microorganisms as they must be evaluated for toxicity and safety. For this reason most industrial microbial enzymes are derived from little more than 11 fungi, 8 bacteria and 4 yeasts and in practice producers normally seek new enzymes from within this group (Table 5. 1). Unless cheaper methods of safety testing can be developed there will be a considerable limitation to novel microbial activity for product development.

Screening programmes for enzyme production are extremely complex and in particular the type of cultivation to be used will determine strain selection. It has been shown

Table 5. 1　Microbial sources and uses of some commercially important enzymes

Enzyme	Microbial source	Uses
Alcohol dehydrogenase	*Saccharomyces cerevisiae*	Assay of ethanol
α-Amylase	*Aspergillus oryzae. Baccillus subtilis*	Wide use in food industry, desizing of fabrics
Amyloglucosidase[2]	*Aspergillus niger, A, oryzae*	Production of glucose from corn syrup
Asparaginase	*A. niger. Baccillus coagulans, Penicillium camemberti*	Treatment of acute lymphatic leukaemia
Catalase	*A. niger, P. vitale, Micrococcus lysodeikticus*	Removal of hydrogen used in many processes
Cellulase	*Trichoderma viride*	Preparation of dehydrated vegetables, drain cleaner
Glucose isomerase	*B. coagulans, Streptomyces phaeochromogenes*	Fructose production from corn syrup
Glucose oxidase	*A. niger, P. chrysogenum, P. notatum*	Oxygen removal from fruit juices and other products
Invertase	*Saccharomyces cerevisiae, S. carlsbergensis*	Preparation of soft-centred chocolates
Lipase	*A. niger, Geotrichum candidum, Rhizopus arrhizus*	Improvement of flavour in ice cream, cheese, chocolate
Pectinase	*A. niger, A. oryzae*	Clarification of fruit juices, coffee bean fermentation
Penicillin acylase	*Escherichia coli*	Production of semi-synthetic penicillins
Penicillinase[3]	*Bacillus subtilis*	Treatment of penicillin allergy

Enzyme	Microbial source	Uses	
Proteases (bacterial)	*B. subtilis*	Biological detergents, meat tenderizers	
(fungal)	*A. oryzae*	Softening of bread doughs	**5**
Pyruvate kinase	*Saccharomyces cerevisae*	ATP generation for protein synthesis	
Pullulanase	*Aerobacter aerogenes*	Treatment of wort	
Rennin	*Mucor* sp.	Cheese production	

that certain strains will only produce high enzyme titres in surface or solid culture **10** whereas other strains respond to submerged cultivation techniques. Thus the selection technique must be related to the final commercial production process.

5. 3　Production of enzymes

Having selected the organism, growth must take place under conditions that will maximize enzyme production. Extracellular enzymes have specific advantages over intracellu- **15** lar enzymes since their production does not require costly cell disruption techniques; furthermore, extracellular enzymes are present in a relatively pure form in the culture liquid whereas intracellular enzymes need more complicated methods of separation and purification (see Chapter 6). Extracellular enzymes make up the bulk of industrial microbial enzyme production but intracellular enzymes are finding an increasingly important role **20** as diagnostic enzymes in medicine and industry.

The chosen microorganisms should be stable with respect to enzyme production and ability to sporulate, able to grow well on cheap substrates, not produce toxic substances, and be free of antibiotic activity.

Current industrial enzyme production relies predominantly on deep tank or solid **25** state fermentation methods.

As microbial enzymes are usually low-volume products, economically it has been difficult to justify the development of special fermentation equipment for deep culture production. Generally, the equipment used is similar in design and function to that used for antibiotic production. A typical enzyme producing bioreactor is made from stainless **30** steel, has strong mechanical agitators and air spargers and has a capacity of $10 \sim$ $50m^3$. Such bioreactors have built-in flexibility and can easily be switched to other product formations. Examples of industrial bioreactors used in industry are shown in Table 5. 2. The reader should consult Chapter 4 for further details.

In general, extracellular enzymes are produced in batch processes lasting from 30 to **35** 50 hours. The optimum time to stop the fermentation falls between the point of maximum productivity and the point of maximum enzyme activity. The optimum will be determined by raw material costs, plant capacity and ease of recovery.

Continuous culture techniques can be used for enzyme production on a laboratory scale but there is little evidence that this method is employed by any commercial manu- **40**

Table 5. 2   Examples of industrial bioreactors used for enzyme production

Enzyme	Bioreactor size(m³)	Company
Glucose oxidase	220	J. & E. Sturge
α-Amylase	80	Novo Industri
Glucose isomerase	80	Novo Industri
Asparaginase	75	Novo Industri
Penicillin acylase	30	Beecham Pharmaceuticals
Cholesterol oxidase	3~5	Genzyme Biochemicals

facturer. Batch methods can often be extended and enzyme production improved by the continuous or fed-batch feeding of carbohydrates or proteins.

There are no general kinetic models of enzyme synthesis but it has been possible to study the regulation of certain enzymes. Only a few commercially important enzymes are produced during exponential growth, the majority being synthesized during the post-exponential growth phase. The yield of useful enzyme proteins can be from 1% to 5% of the initial dry substance of the medium while the cell yield in a typical enzyme fermentation can vary from 2% to 10% on a similar basis.

How can enzyme production be regulated in the bioreactor to the advantage of the commercial operator? There are a number of methods that can be used to overcome any one of the established control mechanisms that can limit production of a given enzyme. In principle, there are two main categories: manipulation of the genetic apparatus of the organism and manipulation of the growing environment of the organism. Often the most successful results are achieved by simultaneous application of both approaches.

Genetic manipulation of microorganisms has already been discussed in Chapter 3 and many if not all of the well-accepted procedures have found use in enzyme regulatory studies. Mutant formation is still the most practised industrial approach but recombinant DNA techniques will be increasingly used, particularly for non-food applications.

Process operators can manipulate the growth environment by the selection of suitable medium composition or culture parameters to overcome the inhibition of enzyme biosynthesis caused by regulatory mechanisms. For inducible enzymes, incorporation into the medium of inducer substances can be very effective. The most widely used inducers are non-metabolizable substrate analogues.

Degradative enzymes are usually controlled by induction and catabolite repression while biosynthetic enzymes are mainly controlled by feedback regulation. Feedback regulation can involve feedback (or end-product) inhibition and feedback repression[④].

End-product repression of enzyme biosynthesis may be prevented by any or all of the following approaches:

    (a) limitation of end-product accumulation by adding an inhibitor to the medium;

    (b) ensuring that end-products do not occur in the medium supplied;

    (c) selection of regulatory mutants (constitutive mutants) which are not repressed
        by end-products.

Many industrially important enzymes are subject to catabolite repression (Table 5. 3). In practice catabolite repression can be avoided by:

(a) mutation to resistance to catabolite repression;

(b) avoidance of the use of repressing carbon sources in the medium;

(c) the derepression of enzyme synthesis by growth limitation involving the slow feeding of the repressive substrate or by the use of slowly metabolizable analogues or derivatives of the substrate.

Table 5. 3   Catabolite repression of enzymes

Enzyme	Organism	Depressive carbon source
α-Amylase	*Bacillus stearothermophilus*	Fructose
Cellulase	*Trichoderma reesei*	Glucose,glycerol,starch cellobiose
Protease	*Bacillus megaterium*	Glucose
Amyloglucosidase	*Endomycopsis bispora*	Starch,maltose,glycerol
Invertase	*Neurospora crassa*	Mannose,glucose,fructose,xylose

In the industrial production of many important secondary metabolites product formation generally only occurs in the idiophase, i. e. after the initial period of rapid growth (trophophase). This phenomenon was first reported for penicillin production but is now known to occur with many others. The factor that initiates secondary metabolism is not known but it does coincide with marked changes in specific enzyme composition of the cells. This derepression of enzyme synthesis is shown for several fermentations in Table 5. 4.

Table 5. 4   Enzymes derepressed at end of trophophase in secondary biosynthesis

Enzyme	Secondary metabolite
Amidinotransferase	Streptomycin
Acyltransferase	Penicillin
Phenoxazinone synthetase	Actinomycin
Synthetase 1 and 11	Gramicidin S

Solid substrate cultivation methods have occupied an important role in commercial enzyme production from fungal sources, particularly in Japan. In particular, amylases from *Aspergillus* and proteases from *Aspergillus* and *Mucor* have long been commercially important. Other enzymes produced include pectinases and cellulases. Originally, cultures were grown in trays with manual handling but increasingly mechanical systems for cleaning, filling and emptying trays have been developed. Rotating drum systems have found increasing use (see Chapter 4). The advantages and disadvantages of solid state systems compared with submerged culture procedures have been well analysed. The main positive aspects of solid state cultivation methods for enzyme production are:

(a) enzyme yields per unit volume of incubator are high;

(b) power utilization is low;

(c) minimal control is required;

(d) extraction yields highly concentrated enzyme solutions;

(e) equipment size is usually small;

(f) scale-up is not too difficult.

Continuous operation is possible together with the feeding of substrates during cultivation.

Undoubtedly, submerged culture methods presently dominate the production of commercial enzymes since handling costs and risks of infection are more easily controlled in these processes. The ultimate decision as to whether an enzyme will be produced either by solid substrate or submerged fermentation will basically depend on the relative economics of the two processes. Yet notwithstanding, solid substrate fermentation resembles more closely the natural environmental growth conditions of many microorganisms, in particular, fungi. It may well be that this offers a more acceptable blend of enzyme activity. Future success of solid substrate fermentation methods for enzyme production will depend largely on the outcome of several lines of research, which include intraparticle mass transfer, enzyme degradation of insoluble substrates and improvements in bioreactor design and process control (see also Chapter 4).

5.4 Enzyme legislation

Microbial enzyme products are required to meet strict specifications with regard to toxicity and other safety aspects. The areas of potential concern in the safety evaluation of commercial enzymes are primarily:

(a) allergenic reactions caused by any proteins present in the product including the enzyme protein and any other extraneous material;

(b) catalytic activity of the enzyme;

(c) the occurrence of toxic compounds such as mycotoxins and antibiotics.

Antigenicity varies from one enzyme to another and though it cannot be changed, the exposure of the user to the enzyme can be minimized by the formulation. Most problems occur with enzymes in dust form but can be eliminated by encapsulation in an inert carrier. Liquid enzyme products are more widely used.

Direct effects due to the catalytic activity of the enzyme are now considered to be of low health concern. In general, pure enzymes are non-toxic.

The presence of toxins in enzyme preparations can occur by two major routes. Toxic materials could be present in the fermentation medium and since most enzyme products only undergo relatively crude purification such materials could occur in the final product. Thus to ensure no carry over of toxic materials, food or feed-grade raw materials should be specified and the whole system should be tested regularly for microbial contamination.

The major toxicological concern from fungal enzymes is the presence of mycotoxins in the producer strains. During the last 25 years there has been a growing awareness of the occurrence of toxic metabolites or mycotoxins produced by many fungi and it is now obligatory to test all fungal enzyme samples for certain mycotoxins. Many of these mycotoxins can express carcinogenic, oestrogenic, mutagenic or teratogenic activity in test organisms. The quantitative assessment of risk is extremely difficult since little information exists on the toxic response of low concentrations of mycotoxins on man. However, if mycotoxins are detectable then the product cannot be used.

The microorganisms used for enzyme production can be classified into three groups. Depending on the classification there will be differing levels of toxicity testing required (Table 5.5). Group A microorganisms have traditionally been used in food or in food processing. No toxicological studies are required in these cases. Group B microorganisms are those accepted as harmless contaminants present in food and only short term toxicity tests are necessary. In group C are all microorganisms not listed in A or B. Such microorganisms require more extensive toxicological studies including long-term feeding studies on several species of animals.

Table 5.5 Safety testing of food enzymes based on the Association of Microbial Food Enzyme Producers classification

Group Tests (X=to be performed)	(a) Microorganisms that have traditionally been used in food, or in food processing	(b) Microorganisms that are accepted as harmless contaminants present in food	(c) Microorganisms that are not included in A or B
Pathogenicity	In general no testing required		X
Acute oral toxicity, mouse and rat; subacute oral toxicity, rat four weeks		X X	X X
Three month oral toxicity, rat		X	X
In vitro mutagenicity		X	X
Teratogenicity, rat; *in vivo* mutagenicity, mouse and hamster			(X)* (X)
Toxicity studies on the final food			(X)
Carcinogenicity, rat; fertility and reproduction			(X) (X)

* Only to be performed under exceptional conditions.

Responsibility for the safety of an enzyme product rests with the manufacturer and new products require the approval of the appropriate authorities. Specifications and recommendations have been made for several enzymes by national and international bodies.

In summary, enzyme products must be uniform, reliable and safe and it is the duty of the manufacturer to meet these specifications.

5.5 Immobilized enzymes

The most important drawbacks in the use of isolated enzymes are that they are not sufficiently stable under operational conditions and as water-soluble free molecules, they are difficult to separate from substrate and products and to reuse repeatedly.

In recent years attempts have been made to overcome these disadvantages by the process of enzyme immobilization. Immobilization can usually be considered to be the
5 conversion of enzymes from a water-soluble, mobile state to a water-insoluble immobile state. Immobilization prevents diffusion of the enzyme in the reaction mixtures and facilitates their recovery from the product stream by simple solid/liquid separation techniques. Thus reaction products are free of enzyme and it is possible to re-use the enzyme. Immobilized enzymes can be used advantageously in continuously operated biore-
10 actors.

Over a hundred immobilization techniques have been developed. These can be divided into distinct groups. In practice, immobilization of an enzyme will be achieved by covalent attachment to the surface of a water-insoluble material; by crosslinking with suitable agents to give insoluble particles; by entrapment inside a matrix or gel that is per-
15 meable to the enzyme, substrate and products; by encapsulation; and by adsorption of enzymes on solid supports. A schematic representation of immobilization methods is shown in Fig. 5. 2 and the methodology of immobilization in Table 5. 6.

20

25

30

35

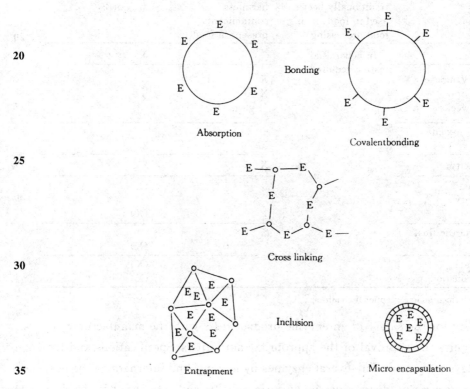

Fig. 5. 2 Immobilization methods

Covalent coupling of enzymes to solid supports Many types of support have been used including porous glass and ceramics (amyloglucosidase), synthetic polymers (trypsin),

Table 5. 6   Immobilization procedures

Covalent binding
  Hydroxyalkyl methacrylate (glutaraldehyde)
  Carboxymethylcellulose (carbodi-imide)

Entrapment
Polyacrylamide	Collagen (gelatin)
Alginate	Polystyrene
Cellulose-triacetate	Urethane
Agar	Nylon (micro-encapsulation)
Carrageenan	
Chitosan	

Adsorption
Anion-exchange resin	Ion-exchange cellulose
Dowex 1	Polyvinylchloride and porous bricks
DEAE-cellulose	
Crosslinked pectate	
Metal oxide	
Bioadsorption:concanavalin A	

Crosslinking
  Glutaraldehyde
  Albumin and glutaraldehyde
  Gelatin and glutaraldehyde

cellulose (asparaginase,amylase),nylon (urease) and alumina (glucose oxidase). Methods derived from peptide and protein chemistry are used to achieve attachment. Formation of covalent bonds has the advantage of forming an attachment that is not reversed by pH,ionic strength or substrate. However,it is possible that the enzyme is rendered inactive in part or whole through the chemical reactions used to create covalent bonding. There are many methods of covalent attachment and the immobilization procedure consists of at least two steps,activation of the support and enzyme attachment *per se*. In practice the groups that are involved in the formation of the chemical bonds are amino, imino,amide,hydroxyl,carboxyl,thiol,methylthiol,quanidyl,imidazole and the phenol group.

Entrapment of enzymes in gels   In principle the methods used are very mild and unlikely to damage enzyme activity. The enzymes can be added to a solution of monomers prior to gel formation. Gel formation will occur either by changing the temperature or by adding a gel-inducing chemical. The enzyme then becomes entrapped in the gel volume. The enzyme is retained in its native state without risk of blocking active sites, groups or enzyme molecules by chemical bonds. However,the main disadvantages of this form of immobilization are continuous loss of enzymes through pores and the retardation of enzyme reaction by diffusional control of the transport of substrates and products, which is of particular relevance with high molecular weight compounds.

  Entrapment materials include silica gel, silicone rubber, starch and polyacrylamides. Polyacrylamides are the most widely used entrapment matrices having been used with asparaginase, glucose isomerase, peroxidase and many others.

Encapsulation of enzymes   This method is a variation of the inclusion method and involves encapsulation within semi-permeable membranes. These membranes are impermeable to enzymes and other macromolecules but permeable to low molecular weight substrates and products. The types of materials used include collodion (catalase, L-asparaginase), cellulose derivatives (lipase), polystyrene (catalase) and, most often, nylon (trypsin, urease). These materials can be used to form thin, spherical semi-permeable membranes which form microcapsules with enzyme inclusion.

Adsorption of enzymes on solid surfaces   The most attractive feature of adsorption methods is their simplicity. The conditions of adsorption involve no reactive species and there are no modifications of the enzyme. The most commonly used adsorbants include many organic and inorganic materials such as alumina (aminoacylase, amylase), cellulose (cellulase), clays (catalase), glass (urease), hydroxylapatite (NAD pyrophosphorylase), carbon and various silicaceous materials (amylase). Ion exchangers readily absorb most proteins and for this reason have been widely employed for enzyme immobilization. The binding of the enzyme is reversible and for this reason adsorbed enzymes may be desorbed in the presence of substrate or increased ionic strength.

Crosslinking with multifunctional agents   If the reaction is carried out in the absence of solid supports, this method results in the formation of a three-dimensional network of enzyme molecules. In practice enzymes are more usually crosslinked after adsorption onto a suitable carrier. Among the most commonly applied crosslinkers are aliphatic diamines, dimethyl adipimidate, dimethyl suberimidate[5], and especially glutaraldehyde. Crosslinking can be both intermolecular (creating water-insoluble aggregates) and intramolecular. Enzymes can become immobilized by copolymerization, i. e. covalent incorporation into polymers, often involving copolymerization with maleic anhydride and ethylene. A widely used method involves initial adsorption on cellophane membrane and crosslinking with glutaraldehyde (amylase, catalase, glucose oxidase). As with entrapment and microencapsulation, these derivatives show little or no activity towards macromolecular substrates.

Commercialized immobilized enzymes   The selection of a suitable immobilization method will depend primarily on how the method affects the catalytic activity of the enzyme. Covalent and crosslinking methods create strong chemical bonds between the enzyme and support. These methods can be relatively laborious and expensive. They may cause significant inactivation of the enzyme and attachment could occur by way of the active centres (Table 5. 7). In contrast, while methods of immobilization by adsorption and gel entrapment are simple and efficient they do not create strong bonds between the enzyme and matrix. Consequently, enzymes often leak from the supports. This problem can mostly be overcome by crosslinking the adsorbed or entrapped enzymes with glutaraldehyde.

Immobilization of many enzymes has been achieved at laboratory level but only in a

Table 5.7 Limitations of immobilized enzyme techniques

Method	Advantages	Disadvantages	
Covalent attachment	Not affected by pH, ionic strength of the medium or substrate concentration	Active site may be modified; costly process	**5**
Covalent crosslinking	Enzyme strongly bound, thus unlikely to be lost	Loss of enzyme activity during preparation; not effective for macromolecular substrates; regeneration of carrier not possible	**10**
Adsorption	Simple with no modification of enzyme; regeneration of carrier possible; cheap technique	Changes in ionic strength may cause desorption; enzyme subject to microbial or proteolytic enzyme attack	**15**
Entrapment	No chemical modification of enzyme	Diffusion effects affect transport of substrate to and product from the active site; preparation difficult and often results in enzyme inactivation; continuous loss of enzyme due to distribution of pore size; not effective for macromolecular substrates; enzyme not subject to microbial or proteolytic action	**20** **25**

few cases has there been successful scale-up to industrial production. Two outstanding commercial successes have been the use of glucose isomerase in the food industry and **30** penicillin acylase in the antibiotic industry.

Glucose isomerase catalyzes the partial conversion of glucose to fructose giving a low cost sweetener which will ultimately change the world pattern of usage of sugar cane and sugar beet, the traditional sources of sucrose sweeteners. At least five companies now supply bulk tonnage quantities of the fructose sweetener making use of differ- **35** ent source organisms (*Streptomyces* spp., *Bacillus coagulans*, *Actinoplanes missouriensis*). In practice these enzymes need high glucose substrate concentrations for optimum (commercial) activity and the feed syrup, derived from a cheap starch source, is supplied to the bioreactor at 40%~50% glucose level. Viscosity problems may arise during continuous pumping operations but these have been overcome by operating at high tempera- **40** ture (60℃) and at high pH value (7.5~8.5). Industrial scale chromatography has been developed to separate fructose and glucose to give enriched fructose syrups containing 55% or higher fructose yields. Thousands of tons of this enzyme are now being used annually to produce millions of tons of fructose syrup. Process data are shown in Table 5.8 Glucose isomerase is used industrially in both the immobilized enzyme and immobilized cell form (Table 5.9).

The second important industrially-used immobilized enzyme is penicillin acylase (derived from *Escherischia coli*) which catalyzes the deacetylation of the side chain of naturally occurring penicillin producing 6-amino-penicillanic acid (6-APA). The 6 APA can be used to synthesize several semisynthetic antibiotics which have important medical applications. In this way the important antibiotic ampicillin was synthesized from phenyl glycine and 6 APA.

$$C_6H_5CHCO_2H + NH_2-CH-CH \quad C(CH_3)_2 \quad \underset{pH7.5}{\overset{pH5}{\rightleftharpoons}}$$

Phenyl glycine   6-aminopenicillanic acid

$$C_6H_5CHCONH-CH-CH \quad C(CH_3)_2 + H_2O$$

α-aminobenzylpenicillin(ampicillin)

At least 3500 tons of 6 APA are produced each year but this requires only about 30 tons of enzyme preparation. The enzyme is used in a granular form in fixed bed column bioreactors. Process data are shown in Table 5.8.

Table 5.8   Typical process data for glucose isomerase and penicillin acylase

	Glucose isomerase	Penicillin acylase
Enzyme form	Rigid granules	Rigid granules or dextran/ Sephadex
Reactor	Column(packed bed)	Column
Feedstock	95% dextrose at 40%~50%(w/w)	Penicillins or cephalosporins at 4%~15% w/w (dependent on enzyme preparation)
Additives	Magnesium sulphate	—
Temperature	58~65℃	35~40℃
Inlet pH	7.5~8.5	7.0~8.0(dependent on enzyme source)
Operating life	1000~2000 hours	2000~4000 hours
Productivity	2000~4000 kg/kg enzyme producing 42% fructose	1000~2000 kg/kg enzyme

Table 5. 9   Immobilized glucose isomerase

Enzyme source	Immobilization method	Company
Streptomyces albus	Temperature fixing inside the cells	Agency of Industrial Science and Technology
*Streptomyces sp.**	Adsorption onto DEAE cellulose	Standard brands
Arthrobacter	Aggregation with a flocculating agent	Reynolds Tobacco Co.
Bacillus coagulans	Crosslinking with glutaraldehyde	Novo Industri A/S
Streptomyces phaeochromogenes	Adsorption on phenol formaldehyde resin	Kyowa Hakko Kogyo
Streptomyces sp	Adsorption on special porous alumina	Corning Glass Works
Streptomyces phaeochromogenes	Adsorption on special ion exchange resin	Misubishi Chemical Industries
Actinoplanes missouriensis	Occlusion in gelatin and crosslinking with glutaraldehyde	Gist-Brocades NV
Streptomyces olivaceus	Crosslinking with glutaraldehyde	Miles Laboratories Inc.
*Streptomyces sp.**	Entrapment in fibres	Snamprogettie SPA

* Enzyme from this source; other entries refer to cells.

5. 6   Properties of immobilized enzymes

Immobilization of an enzyme can result in significant changes in its properties. These alterations can be attributed to (1) chemical and/or conformational changes in the enzyme structure, (2) the heterogeneous nature of catalysis by immobilized enzymes, and (3) the physical and chemical nature of the carrier used.

One of the most challenging problems in biotechnology is to improve the stability of enzymes. When enzymes are used in bioreactor systems the environment is usually much more severe than would have occurred *in vivo*[⑥]. In particular they will be subjected to higher temperatures, inactivating impurities, and absence of the protective balanced environment of the living cell. Even after many years of enzyme chemistry little is known about mechanisms of enzyme inactivation.

Although there are some examples of increased stabilization of enzymes by immobilization, in general immobilization is not a method of enzyme stabilization. Immobilization is as likely as any other random treatment to increase, decrease or have no effect on the stability of enzymes.

Heat represents one of the main causes of enzyme inactivation in bioreactors. Thermal inactivation of enzymes undoubtedly results from conformational changes in the protein molecule. When enzymes become covalently linked to a solid support the protein molecules become more rigid and less able to unfold and are thus much less readily inactivated. Unfolding of protein structure is a common feature of different modes of enzyme inactivation and is caused by, for example, organic solvents, denaturing agents and pH changes. Thus immobilization by multipoint binding to solid supports will offer a general approach to the stabilization of enzymes.

The immobilization of enzymes can often result in the alteration of certain of their functional characteristics. When enzymes function in a free state the system will be homogeneous with respect to all components of the process substrate, products, activators, inhibitors, co-factors. However, when they are immobilized, the physico-chemical properties of the new system will create partitioning between the immobilized enzyme and the aqueous phase thus creating a heterogeneous system. Thus, it can be expected that certain characteristics of the enzymes will be altered significantly compared with enzymes in free solution. Similarly, the transport of substrates to catalysts is affected by diffusional resistances. Diffusional limitations arise when substrates need to be transported from the bulk liquid across a boundary layer of water to the immobilized enzyme and again at the inside of the immobilized enzyme particle which could be a gel, a microcapsule or a hollow fibre.

Immobilized enzymes will be used either to improve an existing process or to create a novel one. As yet their penetration into commercial practice is small. By early 1983, commercial industrial operation by immobilized systems was restricted to seven glucose isomerases, four penicillin amidases, three amino acylases and lactases, two glucoamylases, one aspartase and one fumarase. Further use of immobilized systems can be anticipated in analytical and medical applications and will result from novel ideas rather than improvements.

What are the reasons for their limited success so far? In principle they can be attributed to a combination of the following factors:

(a) soluble enzymes used in many industrial processes are relatively cheap;

(b) introduction of new capital equipment to existing processes is high;

(c) the disappointing performance in practice of immobilized systems in relation to overall operational economy and plant design scale.

The further industrial applications of enzyme technology can be seen in two contexts: those already in use or nearing application and those that will require a major research commitment before they can realistically become technically and commercially available.

This second generation of enzyme engineering is undoubtedly one of the most exciting and intellectually demanding of the many facets of biotechnology (Table 5. 10).

Table 5.10 Second generation of enzyme engineering

Present state	Present knowledge of enzyme technology. Basic knowledge in molecular biology, enzymology, physical chemistry.

$$\Downarrow$$

Goals of the research	Technical use of more sophisticated enzyme reaction to perform synthesis with multi-enzyme systems including co-factor regeneration; stabilized subcellular structure; immobilized whole cells; use of enzymes in organic solvents.	5
Expertise needed	Organic and polymer chemistry Biochemistry Microbiology Genetic engineering	Biochemical engineering Electrochemistry Biophysics 10

	New medical applications	New analytical applications	New industrial applications 15
Impact of the research	Biochemical prosthesis (e.g. artificial liver functions)	Enzyme electrodes for both medicine and industry (e.g. line control of bioreactors, artificial pancreas)	Fine chemicals, pharmaceuticals, foods 20

5.7 Immobilization of cells

Cells and organelles are normally the smallest feasible units for biochemical synthetic 25
purposes since they contain coenzyme regenerating systems, ordered multi-enzyme sequences, etc. It is therefore surprising that microbial cell immobilization technology was
developed mainly after enzyme immobilization. However, in practice, immobilization techniques for enzymes have been primarily concerned with single enzyme systems that catalyse single reactions such as oxido-reduction, isomerization, hydrolysis, etc. Attempts to 30
use immobilized enzymes other than for simple one-stage reactions have encountered severe limitations first with developing a practical, feasible technology for coenzyme regeneration and secondly with the paucity of methods to arrange enzyme molecules in ordered
clusters to perform multistep enzyme-catalysed reactions. Can immobilized cells overcome the disadvantages of immobilized enzymes and will it still be possible to manipulate 35
the total cell metabolism after immobilization of the cell?

During the last decade there have been rapid advances in the methods available for
immobilizing cells and organelles and the range of preparations include cell fragments,
organelles, cell homogenates, dead cells, permeabilized cells, resting cells, starving cells
and mixed cell cultures. In most cases the preparations have been used as biocatalysts 40

while some recent studies have used them as affinity adsorbents. It is now possible to im-
mobilize almost any cell structure and keep the cell viable. The procedures are not without drawbacks, for example the increased difficulty in delivering a good oxygen supply to
dense cell preparations, the growth of the cells within the support structure, and even
5 changed metabolic patterns.

The promise of immobilized cell technology is considerable and is undoubtedly
wider than for immobilized enzymes. Some industrial applications are now in operation. Immobilized cells of *Bacillus coagulans* produce a major proportion of high fructose
syrups, and aspartic and malic acids are produced in large tonnage quantities each
10 year. Anchorage-dependent mammalian cells growing on microcarrier spheres represent
an outstandingly important immobilized cell technique which is being used for the production of vaccines, enzymes, hormones, antibodies and interferons.

Artificial Immobilization　　The previous methods described for immobilization of enzymes can be used for whole cells. However, in practice the main methods that have been
15 used for microbial, animal and plant cells have been entrapment of the cells in gels and
by adsorption, but care must be taken to avoid inactivation of necessary metabolic activity. Such systems allow easy separation of the biocatalyst from products and make the
biocatalyst more stable.

In some cases the cells used may be dead but still retain the necessary enzyme activ-
20 ity. Cells may be treated to allow easy entry and exit of certain molecules through the
membranes. This process, permeabilization, involves the formation of small pores in the
cell membrane but leaves the entire enzyme package intact. Treatment of cells can occur
before or after immobilization. However, a wide variety of reactions can be carried out by
immobilized living cells, either in a resting state or actively growing in gel matri-
25 ces. Immobilized growing cells can be seen as renewable or self-proliferating biocatalysts, existing in a particular defined region of space and being protected against unfavourable environmental parameters outside their area of functioning.

One of the main advantages of the immobilized cell procedure is the capability for
re-use. This provides a means of making a batch process continuous and further allows
30 the maintenance of a high cell population to achieve fast reaction rates. The support material retains the organism in the bioreactor, allowing high dilution rates which exceed the maximum specific growth rate (μ_{max}) of the organism (thus overcoming the
wash-out problem in continuous systems). The ability of microbial cells to regenerate
the cofactors necessary for many biosynthetic reactions gives immobilized cells a major
35 advantage over isolated enzymes which require the cofactors to be supplied; the cost of
cofactors is prohibitively high. The spatial organization of multi-enzyme reactions is
more advantageously achieved in whole cells as opposed to isolated and/or immobilized
enzymes.

There are, however, several disadvantages in the use of immobilized whole
40 cells. Cells contain numerous catalytically active enzymes and in some processes enzymes

may catalyze unwanted side reactions. The destruction of certain unwanted enzyme reactions has been achieved simply by heating or by treatment with alkali or bile salts. Immobilization may also result in the loss of the desired catalytic ability but this problem can be reduced by the appropriate choice of immobilization method. Losses of catalytic activity can occur due to diffusional barriers impeding substrate access or product removal. With immobilized resting and growing cells yields of products may be lowered by the consumption of substrates as a source of carbon or energy for maintaining the cell in a growing state; with immobilized growing cells, products can become contaminated by cells leaking through gel matrices.

Immobilized enzyme or cell bioreactors   Bioreactor design and operation have been previously described in Chapter 4 for use in fermentation processes. Some of these bioreactor types can be used for immobilized enzymes and cells, but in general the types of reactions used for fermentations are radically different to those for immobilized enzymes and cells. The first consideration when designing an immobilized process is whether batch or continuous operation will be used. In most cases the continuous process has been selected.

Kinetic considerations are an important part in the choice of a bioreactor. In general packed bed reactors have kinetic advantages over continuous stirred tank reactors for most types of reaction. In a continuous stirred bioreactor the average reaction rate is lower than in a packed bed bioreactor due to the different operational concentration of substrates. However, stirred bioreactors are more suitable for reactions requiring high rates of oxygen transfer or the addition of base or acid for pH control. The volume of liquid to be processed must also be taken into consideration. For the unit production of a desired compound the volume of fermentation broth will be much smaller when using a continuous method.

The types of bioreactor systems commonly used with immobilized enzyme and cell technology are shown in Fig. 5. 3. Of special interest are the packed bed and fluidized bed bioreactors. Continuous packed bed bioreactors are widely operated and present three possibilities as regards substrate flow, downward flow, upward flow, or recycling.

When the reaction rate is affected by the rate of substrate availability, recycling is the method of choice. Since down flow of substrates can cause compression of the beds, upward flow methods have usually been selected for industrial practices. Similarly, upward flow is to be preferred when gas is released during a reaction. Immobilized growing cell systems can be problematic since liberated cells may cause blockage of the void space (i. e. space between particles) causing channelling of the substrates.

In fluidized beds the particles are held in suspension when the pressure drop across the bed is equal to the weight of the bed. Reduced pressure results in a packed bed while increased pressure causes elutrition or removal of the particles from the system.

Fluidized bed reactors are of special value when substrate solutions of high viscosity or a gaseous substrate or product is involved in a continuous bioreactor system. Particle size of the immobilized system can be important for the formation of a smooth fluidized

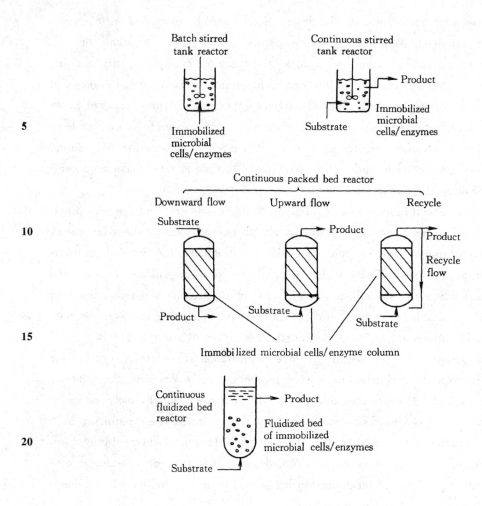

Fig. 5.3 Immobilized cell/enzyme bioreactors

bed.

Immobilization by natural adhesion In this category of immobilization, cells become attached to surfaces by natural mechanisms of adhesion and subsequent film growth. Several such categories of bioreactor include: (a) microbial film growth on fixed bed bioreactors, for example percolating or trickling filters in effluent treatment processes; (b) film growth on rotating surface bioreactors or rotating biological contactors in which microorganisms or animal cells can develop on partially submerged discs which rotate through a reservoir of nutrient exposing the film growth to liquid and air in sequence; and (c) film growth on small support particles which can exist in stirred tanks or fluidized bed bioreactors creating extensive surface areas for organism colonization. The physical contact or abrasion between the particles removes excess surface growth and maintains a relatively constant film thickness. Such particles can exist in a variety of shapes, sizes, porosities and densities and can be colonized by a wide range of cell types.

The phenomenon of film growth can also occur where it is not required, for example in traditional bioreactors where cell growth is desired only in the agitated liquid. Many microorganisms are difficult to cultivate in liquid bioreactors because they readily be-come attached to reactor walls, impellers, and ports of entry for probes. Such growth can lead to a deterioration in the performance of the equipment downstream of the bioreactor as well as encouraging corrosion.

Film growth systems show advantages similar to other immobilization techniques including the prevention of cell wash-out, separation of cell production and the bio-catalytic process, bioreactor stability under differing substrate feed rates, high substrate conversion and easier product recovery. The main disadvantages are concerned with the heterogeneous nature of film growth and the special problems of substrate and gaseous diffusion.

The thickness of the film is an important factor influencing the biological activity of these cell films. It has been shown that substrate uptake by microbial films occurs only at the outer $70\sim100$ μm of the film and that the aerobic layer is $50\sim150$ μm, depending on substrate concentration.

5.8 Summary

Enzymes are highly specific biocatalysts, functioning at high conversion rates under mild physiological conditions in aqueous solutions. They occur naturally inside all living organisms but can also occur in nature as extracellular enzymes secreted by organisms into the environment. Over 2000 enzymes have been isolated but only about 20 have gained significant commercial importance and most of these are hydrolases, for example amy-lases, proteases, pectinases and cellulases. Other enzymes of importance are glucose iso-merase and glucose oxidase.

Most important commercial enzymes are produced from a limited number of mi-croorganisms which have a long history of acceptability as food and beverage produc-ers. Safety regulations impose severe limitations to novel enzyme products.

Extracellular and intracellular microbial enzymes are produced industrially by sub-merged, deep tank, and solid substrate fermentation techniques. Most liquid media are mixtures of several complex undefined materials, such as molasses, starch hydrolysates, corn steep liquor, yeast extract. Batch cultivation is the most utilized method of produc-tion. Enzyme production can be controlled by environmental and genetic manipulation.

Enzymes may be used in the free water-soluble state or in an immobilized form. Immobilization prevents diffusion of the enzyme in the reaction mixtures and al-lows easy recovery from the product stream; immobilized enzymes can be used best in continuously operated bioreactors. Enzyme immobilization can occur by covalent cou-pling, entrapment in gels, encapsulation, adsorption on solid surfaces and crosslinking with multifunctional agents. Immobilized enzymes have so far found limited industrial use but further applications should come in medical and analytical use.

Whole cell immobilization techniques have now been widely developed using the principles derived from enzyme studies. These techniques allow simple and multi-enzyme

systems to be utilized and avoid the hazards of long enzyme purification procedures. In practice the immobilized cells may be dead, in a resting state, or actively growing and can be treated to allow easy entry and exit of specific molecules through the
plasma membranes. Such 'permeabilization' involves the formation of small pores in the
cell membrane but retaining the enzymes inside the cell. Cofactor regeneration by immo-
5   bilized living cells is an important commercial advantage. Multi-enzyme reactions are
more advantageously carried out in whole cells as opposed to isolated and/or immobilized ensymes.

The most commonly used bioreactor systems for immobilized enzymes and cells are
packed bed bioreactors and fluidized bed bioreactors.

10   Cells may also be immobilized by attachment to surfaces by natural mechanisms of
adhesion and subsequent film growth. Examples of these techniques include percolating
or trickling filters, rotating surface bioreactors or biological contactors, or film growths
on support particles in stirred tanks or fluidized bed bioreactors.

Words and Expressions

Page	line		
142	5	inanimate ［in'ænimit］ a. 无生命的	not living
	8	urease ['juərieis] n. 脲酶	
143	8	hydrolase ['haidrəleis] n. 水解酶	
	12	glucose oxidase n. 葡萄糖氧化酶	
	18	papain ［pə'peiin］ n. 木瓜蛋白酶	
		ficin ['faisin] n. 无花果蛋白酶	
		bromelain ['brəuməlin] n. 菠萝蛋白酶	
		lipoxygenase ［li'pɔksidʒəneis］ n. 脂氧合酶	
144	1	pancreatic ［ˌpæŋkri'ætik］ a. 胰的	
		lipase ['laipeis] n. 脂肪酶	
	2	rennet ['renit] n. 粗制凝乳酶	
	7	recourse ［ri'kɔːs］ n. 求助 turning to something or somebody for help; resort	
	24	desizing ［diː'saiziŋ］ n. (布)褪浆	
	25	amyloglucosidase ［ˌæmiləu gluˈkəusideis］ n. 淀粉葡糖苷酶	
	27	lymphatic leukaemia ［limˈfætik ljuːˈkiːmiə］ n. 淋巴性白血病	
	29	catalage ['kætəleis] n. 过氧化氢酶	
	43	penicillin acylase ［ˌpeniˈsilin 'æsileis］ n. 青霉素酰化酶	
	45	penicillinase ［ˌpeniˈsilineis］ n. 青霉素酶	
145	6	pyruvate kinase ['kaineis] n. 丙酮酸激酶	
	8	pullulanase n. 支链淀粉酶 催化支点上的 α-(1,6)糖苷键 水解的一种酶	
		wort ［wɔːt］ n. 麦芽汁 生产啤酒的原料,主要来自大麦麦芽和蛇麻子	
	9	rennin ['renin] n. 凝乳酶 一种酸性蛋白酶,能使牛乳中酪蛋白凝结	

Page line

145 10 titre ['taitə] n. 滴定度 the concentration of a substance in a solution determined by titration

23 sporulate ['spɔːrjuleit] vt. 形成孢子

32 built-in a. 固有的 inherent

147 14 mannose ['mænəus] n. 甘露糖

xylose ['zailəus] n. 木糖

16 idiophase n. 繁殖期 在分批培养中,相当于指数生长期后期和整个稳定期,主
要产生次级代谢产物

17 trophophase n. 生长期 在分批培养中,相当于滞后期的后期和指数生长期的
初期和中期,主要发生初级代谢和菌体生长

24 amidinotransferase [ˌæmiˈdinəˈtrænsfəreis] n. 转脒基酶

25 acyltransferase [ˌæsilˈtrænsfəreis] n. 转酰基酶

26 phenoxazinone n. 吩嗪嗪酮

27 synthetase ['sinθiteis] n. 合成酶

gramicidin [ˌgræmiˈsaidin] n. 短杆菌肽

148 17 legislation [ˌledʒisˈleiʃən] n. 法规 law

21 allergenic [ˌæləˈdʒenic] a. 变应原的,引起变态反应的

22 extraneous [eksˈtreinjəs] a. 外来的 foreign, alien

24 mycotoxin [ˌmaikəuˈtɔksin] n. 真菌毒素 由真菌产生的毒素,包括黄曲霉毒
素等

25 antigenicity [ˌæntidʒiˈnisiti] n. 抗原性

37 toxicological [ˌtɔksikəˈlɔdʒikəl] a. 毒理学的

149 2 carcinogenic [ˌkɑːsinəuˈdʒenik] a. 致癌的

oestrogenic [iːstrəˈdʒenik] a. 雌激素的

teratogenic [ˌterətəuˈdʒenik] a. 致畸形的

24 subacute [ˌsʌbəˈkjuːt] a. 亚急性的

35 fertility [fəˈtiliti] n. 能育性

37 rest with vi. 归属于,在于,存在于 be left in the hands or charge of

42 immobilized enzyme 固定化酶

150 14 entrapment [inˈtræpmənt] n. 包埋

15 encapsulation [inˌkæpsəˈleiʃən] n. 胶囊封装

32 inclusion[inˈkluːʒən] n. 包含 the state of being included

151 3 methacrylate [meˈθækrileit] n. 甲基丙烯酸盐(酯)

glutaraldehyde [ˌgluːtəˈrældihaid] n. 戊二醛

4 carboxymethylcellulose n. 羧甲基纤维素

carbodi-imide [ˌkɑːbəudaiˈimid] n. 碳二亚胺

6 polyacrylamide n. 聚丙烯酰胺

collagen ['kɔlədʒen] n. 胶原 一种纤维状蛋白质,存在于骨、软骨和结缔组织
中

Page line

7 alginate ['ældʒineit] n. 海藻酸盐

8 urethane ['juəriθein] n. 氨基甲酸乙酯,聚氨酯

10 carrageenan [ˌkærə'giːnən] n. 卡拉胶,角叉菜胶

11 chitosan ['kaitəsæn] n. 脱乙酰壳多糖,脱乙酰儿丁质

14 polyvinylchloride [ˌpɔliˌvainil'klɔːraid] n. 聚氯乙烯

16 pectate ['pekteit] n. 果胶酸盐(酯)

18 concanavalin [ˌkɔnkə'nævəlin] n. 伴刀豆球蛋白

23 alumina [ə'luːminə] n. 氧化铝,矾土

29 per se [ˌpəː'siː] (拉丁文) ad. 本身 by, of, or in itself or oneself or themselves; as such; intrinsically

31 imino ['iminəu] 亚胺基=NH

amide ['æmaid] n. 酰胺

thiol ['θaiɔl] n. 巯基,硫羟基 —SH

methyl thiol n. 甲硫基 CH$_3$S—

guanidyl 胍基 —HN—C$\begin{smallmatrix}NH\\NH_2\end{smallmatrix}$

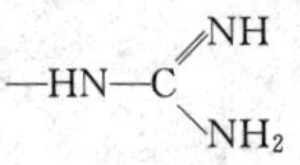

31 imidazole [ˌimi'dæzəul] n. 咪唑

42 silica gel ['silikə] n. 硅胶 无定形二氧化硅

silicone rubber ['silikəun] n. 硅橡胶

152 5 collodion [kə'ləudjən] n. 火棉胶 火棉(焦木素)在醚或醇中溶液,用于形成
表面覆盖层

12 aminoacylase [ˌæminəu'æsileis] n. 氨基酰化酶

13 hydroxylapatite [haiˌdrɔksi'læpətait] n. 羟基磷灰石

pyrophosphorylase n. 焦磷酸化酶

22 dimethyl adipimidate 二甲基己二亚氨酯 CH$_3$OC(=NH)CH$_2$(CH$_2$)$_2$CH$_2$C
(=NH)OCH$_3$

dimethyl suberimidate 二甲基辛二亚氨酯 CH$_3$OC(=NH)CH$_2$(CH$_2$)$_4$CH$_2$C
(=NH)OCH$_3$

25 maleic anhydride [mə'liːiːk] n. 马来酐

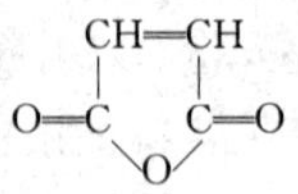

26 cellophane ['seləfein] n. 赛璐玢,玻璃纸 由木质纸浆制得的薄膜状透明纤维
素材料

153 33 sweetener ['swiːtənə] n. 甜味剂

154 3 6-amino-penicillanic acid (6-APA) n. 6-氨基青霉烷酸

5 ampicillin [ˌæmpi'silin] n. 氨苄青霉素

phenyl glycine ['fenil 'glaisiːn] n. 苯基甘氨酸

Page line

     20 dextrose ［'dekstrəus］ n. 右旋糖,葡萄糖

155   17 occlusion ［ə'kluːʒən］ n. 吸留,包藏 adsorption in great quantity

     29 challenging ［'tʃælindʒiŋ］ a. 困难但引起兴趣的 difficult but stimulating

156   4 unfold ［ʌn'fəuld］ vi. 展开

     24 penicillin amidase ［'æmideis］ n. 青霉素酰化酶

     25 aspartase ［'æspɑːteis］ n. 天冬氨酸酶

         fumarase ［'fjuːməreis］ n. 延胡索酸酶

     36 commitment ［kə'mitmənt］ n. 承担的义务

157   18 prosthesis ［prɔs'θiːsis］ n. 修复术

     33 paucity ［'pɔːsəti］ n. 量少,不足,缺乏 quantity of something that is small and especially less than what is needed. dearth

     34 cluster ［'klʌstə］ n. 群,束 a number of things of same kind being close together

     39 cell homogenate ［hɔ'mɔdʒineit］ n. 细胞匀浆液 细胞经匀浆器破碎后的悬浮液

159   2 bile salt ［bail］ n. 胆汁盐

     36 elutriation ［iˌljuːtri'eiʃən］ n. 淘析 purification or separation by washing, settling and decanting

160   29 percolate ［'pəːkəleit］ vi. 渗滤 to pass through a porous substance

         trickle ［'trikl］ vi. 滴流 to flow in drops

     35 abrasion ［əb'reiʒən］ n. 磨损 the process of wearing down or rubbing away by means of friction

Notes

① It was not until 1878……这是强调的双重否定句,强调 it 形式主语所代表的 that 起首的从句。意为"直到 1878 年,才……"。参见 Ch. 1,Note⑩.

② amyloglucosidase 淀粉葡萄糖苷酶,一般称为 glucoamylase 葡萄糖淀粉酶,是一种外切酶,它能连续地从支链和直链淀粉的非还原性末端水解 1,4-α-糖苷键,生成 β-D-葡萄糖,也可水解 1,6-α-糖苷键,但速度较慢,工业上由真菌 Aspergillus niger 产生。用于使极限糊精转变为 D-葡萄糖。也称为糖化酶。此酶应和 α-淀粉酶相区别。后者是一种内切酶,能水解1,4-α-糖苷键,作用于支链淀粉形成葡萄糖、麦芽糖和分支的 α-极限糊精;作用于直链淀粉形成麦芽糖和葡萄糖,但对两端 1,4-α-糖苷键和分支点的 1,6-α-糖苷键无作用。

③ penicillinase 青霉素酶,也称为 β-lactamase β-内酰胺酶,使青霉素 β-内酰胺环裂解,生成青霉噻唑酸 penicilloic acid。此酶和青霉素酰化酶 penicillin acylase 相区别,后者也称为 penicillin amidase,penicillin amidohydrolase,能裂解青霉素侧链,形成 6-氨基青霉烷酸。

④ feedback regulation 反馈调节包括 feedback inhibition 反馈抑制和 feedback repression 反馈阻遏两种形式。前者指最终产物对代谢途径中的第一种酶的抑制作用,即最终产物能和该酶结合,使酶分子变形(变构作用)而降低活性。反馈阻遏是指最终产物可作为一种共阻遏物(corepressor),能使调节基因产生的阻遏蛋白质激活,从而使后者与操纵基因作用,阻

止结构基因转录成 m RNA。

⑤ dimethyl adipimidate 二甲基己二亚氨酯 是一种双功能亚氨酯,能和—NH₂ 基起作用,起交联作用

$$protein—NH_2 +NH_2=C\underset{|}{\overset{OCH_3}{|}}—(CH_2)_4—C\underset{|}{\overset{OCH_3}{|}}=NH_2^+ \longrightarrow NH_2^+=C\underset{\underset{protein}{\overset{|}{NH}}}{\overset{\overset{protein}{|}\\ NH \\ |}{|}}—(CH_2)_4—C^+\overset{|}{\underset{|}{}}=NH_2$$

dimethyl adipimidate

dimethyl suberimidate 的反应与此类似。

⑥ 本句为虚拟态,可译为:当酶用于生物反应器系统时,其所处环境通常要比在生物体中恶劣得多。由于酶过去已经加以固定化,所以'酶处于生物体中的环境'(would have occurred in vivo)要用虚拟态过去时。

Comprehension

1. How can some microorganisms utilize polysaccharides to which cell wall is impermeable? (p. 142)

2. In fact all fermentations are the resultant activities of a whole range of enzymes. Why, up to now, has little success been gained in replacing producer organism by enzymes in fermentations? (p. 142)

3. Which kinds of enzymes are mostly being produced in industry? (p. 143)

4. Compare the production of extra cellular enzymes with that of intracellular ones. (p. 145)

5. What percentage by weight does an enzyme usually account for of the biomass in fermentation? (p. 146)

6. Enumerate the methods for increasing the production of enzymes during fermentation. (p. 146~147)

7. What is the major concern with the fungal enzyme in respect of safety? (p. 148)

8. For which reason does an enzyme need to be immobilized? (p. 150)

9. What categories could the methods of immobilization be classified into? (p. 150)

10. Describe the process of covalent coupling in enzyme immobilization (p. 151)

11. Compare the merits and demerits of various immobilization methods? (p. 151~153)

12. Which industries have succesfully made use of immobilized enzymes? (p. 153~155)

13. Discuss the advantages and disadvantages of immobilized enzyme in comparison with free enzyme. (p. 155~156)

14. What are the advantages and disadvantages of cell immobilization compared with enzyme immobilization? (p. 157~159)

15. When would the continuous packed bed bioreactor with recycle flow be the type of choice and why? (p. 159)

Vocabulary

Give another word or phrase to replace these words or phrases as they are used in the text:

locus (142/14); blend (148/12); formulation (148/26); carry over (148/34); gel-inducing

(151/36);level(153/39);context(156/34);promise(158/6);as regards(159/27);in se-
quence(160/32).

Word usage

1. Write sentences to bring out the difference between the following pairs of words:
   catalyse(142/11),catalysis;subsequently(142/11),later;analyses(143/13),analyse;seek
   (144/15),find;method(150/16),methodology(150/17);ultimately(153/33),lastly.
2. Make sentences with the following words or phrases:
   render(151/26);cause(152/34);be attributed to(156/28);rather than(156/26).

Patterns

1. Expressing contrast or difference.

   Here are the structures commonly used to show the contrast or difference between two
   facts:

   Degradative enzymes are usually controlled by induction and catabolite repression, <u>while</u>
   (<u>whereas</u>) biosynthetic enzymes are mainly controlled by feedback regulation. (146/32~
   33)

   Biosynthetic enzymes <u>differ</u> (<u>are different</u>) from the degradative enzymes in that they are
   mainly controlled by feedback regulation.

   <u>In contrast to</u> the crude bulk enzymes there is a rapidly expanding market for certain highly purified enzymes such as glucose isomerase and glucose oxidase. (143/10~12)

   Multi-enzyme reactions are more advantageously carried out in whole cells <u>as opposed to</u>
   (<u>as against</u>,<u>as compared with</u>) isolated and/or immobilized enzymes. (162/5~6)

   The advantages and disadvantages of solid state systems (<u>as</u>) <u>compared with</u> submerged
   culture procedures have been well analysed. (147/35)

   Exercises

   Complete these statements:

   (a) Biochemical engineering… chemical engineering… that it deals with biological materi-
       al

   (b) We are not sure what it means if a cell is quoted as having an energy charge of 0. 7…
       0. 8 or 0. 6.

   (c) …protoplast fusion where entire genomes are mixed,recombinant DNA technology is
       primarily concerned with small numbers of individual genes controlling known gene
       products.

2. Allow,permit,enable,cause,make,etc. +infinitive.

   Note:Enable really means to make possible,but it is often used in the same sense as allow
        and permit. With make and let,the word 'to' is not used before infinitive.

   Examples.

   These techniques allow simple and multi-enzyme systems to be utilized. (161/39~162/1)

   The rich medium <u>caused</u> the organisms <u>to</u> grow rapidly.

   The rich medium <u>made</u> the organisms grow rapidly.

   The microscope <u>enables</u> scientists <u>to</u> examine very small objects.

Exercises

Complete these statements using the verbs shown above:

(a) These parameters can be independently controlled… the experimenter to obtain realistic information on the role of each… the growth of the organism.

(b) The risk of an explosion… the workers… leave the factory.

Sentence analysis and translation

First analyse the following sentences as in Ch. 1, Note① and then translate into chinese:

1. The 2nd paragraph on page 144 (line 9 to line 17)

2. The last part of section 5.6 (156/28~39)

3. The last paragraph of the section Immobilization by natural adhesion(161/11~14)

4. Attemps to use immobilized enzymes other than……to perform multistep enzyme-catalysed reactions. (157/30~34)

Writing

Certainly you need to write business letters throughout your lives. You will improve your chance of success by writing a good business letter which should be concise, courteous and adherent to standard form.

Here is a typical piece of business correspondence with some explanations in Chinese.

Journal of
Chemical Technology and Biotechnology

14/15 Belgrave Square
London SW1X 8PS. UK
Tel:+44-(0)171-235 3681
Fax:+44-(0)171-823 1698

发信人地址,如果不用印有单位名
称的信纸,也可以放在右上角.

Dr Shaoxun Huang
Department of Biochemical Engineering
East China University of Science and Technology
Shanghai 200237

China

收信人及地址

13 April 1995

Dear Dr Huang

<u>JCTB 273/94 APPLICATION OF MEMBRANE FIL TRATION TO
GLUTAMIC ACID RECOVERY</u>　　信的主题内容,一般
情况下也可省去

Thank you for submitting a revised version of your paper to the Journal of Chemical Technology and Biotechnology.

Your paper is now acceptable to the Editors for publication. In due course, you will receive proofs directly from the publishers, together with instructions how to proceed. Please check the proofs carefully for typographical errors.

I would like to thank you for your interest in the Joumal and I look forward to receiving future potential publications from your group.

Yours sincerely

Signature   信尾客套话，签名和头衔等
（发信人签名）   如果发信人地址放在右上角，
                则这部分应移至右下角
DR A M PICKETT
Technical Editor ll

AMP/Smb   表示发信人姓名的开首字母/打字员姓名的开首字母
cc：Wang   表示抄送给某人
enc.   表示有附件，在信中也应提及

Write a letter for job application to personnel department of Biotech Company，whose address is：400 Caobao Road，Shanghai 200233

Chapter 6　Downstream Processing in Biotechnology

6. 1　Introduction

'Downstream processing' is a useful collective term for all the steps which are required in order actually to recover useful products from any kind of industrial process. It is particularly important in biotechnology where the desired final forms of the products are usually quite far removed from the state in which they are first obtained in the bioreactor. For example, a typical fermentation process gives a mixture of a dispersed solid(the eell mass, perhaps with some components from the nutrient medium, etc.) and a dilute water solution; the desired product may be within the cells, as one constituent of a very complex mixture, or in the dilute aqueous medium, or even distributed between the two. In any case its recovery, concentration, and purification will require careful and effective operations which are also constrained by manufacturing economics. Any special requirements, such as a need to exclude contaminants or to contain the process organism, will only add to the difficulties.

Many operations which are standard in the laboratory will become impractical, or uneconomic, on the process scale. Moreover, bioproducts are often very labile or sensitive compounds, whose active structures can survive only under defined and limited conditions of pH, temperature, ionic strength, etc. Bearing in mind such restrictions[①], much ingenuity is called for if the available repertoire of scientific methods is to be used to best effect. It will also be apparent that there is no one unique, ideal, or universal operation, or even sequence of operations, which can be recommended; individual unit operations must be combined in the most suitable way for a particular problem.

6. 2　Separation of particles

At the end of a fermentation, the first step in many cases is to separate the solids(usually cells, but alternatively cells or enzymes on a particulate support, and not excluding solid components of the reaction medium)from the liquid continuum which is almost always aqueous. Some properties of cells which are relevant to such separations are listed in Table 6. 1; note that the specific gravity of the cells is not much greater than that of the fermentation broth. The cell size can also cause difficulties with bacteria, but larger cells are more easily separated, sometimes even by simple settling in decanters. Ease of separation will also be dependent upon the nature of the fermentation broth, its pH and temperature, etc. , and in many cases it must be improved by the addition of filter aids, flocculating agents. etc. (see later). Table 6. 2 gives a general classification of separation methods.

Table 6. 1 Properties of cells with reference to separation

Properties	Bacteria	Yeast	Fungi
Shape	Rods, spheres chains	Spheres, ellipsoids filaments	Filaments
Size	$0.5\sim3\mu m$	$1\sim50\mu m$	$5\sim15\mu m$ diameter; $50\sim500\mu m$ length
Specific weight	$1.05\sim1.1$	$1.05\sim1.1$	$1.05\sim1.1$
Cell weight	$10^{-12}g$	$10^{-11}g$	—

Table 6. 2 Classification of separation methods

Separation principle	Separation method	Particle size(μm)
Particle size	Fibre filtration	$>200\sim10$
	Microfiltration	$20\sim0.5$
Molecule size	Ultrafiltration	$2\sim0.005$
	Hyperfiltration	$0.008\sim0.00025$
	Gel chromatography	$2\sim0.0003$
	Dialysis	$0.002\sim0.00025$
Temperature	Crystallization	<0.002
Solubility	Adsorption	<0.002
	Extraction	
Electric charge	Electrophoresis	$2\sim0.02$
	Electrodialysis	$0.02\sim0.00025$
	Ion exchange	$0.02\sim0.00025$
Density	Sedimentation	>1000
	Decantation	$1000\sim5$
	Centrifugation	$1000\sim0.5$
	Ultracentrifugation	$2\sim0.02$

6.2.1 Filtration

This method is most widely and typically used to separate filamentous fungi, and filamentous bacteria (i. e. streptomycetes)from fermentation broths. It can also be used for yeast flocs. According to the mechanism, filtration can be performed as surface filtration, or depth filtration[2]; or centrifugal filtration; in all cases, the driving force is pressure, whether created by overpressure or by a vacuum.

The rate of filtration, i. e. the volume of filtrate which can be collected in a given time, is a function of filter area, the viscosity of the fluid, and the pressure drop across the filter medium and the deposited filter cake. The resistance of the filter medium and the filter cake together is therefore critical, and this resistance depends upon its compressibility. For noncompressible cakes the filtration rate becomes independent of pressure, but most biological materials are compressible, so the resistance of the cake increases with time quite independently of the increased overall resistance as the filtration proceeds and the cake builds up.

A considerable improvement in filter flow is attained by cross-flow filtration, in which the solids which do not pass through the filter are kept in suspension by a turbulent flow across the membrane. This can be brought about by arranging for the suspension to flow across the membrane, or by fitting moving blades or an impellor inside the

5 filter. Simple plate filters are widely used for the clarification of liquids, and can be used for the filtration of small amounts of suspensions, but their loading capacity is limited; filter-press assemblies are sometimes used, especially for batch operations.

Rotary drum vacuum filters are perhaps the most widely used devices for the separation of microorganisms from the fermentation broth; in these, the filtration element is

10 a rotating drum maintained under reduced internal pressure. The drum rotates into the liquor to be filtered, and its continuing rotation allows essential subsequent operations on the filter cake, as shown schematically in Fig. 6. 1. To avoid build-up of biomass on the filter surface. which will increase filtration resistance, such filters are frequently fitted with a knife discharge, as illustrated; if a mycelium which forms a coherent 'carpet'

15 is being separated, it can be lifted from the filter by strings. The drum is often precoated with a filter aid which helps to prevent blocking and to allow a constant pressure drop to be maintained. Major advantages are the effectiveness of filtration, with minimal temperature rise, low power consumption, and the integration of filtration with washing and partial dewatering; contamination of the filtered-off material with filter aid can be a seri-

20 ous drawback. Rotary filters operating under positive pressure can also be used, while

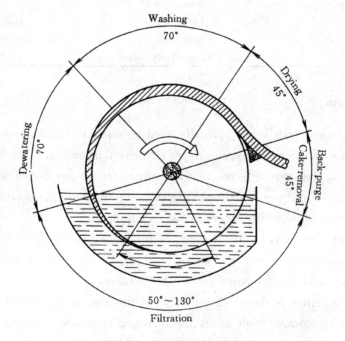

25   Fig. 6. 1   Schematic representation of a rotary vacuum filter (Section of filtration depends
on immersion depth of the filter drum)

belt filters are an obvious modification of the principle, and are very suitable for readily-filtered precipitates requiring extensive washing. Belt filters can be combined with a press to promote dewatering.

6.2.2 Centrifugation

Bacteria are usually too small to separate on simple filter media, but their separation by centrifugation is also difficult because of the small difference in density between the particles and the suspension. Protein precipitates must very often be separated by centrifugation, with similar difficulties. The performance of a centrifuge can be characterized by the expressions:

$$Q=d^2\Delta\rho gZF/18\eta$$

and

$$Z=R\omega^2/g\simeq Rn^2/900$$

in which Q = volumetric feed rate, d = particle diameter, $\Delta\rho$ = density difference, g = acceleration due to gravity, F = sedimentation area, η = viscosity, R = radius, ω = angular velocity and n = number of revolutions per minute.

The function $\sum=FZ$ is useful in comparing different centrifuges. Because F increases with the axial length of the rotor, and Z with its diameter and speed, performance improves by using longer rotors (F) or faster, wider rotors (Z); attainable values of Z are limited by the materials of construction. Fig. 6.2 shows some rotor arrangements schematically, and the critical characteristics of different arrangements are summarized

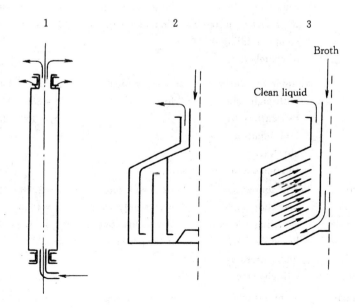

Fig. 6.2   Examples of solid centrifuges. 1,tubular bowl;2,multichamber solid bowl; 3,disc bowl centrifuge

in Table 6. 3. All designs have individual disadvantages, to which must be added the general ones of cost(including maintenance), power consumption, and (except where refrigeration is incorporated)temperature rise.

Table 6. 3 Properties of different centrifuges

	Type of centrifuge	Advantages	Disadvantages	Technical details
5				
10	Perforated basket	Good dewatering; easy to clean; washing of cake possible	Limited solids capacity; solids recovery laborious; low centrifugal force; discontinuous operation	$n=500\sim2500\mathrm{min}^{-1}$ $Z=300\sim1500$ $\Sigma=900\sim1800$
15	Sieve-scroll-centrifuge	Possibility for classification of different solids; washing of cake possible; continuous operation	Low centrifugal force	$n=500\sim1000\mathrm{min}^{-1}$ $Z=300\sim1500$
20	Tubular bowl	Good dewatering; high centrifugal force; easy to clean; bowl easy to remove	Limited solids capacity; solids recovery laborious; discontinuous operation; low Σ	$n=13000\sim18000\mathrm{min}^{-1}$ $d=75\sim150\mathrm{mm}$ $Z=13000\sim17000$ $\Sigma=1500\sim4000$
25	Multichamber solid bowl	Increase in solids capacity; no loss of efficiency up to complete filling of chambers	Solids recovery laborious; discontinuous operation	$n=5000\sim10000\mathrm{min}^{-1}$ $d=125\sim530\mathrm{mm}$ $Z=6000\sim11400$
30	Scroll discharge centrifuge	Suitable for slurry with high solids concentration; high input of slurry; continuous operation	Low centrifugal force	$n=700\sim2500\mathrm{min}^{-1}$ $Z=350\sim1400$ $\Sigma=900\sim2300$
35	Disc bowl centrifuge	Partly continuous operation; high centrifugal force; liquid discharge under pressure; CIP cleaning	Poor dewatering; works only with low solids content in suspension	$n=3000\sim10000\mathrm{min}^{-1}$ $Z=4000\sim7500$ $\Sigma=\mathrm{up\ to\ }270000$
40	Nozzle bowl centrifuge	Continuous operation; high centrifugal force	Poor dewatering	$n=\mathrm{up\ to\ }10000\mathrm{min}^{-1}$ $Z=\mathrm{up\ to\ }14000$ $\Sigma=\mathrm{up\ to\ }80000$

6.2.3 Flocculation and flotation

Where the small size of bacterial cells makes their recovery from fermentation broth very difficult, even by centrifugation, an improvement can often be achieved by flocculation; the sedimentation rate of a particle increases with its diameter (Stokes's law). Flocculation can occur reversibly if charges on the cell surface can be neutralized by oppositely charged ions, and irreversibly if charged polymer molecules form bridges between the cells. Thus flocculating agents include inorganic salts, mineral hydrocolloids, and organic polyelectrolytes. As well as choice of flocculating agent, flocculation also depends on such other factors as the nature (and physiological age) of the cells, the ionic environment, temperature, and surface shear stress.

If a sufficiently dense floc does not form. flotation can be used, in which small gas bubbles adsorb and entrain the organisms. The separation depends on the size of the gas bubbles; gas can be sparged in, or (better) very fine bubbles can be created from dissolved gases by releasing the overpressure or by electrolysis. Formation of a stable foam is promoted by insoluble 'collector substances' such as long-chain fatty acids or amines, and the particles collected in the foam layer can be removed. In some cases, a combination of flocculation and flotation is most efficiently applied for biomass recovery.

6.3 Disintegration of cells

6.3.1 Microorganisms

Disruption of microorganisms is usually difficult because of the strength of the cell wall and the high osmotic pressure inside; the particles are too small to be subjected to simple mechanical means, such as milling, whereby the necessary strong forces can be obtained. At the same time the disintegration must be effected without damaging the desired cell components, and often the requirements are contradictory. Methods used for breaking microorganisms are summarized in Fig. 6. 3. Their effect can often be assessed in terms of the level of activity of a cellular enzyme recovered in the disrupted suspension, combining a measure of the efficiency of disruption with an assessment of the degree of damage.

Mechanical methods

Mechanical methods may use shear (grinding in a ball mill, colloid mill, etc.), pressure and pressure-release (homogenizer), and ultrasound. A widely used process method uses high pressure followed by sudden decompression, resulting from the flow of the cell suspension through a fine nozzle. One such arrangement is shown in Fig. 6. 4; here disintegration is due to hydrodynamic shear and to cavitation. Ultrasound works mainly through cavitation, but is mainly used in the laboratory, since on a larger scale heat removal is difficult.

Non-mechanical methods

Cells can also be broken by thermal, chemical, or enzymic means. One widely used method is drying, which causes changes in the cell-wall structure and often allows a subsequent extraction of the cell contents by buffer or salt solutions; a well-known procedure is to prepare an 'acetone powder' by introducing the cells into a large excess of cold

5   acetone. Lysis of cells can be caused by chemical means, such as salts or surfactants, or

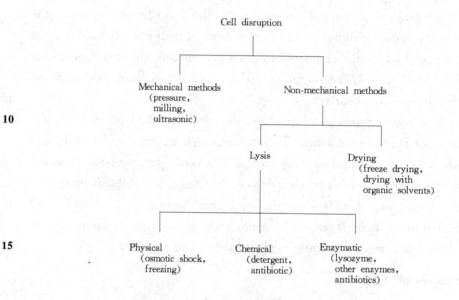

Fig. 6. 3   Methods for the disruption of microorganisms

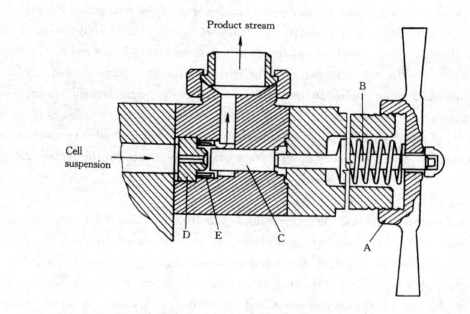

Fig. 6. 4   Pressure valve for disintegration of microorganisms on suspension. A, handwheel; B, rod for valve adjustment; C. valve; D, valveseat; E. impact ring

by osmotic shock, or by the application of appropriate lytic enzymes, which are now available in considerable variety and can be matched to the specific nature of the microorganism in question. Where the full variety of methods can be used, and compared, the recovery of active cellular enzymes following disruption is usually best after enzyme treatment or ultrasound; thermal or osmotic methods are less good, and mechanical disruption is commonly the least effective method.

6.3.2 Plant and animal cells

Cells from animal tissue or from plants are usually less stable and can be more easily disrupted by mechanical means. Additional shear can be applied if the material is first frozen, while appropriate enzymes can assist extraction from either animal or plant materials. Technically, considerable attention has been given to increasing the yield of plant extractives of all kinds by treatment with appropriate lytic enzymes (cellulases and hemicellulases) prior to conventional extraction methods.

6.4 Extraction methods

Extraction as applied to bioproducts has the function both of separation and also of concentration. It is especially useful for the recovery of lipophilic substances, whether these are initially extracellular or are liberated by suitable treatment of the cells. The solution, or even suspension, containing the desired product is mixed with an immiscible solvent in which it is preferentially dissolved and from which it can be more easily and specifically recovered. The distribution of a substance between the two phases is governed by its characteristic partition coefficient, K:

$$K = \frac{\text{concentration of substance in phase A}}{\text{concentration of substance in phase B}}$$

However, the efficiency of any practical extraction process also depends upon the relative volumes of the two phases which are brought to equilibrium. Simple calculation confirms that where the substance is to be[3] extracted into a given volume of solvent the extraction is more efficient if it is carried out with successive smaller aliquots, and where differential extraction of one component rather than others is sought, back-extraction will increase any selectivity[4]. Thus liquid-liquid extraction can be performed in a single step (if the partition coefficient is very favourable), by multistage parallel-flow extraction, or by counter-current extraction (the most complex arrangement but one which is also capable of fairly good resolution of mixtures).

In the recovery of antibiotics, solvent extraction is often an early step after the removal of cells or cell debris. The extraction of whole broth can also be achieved using extraction-decanters, extraction columns, or mixer-settlers using centrifuges. Fig. 6.5 shows a process for whole broth extraction for recovery of antibiotics direct from the fermentation broth.

5

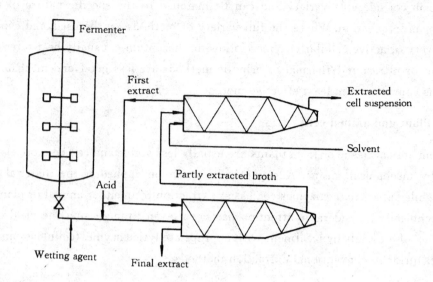

Fig. 6. 5　Whole-batch recovery process for antibiotics extraction

10　　　Whole broth recovery methods clearly lead to a reduction in the number of recovery stages, and should therefore reduce stage-by-stage losses even though the extraction may be impaired by the presence of cells. Reducing the time in which products are left in the aqueous phase, in which degradation is usually most rapid, will also be advantageous.

15　　　Separation of enzymes from cells or cell debris can be achieved using extraction with aqueous multiphase systems. Cell debris and enzymes are distributed in aqueous polyethyleneglycol-dextran mixtures, which form separate phases and can thus be separated easily. This method avoids some of the difficulties which arise in centrifugation (small particle dimensions) and gives high yields.

20　6. 5　Concentration methods

The products formed at low concentrations in bioprocesses may well be more concentrated as a result of some initial separation step, as in extraction (see above), but in general they must be further concentrated before economic purification is possible. Again, because of the lability of many products, methods for their concentration must be very

25　gentle. Some suitable methods will include:

- extraction(already considered)
- evaporation
- membrane processes
- ion exchange methods
- adsorption methods.

30

6.5.1　Evaporation

Evaporation is usually applied to solutions obtained by solvent extraction, in which case careful arrangements for recovery of the evaporated solvent are obligatory; because of the higher specific heat of evaporation, it requires more critical arrangements when it is applied to an aqueous preparation. Direct evaporation of whole culture broth is often   **5** used for relatively lowgrade products, usually by the use of some sort of spray-dryer.

　　Quite generally, evaporators with a short residence time are used to minimize losses due to⑤ thermal lability. The continuous flow evaporator allows concentration of labile products in one rapid throughput; in falling film evaporators the heat transfer is better, based on the large heat transfer surface, which allows a minimal temperature difference   **10** between the heating medium and the solution. Residence times are in the order of a minute. In thin-film evaporators the thin layer is created mechanically and is very turbulent; heat transfer is very effective and these evaporators can be used for the concentration of viscous liquids and even for concentration up to dry products. Centrifugal thin-film evaporators. in which evaporation takes place on heated conical walls inside a rotat-   **15** ing bowl, give even shorter residence times.

6.5.2　Membrane filtration

Membrane filtration is a versatile procedure which can be used for both the enrichment and the separation of different molecules or particles. Under hydrostatic pressure, small particles will pass through a suitable membrane if the applied pressure exceeds the os-   **20** motic pressure of the solution. which tends to drive solvent from the concentrate into the more dilute solution. In ultrafiltration the membrane can be considered as a sieve (microporous membrane) whose pore size governs the separation, but this simple model is not applicable in the case of reverse osmosis in which molecules of similar sizes may still be separated. This depends upon diffusion and solution interactions between the molecules   **25** and the membrane material. Examples of the application of membrane filtration processes are given in Table 6.4.

　　To obtain high flux rates it is usual to use asymmetric membranes, with a dense thin layer of membrane material supported mechanically by a coarser sponge-like structure. One serious problem in ultrafiltration is the phenomenon of 'concentration polar-   **30** ization'. On the concentrate side of the membrane the concentration of solutes increases with approach to the membrane, and is zero on the other side of the membrane. This results in the formation of what is, in effect, a 'secondary membrane', with different flux and separation characteristics. As in cross-flow filtration (see above, Section 6.2.1), the effect can be minimized, though not completely abolished by high flux rates across the   **35** membrane surface, achieved either by high pumping speeds, inducing turbulent flow, or by equipment with thin channels for high-velocity laminar flow. Typical arrangements are illustrated in Figs 6.6 and 6.7.

Table 6.4　Use of membrane processes

Type of membrane	Application	Relative molecular mass
Microfiltration	Concentration of bacteria and viruses	>1000000 (or particles)
Ultrafiltration	Fractionation;dialysis;production of enzymes;production of protein; processing of whey	>10000 (macromolecules)
Reverse osmosis	Concentration of pharmaceutical substances,production of lactose;part-desalination of solutions	>200 (organic compounds)
Electrodialysis	Purification and fractionation of charged substances;desalination	>100 (organic compounds)

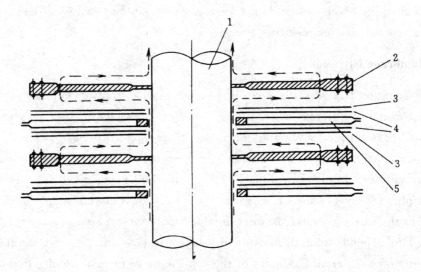

Fig. 6. 6　Sectional drawing of 'plate-and-frame' ultrafiltration module(The Danish Sugar Co.). 1, centre bolt;2,frame;3,membrane;4,filter paper;5,membrane support plate

　　Miorofiltration can replace filtration for the separation of cells, or even specific metabolites,from fermentation broths;the closed system facilitates sterile work and also containment,where necessary[6].

6. 5. 3　Ion exchange and adsorption resins

The use of adsorbents to recover substances from fermentation broths is a method of long standing,originally based on the use of active charcoal. Such methods can give a very large concentration effect in a single step, and with the availability of a wider range of more specific adsorption agents they are being used increasingly. For example, their exploration is usually one of the first steps in re-searching recovery methods for any new antibiot-ic.

Ion exchange resins

Ion exchange resins are polymers carrying firmly attached ionizable groups, which may be anions or cations according to choice, and which will be in the ionized or non-ionized forms according to the environment. Available types are listed in Table 6.5; the solid ion exchangers are used either by batchwise addition, followed by removing the resin by decantation, or else by column proce-dures, Chromatographic separations involving such ion exchange columns are dealt with below, Section 6.6.2.

Liquid ion exchangers operate through simi-lar principles, but with ionizable substances which dissolve only in a non-aqueous solvent carrier; the separation is then by liquid-liquid extraction. The desired substance, in either case, is recovered from the ion exchanger by ion displacement, and the ion exchanger is then regenerated.

In suitable cases, antibiotics may be recov-ered from whole broth, as an alternative to clari-fied broth, by the use of ion exchange resins in the batch mode.

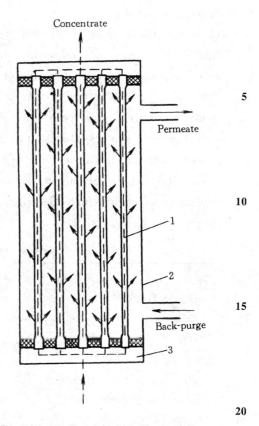

Fig. 6.7 Schematic drawing of a hollow-fibre ultrafiltration module (Romicon).
1, hollow fibre; 2, housing;
3, mounting of fibres

Table 6.5 Chemical nature of solid and liquid ion exchangers

Ion exchanger	Matrix	Functional Group
Solid exchange resin	Styrene-divinyl-benzene	Carboxyl
	Acrylate	Sulphonic acid
	Methacrylate	Primary, secondary and
	Polyamine	tertiary amines
	Cellulose	Quaternary amines
	Dextran	
Liquid ion exchange compounds	Solvent is used as carrier for functional group	Primary, secondary and tertiary amines
		Phosphoric acid-monoester
		Phosphoric acid-diester

Adsorption resins

These are resins which, in effect, provide a solid phase with similar properties to an immiscible liquid solvent, and so may be used in place of extraction procedures. Today a wide range of such resins is available, and their important properties are summarized in Table 6.6. The resins are porous polymeric matrices whose functional groups, if any, modify the overall polarity of the matrix, without ionization. Most compounds are adsorbed in their non-dissociated state, usually from aqueous solutions; they are recovered by extraction into organic solvent or by changing the pH or ionic strength of the aqueous phase. The porosity of the adsorption resins is important, because this determines the available surface on which adsorption can occur, and thus the total capacity of the resin for the adsorbed substance.

Table 6.6 Properties of adsorption resins

physical properties
surface 20～800 $m^2\ g^{-1}$
volume of pores 0.5～1.2ml g^{-1}
average pore size 5～130nm
Chemical nature
apolar: styrene-divinyl benzene
semipolar: acrylic ester
polar: sulfoxide. amide. N-O-groups

6.6 Purification and resolution of mixtures

In a properly conceived process sequence. product recovery and concentration will already have been accompanied by some substantial degree of purification. However, the need for further steps to purify the product will usually remain, particularly when the desired product is accompanied by essentially similar cometabolites, which will usually accompany it through the earlier stages of recovery. Thus the situation to be faced in purification may or may not call for a high degree of resolution. The two methods most generally applied are crystallization and various kinds of chromatographic procedure; crystallization is more readily scaled up, but chromatographic methods lend themselves to a better resolution of mixtures.

6.6.1 Crystallization

Crystallization is mainly used for the purification of low molecular weight compounds, such as antibiotics. For example, penicillin G is usually extracted from the fermentation broth with butyl acetate and crystallized by the addition of potassium acetate in ethanolic solution. A similar sequence for the isolation and purification of actinomycin is set out in Fig. 6.8. The crystallization is from a concentrated solution in ethyl acetate at 50℃, by adding light petroleum until the solution becomes turbid; the solution is

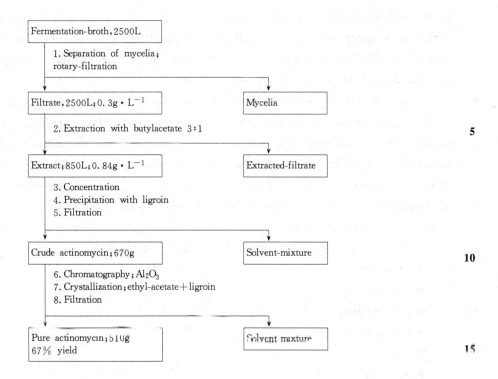

Fig. 6. 8   Isolation and purification of Actinomycin

heated to 65℃ and then cooled.

On a much larger scale, crystallization is the final stage in the purification of such products as citric acid and sodium glutamate, etc.

6. 6. 2   Chromatographic methods

Chromatographic methods are used for low molecular weight compounds where resolution of mixtures is needful(e. g. homologous antibiotics)and for macromolecules, particularly enzymes, where accompanying products are of rather similar nature. The necessary equipment is an arrangement of columns, packed with the carrier material which is usually particulate, reservoirs and pumping systems for the eluting liquids, and a means of selectively collecting specific eluate fractions.

According to the specific separation problem, the column proportions may vary, from relatively tall narrow columns to short wide ones; an example is pharmacia segment column, where the construction is in stainless steel. For optimal resolution, column particles with an even size distribution are used; packing the column is usually effected by mixing the adsorbent with the solvent system in a separate tank, degassing under reduced pressure if necessary, and transferring to the column as a thick slurry. Some materials, especially those used in molecular-sieve chromatography, change their volume when equilibrated with mixtures of buffer and organic solvents, or with buffer solutions of varied ionic strength(salt gradient elution), and must then be fixed into the column by adjustable end-plates. Columns may be run with upwards or downwards flow, usually with a flow meter for the pumped liquid and an entry pressure control device. Installation of a sterile filter at each end of the column, to eliminate bacterial contamination and possible destruction of products, may be desirable.

5   It is normally necessary to monitor what is being eluted from the column at every stage, e. g. by following the ultraviolet absorption of the eluate at 254nm or 280nm for nucleic acids or proteins respectively; buffer gradients can be monitored by measurements of conductivity, or in extreme cases a by-pass leading to an autoanalyser can be fitted. To isolate the separated products some form of fraction collector is needed, and

10 for largescale separations using organic solvents this must be a flame-proof installation in an explosion-proof room.

    Different chromatographic procedures can be distinguished, as follows:
- adsorption
- ion exchange

15   • gel filtration
- hydrophobic
- affinity
- covalent
- partition

20 Particular features of these are described below.

Adsorption chromatography separates products according to their different affinities for the surface of a solid matrix, either an inorganic carrier such as silica gel, alumina or hydroxyapatite, or an organic polymer.

Ion exchange chromatography uses resins of the kind already described (see Section

25 6. 5. 3 and Table 6. 5), or insoluble or cross-linked polysaccharides (cellulose, sepharose) to which ionized functional groups have been attached. It can give high resolution for macromolecules; an example of the resolution of a complex mixture of proteins is given in Fig. 6. 9. This shows the fractionation of human plasma proteins, on a production scale, by a combination of ion exchange chromatography, Steps 4 and 6, with gel filtra-

30 tion, Steps 2 and 9.

Gel filtration uses a 'molecular sieve', that is, a neutral cross-linked carrier with a definite pore size for molecular fractionation. Molecules larger than the largest pores cannot enter the matrix and pass directly through the column; smaller molecules enter the carrier and are retained; diffusion into the pores is then a function of the molecular size, so

35 that the retained molecules are eluted in order of decreasing size.

    Corresponding to the range of molecular weights, from a few hundred to a million or more, a wide range of carriers with controlled pore sizes is called for; they are generally produced from linear polymers (dextrans, agarose) subjected to varied degrees of crosslinking. These are generally used in aqueous systems, and gel filtration can also be used

40 for desalting of peptide or protein solutions. Molecular sieves into which relatively

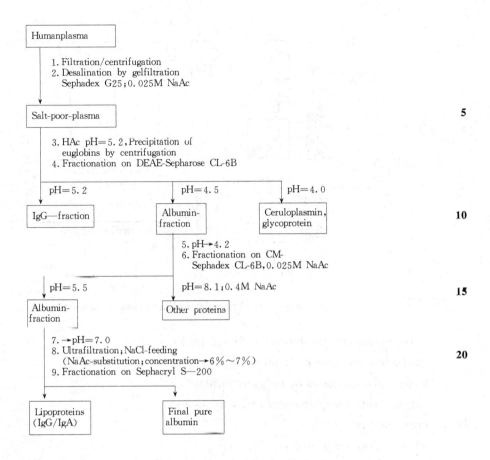

Fig. 6. 9　Human plasma fractionation by ion exchange and molecular sieve chromatography

hydrophobic groups have also been introduced can be used in organic solvents to sepa-　**25**
rate lipophilic substances in the same manner.

Hydrophobic carriers. Molecules with different hydrophobicity can be separated on a carrier containing hydrophobic groups. Thus many enzymes and other proteins have hydrophobic regions, where there is an accumulation of neutral aminoacids (e. g. valine,
phenylalanine), and will interact to varying degress with a carrier on to which alkyl　**30**
residues of varying lengths have been attached.

Affinity chromatography uses more specific interactions to obtain separations; a specific
structure is attached to a solid support carrier and interacts specifically with the component to be isolated. The principle is shown in Fig. 6. 10. The specific effector, such as an
enzyme inhibitor (I) is immobilized on a water-insoluble carrier (C) which is packed into　**35**
a column. A complex mixture of different enzymes (E_1, E_2, E_3, E_4 ...) in a neutral buffer
solution is introduced, and while the enzyme E_1 is complexed by the inhibitor I, all the remaining enzymes pass through the column. Using a buffer solution at a different pH the
enzyme E_1 can now be selectively eluted from the column. Typical specific effectors, and
the complementary molecules that can be separated, include:　**40**

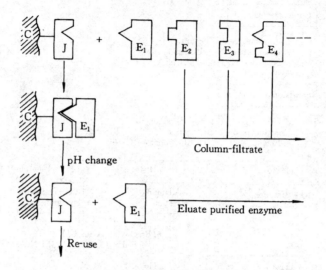

Fig. 6.10   Principle of affinity chromatography

enzymes/enzyme inhibitors (or vice versa)

antibodies/antigens or haptens⑦ (or vice versa)

lectins/glycoproteins or polysaccharides

nucleic acids/complementary base sequences

10   hormones/receptors

vitamins/carrier proteins

etc.

This type of separation, therefore, depends upon the same high specific interactions that mediate biological processes. For example, dehydrogenase enzymes can be separated by

15   virtue of their specific coenzyme interactions using a sepharose matrix carrying bound NAD^+. Antigen/antibody reactions can be used; for example human leucocyte interferon is recovered in high yield and in highly purified form after chromatography on sepharose carrying an immobilized monoclonal antibody. Obviously such specific immoblized effectors can be very costly, and have to be used for many cycles.

20   To prepare the specific immobilizate, a carrier such as agarose gel in head form is activated by reaction with, for example, cyanogen bromide; it can then be coupled directly when small molecules, such as coenzymes, are to be bound, or through a bifunctional 'spacer' molecule when a larger effector molecule is to be attached.

Group-specific affinity chromatography uses somewhat less specific 'chemical' interac-

25   tions in a similar way; for example polymers carrying dihydroxyboryl groups can be used to separate both glycoproteins and nucleotides because of the reversible complex formation between boric acids and 1,2-diols⑧.

Covalent chromatography is a minor variant using reversible covalent bond formation between an immobilized functional group and the material being purified; in particular, thiolated polymers can be used to separate SH-containing proteins because of reversible disulphide formation[9].

6.7 Drying

Drying of bioproducts is in many cases the eventual method by which the products are brought to a stable form suitable for handling and storage; the heat sensitivity of most biological products means that the only methods which can be used are ones leading to water removal with minimal temperature rise. In some cases, the thermostability of products such as enzymes or pharmaceutical preparations is improved by the addition of sugars or other inert stabilizers.

To remove water as vapour, heat energy must be transferred and strictly controlled conditions are required to ensure that the temperature rise, which results from the balance between the rate of heat input and the latent heat equivalent of the evaporation rate, is within the tolerable limit. The heat transfer may be effected by contact (conduction). convection. or radiation, or by combinations of these; Table 6.7 shows examples

Table 6.7 Methods for drying of bioproducts

	Convection dryer	Contact dryer	Freeze dryer (radiation)
Addition of energy	gas current	heated surface	heated surface
			radiant heat
Removal of water	convection by heated gas current		
		drain by pumping	sublimation
Mode of operation		batchwise	batchwise
	continuous	continuous	continuous
Status of drying material	resting layer		resting layer
	pneumatic movement	mechanical movement	mechanical movement
Apparatus	chamber dryer		
	shelf dryer	drum dryer	
	spray dryer	tumble dryer	
	belt dryer	film dryer	
	fluidized bed dryer		chamber freeze dryer
	pneumatic-conveyor dryer		belt freeze dryer
			plate freeze dryer
			tunnel freeze dryer

and operating conditions for the three most important drying methods. For fuller information the reader should refer to standard books; here we describe the most important techniques in outline.

Vacuum drying is applied in batch mode in chamber dryers, or continuously, as in rotating drum vacuum driers. Heat transfer occurs mainly by contact with heated surfaces, and changes in the characteristics of the liquid phase as it becomes more concentrated must be taken into account.

Spray drying provides the most important example of a convective method. in which heat transfer, movement of product, and vapour removal are all effected by a gas current. Large quantities can be dealt with in continuous operation. The liquor to be dried is applied as a solution or slurry and is atomized by a nozzle or a rotating disc. A current of hot gas(150~250℃) causes such rapid evaporation that the temperature of the particles remains very low. Spray drying can be used for drying of enzymes or antibiotics, and when the presence of other materials is not deleterious it can be used for the drying of whole fermenter broth, e. g. for detergent-grade enzymes or feed-grade antibiotics. The method is also widely used in food industries.

Freeze drying is the most gentle drying method because water is sublimed from a frozen mass. For the sublimation of water vapour approximately 680kcal per kg water have to be transferred to the sublimation surface by conduction from heated plates and by radiation on to the surface; to promote rapid sublimation, a very low pressure is maintained and the vapour must be removed by low-temperature condensation. The solid temperature is regulated through control of the pressure in the drying chamber, and measurement of the electrical conductivity of the material being dried provides a very sensitive check for the presence of any liquid water in the mass.

Many pharmaceutical products are freeze-dried, e. g. viruses, vaccines, plasma fractions, hormones and enzyme preparations, as well as labile and costly ingredients in diagnostics; at the same time, very large-scale applications of the technology are important in food industries.

Words and Expressions

page line

170　　1　downstream processing　['daun s'tri:m 'prɔsesiŋ]　n.下游加工(技术)

　　　12　constrain　[kən'strein]　vt.限制　restrain

　　　13　contain　[kən'tein]　vt.限制,保持在某一范围内　to hold or keep within certain limits; confine, restrain

　　　18　ingenuity　[ˌindʒi'nju:iti]　n.创造性

　　　19　repertoire　['repətwɑ:r]　n.全部技能　all skills; the complete list or supply of skills, devices, or ingredients used in a particular field, occupation or practice

　　　26　continuum　[kən'tinjuəm]　n.连续均匀系统　a continuous extent, no part of which can be distinguished from neighbouring parts

page　line

185　　7　　euglobin　[juːˈglɔbin]　n. 优珠蛋白

　　　10　　IgG (immunoglobulin G)　n. 免疫球蛋白 G

　　　　　　albumin　[ˈælbjumin]　n. 白蛋白,清蛋白

　　　　　　ceruloplasmin　[siˌruːləuˈplæzmin]　n. 血浆铜蓝蛋白

　　　11　　glycoprotein　[ˌglaikəuˈprəutiːn]　n. 糖蛋白

　　　22　　lipoprotein　[ˌlipəˈprəutiːn]　n. 脂蛋白

　　　27　　hydrophobicity　[ˌhaidrəufəuˈbisiti]　n. 疏水性

　　　29　　valine　[ˈvæliːn]　n. 缬氨酸

　　　30　　phenylalanine　[ˌfeniˈlæləniːn]　n. 苯丙氨酸

　　　32　　affinity chromatography　n. 亲和层析

186　　7　　hapten　[ˈhæpten]　n. 半抗原

　　　8　　lectin　[ˈlektin]　n. 外源凝集素

　　　10　　receptor　[riˈseptə]　n. 受体

　　　16　　leucocyte　[ˈljuːkəsait]　n. 白细胞

　　　21　　cyanogen bromide　[saiˈænədʒin ˈbrəumaid]　n. 溴化氰 CNBr

　　　25　　boryl　n. 硼基

　　　29　　thiolate　v. 硫醇化

187　　25　　pneumatic　[njuːˈmætik]　a. 气体的

　　　28　　shelf dryer　n. 柜式干燥机

　　　29　　tumble dryer　n. 滚筒式干燥机

　　　34　　pneumatic conveyor dryer　n. 气流干燥机

　　　37　　tunnel freeze dryer　n. 隧道式冷冻干燥机

188　　11　　atomize　[ˈætəmaiz]　vt. 雾化

Notes

① Bearing in mind such restrictions, much ingenuity is called for…句中包含一分词短语。使用分词短语时，一定要留心其逻辑上的主语，应该是主句中的主语。但也有例外，如：

When lifting or carrying heavy weights, it is important to keep the arms close to the body.

这种句子虽然主语是 it，但为无人称，一般泛指未表示出来的某人，这种结构可扩展至无人称被动态和 there is/are 结构，如：

When working with the heavy machinery, there is always a certain amount of risk present. (i. e. for the worker)

Before using dangerous chemicals, certain precautions must be taken (i. e. by the user).

这一句的结构与所引的书上的句子相同。

　上述分词短语的逻辑主语与主句的主语不一致的情况称为垂悬分词，为垂悬修饰语 (dangling modifier) 的一种。其他垂悬修饰语尚有下列三种，请读者注意：

a. 垂悬动名词（在介词短语中）

     误　With training, he will have a talking bird.

     正　With training, his bird will learn to talk.

b. 垂悬不定式

     误　To promote rapid sublimation, low pressure is the first requirement.

     正　To promote rapid sublimation, low pressure should be maintained.

c. 垂悬简化从句（参见 p.63，Ch.2，Pattern 1）

     误　When full of gas, he found the car rode uncomfortably.

     正　When it was full of gas, he found the car rode uncomfortably.

② surface filtration 表面过滤，即大于介质孔径的颗粒直接被截留在表面。depth filtration 深层过滤，过滤介质有相当的厚度，过滤机理较复杂：大颗粒在表面被截留，而较细颗粒则在下面几层被截留。当欲过滤的粒子大小不均一时，采用深层过滤是有利的；如果是均匀的，则采用表面过滤也同样有效。

③ the substance is to be extracted into a given volume of solvent⋯

（要将该物质萃取到一定体积的溶剂中）。

这是 be＋inf. 的一种用法，表示想要做的事，此外尚可表示按计划要做的事或应当、必须、能够做的事。如：

    The meeting is to be held next Monday.（按计划要做的事）

    if the available repertoire of scientific methods is to be used to best effect. (170/19～20)（要求要做之事）.

    At the end of a fermentation, the first step in many cases is to separate the solids from the liquid continuum(170/24～26)（应当要做之事）.

④ Simple calculation confirms that where⋯back-extraction will increase any selectivity, 本句可译为：由简单的计算可知，当以一定体积的溶剂萃取某一物质时，如将溶剂分成若干等分，分数次相继进行，则萃取的效率较高；而当欲差别地萃取一种组分，而非其他组分时，则反萃取必能提高选择性。

⑤ ⋯to minimize losses due to thermal lability（减少由于热不稳定性而引起的损失）这里 due to 短语作为形容词修饰名词 losses。due to 短语也可以作为联系动词的补语，如：

    His hesitancy was due to fear.

但 due to 短语不能用作状语（虽然有时也有人用，但最好不用），如：

    He hesitated due to fear.

此时应把 due to 改为 owing to 或 because of.

⑥ where necessary 是 where it is necessary 关系从句的省略形式（参见 p.63，Ch.2，pattern 1），以 when, if, while, once, although/though 等连词＋形容词或短语构成，在科技文献中很常见。如：

    I shall buy a new machine, if available.　如果有货的话，我想买一架新机器。

    When not in use, the machine must be turned off.　不用时，应将机器关闭。

⑦ 半抗原是一种低相对分子质量物质，能和一种抗体起反应，但不能刺激抗体产生，除非和一种载体蛋白质相结合。

⑧ 二羟硼基（dihydroxyboryl）与糖蛋白中糖基或核苷酸中核糖环的邻接二羟基发生如下反应。

$$B \diagup^{OH}_{OH} + \begin{matrix} HO \\ HO \end{matrix} + H_2O \rightleftharpoons \stackrel{\ominus}{B} \begin{matrix} O \\ O \end{matrix} \diagdown_{OH} + H^+$$

1,2-cis-diol

⑨ 共价层析法最常用的是利用硫醇和二硫化合物间的交换反应：

蛋白质吸附在载体上：

$$—S—S—\langle O \rangle_N + P—SH \rightarrow —S—S—P + \langle \rangle_{N—H} S$$

蛋白质
（含巯基）

以低相对分子质量的巯基化合物（如二硫苏糖醇）洗脱

$$—S—S—P + RSH(过量) \rightarrow —SH + P—SH + R—S—S—R$$

Comprehension

1. Why did the author say that much ingenuity is required for using the available scientific methods to best effect? (p. 170)

2. What are the advantages and disadvantages of rotary drum vacuum filter precoated with a filter aid? (p. 172)

3. What parameter is usually used in comparing performance between different kinds of centrifuges? (p. 173)

4. Enumerate the parameters which affect flocculation. (p. 175)

5. Why it is much more difficult to disintegrate cells of microorganisms compared with those of plants and animals? (p. 175)

6. What kinds of substances does the extraction method usually used for? (p. 177)

7. What are the mechanisms underlying ultrafiltration and reverse osmasis? (p. 179)

8. What is the differences between ion-exchange resin and adsorption resin? (p. 181~182)

9. Discuss the principles of gel filtration chromatography. (p. 184)

10. What kinds of high specific interactions are frequently used in affinity chromatography? (p. 186)

11. Compare spray drying vs. freeze drying with respect to their field of application. (p. 188)

Vocabulary

Give another word or phrase to replace these words or phrases as they are used in the text：

removed(170/6);in any case(170/11);assembly(172/6);in question(177/3); throughput(179/9);flux rate(179/28);mode(181/26);in effect(182/2); diagnostics(188/26).

Word usage

1. Write sentences to bring out the difference between the following pairs of words： clean(173/22),clear(178/10);respectively(184/7),separately.

2. Make sentences with the following words or phrases:

in terms of (175/25);or else (181/12);conceive(182/22);

lend oneself to (182/29);mediate (186/14);by virtue of (186/14).

Patterns

such···that;so···that;so···as to;such···as to;so that.

These are common structures for expressing result. (see p. 102,Ch. 3,pattern 3)

Examples

A current of hot gas causes <u>such</u> rapid evaporation <u>that</u> the temperature of the particles remains very low. (188/11~13)

The bisulphite forms a complex with acetaldehyde,<u>so that</u> ethanol can no longer be produced,···(37/31~32)

The increase in population is <u>so</u> rapid <u>as to</u> cause a food shortage.

There are <u>such</u> rapid increases in population <u>as to</u> cause a food shortage.

Exercises

Complete these statements with the appropriate words:

1. Membrane filtration is ··· versatile ··· it can be used for both the enrichment and the separation of different molecules or particles.

2. Affinity chromatography uses ··· specific interaction ··· make it being increasingly exploited both in laboratory and in industry.

3. Most nutrients are taken up by specific transport mechanisms, ··· they may be concentrated within the cell from dilute solutions outside.

Sentence analysis and translation

First analyse the following sentences as in Ch. 1,Note ① and then translate into chinese:

1. First paragraph on page 178(line 10 to line 14).

2. Last paragraph on page 179(line 18 to line 27).

3. Fourth paragraph on page 188(line 17 to line 24).

Writing

A letter for job application is usually accompanied by a résumé. The résumé is an outline of applicant's educational and professional background,and of his interests. Here is a sample résumé.

RÉSUMÉ

name: PANG Zhengyu	sex: Male
date of birth: Nov. 25,1971	place of birth: Jiangsu,P. R. China
tel: 86-21-64700892 ext:370	fax: 86-21-64700244
address: 500 Caobao Rd. Shanghai,200233,PRC	

EDUCATION:

Sep. 1993··· July,1996   East China University of Science and Technology
Department of Biochemical Engineering

	Research area Downstream Processing Master of Engineering
Sep. 1989··· July,1993	Nanjing University of Chemical Technology Department of Chemical Engineering Bachelor of Science

PROFESSIONAL EXPERIENCE:

July,1996···Present	Shanghai Research Center of Biotechnology, Chinese Academy of Sciences Junior Researcher Research Field: 　1. Genetic engineering 　2. Downstream processing 　3. Bioinformatics(associated with EMBL)
Sep,1994··· July,1995	East China University of Science and Technology Department of Biochemical Engineering Teaching Assistant
Sep. ,1993··· July,1994	East China University of Science and Technology Department of Mathematics Teaching Assistant

PUBLICATIONS:

1. Affinity Chromatography Purification of Urokinase with a Polystyrene-based Medium,*J. of East China University of Science and Technology.* V22,417～422,1996
2. Purification of Urokinase from Human Urine Using HD-2 Weakly Acidic Resin,*Chinese Pharmaceutical Industry*

REFERENCES:

1. WU Xingyan,Prof. ,East China University of Science and Technology,Shanghai,200237. P. R. China
2. YANG Shengli. Prof and Chairman of Advisor Committee of Biotechnology,Chinese Academy of Sciences. Shanghai Research Center of Biotechnology,Shanghai,200233,P. R. China
3. CAI Yudong,Prof,EMBL. Meyerhofstr. 1,69012 Heidelberg,Germany

Write a résumé of your own as an enclosure to the letter for job application,assuming you will graduate soon.

Chapter 7　Instrumentation

7.1　Introduction

This chapter deals with instruments used in measurement and control of fermentation processes. It will be seen that they are by no means exclusive to fermentation technology, and most find widespread application in biotechnology and related technologies. In fact the majority of the analytical instruments used in biotechnology are not biotechnological developments, and until quite recently, biotechnologists usually employed instruments which were developed for use in the chemical industry. Though excellent instruments in their own right, they were not designed for the higher degree of complexity of biological reactions and with the onset of computer control, this became very obvious.

The development of fully automated computer controlled fermentation processes depends upon the availability of sensors producing meaningful sginals which can be translated into control action. Considerable effort is now being devoted to the development of more suitable instruments which can provide more detailed information about biological processes, needed for continued improvements in process yields and productivity. Unfortunately, few ideas or developments have yet been realized on a commercial scale, but it is only a matter of time before this will change. However, this chapter concentrates on current instruments, their application (on all scales) and their present limitations.

Computer control is the current by-word in fermentation technology and will soon reach the point where you dare not admit that your fermenters are not coupled to a computer; unfortunately, amidst the improvements this brings, we are beginning to see cases of the old dogma 'instruments prevent creative thinking'. Computer control requires on-line instruments (or at least off-line instruments where the time lag between sampling and analysis is short) and this is reflected in this chapter.

7.2　Terminology

Given our total dependence on the instrumentation for understanding biotechnological processes, it is important that we understand the instruments we use, otherwise we can easily make incorrect assumptions about their suitability or performance[①]. Some common characteristics are explained below.

Response time is normally defined as the time required for the output signal to change from the initial value to 90% of the final value following a step change. As a rule of thumb instruments used in biological systems should have a response time less than 10% (preferably much less) of the system doubling time. Thus, in a typical fermentation, with doubling time around 3h, instruments with response time above 18 min are not suited to on-line control. Most instruments have much lower response times and it is often the time taken for other operations associated with the sampling (e. g. pumping fluid through tubing, sample preparation, etc.) which produces an excessive lag between the measurement and the control action.

Sensitivity is a measure of the change in output of an instrument resulting from a change in input. Generally, instruments with high sensitivity are preferred, making it possible to measure small input changes. However other instrument parameters such as linearity (of output to input), accuracy and range should be taken into consideration when choosing an instrument.

Linearity between input and output is the simplest and most desired relationship between the two. The greatest simplification is in calibrating (or recalibrating the instruments) with a minimum number of calibration points required.

Accuracy indicates an uncertainty about the output signal. It is usually expressed as a percentage of the instrument range. The higher the accuracy, the smaller is the uncertainty about the output signal as an indicator of the true value of the input signal.

Drift is the variation in the output independent of input. Normally this is seen as an output signal which falls with time. This is an inherent property of the instrument and can only be overcome by recalibration at regular intervals. Given the high demand for asepsis over long runs, drift may be a severe problem with instruments applied to fermentation processes[1].

Resolution is the smallest measurable value of changes in the input and is normally expressed as a percentage of full scale deflection.

Offset (error, static error or residual error) is a deviation in the output from the true value of the input when the latter is held constant.

Reproducibility should never be assumed and instruments should be recalibrated whenever possible, particularly instruments involved with O_2 and CO_2 measurements. Often the absolute value of the measured variable is not as important as its relation to the input value. Constant recalibration will, therefore, compensate for changing instrument characteristics.

7. 3 Process control

There are three possible aims for process control:
    (1) maintain a variable constant through time
    (2) force a variable to follow a prescribed path through time
    (3) optimize some function of the system variables.

The first is achieved by regulation, the second by servomechanisms and the third by optimal controllers. All these items of hardware are generally termed automatic controllers.

In a process control system, we have four classes of variables:

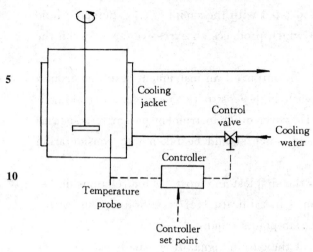

5

10

Cooling
jacket

Control
valve

Cooling
water

Controller

Temperature
probe

Controller
set point

15

Fig. 7. 1 A scheme for controlling bioreactor temperature illustrating how the four types of process control variables are linked . In this case the temperature of the reactor content is the con - trolled variable . the controller set point is the ref -

20

erence variable and the flow of cooling water is the manipulated variable with the temperature of the cooling water acting as a disturbance variable

(1) controlled variables

(2) disturbance variables

(3) manipulated variables

(4) reference variables.

The controlled variable is the output variable we want to control and the manipulated variable is the input variable with which we are controlling it. A disturbance variable is an input variable affecting the controlled variable through variation in other inputs than the manipulated variable and the reference variable is the desired value of the controlled variable. An illustration of the way in which these four classes of variables are linked is given in Fig. 7. 1.

The three control structures commonly referred to, open loop, feed forward and feedback, are shown in Fig. 7. 2. Open loop control can only be used if disturbances are absent and process

25

conditions never change. (Feed forward control can be used as long as disturbances can be measured and a process model is available.) Manual control systems are normally described as feed forward. Feedback(or closed loop)control can accommodate any number of disturbances and no knowledge of the process is (in principle)necessary.

30

Typically, temperature control systems will be based on feedback control. A typical feed forward system is a continuous fermenter in which feed is pumped into and broth taken out of the fermenter continuously.[2] Here, the dilution rate

35

will be the controlled and the feed flow rate the manipulated variable.

The speed at which a system corrects a transient input or adjusts to a new set point is decided by its dynamic response. This may be adjusted for

40

cyclic or damped response as illustrated in Fig. 7. 3 by selecting suitable control strategies.

The simplest type of control is the on-off or two position action which is used extensively in

D
R

M

C

Open loop

D
R

M

C

Feed forward

D
R
[2]
+
−

M

C

Feedback

Fig. 7. 2 Three common control structures

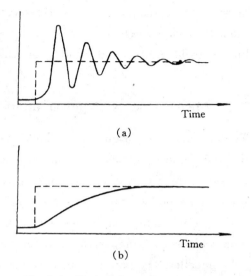

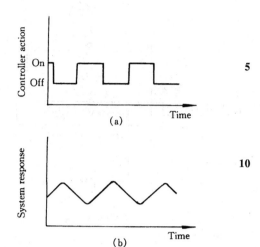

Fig. 7. 3 Typical dynamic responses of a system to a set point change. (a)Cyclic response; (b)damped response; ···input—system response

Fig. 7. 4 Relationship between (a)controller action and (b)system response

control of fermentation processes. The controlled variable will cycle between the two set points but the dynamic response of fermenter broths are sufficiently poor to dampen the effect of the control action, thus avoiding overshooting. A typical relationship between controller output and response is illustrated in Fig. 7. 4.

Process control technology is well advanced and typical fermentation processes will only need relatively simple controllers. The problems are encountered in measurements and actuation of control action demanded by the controller and this chapter has sought to highlight the present state of the technology.

7. 4 Air flow monitoring

In aerobic fermentations, air is passed through the fermenter to provide oxygen and also to remove carbon dioxide which would otherwise affect metabolic activity. In tower and air-lift bioreactors, the air also promotes bulk mixing. Normally, the air flow rate lies in the range 0. 5～1. 5 vvm (volumes of air per reactor volume per minute). Higher flow rates should be avoided as this will lead to impractically high superficial gas velocities $(m \cdot s^{-1})$ in large reactors when scaling-up is attempted.

The air flow is normally monitored by manually controlled variable area flowmeters (rotameters) (usually calibrated for flow at NTP conditions.) If the line pressure changes, a control valve should be used to keep the flow rate constant. The position of the rotameter float can be detected by a proximity sensor, but if a signal is required for process control purposes, it is more common to replace the flow meter with a thermal mass flow meter, as illustrated in Fig. 7. 5. Here two probes read the temperature difference between inlet and outlet gas as it passes through a heated tube. Incorporating the probes in a Wheatstone bridge allows the temperature difference to be translated into an

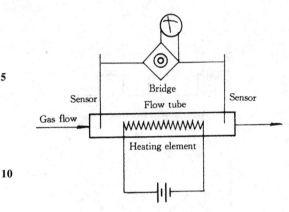

Fig. 7. 5   Thermal mass flow meter

air flow rate. Such flow meters are usually more accurate than rotameters. However, their flow rate range is more restricted, limited to laboratory and small pilot-scale operation.

7.5　Measurements of power input

The unit of work (or quantity of heat) has the unit joule (J). Power is the rate of work, or rate of flow of energy, and is measured in watts (W) where $W = J \cdot s^{-1}$. To assess fermentation processes in stirred tank reactors, it is important to determine how much energy is imparted to the liquid by the impeller. The power input per unit of fermenter volume has often been used as a scale-up parameter and the convention of 1 HP/100 gal is often quoted. In SI units, this is equal to $1.64 kW \cdot m^{-3}$.

　　Total power uptake can be determined by employing a wattmeter measuring the rate of power consumption by the drive motor (also a convenient way of measuring money spent, which on large-scale fermenters can be of the order of 10% of the operating cost!). For industrial-scale vessels, this will also give the power input to the liquid (shaft power). On pilot and laboratory-scale fermenters, however, friction losses in stirrer glands and motor inefficiency cannot be neglected and other methods must be employed. Dynamometers and strain gauges[3] are used in pilot plants; the latter can be incorporated in the stirrer shaft providing direct measurements of the shaft power input. A simple dynamometer for small fermenters can be made by mounting the motor in two load bearings on the motor shaft positioned vertically above the fermenter. The power input is determined by the torque required to prevent the motor from turning during operation.

　　Another scale-up criteria is constant tip speed, being defined as ND where N is the speed of rotation of the impeller and D is the impeller diameter. It is quite common for

Table 7. 1　Scale-down on constant impeller tip speed in a stirred tank reactor.
Data based on impeller speed of 100 r. p. m. in a 100 m³ fermenter

Fermenter volume (m³)	$\dfrac{\text{Liquid height}}{\text{Vessel diameter}}$	$\dfrac{\text{Impeller diameter}}{\text{Vessel diameter}}$	Impeller speed (r. p. m.)
0.001	1	1/3	2775
0.01	1	1/3	1191
0.1	1.5	1/3	633
1	2	1/4	431
10	2	1/4	200
100	2.5	1/4	100

large reactors to have fixed speed motors, typically 100 r. p. m. in 100 m^3 vessels. The impeller speeds in smaller reactors can be determined using tip speed as a scaling-down factor, as shown in Table 7.1. In this case, the impeller diameter and the aspect ratio (liquid height to diameter) reflect typical units. The table indicates that small fermenters must be operated at excessive impeller speeds. Note that power per unit volume is not kept **5** constant when tip speed is used as a scale-up parameter.

7. 6　Temperature measurements

Most microorganisms have a very narrow temperature range for optimal biological activity. Heat energy is readily transported into cells and temperature control is, therefore, an **10** important process parameter. Moreover, temperature affects the performance of a range of instruments not usually associated with temperature control and it is important that these are fitted with manual or, preferably, automatic temperature compensation circuitry.

　　The temperature probes which have found widespread application are resistance thermometers and thermistors. **15**

7. 6. 1　Resistance thermometers

These are based on the principle that metal resistance increases with temperature. They are constructed as a length of wire, often wound in a coil to reduce size. When current is passed through the coil, a voltage change is produced which can be related to the temper- **20** ature. The thermometer itself will have a response time of the order of 1 s, but normally it is inserted in a sheath to protect it from the environment, which may increase the response time by up to 5~10 s[④].

　　Resistance thermometers have a considerable range (typically −100 to 650℃ for a platinum thermometer). The relationship between temperature and thermometer resis- **25** tance is not linear over the whole range, but can safely be assumed for the limited range required for biotechnological processes. In a few cases, particularly in fermentation systems with a high solids content and little mixing, it has been found that the current passing through the thermometer may heat the probe and its environment, thus producing erroneous readings. **30**

7. 6. 2　Thermistors

These are semiconductors exhibiting increasing conductivity with temperature. They have response times of the order of 1 s when the thermal contact is good. Encapsulating the thermistor (usually in teflon or stainless steel) may increase this to 10 s. **35**

　　Thermistors are very sensitive, but the output is highly non-linear. The considerable response to small changes in temperature makes thermistors well suited to application over a limited temperature range (as in fermentation technology), over which the response to temperature changes may be assumed to be linear. Thermistors are also relatively inexpensive. **40**

Temperature control based on temperature sensor outputs, is normally achieved by using steam or electric energy for heating and water for cooling. The technology is highly developed, giving control to $\pm 0.1℃$ for laboratory-scale and $\pm 0.5℃$ for large-scale. The main problem in temperature control is encountered in large fermenters where the surface area designed for heat transfer may not be sufficient to remove the metabolic heat and heat of mixing.

7.7 Rheological measurements

Viscosity, the resistance of a fluid to flow, may be used to indicate the rheological properties of a fluid, and is an important process parameter which is seldom given the attention it merits. The performance of bioreactors can be significantly affected by the flow characteristics of the broth, and it is important to have instruments which can measure rheological properties quickly and reliably.

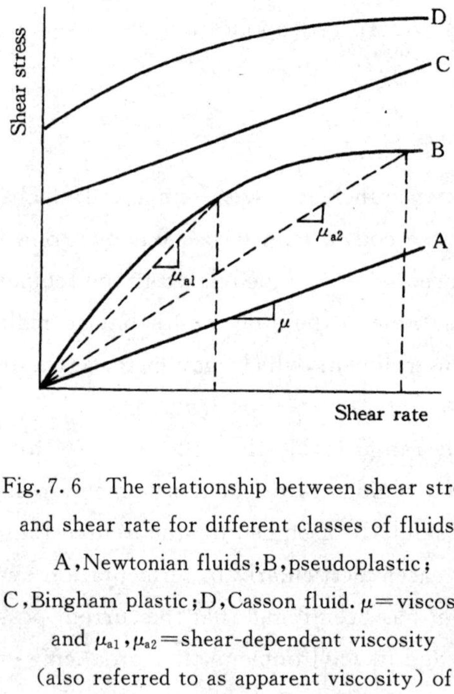

The viscosity of a fluid is determined in a shear stress-shear rate diagram as shown in Fig. 7.6 with a unique curve for different types of fluids. In the case of a Newtonian fluid, the viscosity is equal to the slope of the straight line, and such a fluid has constant rheological properties. This is not the case with the other fluids for which the viscosity changes with shear rate, making it important to state at which shear rate the viscosity is measured. In general, one tries to work at the same shear rate as that near the fermenter impeller, which can be difficult to determine as shear rate will change with distance from the impeller.

Unfortunately, rheological measurements can, with a few exceptions, only be carried out off-line. The most common viscometers are described below and shown in Fig. 7.7 (a)~(d).

Fig. 7.6   The relationship between shear stress and shear rate for different classes of fluids. A, Newtonian fluids; B, pseudoplastic; C, Bingham plastic; D, Casson fluid. μ=viscosity and μ_{a1}, μ_{a2}=shear-dependent viscosity (also referred to as apparent viscosity) of pseudoplastic fluid determined at two different shear rates

7.7.1 Tube viscometers

There are two types of tube viscometers. In a capillary viscometer, the liquid flows under gravity through a tube of known diameter, The time taken for a given volume to pass can be related to viscosity, using the viscosity of pure water as a reference.

In the second type of tube viscometer, the liquid is pumped through a narrow tube under laminar flow conditions; the pressure drop over a fixed length of tube is measured and related to viscosity.

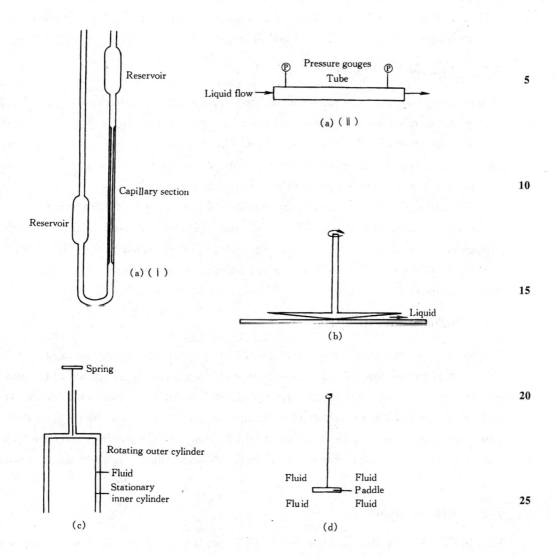

Fig. 7. 7 The most common viscometers. (a)Tube viscometers
(i) and (ii); (b)cone and plate viscometers; (c)concentric
cylinders (cub and bob viscometer); (d)infinite sea viscometer

Tube viscometers are simple and can be used for quick and reliable off-line viscosity determinations of Newtonian fluids. A few reports on on-line applications have been published. In general, however, tube viscometers are not well adapted to fermentation broths. which are often non-Newtonian and will usually contain solids which can block the tube.

7.7.2 Cone and plate viscometers
The fluid is placed between a rotating cone and a stationary plate. Provided the angle between the cone and plate is less than 4° and edge effects can be neglected, the shear rate is uniform throughout the liquid and the shear stress and, hence viscosity, can be evaluated.

This instrument is of a much more complex construction; a high degree of engineering skill is required in making the cone and matching it with the plate. It is not suited to fluids with solids such as mycelium or cell aggregates.

7.7.3 Concentric cylinders (cup and bob)

Concentric cylinders, also termed cup and bob viscometers, are used extensively. The fluid is placed in the annulus between the cylinders and the shearing action is produced by rotating one (normally the inner) while the other is kept stationary. The torque exerted on the second cylinder is related to the viscosity of the fluid. Strict demands on the engineering of these viscometers are essential for reliable readings.

The cup and bob viscometers are excellent for Newtonian fermentation fluids and manufacturers have produced modified versions which can be used on fluids containing filamentous organisms or other high viscosity imparting substances[5]. However, there may be the problems of solids blocking the annulus or wall slip which will lead to inaccurate readings.

7.7.4 Infinite sea viscometers

In these instruments, the torque is measured on an impeller or disc rotating in a large volume of the fluid; the fluid is free flowing and not affected by the walls of its container. Theoretically, these instruments are suitable for all kinds of fluids, and unaffected by suspended solids. However, shear rate changes with distance from the rotating disc and there will be a problem in determining at which shear rate the readings should be taken. Normally an average shear rate can be defined, allowing these relatively simple viscometers to be used.

7.8 Foam control

Foaming can be a serious problem in fermentation. If allowed to form it may block outlet filters, encourage contamination, or reduce yield. Unfortunately, most fermentation media encourage foam formation, and its depression can be achieved mechanically and/or chemically.

The simplest form of mechanical foam break-up for a stirred tank is to fix an additional impeller on the stirrer shaft above the liquid level. A number of manufacturers supply separate mechanical devices including specially designed impellers operating under their own power independent of the agitation system and sophisticated gas-liquid separation devices. They normally give good foam control, but their relatively high power consumption can lead to high operating costs.

Commonly, foam control is achieved by using a simple break-up device aided by chemical foam control, for which a range of antifoam agents are available. Automatic antifoam addition systems incorporate a conductivity probe immersed through the top of the fermenter vessel. The probe can simply be a stainless steel rod, coated with teflon, but

205

exposing the tip. The probe will be activated by foam touching the tip of the probe. A signal will be sent to the control system leading to the addition of antifoam by a pump (small fermenters) or pneumatically (large-scale) . Antifoam will enter the fermenter, break down the foam which will leave the tip of the probe,and the circuit is broken.

It is important to ensure that the correct amount of antifoam is added. Too much antifoam will reduce the gas hold-up,thus affecting the oxygen transfer rate,and may complicate product recovery. As there is always a lag between controller activation and foam breakdown,it is important to incorporate a lag in the control circuit to prevent addition of too much antifoam. It should also be possible to alter the sensitivity of the probe to avoid splashes from the broth surface activating the probe.

Some antifoam 'controllers' rely simply on addition of a fixed amount of antifoam at regular intervals. This can only be used satisfactorily when the necessary experience about a fermentation has been gained. Unfortunately,foaming often occurs in short,irregular bursts and there is little way of predicting these.

There a number of antifoams on the market including natural oils,higher alcohols, silicon oils and n-paraffins. Some antifoams are metabolized by the microorganisms and regular addition to the fermenter is necessary;indeed by careful design of the medium, the antifoam can be used as an additional carbon source,often more efficiently than the main carbon source.

7.9   pH probes

External pH has little direct influence on the internal pH of microbial cells,but the breakdown of substrates,their transport through the cell wall,and the excretion of cell products are all affected by the pH value of the environment. The effect of pH on specific growth rate is well-known and it is clear that pH represents an important process parameter.

pH is a measure of hydrogen ion activity,defined as $pH = -\log a_{H^+}$,and its determination is given by employing the Nernst equation,which is temperature dependent (see Section 7.12.2). Thus,probe output will change with temperature and it is important to have temperature compensation (preferably automatic) in the contoller/indicator circuitry.

Probes which combine a glass electrode with a reference electrode are now used extensively,making external reference probes obsolete. As the demand for sterility is normally strict in biotechnology,steam-sterilizable probes are gaining favour. However,one drawback is that repeated sterilization affects the probe performance (irrespective of manufacturers'claims,though it must be said that progress is being made in this respect). The pH-sensitive glass tip is very brittle (again improvements are made),but the major drawback is that the best probes are unnecessarily expensive. However,new manufacturers are entering the market producing adequate probes compatible with most pH meters , at reasonable prices . There are a number of excellent pH meters / controllers on

206

the market which can be used for control of pH;it is important to be able to adjust the sensitivity and response time of the controller since the addition of acid or alkali to restore the set pH has to take effect over the whole fermenter contents.

5　　The pH probe is referenced to the pH meter ground, but sometimes interference through a different ground may be experienced (indicated by erratic reading indicator off-scale etc.). This can be overcome by employing a common ground for the pH meter and the fermenter itself.

7. 10　Redox probes

It has been suggested that redox potential may be a better indicator of the state of a fer-
10　mentation than either pH or dissolved oxygen. There are a number of steam sterilizable redox probes available and most manufacturers of pH probes will also supply redox probes. One reason for the lack of application of redox probes in the fermentation industry is the difficulty in interpreting results as dissolved oxygen and the presence of oxidizing or reducing compounds will all affect the probe output.

15　## 7. 11　Dissolved oxygen probes

The critical role played by dissolved oxygen (DO) in fermentation processes was discussed in Chapters 4. Thus, the advent of DO probes has offered a significant contribution to our understanding of the performance of bioreactors.

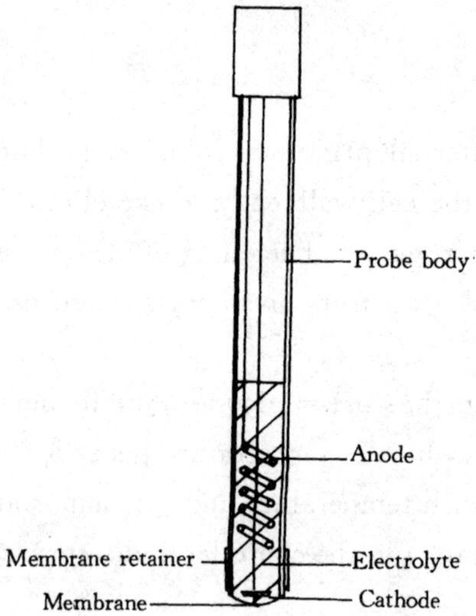

20

DO probes basically consist of a stainless steel or glass sheath containing two electrodes and a suitable electrolyte. To separate the electrodes and electrolyte from the fermentation broth, the probe is covered with a membrane. Oxygen diffuses through the membrane and is reduced at the cathode, which is negatively polarized with respect to the anode. This produces a current which can be translated into oxygen concentration. The DO probe construction is shown in Fig. 7. 8.

25

30

Fig. 7. 8　The dissolved oxygen probe

7. 11. 1　Polarographic DO probes

35　Polarographic probes have an external power source to set up an 0. 6～0. 8V polarization voltage between the two electrodes. The cathode is typically platinum, with Ag/AgCl as a reference anode. The electrode reactions are shown on the next page.

It can be seen that the electrolyte, in this case potassium chloride solution, takes
40　part in the reactions, and must be replenished at regular intervals.

$$Cathode : O_2 + 2H_2O + 2e \longrightarrow H_2O_2 + 2OH^-$$
$$H_2O_2 + 2e \longrightarrow 2OH^-$$
$$Anode : Ag + Cl^- \longrightarrow AgCl + e$$
$$\overline{Overall : 4Ag + O_2 + 2H_2O + 4Cl^- \longrightarrow 4AgCl + 4OH^-}$$

7.11.2　Galvanic DO probes

Galvanic probes do not use an external power supply, relying on the natural polarization potential set up between a noble cathode and a basic anode. The most common materials are silver and lead respectively. In this case, the probe reactions are :

$$Cathode : O_2 + 2H_2O + 4e \longrightarrow 4OH^-$$
$$Anode : Pb \longrightarrow Pb^{2+} + 2e$$
$$\overline{Overall : O_2 + 2Pb + 2H_2O \longrightarrow 2Pb(OH)_2}$$

In galvanic probes, the anode is oxidized and the probe performance depends on the available anode surface area, hence the extensive use of coil-shaped[5] anodes, to maximize the available surface area.

The main difference between polarographic and galvanic probes is price, with the latter being much the cheaper. Polarographic probes may be fractionally faster and may have a longer life, though this depends very much on make of probe and care taken in handling.

Probe responses to step changes in DO level are shown in Fig. 7.9. Response times of 90 s are common and it is doubtful if these probes are sufficiently fast to be used in dynamic k_La measurements or to study

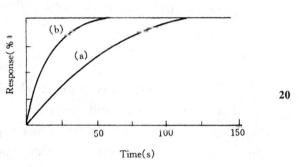

Fig.7.9　Typical dissolved oxygen probe responses to a step change in dissolved oxygen level.
(a)Slow response, and (b) fast response

transients. Reducing the response time to below 30 s, which is possible for a limited number of probes, decreases the significance of the probe characteristics and makes the readings more reliable.

Drift and fouling (microorganism sticking to the probe surface) are the two main problems associated with DO probes. Reproducibility is rarely achieved particularly if a probe is steam sterilized, and repeated calibration is essential.

Electrolytes In polarographic probes, KCl is the most common electrolyte with lead acetate used for the galvanic probes. For both, a number of other solutions have been used (see Table 7.2). The choice of electrolyte may not be critical for probe performance, and it is advisable to experiment with suitable solutions rather than buying expensively from manufacturers.

The loss of solvent through evaporation is a common problem, often leading to premature deterioration of probe performance. It should be remembered that loss of elec-

Table 7.2   Typical electrolytes for DO probes

KCl

KCl+NaHCO$_3$

KCl+KH$_2$PO$_4$+AgCl

KOH

KHCO$_3$

NaHCO$_3$

Acetate buffer

KI

K$_2$CO$_3$+KHCO$_3$

Often chemicals will be added to protect the electrolyte during autoclaving.

trolyte occurs during storage as well as during operation.

Membrane properties are vital for good probe response. Membranes with high O$_2$ diffusivity and low CO$_2$ permeability are preferred. Teflon, polyethylene and polypropylene are the most common membrane materials.

A simple analysis of the behaviour of DO probes indicates that their response is related to the probe constant, k:

$$k = \frac{\pi^2 D}{d^2}$$

where D=oxygen diffusivity in the membrane, and d=membrane thickness.

Fast response probes will have a large value for k, implying a thin membrane and/or high oxygen diffusivity. However, this is a gross simplification of the workings of DO probes; the construction of the electrodes (in particular their relative surface area) will greatly influence probe behaviour.

It should be noted that DO probes do not *measure* dissolved oxygen concentration, but the activity or partial pressure of oxygen. For this reason, DO probes are often calibrated to read percentage saturation, using air and oxygen-free nitrogen as the 100 and 0% points for calibration. The actual amount of oxygen dissolved in the liquid can be determined by chemical methods. It is possible, however, to relate the partial pressure of oxygen (or oxygen tension) to dissolved oxygen concentration by using Henry's law, as the oxygen solubility in fermentation broths is very low (see Chapter 4).

7.11.3   The tubing method

A different approach to dissolved oxygen measurements is provided by the tubing method, which is outlined in Fig. 7.10.

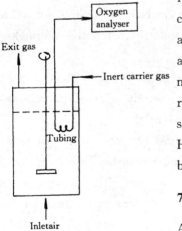

Fig. 7.10   Measuring dissolved oxygen using the tubing method

The tube,often coiled to increase gas residence time and surface area,is made of a permeable material such as teflon or polypropylene. Inert gas. e. g. N_2 or He passes through the coil at a fixed flow rate,picking up the oxygen which has diffused through the tube wall from the fermenter broth. The oxygen content of the gas is determined by an oxygen analyser,see Section 7. 13.

The tubing method is not suited to the control of DO or dynamic measurements, having a response time of the order of $2\sim3$ min,but the simplicity of assembly and operation enhances stability,allowing operation for weeks between calibration. It is necessary to use an analyser which will detect the very low concentrations of O_2 in the carrier gas and erroneous readings can result from microbial fouling and air bubbles contacting the tubing.

7. 11. 4 Dissolved CO_2 probes

We have probably been very slow to realize the importance of dissolved CO_2 as an affector and indicator in fermentation processes. For this reason,dissolved CO_2 probe technology lags far behind DO probes,and has only recently emerged on the market.

Dissolved CO_2 probes contain a bicarbonate solution encapsulated on to a pH probe by a CO_2-permeable membrane. Present probes are not steam sterilizable,and response times are quoted as about 1 min.

It is also possible to use the tubing method (Section 7. 11. 3) for dissolved CO_2 analysis. In this case,a high CO_2-permeable tubing is used together with a sensitive CO_2 analyser,see Section 7. 13. 2.

7. 12 Enzyme probes

A major difficulty for the application of computers to fermentation processes is the lack of sensors providing direct information on the state of the culture. In recent years,considerable progress has been made in the design of ion-selective electrodes[6],but,so far,this has been limited to inorganic ions and is of little direct use in fermentation processes. However,the rapid response and reliability of ion-selective electrodes has been combined with the sensitivity and selectivity of enzyme reactions in the production of enzyme probes.

These are manufactured by immobilizing an enzyme on to the surface of a probe such as DO or pH electrode. The principle involved is illustrated in Fig. 7. 11. The substrate to be[7] assayed diffuses into the enzyme layer and the electrode is chosen so that it will respond to reactants or products in the ensuing enzymic reaction.

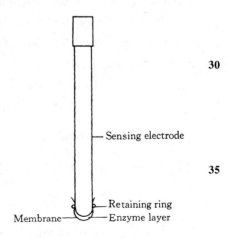

Fig. 7. 11 Construction of an enzyme probe

210

Normally,estimation of fermentation products requires sampling followed by subsequent sample preparation and analysis. The combination of a fast response probe and the selectivity of enzyme reactions means that,in principle,sample, preparation is not necessary with enzyme probes,allowing on-line application. However,most enzyme probes are
5   not steam sterilizable.

7. 12. 1 Enzyme immobilization methods

The enzyme chosen must react specifically or highly selectively with the substance being assayed. Stability is important;this depends on the enzyme system as well as on the
10   method of immobilization. Most solubilized enzymes are unstable and if used in this form,large amounts may be required. Immobilizing the enzyme reduces both the amount required,and the loss of activity thus cutting down the cost. A number of immobilization techniques are employed.

Chemical immobilization usually involves covalent bond formation. Covalent cross-
15   linking by bifunctional reagents,such as glutaraldehyde,is simple and it is possible to control the physical properties and particle size of the final product,but many enzymes are sensitive to the coupling process and lose activity. Binding to water-insoluble materials places the enzyme in a more natural environment with favourable effects on enzyme efficiency and stability. The carriers used include inorganic materials such as porous
20   glass and natural and synthetic polymers such as cellulose and polyacrylamide.

Physical immobilization is generally quicker and easier than chemical methods. Microencapsulation holds much promise but has not yet found widespread application. In this method the enzyme is inside semi-permeable particles,the particle wall allowing transport of reactant and products through the wall but retaining the enzyme[8].
25   Adsorption onto insoluble supports,such as glass or silica gels,is very simple but the enzymes are often easily desorbed by pH,temperature or substrates. This method has been used in the construction of glucose oxidase probes.

Inclusion in gel-lattices is achieved by carrying out a polymerization,e. g. of acrylamide,in an aqueous solution of the enzyme. Very mild reaction conditions favour reten-
30   tion of enzyme activity.

The immobilized enzyme is normally placed on a permeable membrane and secured to the electrode as shown in Fig. 7. 11.

7. 12. 2 The electrode

35   The electrode must be chosen so that in responds to changes in A,B,C or D in the enzymic reaction:

$$A + B \longrightarrow C + D$$

Provided the stoichiometry is known,the reading of the probe can be translated into the concentration of any of the reactants or products. The probe reading will also be cali-
40   brated against a standard concentration of the desired substance.

The electrodes can be divided into two groups according to their principle of operation.

Amperometric electrode measures flux of electroactive species. The response is a linear function of concentration. Amperometric electrodes are used in the detection of substances such as O_2 and H_2O_2 using a polarographic electrode.

Potentiometric electrodes measure concentration of the reactants or products. For these electrodes the response is logarithmic according to the Nernst equation:

$$E = E^0 + \frac{RT}{ZF}\ln[H^+]$$

where E=electrode potential, E^0=standard electrode potential, F =Faraday constant, R=gas constant, T=absolute temperature, Z=charge, and $[H^+]$=hydrogen ion concentration.

This principle is used in ion-sensitive electrodes for hydrogen ion $[H^+]$ and ammonium ion $[NH_4^+]$. It is also used in gas electrodes for CO_2 and NH_3.

Gas electrodes normally have a higher resolution than ion-sensitive electrodes and will, therefore, detect substrates at lower concentration.

In most cases the limiting factor in designing an enzyme electrode will be the availability of a sensor that can monitor the reaction. Here, other possibilities exist. For example, a thermistor covered with an immobilized enzyme could measure the temperature change resulting from the enzymic reaction, proportional to the substrate concentration.

Generally, potentiometric electrodes are currently the most common and most successfully used electrochemical sensors.

7. 12. 3   Probe response

The response characteristics of enzyme probes are determined by a number of parameters. The useful lifetime of a probe will vary from one probe to another. In most cases it will depend on probe stability, which can be divided into:

(a) electrode stability

(b) enzyme stability

(c) probe storage

The stability of the electrode is normally not a factor, being more stable than the enzyme. However, electrochemical electrodes may exhibit drift and regular checking of the response is recommended.

The stability of the enzyme depends largely on the method of immobilization. It has been suggested that chemical methods will give the better stability compared with physical techniques. Enzyme probes have been known to be stable for several months. The amount of enzyme present and the operating conditions will also affect probe stability.

In general, stability of enzyme electrodes is difficult to define; both time and number of assays have been used as parameters. It may also be difficult to determine when an electrode is no longer analytically useful . As the enzyme loses activity , daily recalibration may prove enough to extend its lifetime.

Response time. The following scenario can be visualized for enzyme probes. Substrate diffuses through the retaining membrane and into the enzyme matrix. Products or reactants in the enzymic reaction diffuse out of the enzyme matrix and on to the surface of the
5 measuring element in the electrode, producing a probe output which is translated into concentration of the relevant substance.

It will be appreciated that this cannot happen instantaneously. Reported probe response times vary from 30 s to more than 24 h. The response time will depend on many factors, as outlined below.

10 *Rate of diffusion.* If the probe is designed to monitor changes which occur in a fermentation broth, it is important that this is well mixed. The substrate for the enzymic reaction will then reach the probe surface quickly. It is also important to use retaining membranes which will not represent a diffusional barrier, the right material normally being found by trial and error.

15 The parameters which influence response time will be substrate concentration, pH, temperature, amount of enzyme present, etc. If the probe is used on-line it must be designed to operate at the conditions which have been optimized for product concentration.

Some examples of enzyme probes having proceeded beyond the research level are given in Table 7. 3. This table is by no means exhaustive, and will rapidly become out of
20 date, but it illustrates the versatility and potential of these instruments.

Table 7. 3 Immobilized enzyme probes

Enzyme	Compound	Sensor
Glucose oxidase	Glucose	Polarographic DO
	Lactose	pH
Glucose oxidase β-galactosidase		Polarographic DO
L-amino acid oxidase	L-amino acids	Ammonia
Urease	Urea	pH
Glutamate dehydrogenase	Pyruvate	Ammonia
Uricase	Uric acid	Polarographic DO
β-lactamase	Penicillin	pH
Alcohol oxidase	Alcohol	Polarographic DO

35

7. 13 Gas analysis

7. 13. 1 O₂ analysers

The importance of oxygen in aerobic cultivation of organisms has been discussed in previous chapters. All students of biotechnology should be familiar with the basic rudiments of O_2 transfer (see Chapter 4).

Oxygen is supplied by passing air (O_2) through the system and there may also be some dissolved oxygen in the various inlet liquid streams. Normally, the latter can be ignored and the difference between the oxygen content of the inlet and outlet gas streams is, therefore, equal to the amount of O_2 transferred into the system. The oxygen content of the gas is normally determined by a gas analyser.

Paramagnetic oxygen analysers are used extensively. Paramagnetism (attraction to the strongest part of the field) is a result of molecules having unpaired electrons. Oxygen has two, and is thus strongly paramagnetic. Compared with oxygen, none of the other gases normally associated with fermentation processes are paramagnetic, as shown in Table 7. 4. Hence. this property can be used for selective oxygen analysis.

Table 7. 4 **Paramagnetism of gases** (in relation to a scale of $N_2=0\%$ and $O_2=100\%$)

$O_2=100\%$	$CH_4=-0.2$
$N_2=0\%$	$He=0.3$
$H_2=0.24$	$SO_2=0.22$
$CO=0.01$	$NH_3=-0.26$
$CO_2=-0.27$	$C_3H_8=-0.86$

The most popular analysers are the magnetic wind (thermomagnetic) and the deflection (magnetodynamic) analysers. In the former, the gas enters a cell inside which there is a heated element. The cell is situated in a magnetic field, thus attracting oxygen. As the gas approaches the filament, the oxygen heats up and suffers a loss in paramagnetism. Cooler oxygen will be attracted by the magnetic field, resulting in a magnetic wind through the cell. The filament is part of a Wheatstone bridge which will become unbalanced when the resistivity of the filament changes due to heat loss to the gas. The imbalance will be proportional to the amount of oxygen in the gas.

These analysers are very susceptible to changes in gas composition and barometric pressure. The main problem concerning the former will be water content, as the gas composition under normal fermenter conditions is relatively constant. The water vapour will affect the analysis in such a way that the measured concentration will be lower than the actual concentration (gas analysers normally estimate vol % in dry gas). This can easily be overcome by drying the gas. Changes in barometric pressure of 1% are said to produce an identical change in O_2 reading. In small-scale operation, where the amount of O_2 consumed is very low, O_2 analysers are normally operated with suppressed zero, being calibrated between 19 or 20 and 21% O_2. Under these circumstances it is very important to take account of pressure changes and water vapour so as not to accentuate errors in the data produced.

Magnetodynamic analysers are less affected by changes in gas composition. In these analysers, the cell contains a body, normally in the shape of a dumb-bell, suspended in a non-uniform magnetic field. The gas is passed through the field; if the paramagnetism of the gas is the same as the dumb-bell, this will have no force acting on it and it will maintain its

5   position in the magnetic field. The paramagnetic property of O_2 will act on the dumb-bell, however, causing a deflection which can be calibrated to measure the amount of O_2 in the gas. By incorporating two cells in the analyser, with one reading the inlet, the other the exit fermenter gas, a direct measurement of the amount of O_2 taken up by the fermenter will be provided. In this case barometric pressure changes are compensated for.

10   Present and potential users of O_2 analysers should be warned that although many models and makes available are reliable and accurate, albeit relatively slow to respond (response times vary from about 1 to 4 min, more related to purge time than to the analysis itself), they are often misused by insufficient drying and infrequent checking of barometric pressure (if required). Also, the gas may be transported to the analyser using

15   oxygen-permeable tubing. With careful application O_2 analysers can provide meaningful and valuable information on a fermentation process. It must be remembered, however, that pressure and temperature compensation on the gas flow may be required. This is often overlooked, producing results which can lead to failure in scale-up attempts. Particularly when the difference in oxygen content of inlet and outlet gas is small, as in small-

20   scale fermenters, great care must be taken to reduce the potential errors involved in oxygen analysis.

7. 13. 2   CO$_2$ analysers

Most gases, including CO_2, absorb infrared radiation (IR) energy at some characteristic

25   wavelength. However, simple gases such as hydrogen, nitrogen and oxygen, will not absorb IR energy, and this principle is used for detection of CO_2 in fermentation processes.

An infrared analyser consists of a light source, optical section and sensor. The most common light sources are the Nichrome coil, the Globar (silicon carbide), and the Nernst glower (a filament of oxides), emitting light at the required wavelength (s) for absorp-

30   tion of the gas, When the gas to be measured enters the analyser, it passes through a cell in the path between the radiation source and the detector. It will absorb some radiation, thus reducing the energy level which reaches the detector. This change in energy is detected and amplified to give an analyser signal related to the partial pressure of CO_2 in the gas, which is translated into CO_2 concentration.

35   There is a logarithmic relationship between IR absorption and CO_2 concentration, which implies a lack of sensitivity at high CO_2 concentration. For this reason, most analysers are supplied with a range selection switch allowing operation in a relatively narrow range in which the response can be assumed linear.

The production of CO_2 can be used as an indicator of the state of a growing culture. For example, when CO_2 is produced by the microorganisms metabolizing carbohydrates according to the equation

$$C_6H_{12}O_6 + 6O_2 \longrightarrow 6CO_2 + 6H_2O + energy$$

one mole of CO_2 is produced for every mole of O_2 consumed. The respiratory quotient (RQ) is defined as

$$RQ = \frac{\text{rate of } CO_2 \text{ production}}{\text{rate of } O_2 \text{ consumption}} \qquad 5$$

In the high energy yielding equation above, RQ has a value of unity. In fermentation processes, deviations from this value will always occur, for example when some of the glucose is to be converted into biomass and metabolic products. Some examples of the stoichiometry and RQ values obtained for a number of fermentation processes with a range   10
of micoorganisms and substrates are given in Table 7.5.

Table 7.5   **Examples of stoichiometric equations and respiratory quotient for growth of microorganisms**

Klebsiella aerogenes
$C_3H_8O_3 + 1.87O_2 + 0.32NH_3 \longrightarrow 1.47CH_{1.74}N_{0.22}O_{0.43} + 1.43CO_2 + 3.24H_2O$ 15
glycerol   biomass
$\qquad\qquad\qquad\qquad RQ = 0.76$

Candida utilis
$C_6H_{12}O_6 + 3.53O_2 + 0.71NH_3 \longrightarrow 3.53CH_{1.84}N_{0.2}O_{0.56} + 2.33CO_2 + 3.67H_2O$
glucose   biomass
$\qquad\qquad\qquad\qquad RQ = 0.66$ 20

Saccharomyces cerevisiae
$C_6H_{12}O_6 + 3.96O_2 + 0.33NH_3 \longrightarrow 1.91CH_{1.70}O_{0.50}N_{0.17} + 4.09CO_2 + 4.48H_2O$
$\qquad\qquad\qquad\qquad RQ = 1.03$

Penicillium chrysogenum
$C_6H_{12}O_6 + 3.3O_2 + NH_3 \longrightarrow 2.98CH_{1.86}O_{0.62}N_{0.14} + 3.0CO_2 + 4.8H_2O$
$\qquad\qquad\qquad\qquad RQ = 0.91$ 25

Citric acid production by *A. niger*
$C_6H_{12}O_6 + 1.83O_2 \longrightarrow 0.91C_6O_8H_7 + 0.5CO_2$
$\qquad\qquad\qquad\qquad RQ = 0.27$

In each case, RQ can be used to monitor and possibly control the fermentation. It must be noted, however, that the composition of biomass is unlikely to remain constant   30
throughout a fermentation and this may affect RQ. In the citric acid material balance, the production of biomass is not included. Most of the biomass is formed in the early part of this fermentation, and during the production phase the amount of sugar converted to cell matter is not very high. It is possible, therefore, to approach the theoretical RQ value indicated, but only for high yielding processes in which few secondary acids are being pro-   35
duced.

The production of CO_2 is also a valuable general process indicator in continuous culture. A steady CO_2 plot is normally the best indicator of a steady state.

In fermentation media with high solids content it can be difficult to determine the cell concentration and, hence, the specific growth rate of the culture. In this case, the data   40

from the CO_2 and/or O_2 analysis can be used to calculate this important process variable. A fixed relationship between CO_2 production, or O_2 consumption, and cell growth rate is usually assumed, implying that it is possible to separate the amount of gas associated with formation of cell material from the gas production/consumption due to energy
5   metabolism and production of metabolites.

7. 13. 3   Mass spectrometers

Mass spectrometry is based on the separation of ionized molecules under vacuum. The separation based on the mass to charge ratio, is achieved by magnetic or quadrupole in-
10   struments. Presently mass spectrometers (MS) are finding increasing application in monitoring fermentations.

    Potentially, MS can be used for both continuous on-line gas and liquid analysis. For liquid analysis a probe supporting a strong permeable membrane is inserted into the fermentation broth and dissolved substances such as O_2 and CO_2 and any liquids of suffi-
15   cient volatility are drawn out of the solution by applying a vacuum. The principle is similar to the tubing method described in Section 7. 11. 3. A problem to be solved for this method is the choice of membrane which must be structurally sound to withstand the vacuum yet sufficiently thin to allow rapid diffusion of the required substance(s). There are also problems with finding proper conditions for analysis of individual components of
20   a mixture.

    These problems are not encountered with direct gas analysis. Potentially MS can be used to analyse for any vapour phase component simultaneously; in fermentation it is traditionally restricted to O_2 and CO_2 (plus sometimes CH_4, N_2 and H_2), as a sophisticated gas analyser. The advantage over conventional analysers are speed of response (of the
25   order of seconds compared to minutes), greater accuracy, and the increased number of channels. allowing many fermenters to be connected to one instrument. A distinct disadvantage, however, is cost; typically some ten times more expensive than an O_2 analyser[9].

7. 13. 4   Gas chromatography

30   Gas chromatography (GC) has been used successfully in offline analysis of biochemical processes. By proper sample preparation, most components in the process liquid can be determined. This application of GC is beyond the scope of this chapter, however, and the reader is recommended to search in the abundance of relevant specialist literature.

    Recently, GC technology has progressed sufficiently to make on-line gas analysis
35   feasible. However, it is not necessary to restrict this to CO_2 and O_2. GC can be used in fermenter head-space analysis, monitoring gas composition and concentration of volatile compounds such as acetaldehyde, ethanol, acetone, etc.

    A disadvantage with a GC is its price and the discontinuous nature of the signal produced. (The retention time for the slowest compound can be several minutes.)Gas chro
40   matographs are very sensitive , however , and will detect the presence of intermediates

even at very low concentrations. For reliable operations, extensive calibration will be required.

7. 14 Determination of cell concentration

It may seem strange that measurements of cells and cell growth have been postponed to the end of a chapter on instrumentation for measurement and control of fermentation processes. The reason is that the technology is still in its infancy; considering the importance of cell growth, this is very unfortunate.

Dry weight measurements are still the most common way of determining the concentration and, hence, cell growth. This involves sampling, separation of the cell from the process liquor and subsequent drying. With the aid of microwave ovens, it is possible to reduce the time lag between sampling and dry weight determination to $20\sim30$ min, providing the broth filters easily. For fermentations lasting 100h or more, this lag may not seem significant and, indeed, there are a number of fermentation processes which are controlled manually on the basis of dry weight measurements. However, the introduction of on-line computer facilities has put this method out of favour (and in a few cases it has proved to be inadequate).

Dry weight determinations are only possible when the solids content in the medium is low; unfortunately, this is not the case for most industrial fermentation media.

Turbidity measurements have been used for cell determination on a limited scale. The principle involved is to measure the turbidity of a fermentation broth by the amount of light transmitted. This method is limited to systems in which the turbidity of the broth is only due to the cells, i. e. yeast or bacterial single cell fermentation. For on-line process control this method is only applicable to fermentation processes with low cell concentration as the relationship between turbidity and cell concentration rapidly deviates from linearity.

Turbidity readings must be translated into dry weight (or cell number) and the calibration should always be checked. Naturally, it is difficult to read the turbidity of complex fermentation media and relate it to cell concentration. However, the method is more useful in continuous culture where complex media are less commonly used.

Cell numbers require specialist counting methods and are only used to a very limited extent, suffering to a larger degree from the same problems as measurements of turbidity.

Impedance. It is known that microorganisms alter the impedance of their growth medium when actively growing. In suitable media, it is possible to obtain growth curves of a number of yeast and bacteria in a relatively short time. The method, or a related one based on resistance measurements, can be used for detection of contaminants in the food industry but its application in the fermentation industry appears limited; in complex media, changes in capacitance are difficult to relate to cell growth.

Metabolic heat can be related to growth since this is an exothermic process . The relationship will be empirical and the errors involved are considerable even on small-scale fermenters. Very accurate temperature control is essential, but given that temperature sensor technology is very advanced, there is some justification for considering this method, as metabolic heat is not directly affected by scale or medium composition, etc.

5   CO_2 *production* (O_2 *consumption*) can be empirically related to cell growth. However, this approach requires intimate knowledge of the fermentation process.

    DNA *content* of cells varies very little with growth rate, environment, metabolism or nutrient uptake. DNA analysis is more complex than dry weight determination, but the methods are well documented. In media with high solids content DNA analysis may be 10 one of the most reliable methods for estimation of cell concentration.

    Other methods, such as measurement of ATP content, have been examined. Most have not proceeded beyond the stage of determining single cells growing at low concentrations in synthetic media. However, the importance of developing on-line or automatic sampling with fast, automatic off-line methods for cell growth determination has been 15 realized, and rapid development should be expected in this field. At the moment, gas analysis appears to be the most promising method.

Words and Expressions

page	line		
196	1	instrumentation [ˌinstrəmenˈteiʃən] n.	仪表化；[总称]检测仪表

the application or use of instrument in the performance of some work

4   exclusive [ˈikskluːsiv] a.   专有的,排他的   not share with others

9   in one's own right   凭本身的资格和特性   by virtue of one's qualifications or properties

10   onset [ˈɔnset] n.   开始   beginning, commencement; outset

19   by-word n.   惯用语   a frequently used word or phrase

21   amidst [əˈmidst] prep.   在……中间   among

22   dogma [ˈdɔgmə] n.   教条   a point of view put forth as authoritative without adequate grounds

25   terminology [ˌtəːmiˈnɔlədʒi] n.   专门术语

31   response time n.   响应时间

32   rule of thumb [θʌm]   经验法则

197   5   sensitivity [ˌsensiˈtiviti] n.   灵敏度

8   linearity [ˌliniˈæriti] n.   线性(关系)

11   calibrate [ˈkælibreit] vt.   标定

21   resolution [ˌrezəˈluːʃən] n.   分辨率

22   deflection [diˈflekʃən] n.   (指针的)偏转角

23   offset [ˈɔfset] n.   残留误差

25   reproducibility [ˈriːprəˌdjuːsəˈbiləti] n.   重现性

36   servomechanism [ˌsəːvəuˈmekənizəm] n.   伺服机构   一种控制机械运转

page　line

　　　　的自动装置。具有输出与输入相比较的机构,使这两个量之间的误差能控制在
　　　　规定的范围之内。

198　1　controlled variable　n.　受控变量

　　　2　disturbance variable　[dis'tə:bəns]　n.　干扰变量

　　　3　manipulated variable　[mə'nipjuleitid]　n.　控制变量

　　　4　reference variable　n.　参比变量

　　19　open loop control　n.　开环控制

　　　　feed forward control　n.　前馈控制

　　20　feed-back control　n.　反馈控制

　　39　dynamic response　n.　动态响应

　　40　cyclic response　['saiklik]　n.　周期性响应

　　　　damped response　['dæmpəd]　n.　阻尼响应

199　21　overshooting　['əuvə'ʃu:tiŋ]　n.　过调节　shooting over so as to miss

　　25　actuation　[,æktju'eiʃən]　n.　驱动　putting into action

　　26　highlight　['hailait]　vt.　使显著　give prominence or emphasis to

　　35　NTP normal temperature and pressure　标准温度和压力(0℃和101.325kPa)

　　37　float　[fləut]　n.　浮子

　　　　proximity　[prɔk'siməti]　n.　邻近

200　15　impart　[im'pɑ:t]　vt.　给予,传给　give,convey or grant from or as if from a
　　　　store

　　22　shaft power　n.　轴(输出)功率

　　24　dynamometer　[,dainə'mɔmitə]　n.　功率计

　　　　strain gauge　['strein geidʒ]　n.　应变仪

201　13　circuitry　['sə:kitri]　n.　电路系统　electric circuit collectively

　　15　thermistor　[θə:'mistə]　n.　热敏电阻　温度的变化由半导体电阻的变化而被
　　　　测定。

　　22　sheath　[ʃi:θ]　n.　护套

202　7　rheological　[ri:ə'lɔdʒikəl]　a.　流变学的　研究物质流动和变形,包括一些基
　　　　本的参数如弹性、塑性和粘度等的科学称为流变学(rheology)

　　14　shear stress　['ʃiə 'stres]　n.　切应力　每单位面积上的促进流体运动的剪
　　　　切力

　　　　shear rate　['ʃiə 'reit]　n.　剪切速率　一层流体与平行邻接各层流体间的速
　　　　度梯度

　　27　Newtonian fluid　[nju:'təunjən]　n.　牛顿流体

　　　　pseudoplastic fluid　[,sju:də'plæstik]　n.　假塑性流体

　　28　Bingham plastic　['biŋəm]　n.　平汉塑性流体

　　　　Casson fluid　['kæsen]　n.　凯松流体

　　34　tube viscometer　[tju:b vis'kɔmitə]　n.　管式粘度计

204　4　bob　[bɔb]　n.　浮子

```
page  line
214   11   make   n.   （产品的）牌子；类型，型号；式样   a specific line of goods, identi-
                 fied by the maker's name  or  the  registered  trademark; A  manufacturing
                 style.

           albeit  [ɔːlˈbiːit]  conj.   尽管   though, Although. 一般用来联结短语
      28   Nichrome  [ˈnaikrəum]  n.   镍铬合金（原为商标名）
           Globar   n.   碳化硅热棒
           silicon carbide   n.   碳化硅，金刚砂
      29   glower   [ˈgləuə]  n.   灯丝
215   38   plot   [plɔt]   n.   图表   a graphic representation
216    9   quadrupole  [ˈkwɔdrəpəul]  n.   四极
      36   headspace   n.   顶部空间
217   13   providing  [prəuˈvaidiŋ]  conj. =provided
      16   out of favour   不受欢迎   no longer liked or approved
      34   impedance  [imˈpiːdəns]  n.   阻抗
      39   capacitance  [kəˈpæsitəns]  n.   电容
```

Notes

① 这两句中都含有分词 given，具有独立词汇的作用，在这里是形容词，有两种意义：假定、设想或考虑到。此处应解释为"考虑到"，参见 p. 61, Ch. 2, Note⑩. 前一句可译为：考虑到我们需依赖仪表了解生物过程，因而了解所用的仪表是很重要的，否则在使用中容易在它们的适用性和功能方面犯错误。

② 在并列句中，句子的结构应是平行的，在文法上是相似的，重复的词一般都可以省去。在本句所含从句中，含两个并列句：

Feed is pumped into the fermenter continuously.

Broth is taken out of the fermenter continuously.

可以合并为：

Feed is pumped into and broth taken out of the fermenter continuously.

③ strain gauge 应变仪是一种测定弹性物质伸长与压缩的装置。应变仪用于力荷仪（load cell）中测重量或附在搅拌轴上测量功率。

④ 本句中的 by 表示增加的量。本句可译为：温度计本身的响应时间在 1s 左右，但通常加一护套，以免受环境的影响，但这样会使响应时间的增加量高达 5～10s。

⑤ high viscosity-imparting (substance) 引起高粘度的物质

coil-shaped (anodes)（制成）线圈状的阳极

上面是复合形容词，在科技文章中用得很多，可使文章紧凑。前者由名词＋现在分语构成，有主动的意义；后者由名词＋过去分词构成，有被动的意义，参见 p. 13, Ch. 1, Note④.

⑥ ion-selective electrode 离子选择性电极。ion-selective 是由名词＋形容词构成的复合形容词，意为对离子具有选择性的。其他例子有：electron-deficient hydrogen（缺少电子的氢原子），pH-independent（与 pH 无关的）等，参见 p. 13, Ch. 1. Note④.

离子选择性电极为一种电化学装置，它对一种离子的活度的变化能产生选择性的响应，以

一种膜将试验溶液与参比电极（或溶液）隔开而产生电位差，其值与离子活度成比例。测量氢离子活度的 pH 电极是最常用的离子选择性电极，其中试液与电极系以玻璃膜隔开。

⑦ The substrate to be assayed…动词不定式的被动形式作为定语，除具有被动意义外，有时还具有将要完成的意义，表示说话人计划或要求发生的行为。全句可译为：欲进行测定的基质扩散进入酶层，进行酶促反应，而选择的电极应能对反应物或反应产物有所响应。其他例子有：

This is the work to be done. 这是要做的工作。

Let us show you the engine to be tested. 让我们给你看一看要作检验的那台发动机。

注意：上句中的 "to be" 不能省，而在下例中，则可仅用过去分词 assayed：

The substrate assayed was a fluorescent component in the mixture. 进行测定的基质是混合物中发荧光的组分（过去时）。

⑧ …the particle wall allowing transport of reactant and products through the wall but retaining the enzyme.

句子中，句末的分词短语有自己的主语，对主句起补充说明的作用，参见 p. 140，Ch. 4，pattern 2. 也称为独立短语（absolute phrase）。独立短语在句中以逗号与主句分开，有时 being 可省去，如：Her father ill, she entertained his friend herself.

⑨ 本句牵涉倍数的表示法。英语中增加几倍的说法与汉语稍有不同，主要是要考虑是否包括原来的底数在内，翻译时要多加注意。英语中仅有包括基数在内的一种表示方法，参见 p. 60,Ch. 2，Note③.

Comprehension

1. From where do the instruments used in biotechnology originate and why are they needed to be improved for efficient application? (p. 196)

2. How does the author define the term 'response time'? For which reason have most instruments too much longer response time? (p. 196~197)

3. Why are the instruments with good linearity preferred? (p. 197)

4. What is the difference in meaning between the manipulated and disturbance variables? (p. 198)

5. State briefly in which cases the three control structures are applicable, respectively and why? (p. 198)

6. Explain the essential principle of the thermal mass flow meter. (p. 199~200)

7. How can we tell the difference between total power uptake and shaft power regarding a fermenter? (p. 200)

8. Illustrate how can we obtain the value of impeller speed (r. p. m.) in the last column of table 7. 1, taking the 10 m^3-fermenter as an example. (p. 200)

9. State briefly how a resistance thermometer as well as a thermistor works. (p. 201)

10. What are the distinctive characteristic of a Newtonian fluid and that of other classes of fluids? (p. 202, Fig. 7. 6)

11. A number of viscometers are illustrated in the text. Which one is most suitable for solid-containing broth? (p. 202~204)

12. What is meant by the statement that it should also be possible to alter the sensitivity of the probe to avoid splashes from the broth surface activating the probe on the 9th line of page 205?

13. For which reasons is pH value considered as an important parameter in fermentation processes? (p. 205)

14. State briefly the basic principle of dissolved oxygen probes? (p. 206)

15. What are the advantages and disadvantages of an enzyme probe? (p. 209~212)

16. What do you understand by the sentence, i. e. In this case barometric pressure changes are compensated for at the end of first paragraph on page 214?

17. What meaning does the respiratory quotient (RQ) have in a fermentation process? (p. 214~215)

18. What is meant by the sentence, i. e. the methods are well documented, appearing on page 218, line 9?

Vocabulary

Give another word or phrase to replace these words or phrases as they are used in the text:

productivity(196/15); around(196/35); version(204/12); fix(204/31); hold-up(205/6); claim(205/36); step change(207/26); feasible(216/35); document(218/9).

Word usage

1. Write sentences to bring out the difference between the following pairs of words:

tubing(197/3), tube(209/1); may be(197/19), maybe(250/25); device(204/37), devise; ensure(205/5), assure; place(210/18), put.

2. Make sentences with the following words:

exclusive(196/4); compensate(197/29); as long as(198/24); impart(200/15); provided(203/38); ensuring(209/39).

Pronoun and antecedent

Pronouns must have clear and definite antecedents. Understanding their relation is vital to the sentence comprehension.

Find out the antecedents of the following pronouns:

it(198/8); this(201/35); it(202/22); these(205/14); this(207/20).

Sentence analysis and translation

First analyse the following sentences as in Ch. 1, Note ① and then translate into Chinese:

1. Last paragragh of the section 7. 1(page 196)

2. Third paragragh of the section 7. 3 (line 5 to 18, page 198)

3. Second paragragh of the section 7. 8 (line 31 to 36, page 204)

4. Fifth paragragh of the section 7. 12. 3 (line 2 to 6, page 212)

Reading and Writing

Patents are important source of information on technology and know-how of industry. Here is an united states patent with the abstract deliberately omitted.

Read it carefully and

1. note the format of the patent

2. note the style of the patent,picking out the words which are far more frequently used in it than in the other technical publications.

3. write an abstract using fewer words as possible,while retaining the essential points.

United States Patent [19]

Toyoshi et al.

[11] Patent Number:4,523,999

[45] Date of Patent:Jun. 18,1985

---

[54] ULTRAFILTRATION METHOD

[75] Inventors:Seiji Toyoshi;Tetsuo Tane-gawa;both of Saga;Masaru Saeki;Fujisawa; Tetsuya Kawakita, Yoko-hama,all of Japan

[73] Assignee:Ajinomoto Co. ,Inc. ,Toky-o. Japan

[21] Appl. No:561,974

[22] Filed:Dec. 16,1983

[51] Int. Cl^3. ·············· B01D 13/00

[52] U. S. Cl. ··········· 210/639;127/48; 127/55;210/651;435/110;435/115

[58] Field of Search ·······················

·················· 127/48,51. 54,55; 210/638,639,650,651,702,724;435/106 110~112,115,276

[56] **References Cited**

U. S. PATENT DOCUMENTS

3,799,806 3/1974 Madsen ······210/639

3,986,933 10/1976 Maldonado et al.

······························ 435/110

4,069,103 1/1978 Muller ······ 127/54

4,278 766 7/1981 Srinivasan

····························· 425/110

4,411,991 10/1983 Hirakawa et al.

······························ 426/43

4,416,700 11/1983 Clark et al.

····························· 210/639

FOREIGN PATENT DOCUMENTS

937058 9/1963 United Kingdom.

973828 10/1964 United Kingdom

·· 435/110

1015637 1/1966 United Kingdom

2113247 8/1983 United Kingdom

·· 127/55

OTHER PUBLICATIONS

Michaels,"New Separation Technique for the CPI", *Chem. Eng. Progress*, Dec. 1968, pp. 31~43.

Primary Examiner —Peter Hruskoci

Attorney, *Agent*, *or Firm* —Oblon, Fisher, Spivak,McClelland & Maier

[57] **ABSTRACT**

(The text of the abstract has been deliberate-ly omitted,leaving as an exercise for the stu-dent)

9 Claims,No Drawings

4,523,999

ULTRAFILTRATION METHOD

DETAILED DESCRIPTION
OF THE INVENTION

The present invention is, on removing polymer impurities such as humic substances, dyes etc. contained in an amino acid fermented liquor or its intermediate treated liquor before the intended amino acid is separated and obtained therefrom, to aggregate the aforesaid impurities by previously adjusting the pH of the liquor to a specified value, thus enhancing the degree of blocking thereof. More specifically, in a system containing polymer impurities, e. g. a fermented liquor starting from cane or beet molasses or its intermediate treated liquor, the kinds of said impurities are varied, for example, dyes, humic substances, gums, polysaccharides, proteins etc. Among those, the humic substances and certain dyes are the so-called acidic substances having a carboxyl group as a functional group, and in a certain acidic region, they become a non-charged state and lose affinity with water, thus resulting in precipitation. The object of the present invention is to aggregate and precipitate these polymer substances by adjusting the pH of such a fermented liquor or its intermediate treated liquor to a specific acidic region by utilizing the aforesaid property, thereby increasing the degree of blocking in the ultrafiltration treating operation.

The certain acidic region as herein

used is pH 2 ～ 5. This region is suitable because the isoelectric points of the certain dyes and humic substances fall within it or its vicinity. However, if the isoelectric point of the intended amino acid falls within this region, it is a matter of course to exclude said isoelectric point and its neighboring region. Adjustment of pH may be satisfactorily achieved by using acid or alkali, and examples of the acid which may be employed are the so-called mineral acids such as hydrochloric acid, sulfuric acid, nitric acid, phosphoric acid etc. and organic acids such as acetic acid etc. , while as the alkali, there are sodium hydroxide, potassium hydroxide, lime, ammonia etc.

Practical points of operations of the present invention are now described.

The liquor to be treated by the present invention is an amino acid fermented liquor employing as a carbon source cane or beet molasses or its intermediate treated liquor as described above, and before subjecting this liquor to the ultrafiltration treatment, the pH thereof is previously adjusted to 2 - 5 (except the isoelectric point of the intended amino acid and its vicinity).

The thus pH-adjusted liquor is subjected to the ultrafiltration treatment, and the ultrafiltration threatment perse may be a conventional known method. For example, the material for the membrane employed in the filtration may be a conventional semipermeable membrane and there is no particular restriction thereon. For

4,523,999

3

example, polyamide, polyacrylonitrile, cellulose acetate type etc. may be contemplated. The shape of the membrane is also not restricted and may be for example, a tubular, flat film, spiral, hollow fiber membrane etc. The conditions, e. g. temperature etc. are also nothing particular.

The effect of the present invention is demonstrated by the following examples. In the examples, the percent of dyes excluded was measured by the absorbance at 400 nm and the percent of polymers removed was by the Lowly Folin method utilizing the reducing property of humic substances.

EXAMPLE 1

A glutamic acid fermented liquor (pH 7. 2) starting from cane molasses was adjusted to pH 4. 8 with hydrochloric acid, then subjected to ultrafiltration treatment employing a polyacrylonitrile hollow fiber-shaped ultrafiltration membrane (molecule fraction 13, 000) at 40° C. , and compared with the case where the fermented liquor (pH 7. 2) was directly treated by ultrafiltration.

The results are shown in Table 1.

Table 1

		Percent of Polymers Removed	Percent of Dyes Excluded
(control)	Glutamic Acid Fermented Liquor (pH 7. 2)	10(%)	20(%)
(Present Invention)	Above Fermented Liquor Adjusted to pH 4. 8	15	30

4

From the above table, it can be understood that by adjusting the pH to a predetermined value. the percent of the polymeric reducing substances removed has been increased by 50% and the percent of the dyes excluded by 50%.

EXAMPLE 2

A lysine fermented liquor starting from cane molasses (pH 7. 0) per se (Control) and that further adjusted to pH 4 (Present Invention) were subjected to ultrafiltration similarly as in Example 1.

The results are shown in Table 2. From this table, it can be seen that by the present invention, the percent of the polymeric reducing substances removed has been increased by 36% and the percent of the dyes excluded by 60%.

Table 2

		Percent of Polymers Removed	Percent of Dyes Excluded
(Control)	Lysine Fermented Liquor (pH 7. 0)	14(%)	15(%)
(Present Invention)	Above Fermented Liquor Adjusted to pH 4	19	24

EXAMPLE 3

A lysine fermented liquor (pH 7. 0) starting from beet molasses was adjusted to pH 3. 0 with sulfuric acid, then subjected to ultrafiltration treatment employing a polyacrylonitrile hollow fiber-shaped ultrafiltration membrane (molecule fraction

4,523,999

5

6,000) at 50℃ ., and compared with the case where the fermented liquor (pH 7.0) was directly treated by ultrafiltration.

The results are shown in Table 3.

Table 3

		Percent of Polymers Removed	Percent of Dyes Excluded
(Control)	Lysine Fermented Liquor (pH 7.0)	30(%)	37(%)
(Present Invention)	Above Fermented Liquor Adjusted to pH 3	50	63

From the above table, it can be understood that the percent of the polymeric reducing substances removed has been increased by 67% and the percent of the dyes excluded by 70% in accordance with this invention.

What is claimed is:

1. A method for removing impurities including humic substances, gums, polysaccharides, proteins or a mixture thereof from an amino acid fermented liquor obtained from cane, beet molasses, or a mixture thereof, said amino acid being selected from the group consisting of glutamic acid, lysine and a mixture thereof; said method comprising:

(a) adjusting the pH of the fermented liquor to a value of from 2~5 to pre cipitate said impurities , said impurities

6

having an isoelectric point falling within a pH range of 2~5;

(b)ultrafiltering said impurities from said fermented liquor using a semipermeable ultrafiltration membrane.

2. The method of claim 1 wherein said amino acid fermented liquor comprises an intermediate liquor obtained from cane molasses, beet molasses or a mixture thereof.

3. The method of claim 1 wherein said pH is adjusted by adding an acid or an alkali to the amino acid fermented liquor.

4. The method of claim 3 wherein said acid comprises a mineral acid, an organic acid, or a mixture thereof.

5. The method of claim 4 wherein said mineral acid comprises hydrochloric acid, sulfuric acid, nitric acid, phosphoric acid, or a mixture thereof.

6. The method of claim 4 wherein said organic acid comprises acetic acid.

7. The method of claim 3 wherein said alkali comprises sodium hydroxide, potassium hydroxide, lime, ammonia, or a mixture thereof.

8. The method of claim 1 wherein said semipermeable membrane is made up of polyamide, polyacrylonitrile, cellulose acetate, or a mixture thereof.

9. The method of claim 1 wherein said membrane has a tubular, flat film, spiral, or hollow fiber membrane shape.

* * * * * *

Chapter 8   Processes and Products Dependent on Cultured Animal Cells

8. 1   Historical

Although many investigators had previously studied the behaviour of animal cells *in vitro*, the first application of such cells which led to a useful product was in 1949 when J. F. Enders demonstrated that polio virus could grow in cultured animal cells from
5 neural and nonneural tissues (kidney) derived from primates.

The pioneering work which led up to this event may be summarized briefly. It began as early as 1880 with the demonstration that leucocytes would divide outside the body (Arnold) which was followed by observations on the behaviour of excised pieces of animal tissues immersed in serum, lymph① or ascites fluid. The hanging drop method of
10 R. Harrison (1907), whereby a piece of tissue (tadpole spinal chord) was held in lymph on the underside of a coverslip which was sealed on to a hollowed-out microscope slide, is regarded as a turning point. This work was extended by Carrel (1913) who developed a complicated methodology for maintaining cultures free of extraneous contaminants (particularly bacteria). Few other people were so capable. However, media were
15 developed to promote animal cell growth so that, by 1928, the Maitlands were able to grow virus in minced mouse or chick embryos maintained *in vitro*. This methodology was used by Enders for his polio work where he and his followers were considerably assisted by the use of antibiotics which had become available during the previous 10 years. The polio vaccines which were produced by Salk in the early 1950s were produced in roller
20 tube cultures of monkey kidney or testicle. Once this technology became established other vaccines were produced from chick or primate embryo cells grown in culture [measles (1958); mumps (1951); adenovirus (1958)].

8. 2   Types of products which can be obtained from cultured animal cells

Animal viruses were, and still are, the most commercial product derived from cultured
25 animal cells. At present, about 1.5×10^9 doses of foot and mouth disease vaccine are produced annually, a figure which is approached by the poultry vaccines for Newcastle ($\sim 1 \times 10^9$) and Marek's Disease (0.5×10^9). Human viral vaccines are administered at the rate of 10^8 doses per annum or below. Processes for the production of interferon② are also under development at scales approaching or exceeding those used for the veterinary
30 vaccines, while the relatively unexploited area of the immunobiologicals, derived from specifically synthesized hybridoma cells, will undoubtedly become an area of significance

during the next decade. In Table 8. 1 the major products which either already are, or are likely to be, generated from cultured animal cells are presented. This is not an exclusive listing but it does represent the major product areas, and the types of materials which can be generated within those areas.

Table 8. 1　Products generated from cultured animal cells

Virus vaccines	*Immunobiologicals*
Foot and Mouth	Monoclonal antibodies
Polio	diagnosis
Mumps	preparative
Measles	drug targeting
Rubella	passive vaccines or therapeutic agents
Rabies	investigative science
Tick Borne Encephalitis	
Newcastle	*Hormones*
Mareks	Growth Hormone
Rinderpest	Prolactin
Fish Rhabdovirus	ACTH
Cellular chemicals	*Virus predators*
α-Interferon (lymphoblastoid)	Insecticides
β-Interferon (fibroblastic)	
Interleukin-2[3]	
Thymosin	
Plasminogen activator (Urokinase)	

8. 3　Overview of methodology for product generation

The basic outline of the generation of a product from an animal cell culture system is depicted in Figs 8. 1～8. 3. It consists of three phases. The first phase is preparative, the second involves the cultivation of the animal cells. While the third phase is that of product generation. This last phase is not separated from the cell production phase in some systems (hormone and immunobiological production), while in others it involves the infection of a cell culture with a virus (for the production of a viral vaccine) or with an inducing agent(s) (for the production of the interferons; Fig. 8. 3).

Much of the effort involved in such production operations goes into quality control of all components, and the on-line and off-line monitoring of as many biological parameters as is feasible. The quality control tests are designed to ensure (a) that the materials used will promote the generation of cells or product, and (b) that they are free of exogenous organisms. i. e. contaminants.

It is clear from Fig. 8. 2 that preparation of the growth medium is a laborious and skilled process. While the defined materials of the medium are relatively easy to control, the two components which provide most difficulty are the water and the serum.

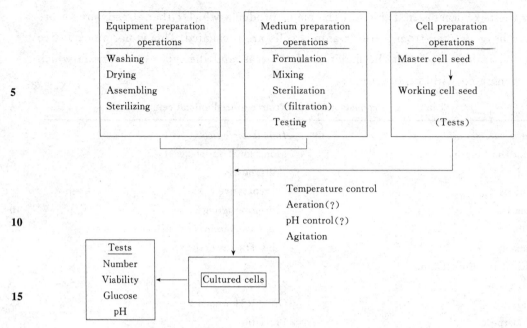

Fig. 8.1 Outline of the steps involved in generating a product from cultured animal cells

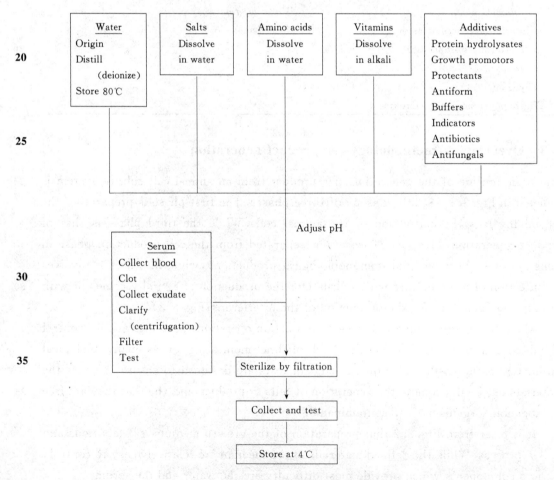

Fig. 8.2 Medium preparation

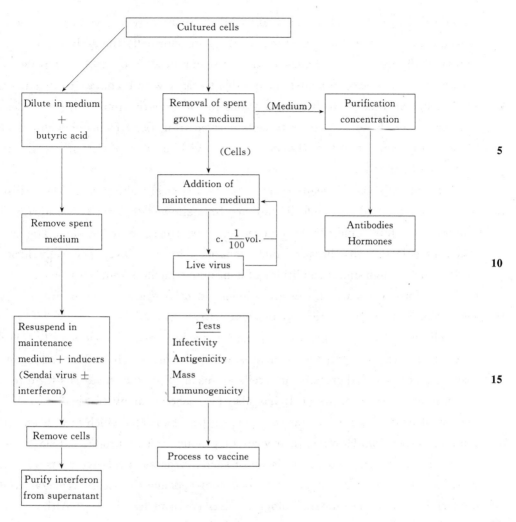

Fig. 8. 3 Production generation

Water can be obtained from a wide variety of sources and even after distillation and deionization it may contain materials detrimental[④] to cell growth. For this reason, melted ice from deep within a Greenland glacier is a useful reference material! Storage of prepared water can lead to difficulties, as bacteria can reach a concentration of 10^5 cells ml^{-1} in distilled water held at ambient temperatures and the products of such bacteria, apart from constituting a variable, can be toxic in very small quantities. This is normally overcome by holding stored water at 80℃, at which temperature it is ostensibly sterile.

Medium can be prepared without serum and some, but by no means all, cells can be induced to replicate in it. However, such cell-medium combinations are not generally used for the production of saleable materials.

Serum which has been treated to remove the immunoglobulin components can be most useful in virus production systems where locally-produced serum contains antibodies to the production virus. Although bought and tested serum is expensive, it is possible to produce it ' in house ' . The thorough quality control of sera is essential for reliable reproducible operations. It is often advisable to maintain a reserve of pretested serum at −20℃, so as to cover for those times of the year (normally the early summer)when the quality of the fresh serum wanes. Fetal calf serum is often used for cell growth, yet this is expensive and scarce. It is also most liable to carry with it contaminants such as phage and mycoplasma. Batch-to-batch variations in the growth promoting properties of fetal calf serum are also observed. With cells derived from Baby Hamster Kidneys (BHK 21 Clone 13) grown in adult ox (bovine) serum a yield of 90% of that of a fetal calf control serum can be obtained.

Animal cells can be made to grow in two basically different modes. Most animal cells can be induced to divide if they are first allowed to attach to a surface or solid substratum, while some can be induced to grow freely in suspension. The former are called monolayer cells because they generally form a layer one cell thick on the substratum, though under conditions of continuous medium renewal tissue several layers thick can form. Cells which can grow independently of a substratum are referred to as suspension cells or anchorage-independent cells.

Cells which can only grow in monolayers are regarded as possessing (or expressing) fewer oncogenes (the genetic sequences which enable a cell to be carcinogenic) than suspension cells and, therefore, such cells are used to produce materials for direct human consumption (virus vaccines). It has also been shown many times that such cells are capable of producing a wider range of virus types than cells which have been selected to grow in suspension. However, if a virus or product can be produced from a cell which grows in suspension, then the scale-up of such a process is relatively easy. Products for veterinary use are made in this way (e. g. foot and mouth disease virus)as well as the α-interferons and the immunobiologicals derived from hybridomas. Although the cells used for the latter two products can be shown to be carcinogenic in selected test

Table 8. 2 Advantages and disadvantages of monolayer cells

Advantages	Disadvantages
Fewer oncogenes expressed	Need a solid surface for growth (an extra component which adds to the cost)
More susceptible to a wider range of virus types	
Produce β-interferons	Scale-up more difficult
Easy to scale down(<1 ml)	More difficult to control (not homogeneous)
More cell types can grow this way (primary cells, limited life-span cells and some continuous line cells)	Surface parameters have to be precisely described
Easier to standardize the karyology (chromosome profile)	Difficult to obtain a fully continuous process
	Need a trypsinization step between successive cultures and scales of operation
	Cannot produce α-interferon
	Tend to need higher concentrations of better quality serum

systems, they do not pose a severe hazard either in the production phase or when the product has been freed of cellular contaminants prior to use. In Table 8. 2 there is a summary of the advantages and disadvantages of using monolayer (substrate or anchorage-dependent) cells. It can be concluded that it is necessary to be in a position to produce commercial quantities of both cell types and that two necessarily different **5** technologies are required. Descriptions of these two technologies are presented in the next two sections.

8. 4 Monolayer cell growth systems

Systems used to produce cells which require a substratum may be divided into two types. There are those in which one increases the *number* of units of equipment when one **10** scales-up a process. These are the *multiple* processes. Alternative systems are now available whereby scale-up is achieved by increasing the *size* of the equipment——*unit* process systems.

8. 4. 1 Multiple processes for the production of monolayer cells

Traditionally, monolayer cells have been produced on the inner surface of stationary **15** glass bottles or Petri dishes. Such bottles have had a variety of configurations and have gone under the names Brockway (USA), Roux, Carrel, Baxter or Medical Flats. Soda glass may be used, yet borosilicate could be preferred because although it is more expensive it is tougher and easier to repair. The bottles may be used individually, but are more usually stacked in customized racks for ease of transportation. **20**

A development of the stationary bottle culture system which enables cells to grow on all of the inner surface of a bottle rather than the base is the rolling bottle system. For this system cylindrical bottles are generally used, although bottles with rectangular cross-sections held in special jigs can also be rotated. There are many variations possible[5], with some bottles reaching lengths of 180cm. The bottles are placed on rollers **25** in mechanized racks. A standard piece of equipment can rotate 72 bottles and 6~10 such racks make a conveniently sized production unit. The rolling bottle system has been developed to its limit at the Istituto Zooprofilattico Sperimentale at Brescia, Italy, where 7000 bottles can be rotated simultaneously in each of four incubators. The addition of medium, cells and virus to such a large number of bottles while maintaining freedom **30** from bacterial contamination presents a formidable, but not insuperable, problem and the high degree of automation of the Brescia unit promotes the economic viability of this methodology.

8. 4. 2 Unit processes for the production of monolayer cells

The development of unit processes for the cultivation of monolayer cells began in earnest **35** in the mid 1960s and has now become an accepted and preferred practical technology.

Many of the details of this development have been reviewed recently by the author elsewhere. so that only the broad outlines of the different systems, along with the most recent developments, will be described below.

Following the reliable and successful operation of the multiple processes, the unit
5   processes which were designed to supersede them followed the basic pattern of the multiple system. Thus, unit processes based on enclosing a stack of plates in a vessel were developed, reminiscent of a rack of bottles. Such systems were made from disposable polystyrene (multitray system) or polycarbonate as well as soda glass. Later developments took a stack of plates and rotated them either with the plane of the plates
10   in the vertical configuration or, more recently, with the plates in the horizontal configuration. This latter system has been scaled-up and is at present under intensive exploitation as a means of producing the β-or fibroblastic interferon. The scale-up of such systems presents engineering difficulties as well as manipulation problems during the cleaning and cell planting operations. The amount of surface which can be packed
15   into a container in this way is limited, which has two consequences:

(a) both sides of the discs have to be used (a methodological problem); and

(b) the product is produced in a dilute form as all the plates have to be irrigated by the growth medium which must either fill, or at least half-fill, the total outer container volume.

20   The development of the roller bottle® system can be seen in the wide variety of multitube cell propagators which have been developed. Such systems have reached a development scale of 2001 volume. In a recent piece of equipment, the Gyrogen, a large surface area for cell growth has been generated from an array of parallel tubes which are rotated by an external drive within an outer cylindrical shell with a volume of 1001. This
25   expensive piece of equipment can be made to work, but whether it is a cost-effective way of conveniently producing useful materials has yet to be demonstrated.

The contraction of tubes into hollow fibres has led to a number of developments which have unique features. At the small scale it is possible to simulate the structure of an animal tissue with cells growing on the outside of fibres and the nutrient medium
30   percolating through the lumen of the fibre. This system could have advantages in two senses, as both waste materials (which could be cytotoxic) and product materials could be separated from the cells which produced them by the semipermeable membrane of the fibre. Systems of this nature have recently been developed up to the 0. 21 scale and are used commercially in well developed computer controlled and monitored systems.

35   Spirally wound films or bags have also been used and, although such systems have been shown to be practicable on the small scale, commercial-scale versions have not yet been launched.

Many groups are currently using packed beds for the production of cells and products such as β-interferon, foot and mouth virus and swine vesicular disease
40   virus . The packings have varied from stainless steel springs through polystyrene jacks

to glass spheres. Yet the basic system of a packed bed through which medium is made to circulate, with most of the control activity (pH, DO_2) conveniently concentrated in the ancillary medium reservoir, is common to most such systems. They are relatively easy to operate and to scale up, as the mechanical problems of handling uniform column packings are easily solved. As glass is often used as a substratum, the reliability of the operations is improved and the relationship between the cell and the glass surface it has 'learned' to grow on in the laboratory is unchanged. Furthermore, the agencies which control the dissemination of new bioproducts raise fewer questions when presented with products made from cells grown on such a familiar substratum.

Clearly, static packed beds are not without their own problems. Gradients across the bed are not uncommon and there is some difficulty in monitoring a culture one cannot put under the microscope. Although this latter problem may be solved with ease by monitoring components of the circulating medium (glucose concentration for cell growth; lactic acid dehydrogenase activity for cell breakdown and hence virus liberation), the problem of the inhomogeneity of a polyphasic system remains.

Quasi-homogeneous systems for the production of animal cells in monolayers have been developed by A. J. van Wezel. In 1967 he showed that cells would grow on 0.2mm diameter particles of DEAE Sephadex⑦ A 50 coated with collodion. Such particles (relative density 1.05) can be held in suspension with very minimal agitation, and cells would attach to such microcarriers while the system was in its agitated mode. Since these initial observations, many investigators have shown that it is possible to generate products from cells grown on such microcarriers at scales of up to 5001. The latest such report is the production of polio virus from a green monkey kidney cell line called Vero, which was grown on a modern microcarrier called Cytodex. Other microcarriers have been produced from polystyrene (Biosilon), polypropylene and even glass microspheres. How-ever, it would seem that for most purposes the Sephadex-based micro-carriers provide the most suitable substratum.

While many investigators have been able to operate successfully and reliably with microcarrier systems, others have experienced difficulty. Some of these difficulties relate to the particular cell the investigator wishes to grow, which in itself is a product of its tissue of origin and the way it has been grown and subcultured. Other problems stem from the improper use of suitable or unsuitable equipment or the inappropriateness of the medium chosen, either for the period when the cells make the first and critical contacts with the beads or during the later replication of the attached cells.

In conclusion then, for the production of substratum-requiring cells, the microcarrier systems is the preferred methodology under those circumstances when it can be made to work well and reliably. However, packed beds of glass spheres can provide a reliable back-up system. Other systems also have a place, for the provision of that particular environment wherein a unique cell type can grow and generate product.

8. 4. 3   Processes for the production of suspension cells

The processes for the production of suspensions of animal cells are little different from those used to produce bacterial cultures. A recent review (by the author) describes many of the parameters which have to be monitored and controlled. The equipment used is a

5 fairly standard fermenter modified to permit lower rates of agitation and aeration. Such a system may be defined as the conventional methodology and has been scaled up to 8000l. At such scales it is used for the commercial production of foot and mouth disease virus from either Baby Hamster Kidney Cells or a different cell line, also derived from hamsters, called IFFA-3. Also, α-interferon produced from the Namalwa lymphoblastoid

10 cell line is currently in production in similar equipment at about the same scale of operation. A basic modification of this agitator-driven system is that equivalent to the air-lift fermenter. Bulk mixing is provided by introducing large air bubbles at the bottom of the fermenter, as these are efficient at moving liquid yet do not damage the cells. Conventional sparging, which attempts to increase the air bubble surface area by

15 creating masses of small bubbles, can cause severe damage to animal cells. The dissolved oxygen level *per se* is not deleterious until it drops below 15% of the amount of oxygen dissolved in the medium at NTP or rises above the amount of oxygen dissolved at NTP, but the interactions of the cell at the air-liquid interface can lead to loss of cell viability. Surprisingly, physical agitation resulting from rapid impeller speed seems to be

20 much less damaging; however, an unambiguous quantitative study of the relative effects of these parameters taken singly and together remains to be made.

While the conventional stainless steel tank system has its place as the work horse of the technology, the system can be modified for use in technologically less developed countries. For this purpose useful quantities of vaccine (5×10^6 doses per annum) can be

25 made in 10l bottles agitated by an externally driven bar magnet. Such systems have been installed at Surabaya, Indonesia, where the plant has been operated at about 250 000 doses a month, and at Polgolla, Sri Lanka, where the installation of basic equipment is nearing completion.

The continuous cultivation of animal cells is a practicable and useful method either

30 for generating cells or for gathering information about those cells. Recent work has demonstrated the advantages of on-line computer monitoring and control of such a system, and the necessary computer hardware can be purchased relatively easily.

However, the exploitation of the continuous production of animal cells and the generation of product from such cells at levels which make it commercially attractive has

35 not yet been achieved.

8. 5   Downstream processing

While many of the downstream processing operations applied to the raw materials generated by animal cells have their equivalents in other areas of the chemical technology of proteins, there are some operations which are unique and will be considered in more detail below. Operations which are common to other process technologies, such as filtration, centrifugation (moderate speed), precipitation, chromatographic purification, and concentration (reverse osmosis) drying, will not be dealt with. The inactivation of **5** living viral products, the generation of active subunits from whole virus particles and the formulation of materials into useful products are areas which may be considered unique to processes based on the use of animal cells.

8. 5. 1 Inactivation

Although many vaccines are made from infectious virus particles, others are made from **10** killed or inactivated virus. In the latter case it is important to ensure that there is almost no risk of the recipient of the vaccine contracting the disease as a result of a residue of infective virus. Agents used for such inactivations are commonly formaldehyde (Waldman-Schmidt process for foot and mouth disease vaccine, killed polio vaccine, influenza), whereas β-propiolactone is used to inactivate Rabies Virus. More recently, **15** the imines (acetylethyleneimine and ethyleneimine) have been used to inactivate foot and mouth disease virus. While the imines contribute to a slight destabilization of the foot and mouth disease virus structure, the formaldehyde treatment cross-links the capsomeres, holding the basic structure together more tightly. Other methods of inactivation such as ultraviolet irradiation or glycidaldehyde can be used, yet in all such **20** cases it is important to ensure that the viral preparation to be inactivated is monodisperse so that the inactivant is not prevented from reaching virus embedded in the middle of a clump.

8. 5. 2 Subunit formation

Viral vaccines which constitute a danger to the recipient of the vaccine if improperly **25** inactivated, can be made into a subunit vaccine whereby whole virus particles are disrupted using a detergent (Tween 80, Triton X®, tri-(n-butyl)phosphate) and the final vaccine is made from an immunogenic fraction of the dissociated virus. Prime candidates for such subunit vaccines are rabies, hepatitis B, herpes simplex, cytomegalovirus and influenza. To date, trials with the isolated haemagglutinin glycoprotein immunogen from **30** the influenza virus have shown that such a vaccine can be effective, although not quite so effective as the native virus. The studies which have been done so far with glycoproteins isolated from viral preparations show that such materials on a weight for weight basis are less efficient than native virus, but when sufficient material is administered adequate protective responses may be obtained. **35**

8. 5. 3 Product formulation

Live virus vaccines generally contain from 1 to 4 different virus types , each of which is represented by about 10^3 live virus particles per dose. Such materials are freeze dried in the presence of bioprotectants such as sucrose, human or bovine serum or albumin glutamine and phosphate ions. Killed virus vaccines, on the other hand, are formulated at about 10^{11} particles per dose and are mixed with materials called adjuvants which

5 potentiate the effect of the injected immunogens. The adjuvants are a heterogeneous group of chemicals such as the cardiac glycoside saponin (or its refined component Quil A), various aluminium salts (hydroxide, sulphate, phosphate) and oleaginous formulations where the aqueous suspension of virus is homogenized with a biocompatible oil, forming a water-in-oil emulsion which is then transformed into an oil-in-water

10 emulsion by a second emulsification with an aqueous salt solution containing a detergent. Such materials may have many coincident effects as they provoke the immune system physically and chemically and make antigen available to the system at a rate which generates the maximum response.

8.6 Genetically engineered animal cells and bacteria

15 The ability to insert defined sequences of nucleotides into both prokaryotic and eukaryotic cells and then to collect, as a product, the proteins which are defined by the inserted nucleic acid, has far-reaching consequences for both bacterial and animal cell biotechnologies. While it is unlikely that animal cell based processes for the generation of live virus vaccines will be superseded by processes based on genetically engineered

20 bacteria, it is clear that some animal cell products such as insulin[9] and some of the α-interferons will be produced commercially from prokaryotes. Other materials such as the killed virus vaccines for foot and mouth disease virus and polio and the various interferons may be made commercially in either cell type. However, genetically engineered animal cells, which are capable of making glycosylated proteins could be the

25 preferred substratum for the production of human growth hormone and the blood clot dissolving enzyme inducer, tissue plasminogen activator[10].

We are at present witnessing the beginning of a new era of augmented biotechnological capability. It is too early to predict prospective developments with confidence, yet it is certain that these multipotential methodologies will make a major

30 impact on the ways in which we manufacture bioproducts in the future.

Words and Expressions

page line

228   4 polio virus ['pəuliəu 'vairəs] n. 脊髓灰质类病毒

5 neural ['njuərəl] a. 神经的

kidney ['kidni] n. 肾

6 primate ['praimit] n. 灵长类动物(包括猴、猿和人)

7 lead up to 把……一直带领到 to result in by a series of steps

9 lymph [limf] n. 淋巴,淋巴液

page	line		

229　26　depict　[di'pikt]　vt.　描述　describe

　　　31　inducing agent　n.　诱生剂

　　　36　exogenous　[ek'sɔdʒənəs]　n.　外源的　-genous　表示由……产生的

230　31　exudate　['eksju:deit]　n.　渗出物　动词形式为 exude

231　15　sendai virus　['sen'dai]　n.　仙台病毒

　　　23　Greenland　['gri:nlənd]　n.　格陵兰(丹麦)

　　　　　glacier　['glæsjə]　n.　冰河

　　　25　ambient　['æmbiənt]　a.　周围的　surrounding the ambient temperature　室温

　　　27　ostensibly　[ɔ'stensəbli]　ad.　表面上地　apparently;明显地

232　 3　wane　[wein]　vi. 减少,衰退　abate,subside

　　　 5　mycoplasma　[maikəu'plæzmə]　n.　支原体　最小的微生物,通常为球状0.3～
　　　　　0.8μm,但也有成丝状的,0.1～0.3μm 直径,长度可达 150μm

　　　 6　hamster　['hæmstə]　n.　仓鼠

　　　11　substratum　[sʌb'strɑ:təm]　n.　底层　an underlying layer

　　　15　anchorage-independent cell　['æŋkəridʒ]　n.　非贴壁依赖性细胞

　　　17　oncogene　['ɔnkədʒi:n]　n.　致癌基因　onco-　表示瘤,癌
　　　　　carcinogenic　[ˌkɑ:sinəu'dʒenik]　a.　致癌的　carcino-　表示癌

　　　36　karyology　[ˌkæri'ɔlədʒi]　n.　胞核学　细胞学的一个分支,特别是研究染色体
　　　　　的结构和性能.

　　　38　trypsinization　[ˌtripsinai'zeiʃən]　n.　胰蛋白酶消化作用　利用胰蛋白酶使细
　　　　　胞和底层分离。

233　 1　hazard　['hæzəd]　n.　危险　danger,risk.

　　　17　soda glass　['səudə glɑ:s]　n.　钠玻璃

　　　18　borosilicate　n.　硼硅酸盐

　　　20　stak　[stæk]　vt.　堆
　　　　　customize　[k'ʌstəmaiz]　vt.　定做　to alter to the taste of a buyer.
　　　　　rack　[ræk]　n.　搁架

　　　22　rolling bottle　n.　滚瓶

　　　24　jig　[dʒig]　n.　夹具

　　　31　formidable　['fɔ:midəbl]　a.　可怕的　causing fear
　　　　　insuperable　[in'sju:pərəbl]　a.　不能克服的　incapable of being overcome;
　　　　　　　insurmountable

　　　35　in earnest　['ə:nist]　认真地　with a purposeful or serious intent

234　 5　supersede　[ˌsju:pə'si:d]　vt.　取代　replace,supplant

　　　 7　reminiscent　[ˌremi'nisənt]　a.　使人联想起……的　tending to recall of the past

　　　 8　disposable　[dis'pəuzəbl]　a.　用后即丢弃的,一次性的　subject to or available
　　　　　for disposal
　　　　　polystyrene　[ˌpɔli'staiərin]　n.　聚苯乙烯

page	line		
238	6	cardiac glycoside ['kɑːdiæk 'glaikəsaid] n. 强心苷	

saponin ['sæpənin] n. 皂素,皂角苷

7　oleaginous [ˌəuli'ædʒinəs] a. 含油的,油质的

11　coincident [kəu'insidənt] a. 同时发生的,偶然的

26　tissue plasminogen activator ['tiʃjuː plæz'minədʒən 'æktiveitə] n. 组织血纤维蛋白溶酶原激活剂

27　witness ['witnis] vt. 目睹　to see for oneself

Notes

① lymph fluid 淋巴液是无色透明液体,成分与血浆相仿,含白细胞和红细胞。经淋巴系统,通过胸导管,回到静脉血。能从组织中去除细菌和蛋白质,从肠中传送脂肪,并供淋巴细胞于血液中。

② interferon 干扰素是一类蛋白质,具细胞调节功能,能干扰病毒的繁殖,因而得名。干扰素具有种特异性,通常在诱导后才产生,诱导剂包括病毒、微生物、内毒素等。人干扰素按来源分成三种类型:α-(或白细胞)干扰素、β-(或成纤维细胞)干扰素、γ-(或免疫)干扰素。

除抗病毒外,干扰素还能抑制细胞繁殖,因此可能具有抗癌能力,以及具有调节免疫系统的能力。

③ Interleukin-2　白细胞介素-2　一种人体蛋白质,当受到感染时,由 T 细胞产生,它能使 T 细胞很快增殖,也能抑制某些肿瘤细胞,防止扩散。

④ 这里 detrimental(有害的)是形容词,置于它所修饰的名词 materials 之后。形容词通常置于被修饰的名词之前,但如形容词本身又被其他的词语所饰时,则置于所修饰的名词之后。

⑤ possible 是少数可以放在所修饰的名词后面的形容词,其他还有 impossible,available 等。如:

This is the only reference book available here on the subject.

这是这里唯一能找到的有关这问题的参考书。

⑥ roller bottle 滚瓶用于培养贴壁依赖型动物细胞。它是一个圆筒状瓶,内置细胞和培养基,连续转动,使整个内壁都能供细胞生长,也可用一些方法以增大瓶内的表面积。

⑦ Sephadex [sefə'deks]　是 Pharmacia 公司生产的交联葡聚糖的商品名。DEAE ＝ diethylaminoethyl 二乙基氨基乙基　$(C_2H_5)_2\overset{+}{N}H\text{—}CH_2\text{—}CH_2\text{—}$ 。

⑧ Triton x-100 ['traitən]　isooctylphenoxypolyethoxyethanol 是 Rohm and Haas 公司生产的一种非离子型表面活剂的商品名,用于溶解细胞膜而不会使蛋白质变性。

⑨ insulin ['insjulin]　胰岛素是一种多肽激素,能控制血糖浓度,用于治疗糖尿病。现已用基因工程菌生产,是第一种用于治疗的基因工程蛋白质。

⑩ tissue plasminogen activator t-pA,TPA　组织血纤维蛋白溶酶原激活剂,是一种能使血纤维蛋白溶酶原 plasminogen 转变为其活性形式的酶,血纤维蛋白溶酶 plasmin;后者能溶解纤维蛋白 fibrin,它是血块的主要组分。t-pA 用于治疗心脏病,溶解血块很有效,它的优点是不会引起出血。其他血纤维蛋白溶酶原激活剂如链激酶 streptokinase 和尿激酶 urokinase 不和纤维蛋白结合而是使血液中所有血纤维蛋白溶酶原活化,引起血液蛋白质

如纤维蛋白原 fibrinogen 降解引起出血，同时也使血块溶解。

Comprehension

1. When, according to the author, was born the animal cell biotechnology? (p. 228)

2. Which type of products from cultured animal cells is being most produced currently? (p. 228)

3. What are the main difficulties experienced during animal cell cultivation in contrast with the conventional bacteria cultivation regarding the medium preparation? (p. 229~232)

4. State briefly the two different modes of animal cell cultivation. (p. 232)

5. What are the two processes used for cultivating anchorage-dependent cells? (p. 233)

6. What difficulties may a multiple process experience during its operation? (p. 233)

7. Give two reasons why a glass substratum is preferred for monolayer cell cultivation. (p. 235)

8. Name three recently developed systems of unit processes for the production of monolayer cells and give a brief account of their merits and demerits. (p. 234~235)

9. What is the main reason causing cell damage when cultivating anchorage-independent cells in a fermenter? (p. 236)

10. What reagents are used in inactivating infectious virus in vaccine production? (p. 237)

11. How can the viral vaccine be dissociated into subunits? (p. 237)

Vocabulary

Give another word or phrase to replace these words or phrases as they are used in the text:

go into(229/32); ostensibly(231/27); in house(231/34); control(232/7);

in a position(233/4); configuration(233/16); unique(234/28); launch(234/37);

currently(234/38); stem(235/31).

Word usage

1. Write sentences to bring out the difference between the following pairs of words:

apart from(231/26); other than(86/25); irradiation(237/20); radiation; formulation(237/36); formula.

2. Make sentences with the following words or phrases:

liable to(232/4); alternative(233/11); from…through…to(234/40~235/1); prospective(238/28).

Sentence analysis and translation

First analyse the following sentences as in Ch. 1, Note ① and then translate into Chinese:

1. Section 8. 2 (228/24~229/4)

2. The second paragraph of section 8. 4. 2 (line 4 to 19, page 234)

3. The third paragraph on page 235 (line 16 to 27)

4. The last paragraph of this chapter (line 27 to 30, page 238).

Writing

The following is the Chinese translation of an abstract of a paper entitled "Effect of Nitrogen/Carbon Ratio on the specific production Rate of Spiramycin by Streptomyces ambofaciens",published in Process Biochemistry,1996. Try to retranslate it into English.

将产二素链霉菌在一种合成培养基上培养生长,其碳源和氮源分别为甘油(10 g·L^{-1})和铵盐(20 mM)。分批培养时,螺旋霉素的比生产率为 0.3mg·h^{-1}·g^{-1}(细胞干重);采用半连续培养可提高螺旋霉素的生产。将甘油和铵盐以不同比例连续加料进行几次发酵的结果表明甘油和铵盐的开始摄取速率对螺旋霉素的比生产速率有显著影响:比生产率增加了 9 倍。低比生长速率对螺旋霉素的生物合成也是必要的。

生词　产二素链霉菌 Streptomyces ambofaciens;螺旋霉素 spiramycin;比生产率 specific production rate;细胞干重 DCW (dry cell weight);开始摄取速率 initial uptake rate.

Chapter 9   Products from Plant Cells

9.1 Introduction

9.1.1 Perspectives

Within the plant kingdom are to be found[①] a vast array of chemical structures. Some are
small and comparatively simple molecules, such as sugars and amino acids, while others
are large and complex, for example starch and cellulose. Between these extremes are to   **5**
be found a whole range of structures of varying degrees of complexity, many of which
are often placed under the general heading of 'secondary products'; many of these
'secondary metabolites'[②] undergo active metabolism within the plant and in many cases
they play a significant part in the protection of the plant from attack by other
organisms.   **10**

Over the centuries man has made extensive use of plant secondary products, for
instance as perfumes, flavours, spices and particularly as medicines. Not all of these uses
are for discrete single substances[③], some, such as cocoa butter fat or 'Attar of roses', are
complex mixtures and blends, whose precise formulation and product quality control have
long been a concern of industry. Where products consist of a single substance, attempts   **15**
have often been made to produce these through chemical synthesis. Such an approach has
however often been constrained by low yield, high costs, difficult chemical conversions, or
the need for high purity of a particular isomer from a complex mixture, and in many
cases the plant itself has continued to be the more effective means of synthesis.

Plants used as a source of fine or speciality chemicals have traditionally been grown   **20**
in large plantations, more often than not located in the tropics or sub-tropics. During
recent years techniques have however been developed which may in time come to rival
and possibly replace traditional plantation systems as a source of plant products. Such
techniques are generally encompassed by the terms 'plant cell biotechnology' or 'plant
cell culture'. The technology involves the large-scale culture of isolated plant cells under   **25**
conditions which induce them to synthesize commercially or socially desirable substances
characteristic of the parent plant from which they were obtained. Plant cell culture offers
many advantages over traditional plantation methods as a route to natural product
synthesis. These advantages include:

  • independence from environmental factors. including climate, pests, geographical   **30**
    and seasonal constraints;

  • a defined production system with greater process control, and production as and when required;

• more consistent product quality and yield.

In consequence more and more research laboratories are investigating plant cell culture as an alternative route for natural product synthesis, and as an enabling tool to allow the further development of the plant kingdom as a major chemicals resource.

9. 1. 2   Historical background

Although cell culture technology has only come to the fore in the last five to ten years, the beginnings of the subject may be traced back to the late nineteenth century. The earliest documented work is that of Haberlandt who, in 1898, attempted to culture single cells isolated from various parts of different plants. Although Haberlandt's cell cultures apparently remained viable for quite some time, they showed no sign of cell division. Undeterred, other workers repeated his experiments and by the late 1930s White and Gautheret in particular were able to report growth and cell division in cultures established from a number of different species. As the requirements for successful culture became understood, more species were established in culture. An important development was the regeneration of whole plants from cultured cells. Many plant cells have the property of totipotency, that is, each cell carries in the genome the complete information required to give rise to an exact copy of the parent plant. In consequence it is possible to regenerate whole plants from cells taken from roots, leaves or stems. This ability to regenerate plants from culture is of key importance in horticulture and agriculture, providing a means of rapid propagation, in large numbers, of 'standard' plants. While plant propagation is not the subject of this chapter, it is none the less an interesting and increasingly important aspect of plant tissue culture. Readers who would like furtherdetails are referred to Murashige (1978).

In the early days the whole approach to cell culture was very 'hit and miss'. The composition of media was relatively unsophisticated and often ill-defined. Typical media consisted of mineral salts together with organic supplements such as glucose, thiamine, glutathione, cystein and indoleacetic acid (a key plant growth regulator). In many cases coconut milk, the liquid endosperm of the coconut and notorious for its variable composition, was an absolute requirement to sustain growth. During the period 1940 ~ 1960 steady progress was made in our understanding of plant cell culture systems; detailed information on the physiology and biochemistry of growth in suspension culture began to be published and studies of natural product synthesis became more extensive. In the mid 1950s the first major proposals for the industrial application of cell cultures to synthesize plant products were openly discussed, and Pfizer Corporation (USA) issued a patent in 1958 encompassing such a possibility. Prospects of achieving such an aim must none the less at that time have seemed limited; cell growth rates were still low, cultures were generally difficult to establish, media were in the majority of cases still undefined, and worse still, products characteristic of the parent plant were either absent in cell cultures or only present in vanishingly low concentrations.

The following decade from 1960 ~ 1970 saw major progress in many of these problem areas. Defined culture media were established and growth rates improved. Cultures were identified which would synthesize substances characteristic of the parent plant, and progress also occurred in the largescale culture of plant cells and our knowledge of the biochemistry and physiology of cell cultures markedly improved.

9.1.3 The plant kingdom as a chemicals resource

The number of chemical structures reported from higher plants runs into hundreds of thousands and is constantly being added to[4]. Something like 1500 new chemical structures from higher plants are reported each year, of which quite a number have some degree of biological activity. Quite obviously not all plants have the same constituents and it is normal to find secondary metabolites confined to a particular plant family, or unique to a particular species . Unfortunately our rudimentary knowledge of plant

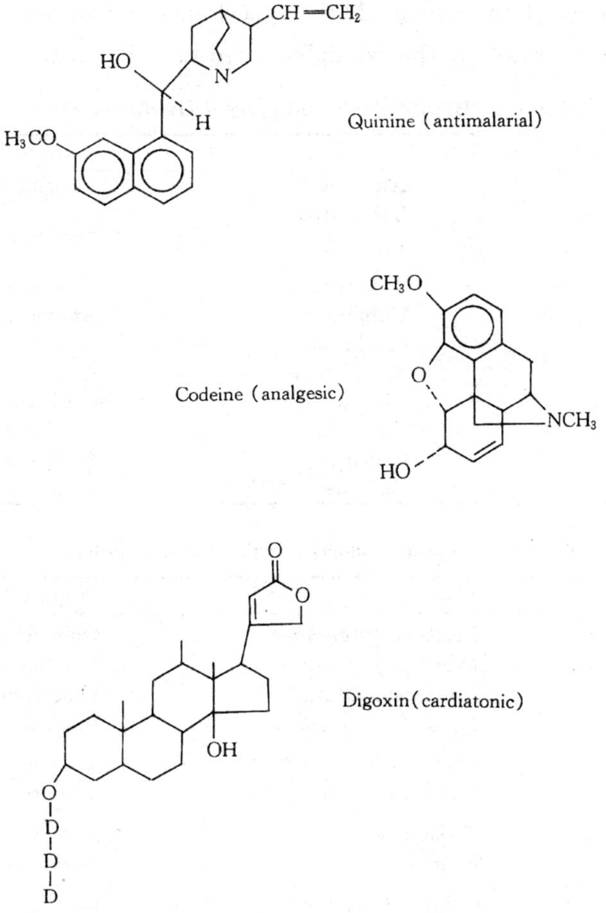
CH═CH2
HO
N
H
H3CO
Quinine (antimalarial)
CH3O
O
NCH3
HO
Codeine (analgesic)
O
O
OH
O
D
D
D
Digoxin(cardiatonic)

Fig. 9.1 Plant natural products : some examples of their diversity of structure and activity.

chemistry and biochemistry still restricts our ability to exploit plant natural product chemistry fully. On the other hand this provides all the more incentive to explore systematically the plant kingdom as a source of novel structures and activities.

Traditionally the plant kingdom is thought of as being a source of illdefined herbal remedies and potions, many of doubtful efficacy. However, some 25% of prescribed and highly purified drugs are derived from the plant kingdom, including such key therapeutic agents as digoxin (a cardiatonic glycoside from *Digitalis lanata*, the foxglove); quinine (an antimalarial alkaloid from the bark of the *Cinchona tree*) and codeine (an analgesic alkaloid from the opium poppy). Not only do these three have different pharmacological properties, but they also serve to illustrate the diversity of chemical structure to be found in plant natural products (Fig. 9. 1) .

The range of therapeutic activity of plant-derived drugs is very wide and includes such properties as anticholinergics, antihypertensives and, antileukaemics (Table. 9. 1). While perhaps having their major social and financial impacts in pharmacology, plant chemicals contribute to a wide range of other products, their properties being utilized in applications as diverse as human food additives, perfumes and agrochemicals. The degree of diversity is well illustrated by the examples listed in Table 9. 2.

Table 9. 1   Higher plants and drugs derived from them

Species	Drug	Activity
Atropa belladona	Atropine	Anticholinergic
Catharanthus roseus	Vincrystine } Vinblastine	Antileukaemic
Chondodendron tomentosum	Tubocurarine	Muscle relaxant
Cinchona ledgeriana	Quinine	Antimalarial
Colchicum autumnale	Colchicine	Anti-inflammatory
Datura metel	Scopalamine	Anticholinergic
Digitalis lanata	Digoxin	Cardiatonic
Dioscorea deltoidea	Diosgenin	Antifertility
Papaver somniferum	Codeine	Analgesic
Uragoga ipecacunha	Emetine	Amoebicide

Table 9. 2   Plant products and the chemical industry

Industry sector	Plant	Product
Pharmaceuticals	*Cinchona ledgeriana*	Quinine
	Digitalis purpurea	Digitoxin
	Pilocarpus jabonanbi	Pilocarpine
	Rauwolfia serpentina	Reserpine
Food and drink	*Cinchona ledgeriana*	Quinine
	Thaumatococcus danielli	Thaumatin
Cosmetics	*Jasminum sp.*	Jasmin
	Rosa sp.	'Attar of roses.'
Agrochemicals	*Chrysanthemum sp.*	Pyrethroids

There are four ways in which cell cultures may contribute to the further exploitation of the plant kingdom . The first we have already touched on ; that is as an alternative route to natural product synthesis. The second occurs where a novel substance with desirable properties has been isolated from a plant, which, for a variety of reasons may be difficult to grow. If that substance is also difficult to synthesize chemically then an alternative synthetic route through cell culture may well provide the answer. The third approach is in many ways a very exciting one. The plant cell genome contains large numbers of 'silent' genes, i. e. genes present and potentially active but which are not normally expressed under the environmental conditions prevailing in the field today. Cell culture is in itself a form of selection pressure which may allow the expression of these genes. As possible evidence of this there are instances where products of potential commercial interest have been obtained from cultures but which have not been identified in the plant from which the culture was initiated. Given the large amount of DNA present in most plant cells we may speculate on the possibility of a whole host of new substances and perhaps new enzymic mechanisms which may be uncovered from studies with cell cultures. The final approach is through 'biotransformations'. Plants possess a wide range of enzyme systems capable of effecting transformations of molecules which through synthetic organic chemistry are either not possible or are too complicated and costly to contemplate as an industrial application. Such biotransformation systems linked perhaps to immobilized enzyme technology could be the most important area for the development of cell culture technology in the future.

9. 2　Nature of cell cultures

Although plant cell culture owes much to standard microbiological practice, there are a number of points of difference which need to be discussed before we move on to review mass growth and product synthesis.

9. 2. 1　Culture initiation

Plant cell cultures are initiated through the formation of a 'callus'[5] which is essentially a mass of non-developed or non-differentiated cells. A callus is obtained by excising a piece of tissue, called an explant, from the parent plant and placing this onto a nutrient base solidified with agar. This nutrient base contains inorganic macro - and micro-nutrients, carbon and nitrogen sources and various plant growth regulators. The whole process must be carried out under aseptic conditions, and before the piece of explant tissue is transferred to the agar it must be carefully surface sterilized (the surface tissues of plants conceal an abundant microflora). The nutrient medium on which the tissue is placed is particularcy rich and provides a good substratum for microorganisms which, unless checked, rapidly outgrow the plant cells, and the need for good aseptic technique cannot be overstressed[6]. Surface sterilization is usually achieved by washing the tissue in 5% sodium hypochlorite, 2% mercuric chloride or 80% ethanol for varying lengths of time, after which the sterilizing agent is removed by repeated washing of the tissue in sterile distilled water. To enhance the effectiveness of the sterilizing agent a wetting agent such as Triton X-100 or Tween is sometimes added.

Caution must equally be exercised not to over-expose the tissues to the sterilizing agent, which may result in deleterious effects, particularly to the surface cells and
5 tissues, and in turn[7] in low cell viability and difficulty in establishing a culture. An alternative approach, with varying degrees of success, is to incorporate antibiotics such as streptomycin and nystatin into the nutrient medium. In some cases such substances not only prevent microbial infection but also affect the growth and metabolism of the cell culture. Instead of taking explants from the plant there is an increasing trend of
10 initiating cultures from seeds. These are generally easier to surface sterilize, without quite the same problems of over-exposure to the sterilizing agent, and in many cases seeds will give rise to callus just as readily as tissue explants.

Once surface sterilized the tissue explant or seed is placed onto the solidified nutrient in a flask covered with material permeable to gases (oxygen, carbon dioxide)
15 but which does not allow the entry of bacterial or fungal spores. Various types of flask closure are in use, ranging from cotton wool bungs, to aluminium foil and sheet polypropylene. Once closed the flask containing the explant is placed in an incubator, generally at 25℃, sometimes with light, sometimes in the dark. It should be noted at this point that although many plant cell cultures are green, there are relatively few reports of
20 cultures which are genuinely autotrophic, a point which is discussed further below. After between 1 and 2 weeks, depending upon a variety of factors including the species, tissue origin, nutrient regime, etc., the explant begins to proliferate cells in the form of a general mass of cell material or callus. The initial sites of proliferation are often aligned with those parts of the explant where cell division had occurred in the parent
25 plant. When twis callus mass has reached a reasonable size, maybe 2~4cm across, it is separated from the parent explant and placed on fresh nutrient media. It then continues to proliferate, typically into a large frizzy mass.

Callus, although an almost obligatory start to the culture process, is far from being an ideal system with which to work. Slow growing and heterogeneous, it is not suitable
30 for scale-up experiments or as a production system, and it is equally unsatisfactory as a tool for biochemical and physiological experiments. Many people who work with cell cultures therefore move quickly on to the next stage, that is into liquid culture.

Successful liquid culture of plant cells depends to a great extent on a 'friable' callus, that is a callus which when placed in liquid in a flask supported on a rotating
35 platform rapidly breaks up under the swirling motion to give a culture composed of a mixture of free cells and cell clumps. Such a system is much more amenable to biochemical investigation and process development studies than callus; growth is generally much more rapid, more cells are in direct contact with the nutrient and the degree of culture heterogeneity is much reduced.

40 Suspension or liquid cultures of plant cells are grown in much the same way as

microbial cells. They are maintained on orbital shakers, at rotational speeds of about 120 r.p.m. (rather lower than with microbial cells) and the temperature is maintained at between 25 and 27℃ (compared with 37℃ typically used for bacterial cultures).

9.2.2 Growth regimes

Some aspects of the regimes under which plant cells are grown have been alluded to above, including temperature, rotational speeds on orbital shakers and general composition of nutrient media. Let us return to this latter topic in more detail.

Early growth media for plant cell cultures were largely undefined, and relied heavily on the addition of complex mixtures such as coconut milk to achieve cell growth and division. Such procedures have been largely superseded by the development of defined media and the use of specific natural and synthetic growth regulators. Examples of media used for plant cell cultures are shown in Table 9.3. Although such media are 'defined', in that their constituents are precisely known, none have been properly optimized. Some attempts have been made to optimize the levels of the various inorganic constituents but only with a very restricted range of media and cell lines.

Table 9.3　Examples of media formulations for the growth of plant cells

Component	Formulation and component concentration $(mg \cdot L^{-1})$	
	Murashige & Skoog (1962)	Gamborg et al. (1968)
$(NH_4)_2SO_4$	—	134.0
$CaCl_2 \cdot 2H_2O$	440.0	150.0
$NaH_2PO_4 \cdot 2H_2O$	—	169.6
KH_2PO_4	170.0	—
NH_4NO_3	1650.0	—
KNO_3	1900.0	3000.0
$MgSO_4 \cdot 7H_2O$	370.0	250.0
$CoCl_2 \cdot 6H_2O$	0.025	0.025
$NaMoO_4 \cdot 2H_2O$	0.25	0.25
$CuSO_4 \cdot 5H_2O$	0.025	0.025
KI	0.83	0.75
H_3BO_3	6.20	10.0
$MnSO_4 \cdot 7H_2O$	22.30	13.20
FeNaEDTA	36.70	40.00
$ZnSO_4 \cdot 7H_2O$	8.6	2.0
meso inositol	100.0	100.0
Nicotinic acid	0.5	1.0
thiamine HCl	0.1	10.0
pyridoxine HCl	0.5	1.0
glycine	2.0	—
sucrose	20×10^3	20×10^3
pH	5.8	5.8

The nitrogen source is typically nitrate or ammonia, although successful growth has been achieved with nitrogen sources as diverse as urea, single amino acids such as glutamate and mixtures such as casein® amino acids. The different nitrogen sources may have an effect on cell morphology. Organic sources tend to give cell cultures
5   characterized by the presence of long thin sausage-like cells, while cells from cultures with inorganic nitrogen sources are generally more rounded.

It has already been mentioned that the majority of cell cultures are unable to maintain themselves autotrophically in spite of their producing chlorophyll. The reason for this is largely unknown although there are indications that a lesion in the fatty acid
10   composition of the chloroplast membranes may much reduce the efficiency of electron trapping and transfer. To maintain cell growth and division it is therefore necessary to provide an exogenous carbon source. The major mobile carbohydrate of plants is sucrose and this has been the carbohydrate source of choice for many cell cultures. However in the last few years attempts have been made to grow cell cultures on a variety of carbon
15   sources, some refined, some waste. Good cell growth has been achieved on glucose, maltose and galactose, and some degree of success has been achieved with more diverse substrates, but biomass yields and productivity levels are generally lower than with sucrose or glucose. Of the non-refined or waste substrates, starch produces variable results, depending upon the source, while molasses and milk whey result in little growth
20   or none at all. With whey the low level of growth is probably due to a very low activity or absence of β-galactosidase needed to hydrolyse the lactose in the milk whey to glucose and galactose, both of which the cell cultures are able to utilize.

The utilization of sucrose by plant cells has interesting features. Plant cells possess an invertase in the cell wall which plays some part in hydrolysing the incoming sucrose
25   to its two monomers, glucose and fructose, prior to entry into the cell through the plasmalemma. The degree of hydrolysis varies depending upon the origin of the cell line, the growth rate and the general growth conditions. So far total hydrolysis of the sucrose has only been found necessary for carbohydrate uptake and subsequent cell growth in one cell line, which was isolated from sugar cane (well known for its high rate of sucrose
30   synthesis and level of sucrose accumulation). There is little understanding of the wide variation in the degree of cell wall sucrose hydrolysis which occurs in different cell lines and under different environmental conditions.

Comparatively little information is available on the need by plant cells for the range of macro-and micro-inorganic nutrients used in culture media. Many can be identified as
35   being important cofactors in enzyme reactions, e. g. molybdenum for nitrate reductase, or magnesium for many of the kinases; others are important in electron transport processes, for instance iron. Variation in the level of phosphate has a marked effect on culture growth and productivity, but again little information is available on the precise interactions.
40   Plant growth regulators (auxin®, kinetin, giberellin, etc.) have major effects on cell

cultures, both quantitative and qualitative. The range of effects varies dramatically, but again our understanding of the biochemistry and physiology of these substances is extremely limited and their use is essentially empirical.

Temperature and pH also exert a major influence. In general, cell culture media are not purposely buffered, the media composition itself ensuring a limited degree of buffering capacity. The nutrient medium is initially adjusted to a pH in the range 5. 2~ 6. 5. Soon after inoculation with cells (2~12h) the pH often declines by as much as 0. 5 unit, to rise again as cell growth proceeds. In later stages of growth the pH generally stabilizes between 6. 5 and 7. 2. In those few instances where attempts have been made to maintain a stable and defined pH level from culture initiation onwards, reduced biomass yields and growth rates have been noted.

Plant cells show a low tolerance to high temperatures. Above 32℃ culture viability is much reduced and productivity declines markedly. The optimal temperature for growth appears to be at about 27℃, although cultures are usually grown at a 'standard' 25℃. On a larger scale, unlike microbial processes which are often highly exothermic and require specialized cooling systems, with plant cells there may even be a need to provide heat to maintain an optimal operating temperature.

9. 2. 3 Growth kinetics

One of the greatest contrasts between the growth of cultured plant cells and microorganisms is in their respective rates of growth. While the pattern of growth may be the same (Fig. 9. 2), plant cells have doubling times or division rates measured in hours and days while many microorganisms have doubling times of the order of minutes or hours.

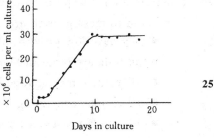

Fig. 9. 2 Growth characteristics of a cellsuspension culture of *Catharanthus roseus*

Fig9. 2 illustrates growth in batch culture of *Catharanthus roseus* cells, which tend to have faster doubling times than many plants but none the less are much slower than microorganisms. One of the fastest (and quite exceptional) recorded doubling times for a plant cell culture is 15h, for tobacco cells.

Attempts have been made to study the kinetics of plant cell growth using chemostat continuous culture systems. Initial studies suggested that, at least in relation to carbohydrate substrates, uptake into plant cells obeyed classical Michaelis kinetics. However more recent studies have questioned this and other kinetic models are now being explored.

9. 2. 4 Culture modes and productivity

Although predominantly grown in batch culture, plant cells have also been grown in semicontinuous, fed-batch or continuous (chemostat and turbidostat[⑩]) culture. Biomass (dry wt) yields in excess of 25 g $\cdot$ L^{-1} have been achieved in batch culture, with carbon conversions greater than 50%. While these figures bear comparison with those from microbial systems, it must be remembered that the data for plant cells are accumulated over days (10~14 days being a fairly typical run time) compared again with hours for microbial cultures. In continuous culture run times of 2~3 months are not uncommon, and productivity figures in excess of 6 g $\cdot$ L^{-1} $\cdot$ d^{-1} have been quoted.

The general approach used to continuous and semicontinuous culture with plant cells is however exactly the same as that for microbial systems and will not be discussed here.

9.3　Mass cell growth and production systems

9.3.1　Mass cell growth and properties of plant cells

The provision of sufficient enzymic machinery as viable biomass underpins all biotechnological processes, whether they be mass cell growth systems, single or multistage biosyntheses, immobilized systems or fluidized beds. This need has in turn led to the development of mass culture systems for plant cells. The approaches to this development are very much dependent on the properties of the cell systems for which they are required. Plant cells have a number of characteristics which not only set them apart from microbial cells and traditional fermenter designs, but also place particular constraints on the approach to vessel design and scale-up. The key features of plant cells in relation to mass growth are as follows:

- they have low growth rates, which necessitate long vessel residence times;
- the cells are large (100μm in diameter) and dense;
- cell volume may change by a factor up to 10^5 during batch culture;
- cell clumps containing between 2 and 200 cells occur to varying degrees;
- older cells possess a large central vacuole which often contains toxic substances;
- metabolic and physiological activity is generally low in comparison with microorganisms (e. g. respiration rates of the order of 1 μmol O_2 h^{-1} $(10^6$ cells$)^{-1}$;
- the plasmalemma is surrounded by a thick cellulose-based cell wall, which has a high tensile strength but low shear resistance.

Plant cells have now been grown in a whole range of vessel shapes and sizes. In Japan, tobacco cells have been successfully grown in conventional turbine-stirred bioreactors up to 20m³ in size. A wide range of cells from other species have been grown in vessels up to about 1.5m³. In general, however, conventional paddle stirred vessels have not been particularly successful. Those designed for handling microorganisms are generally designed to achieve high gas transfer rates, to cope with a very active metabolism and physiology, and therefore with a high level of shear. Unfortunately such levels of shear are deleterious to plant cells and may rapidly result in cell lysis and death. To maintain plant cells in conventional bioreactors, internal baffles are normally removed, and the rotation speed of the turbine is reduced to 300 r.p.m. or less. Unfortunately while lowering the turbine rotation speed may reduce shear and cell lysis, problems of maintaining good mixing may then arise, particularly as the nutrient broth of plant cells tends to have a fairly high viscosity which increases during culture growth. One alternative is to modify the usual flatbladed impeller to a marine impeller to decrease shear but aid bulk mixing. Another approach finding increasing favour is to dispense with the impeller system and utilize the incoming gas stream not only to aerate the culture but also to provide mixing, using the air-lift approach with either an internal draught tube or an external loop (Chapter 4). Both systems have the major advantage of low shear characteristics. Bulk mixing in draught tube and loop reactors can however be poor, particularly at high biomass levels (over $15 \sim 20$ g $\cdot$ L^{-1}), though scale-up to some extent ameliorates this problem. The much lower metabolic and physiological activity of plants results in a much lower respiratory oxygen demand, and in consequence venting rates need not be so high, which also reduces foaming problems. On the whole plant cell cultures do not tend to suffer from foaming problems to the degree observed with microbial systems, but a rather different problem arises. Many plant cell cultures in later stages of growth excrete large amounts of polysaccharide and protein which tends to accumulate around the foam bubbles at the top of the culture. Here it traps cells which are carried up into the foam, and a crust of cell material gradually forms in the head space above the culture. Accretion of cell material may also occur on the underside of the crust, which then 'grows' down into the culture broth aggregating more and more cell material as it does so. This soon results in a breakdown of mixing within the vessel and a highly heterogeneous culture. Though plant cells are not as sticky as many animal cells (Chapter 8), and do not adhere to the general surfaces of the vessel, they will often aggregate around probes, causing problems with sensing devices such as pO_2 and pH electrodes, as well as blocking orifices making the use of recycling systems or weirs in continuous cultures difficult. While the excretion of the polysaccharide may be regulated to some degree through the nature and manner of carbon supply to the culture, no really satisfactory way, either physical or chemical, has yet been found of controlling this phenomenon.

Another important aspect of plant cell mass growth involves the gas regime and the venting rate. As already stated, plant cells have a much lower oxygen demand than microbial cells. It is in fact easy to 'overgas' a plant cell culture, with deleterious effects on both growth rate and final biomass yield. At air flow rates of much more than about 0.5 v.v.m. or K_La values of 20 h^{-1}, there is a marked extension of lag phase in batch culture, with a following reduction in μ_{max} and an eventual reduction in biomass yield, which can be up to 40% less than in cultures operated at K_La values of less than 20 h^{-1}. The precise nature of this effect is not understood. One possibility is that high K_La and dissolved oxygen values may in some way reduce citric acid cycle activity (there are precedents for this from work with intact plant tissues). Another explanation is that high air flow rates lead to the stripping off of key volatiles. With nutrient broth pH values in the range of $5.5 \sim 6.5$, loss of carbon dioxide is a strong possibility, and in experiments where a carbon dioxide bleed has been administered to cultures at high K_La

5   values, some recovery of biomass yield has been noted.

9. 3. 2   Production systems

Only in exceptional cases can plant cell cultures, with their slow growth rates, be envisaged as a biomass source. The principle exception is for tobacco biomass, and possibly tea, coffee and ginseng powder. The major thrust of plant cell culture is

10   therefore directed towards production systems for single, typically high added-value, speciality chemicals (see Section 9. 4). Secondary product synthesis by plant cell cultures follows, in general, a pattern very similar to that observed in microbial systems; major synthesis typically occurs in the late log or stationary phase of batch culture when cell division has ceased and growth (as increase in biomass) has begun to decline. There are

15   occasional exceptions to this, a good one being the alkaloid serpentine which is synthesized by cultures of *Catharanthus roseus* during active growth. Because of the apparent lack of coupling between cell division, active growth and secondary product synthesis, the general approach to product synthesis with plant cell cultures has either been to use two-stage systems, the first stage being for biomass production and the

20   second for natural product synthesis, or more recently to move to 'zero' growth conditions, such as with immobilized cells or fluidized beds.

A number of nutrient regimes have now been developed which allow for effective two-stage operation. The first stage may be some form of continuous culture where conditions are adjusted for maximum biomass productivity, but which result in little or

25   no product formation. Biomass is then transferred to a second vessel system and the nutrient regime geared to high natural product synthesis. This latter system is usually a batch culture and is characterized by low cell viability if the cells are subsequently subcultured. This two-stage approach has been particularly useful in the development of a process for cardiac glycoside formation.

30   During the last two or three years a number of laboratories have begun to study immobilized cells or fluidized beds; this is also a form of two-stage process. A wide range of plant cells have now been successfully immobilized and on a wide variety of supports, including starch, agarose and polyacrylamide. Cell viability has been retained for periods in excess of 150 days and continued product synthesis has been observed. A number of

35   problems still remain: first, it is difficult to prevent cell growth and division; second, gas transfer in the immobilizing support may be critically restricted. A third problem, not unique to immobilized systems, concerns the 'leakage/excretion' of product from the cells. With immobilized systems release in some way of the desired product into the bathing nutrient is of key importance for product recovery. In general, it is still uncertain

whether products appearing in the medium result from active release[①], or through cell lysis subsequent to cell death.

9. 4　Products from cell cultures

9. 4. 1　The development of productive cell lines

The years 1973~1974 appear to have marked a major watershed in the development of plant cell culture technology. Prior to this, although many species had been established in culture, few had been shown to synthesize substances characteristic of the parent plant, and none at concentrations observed in high-yielding plant tissues. Even where desirable substances were synthesized it appeared that their production was linked to the development of shoots, roots and other tissue and organ systems. From a biochemical engineering standpoint, the development of tissues, organs and large slow-growing complex masses of cell material is far from desirable in large-scale bioreactors.

The period 1973 ~ 1974 was characterized by three major steps forward: the discovery of increasing numbers of cell lines which synthesized products characteristic of the parent plant, the observation of levels of desirable products equivalent to those found in the parent plant, and an increasing number of examples where product synthesis occurred in cell cultures and did not appear to be obligatorily linked to tissue or organ development. Examples which fulfil all of these criteria are listed in Table 9. 4; note the wide range of plant species and chemical structures involved. The more general list, Table 9. 5, illustrates the range of structures and activities which have been reported. A degree of caution must be exercised when appraising such a list; only a relatively small proportion of the total number will ever[②] be economically viable targets for commercialization through plant cell culture.

Without a detailed discussion of the various products, it is worth noting the more important ones which are obvious targets. Under the heading medicinal agents there are a variety of substances including such important agents as the antileukaemic drugs vincrystine and vinblastine from the Madagascan periwinkle, *Catharanthus roseus.* These are complex dimeric alkaloids of very high added value and a major target for a number of research groups, but not one has yet succeeded in their synthesis through plant cell culture. The related monomeric alkaloids serpentine and ajmalicine, used as arrhythmic agents and also obtained from periwinkle, have likewise been intensely investigated and in this case cell lines have been isolated which synthesized both alkaloids at levels well above 1% of the dry weight, equivalent to or better than the parent plant. This could provide one of the first major plant cell culture processes. The opiate alkaloids, morphine and codeine, extensively used as painkillers, have been demonstrated in cultures of opium poppy cells (*Papaver somniferum*) and are perhaps an obvious target, not only from the viewpoint of drug supply but also in terms of control of narcotics abuse.

Table 9. 4   Natural product yields from cell cultures and whole plants

	Natural product	Species	Cell culture yield	Whole plant
	Anthraquinones	*Morinda citrifolia*	900 nmol (g dry wt)$^{-1}$	Root，110nmol (g dry wt)$^{-1}$
5	Anthraquinones	*Cassia tora*	0. 334% fr wt	0. 209% seed，dry wt
	Ajmalicine and serpentine	*Catharanthus roseus*	1. 3% dry wt	0. 26% dry wt
	Diosgenin	*Dioscorea deltoidea*	26mg (g dry wt)$^{-1}$	20 mg (g drywt)$^{-1}$tuber
10	Ginseng saponins	*Panax ginseng*	0. 38% fr wt	0. 3%～3. 3% fr wt
	Nicotine	*Nicotiana tabacum*	3%～4% dry wt	2%～5% dry wt
	Thebaine	*Papaver bracteatum*	130 mg (g dry wt)$^{-1}$	1400 g (g dry wt)$^{-1}$ leaf and 3000 mg (g dry wt)$^{-1}$ root
15	Ubiquinone	*N. tabacum*	0. 5mg (g dry wt)$^{-1}$	16 mg (g dry wt)$^{-1}$ leaf

Table 9. 5   Substances reported from plant cell cultures

Alkaloids	Latex
Allergens	Lipids
Anthroquinones	Naphthoquinones
Antileukaemic agents	Nucleic acids
Antitumour agents	Nucleotides
Antiviral agents	Oils
Aromas	Opiates
Benzoquinones	Organic acids
Carbohydrates (including polysaccharides)	Proteins
Cardiac glycosides	Peptides
Chalcones	Perfumes
Diathrones	Pigments
Enzymes	Phenols
Enzyme inhibitors	Plant growth regulators
Flavanoids, flavones	Steroids and derivatives
Flavours (including sweeteners)	Sugars
Furanocoumarins	Tannins
Hormones	Terpenes and terpenoids
Insecticides	Vitamins

Plants are increasingly being turned to as a potential source of antimicrobials, particularly antifungal agents. Many cell cultures have some level of antimicrobial activity, but few have undergone any degree of rigorous screening. Undoubtedly this could be a most fruitful area for further study.

One of the classical plant products used in medicine is the cardiac glycoside digoxin. Not only have cell cultures of *Digitalis lanata* (the foxglove) been established which will synthesize this cardiatonic but also cell lines have been isolated which will carry out[13] the chemically difficult single-step conversion of the low-value digitoxin to   **5** high-value digoxin. This particular biotransformation was perhaps the first to find a true process application.

In addition to the more obvious pharmaceutical targets, there are substances of importance in foods and agrochemicals. Cell cultures of *Cinchona ledgeriana* have been isolated which will produce the alkaloid quinine, which is a bittering agent and ingredient   **10** of many soft drinks, and is still used as a key agent against malaria. Although the alkaloids tend to predominate in secondary product applications, other chemical structures do make an important contribution, for instance terpenoilds and the aromatic oils in perfumes and aromas. Cultures have now been established which possess very pleasant aromas, but in perfumery the precise aroma is often a product of a complex mix   **15** of chemical structures, difficult to reproduce or mimic. Steroids also have been isolated from cell cultures, in particular diosgenin, which is a key precursor in the steroidal component of the oral contraceptive steroids. However in this case the raw material from traditional plantations has such a low market value that it is doubtful if plant cell culture will ever[12] compete commercially.   **20**

Natural colours provide an interesting target. With the increasing problems caused by the various regulatory agencies in response to public concern over synthetic colours in foods, the plant kingdom is an obvious search area for reds, blues, yellows, etc. A variety of reds have now been produced, and recent work has shown that both blue and yellow may be feasible. However in this case there are likely to be problems with the stability of   **25** the natural product. Many foods are either near neutrality or slightly alkaline in pH, whereas most natural colours are more stable in acid conditions. Whether it will prove possible to stabilize these products in an acceptable way is difficult to say.

Some of the plant neurotoxins match anything that some groups of the animal kingdom, such as reptiles and arachnids, are able to synthesize. Ricin and curare are   **30** particularly good examples. Whether they will ever[12] be targets for plant cell culture one hesitates to contemplate.

9.4.2 Selection and screening

A key aspect of the development of a plant cell culture process in to select cells with a high yield of the desired product. The importance of this cannot be overemphasized[6].   **35** Equally this has so far proved to be one of the most problematical areas of plant cell culture. It is exceedingly difficult to isolate and properly clone single plant cells which may be high yielding. At the same time techniques for the assay of desired substances are often insufficiently sensitive to measure the minute traces of substances present in a single cell. Over the last two or three years developments in radioimmunoassay[⑭] and enzyme immunoassay have helped overcome this particular problem. Coupled with classical microbial approaches to application of selection pressures this should bring major progress in the years ahead. Yield increases in the region of 10-fold would dramatically change the economic viability of a number of potential products.

9.4.3 Future horizons

In the long term it is likely that the most important applications of plant cell culture will be in biotransformations and in novel products. The potential for a wide range of biotransformations using either immobilized cells or extracted plant enzymes undoubtedly exists, the major restriction to development being our lack of fundamental knowledge of the general biochemistry and enzymology of natural product synthesis. Novel products raise all sorts of possibilities.

The availability of plant cell culture technology brings with it a possible field of applications for gene manipulation techniques, and where a desirable plant product is an enzyme or a simpler peptide then undoubtedly this will be a target for transfer to a more amenable host/production system for process development. The non-nutritive protein sweetener thaumatin is a good example. However where the product is non-proteinaceous, of low molecular weight and at the end of a long multienzyme sequence it is extremely unlikely that gene transfer to another host will be feasible. In this case gene manipulation within the plant cell itself may be of assistance in de-controlling a pathway to allow greater throughput.

9.5 Conclusion

Our knowledge of both plant natural product biochemistry and of plant cell culture lags far behind that for microbial systems. In consequence our time horizons for plant cells must be extended that much further, possibly into the next century, while the fundamental science base is established. The prize is worth working for, but the level of patience required may be very high.

Words and Expressions

page	line				
245	3	array	[ə'rei]	n.	大量，（排列整齐的）一批 large number
	7	secondary product	['sekəndəri 'prɔdəkt]	n.	次生产物
	8	secondary metabolite	[mə'tæbəlait]	n.	次级代谢产物
	12	perfume	['pəːfjuːm]	n.	香水
		spice	[spais]	n.	香料
	13	discrete	[dis'kriːt]	a.	各别的，分离的 individual, distinct, consisting of unconnected distinct parts.

page	line		
245	13	cocoa butter fat	['kəukəu 'bʌtə fæt] n. 可可脂

Attar of roses   ['ætə əv rəuzis]   n.   玫瑰油

14   blend   [blend]   n.   混合物   mixture

17   constrain   [kən'strein]   vt.   限制，约束   restrain

18   isomer   ['aisəumə]   n.   同分异构体

20   speciality chemical   n.   特种化学品

21   plantation   [plæn'teiʃən]   n.   种植园

more often than not   多半   very frequently

tropics   ['trɔpiks]   （复）   n.   热带

subtropics   [sʌb'trɔpiks]   （复）   n.   副热带，亚热带   area adjacent to the
   tropics

22   in time   总有一天   in the course of time；eventually

rival   ['raivl]   vt.   与……竞争   to attempt to equal or surpass

24   encompass   [in'kʌmpəs]   vt.   包含   include，comprise

30   pest   [pest]   n.   有害的动、植物   an injurious plant or animal

31   constraint   [kən'streint]   n.   约束，限制   something that restricts，limits，
   or regulates

246   7   come to the fore   涌现出来   be in or toward a position of prominence

12   deter   [di'tə:]   vt.   使吓住   to prevent from acting (as by fear)

17   totipotency   [təu'tipətensi]   n.   全能性   a characteristic of having all the
   'potency' of the original plant. ability to generate or regenerate a whole
   organism from a part

21   horticulture   ['hɔ:tikʌltʃə]   n.   园艺（学）   the cultivation of a gardon

22   none the less   还是，仍然   nevertheless

25   hit and miss   有时打中，有时打不中的；碰巧的   sometimes successful，somtimes
   not；random.

26   ill-defined   ['ildi'faind]   a.   不确定的

28   thiamine   ['θaiəmin]   n.   硫胺素，维生素 B_1

glutathione   [ˌglu:tə'θaiəun]   n.   谷胱甘肽

indole acetic acid   n.   吲哚乙酸

29   coconut milk   ['kəukənʌt milk]   n.   椰子汁

endosperm   ['endəuspə:m]   n.   胚乳   a nutritive tissue in seed plants formed
   within the embryo sac.

30   notorious   [nəu'tɔ:riəs]   a.   著名的   generally known and discussed

247   8   run into   （累积而）达到   to mount up to

9   something like   大约

13   rudimentary   [ˌru:di'mentəri]   a.   基本的，初步的   essential

248   2   all the more   更加，更多

incentive   [in'sentiv]   n.   刺激，鼓励   something that incites

262

page	line			
248	4	herbal	['hə:bəl]	a. 草药的

248　4　herbal　['hə:bəl]　a.　草药的

　　　5　potion　['pəuʃən]　n.　药水　a liquid dose of medicine

　　　7　digoxin　[di'dʒɔksin]　n.　地高辛（一种强心剂）

　　　　　cardiatonic　[ˌkɑ:diə'tɔnik]　a.　强心的　tonic　滋补的

　　　　　foxglove　['fɔksglʌv]　n.　（植）毛地黄

　　　　　quinine　[k'wini:n]　n.　奎宁，金鸡钠碱

　　　8　antimalarial　[ˌæntimə'leəriəl]　a.　抗疟疾的

　　　　　alkaloid　['ælkəlɔid]　n.　生物碱　天然存在的有机物质，具药理活性，通常
　　　　　　为结构复杂的杂环化合物.

　　　　　codeine　['kəudi:n]　n.　可待因（用以镇痛、镇咳、催眠等）

　　　　　analgesic　[ˌænæl'dʒi:sik]　a.　止痛的　an-非

　　　9　opium poppy　['əupiəm 'pɔpi]　n.　罂粟

　　　13　anticholinergic　['ænti ˌkɔuli'nædʒik]　a.（n.）　抗胆碱能的（药物）

　　　　　antihypertensive　['ænti ˌhaipə'tensiv]　a.（n.）　抗高血压的（药物）

　　　　　antileukaemic　[ˌæntilju:'ki:mik]　a，（n.）　抗白血病的（药物）

　　　14　pharmacology　[ˌfɑ:mə'kɔlədʒi]　n.　药理学

　　　16　agrochemical　[ˌægrəu'kemikəl]　n.　农用化学品

　　　20　atropine　['ætrəpin]　n.　阿托品，颠茄碱

　　　21　vincrystine　[vin'kristi:n]　n.　长春新碱

　　　23　vinblastine　[vin'blæsti:n]　n.　长春（花）碱

　　　24　tubocurarine　[ˌtju:bəukju'rɑ:rin]　n.　筒箭毒碱

　　　　　relaxant　[ri'læksənt]　n.　弛缓药

　　　26　colchicine　['kɔltʃisi:n]　n.　秋水仙碱

　　　　　anti-inflammatory　[ˌæntiin'flæmətəri]　a.n　消炎的（药）

　　　27　scopalamine　[ˌskəupə'læmi:n]　n.　东莨菪碱

　　　29　diosgenin　[dai'ɔzdʒənin]　n.　薯蓣皂苷配基

　　　　　antifertility　[ˌæntifə'tiləti]　a.　抗生育的

　　　31　emetine　['eməti:n]　n.　依米丁，吐根碱

　　　　　amoebicide　[ə'mi:bicaid]　n.　抗阿米巴药　-cide　杀灭剂

　　　35　digitoxin　[ˌdidʒi'tɔksin]　n.　洋地黄毒苷

　　　36　pilocarpine　[ˌpailəu'kɑ:pain]　n.　毛果芸香碱（一种眼科缩瞳药）

　　　37　reserpine　['resəpin]　n.　利血平（一种降压药）

　　　39　thaumatin　['θɔ:mətin]　n.　非洲竹芋甜素（比砂糖甜 3000 倍）

　　　40　jasmin　['dʒæsmin]　n.　茉莉

　　　42　pyrethroid　[ˌpaiə'ri:θrɔid]　n.　拟除虫菊酯　-oid　类似……的东西

249　8　selection pressure　n.　选择压力（反映环境条件和营养条件的各种力量之和，能
　　　　　促进群体中某些生物生长，而阻碍另一些生物生长）.

　　　12　speculate on　['spekjuleit]　vi.　推测　conjecture, guess
　　　　　a host of　一大群　a very large number

page	line	

249　17　contemplate　［'kɔntempleit］　vt.　预期，视……为可能　to regard or take account of as a possibility

23　move on　继续前进

26　callus　['kæləs］　n.　愈伤组织

28　excise　［ek'saiz］　vt.　切除　to remove by or as if by cutting out

explant　［ek'splænt］　外植体　切除的组织，用于在体外进行组织培养

33　conceal　［kən'siːl］　vt.　隐藏　hide

microflora　［ˌmaikəu'flɔːrə］　n.　微生物群落　flora　菌群

37　sodium hypochrolite　［'səudjəmˌhaipəu'klɔːrait］　n.　次氯酸钠　NaOCl

hypo-次

250　7　nystatin　［'nistətin］　n.　制霉菌素（抗霉菌药）

16　closure　['kləuʒə］　n.　关闭物　something that closes or shuts

bung　［bʌŋ］　n.　塞子　stopper

aluminium foil　［ˌælju'miniəm fɔil］　n.　铝箔

20　autotrophic　［ˌɔːtə'trɔfik］　a.　自养的

22　proliferate　［prəu'lifəreit］　vt.　使增殖　to cause to grow or increase rapidly

23　align (with)　［ə'lain wið］　vt.　使一致　bring into agreement

27　frizzy　['frizi］　a.　卷曲的　tightly curled

28　obligatory　［ɔ'bligətəri］　a.　必须履行的　mandatory

33　friable　['fraiəbl］　a.　易碎的　brittle, readily crumbled

36　amenable　［ə'miːnəbl］ (to)　a.　顺从的　willing to be guided or controlled

40　much the same　几乎相同的　about the same

251　5　allude (to)　［ə'ljuːd］　vi　略为一提，间接提到　refer indirectly

10　supersede　［ˌsjuːpə'siːd］　vt.　取代　replace

16　formulation　［ˌfɔːmju'leiʃən］　n.　配制（按方配制）　the action of preparation according to a specific formula

35　meso inositol　［'mesəu i'nəusitɔl］　n.　内消旋肌醇

36　nicotinic acid　［ˌnikə'tinik 'æsid］　n.　烟酸，尼克酸

38　pyridoxine　［ˌpiri'dɔksiːn］　n.　吡多醇，维生素 B₆

252　3　casein　['keisiːn］　n.　酪蛋白

9　lesion　['liːʒən］　n.　损害　injury

10　chloroplast　['klɔːrəuplæst］　n.　叶绿体　-plast　表示'体'、'粒'、'团'一种在植物和藻类中存在的细胞器，内含叶绿素，能进行光合作用

16　maltose　['mɔːltəus］　n.　麦芽糖　-ose　糖

galactose　［gə'læktəus］　n.　半乳糖

24　invertase　［in'vəːteis］　n.　转化酶　-ase　酶　一种酶能将蔗糖水解为等量的葡萄糖和果糖的混合物（转化糖 invert sugar）

26　plasmalemma　['plæzməˌlemə］　n.　质膜，细胞膜　the outermembrane that surrounds the protoplasm of a cell

264

page	line				
258	11	nicotine	['nikəti:n]	n.	烟碱，尼古丁
	13	thebaine	['θi:bəi:n]	n.	蒂巴因，二甲基吗啡
	14	ubiquinone	[ju:'bikwinəun]	n.	泛醌，辅酶　Q. ubiquitous 与 quinone 缩合
	19	latex	['leiteks]	n.	胶乳
	20	allergen	['ælədʒən]	n.	过敏原，变（态反）应原
	21	naphthoquinone	[ˌnæfθəukwi'nəun]	n.	萘醌
	25	aroma	[ə'rəumə]	n.	香味
		opiate	['əupiət]	n.	鸦片制剂，麻醉剂，镇静剂
	26	benzoquinone	[ˌbenzəukwi'nəun]	n.	苯醌
	29	chalcone	['kælkəun]	n.	苯基苯乙烯酮
	33	flavanoid		n.	类黄酮
		flavone	['fleivəun]	n.	黄酮
	35	furanocoumarin	[ˌfjuərənəu'kumərin]	n.	呋喃香豆素
		tannin	['tænin]	n.	丹宁，鞣酸
	36	terpene	['tə:pi:n]	n.	萜
		terpenoid	['tə:pinɔid]	n.	类萜
259	15	perfumery	[pə'fju:məri]	n.	香料制造厂　-(e)ry　表示场所
	18	contraceptive	[ˌkɔntrə'septiv]	a.	避孕的
	29	neurotoxin	[ˌnjuərəu'tɔksin]	n.	神经毒素
	30	reptile	['reptail]	n.	爬行动物
		arachnid	[ə'ræknid]	n.	蛛形纲动物
		ricin	['raisin]	n.	蓖麻（子）蛋白
		curare	[kju'rɑ:ri]	n.	箭毒马钱子
260	6	horizon	[hə'raizən]	n.	（复）范围、眼界
	21	throughput		n.	生产量　output

Notes

① 助动词 be 和动词不定式构成谓语，可以有几种不同的用法，这里表示可能（can，may），如：

I am not sure whether he is to turn up tonight. 今晚他能否来，我不能肯定．

本句可译为：在植物界可发现很多不同化学结构的化合物。

　　最常用的是表示按计划安排要发生的事，如：

The meeting is to be held Monday morning.（会议订在星期一上午举行）参见 . p. 192，Ch. 6，Note③.

详见张道真：实用英语语法，商务印书馆，1979，p. 184～186.

② Secondary metabolites 次级代谢产物是指对生物的生长非必需的代谢产物或中间产物，通常在微生物生长的稳定期产生。这些产物的作用，人们还不甚了解，但它们很有价值，如大多数由微生物产生的抗生素都是次级代谢产物。

③ 本句可译为：用于这些用途的物质并不都是单一的物质（有些是混合物）。本句为部分否定句。一般说来，含有全体意义的代词和副词，如 all，every，each，total，both，whole，always，totally，completely，wholly 等和 not 同时出现在一个句子中时，不管它们的前后位置，句子的含义一般都是部分否定。本句的表达方式和汉语相同，在理解上不会有问题。但下面的部分否定句，容易发生错误，需要特别注意：

All the answers are not right. 答案并非全对。

I do not know all of them. 对于他们，我不是个个都认识的。

Every body，it is true，wouldn't like it. 的确并不是人人都喜欢它。

They don't go to work by bus every day. 他们并不是每天都坐公共汽车上班。

Both the engines are not running. 两部发动机并不都在运转。

④ add to vi. 增添，这里是其被动态。通常只有及物动词才有被动语态，但有些短语动词在意义上相当于及物动词，也有被动语态。短语动词在主动结构中是一个不可分割的词组，在被动结构中也是如此，不可丢掉后面的介词或副词。如：

We have sent for the doctor. （主动态）

The doctor has been sent for. （被动态）

本句可译为：从高等植物得到的物质具有各种化学结构，据报道，其结构的数目已达几十万种，而且还在不断增加。

⑤ callus 愈伤组织，指含未分化细胞的植物组织，本来指植物体创伤部分新生的组织，现已扩大到包括外植体在琼脂培养基上的培养物。

⑥ 这两句属于一种特殊的强调句型：

can not（can hardly，can scarcely）或 It is impossible…too（enough）/over，这种句型可分两个部分：前面部分的谓语中带有否定词；后面部分含有 too，over 等表示"过分"或 enough 等表示"足够"的词。意为"无论怎样……也不算太过分"或"必须……"、"非常……"之意。

此句可译为：对好的无菌技术的需要，怎么强调也不过分（好的无菌技术是非常需要的）。又如：

1. We cannot estimate the value of modern science too much（或 enough）.

   We cannot overestimate the value of modern science.

   It is impossible to estimate the value of modern science too much（或 enough）

   现代科学的价值，无论怎样重视也不过分（我们必须高度重视现代科学的价值）。

2. There can never be too much deception in war. 兵不厌诈。

3. We can hardly（或 scarcely）pay too high a price for liberation.

   我们不惜任何代价去争取解放。

   也可以把本句型看作双重否定形式，即用两个否定来表示一个肯定的意思。第一个否定由 "not" 表示，而第二个否定由含有否定意义的副词 "too" 或词缀 "over" 来表示，如：

   Practice cannot be done too soon.

   实践越早越好。

⑦ in turn 这里意义为'转而'，如：A affect B，B in turn affects C（A 影响 B，B 则影响 C）.

本句可译为：过分使用灭菌剂，会对表面细胞和组织有损害，因而造成细胞成活率低和对建立培养物造成困难。

注意 in turn 的另一个意义为'依次'或'轮流'。

⑧ casein 酪蛋白，牛乳中的主要蛋白质（占全奶的 2.6%），酪蛋白不是一种单一蛋白质，而是一组磷蛋白的混合物，主要含有三种 α-，β-和 κ-酪蛋白。

⑨ auxin 植物激素，一组内源的植物生长物质，其结构和吲哚乙酸有关，能通过使细胞伸长和根的形成而促使植物生长。在植物细胞培养中常用的植物激素有 1-萘乙酸和 2，4-二氯苯氧乙酸等。

⑩ chemostat 恒化器，它和 tubidostat 恒浊器都是连续发酵的一种操作方式，前者以一种限制性基质的浓度控制加料速度，后者则以浊度来控制加料速度。

⑪ 这里的 active release 相当于以主动传递（active transport，见 Ch. 2，Note⑦）使产物释放。

⑫ 这三句中都含 'ever'，用法也相同，（用在疑问句，否定句以及表示条件和比较的从句中）表示在任何时候'从来'有时或在某时。

第一句可译为：在评价这个表时，需要谨慎；只有较少一部分物质将会在经济上有竞争力，以植物细胞培养的方法进行工业生产。（表示'在某时'）。

又如：

Have you ever been to Beijing？你到过北京吗？（表示'在任何时候'）

It was the first ever meeting to discuss this matter 这是首次讨论这个问题的会议。（表示'从来'）

⑬ carry out（动词＋副词）称为短语动词（phrasal verb），在口语中常用。在科技文章中，为了正确表达含意，很多作者喜欢用一个规范动词来代替，如：

短语动词	规范动词
carry out（249/31，259/5）	conduct，accomplish
break up（250/35）	disintegrate
set out（182/35）	describe
make up（145/19）	form
stand up to（121/33）	endure
set up（110/26）	establish
give rise to（78/38）	cause
open up（77/29）	disclose
show up（76/35）	appear
bring about（40/24）	effect
take up（38/28）	absorb
build up（38/1）	compose

但是也有一些短语动词，广泛应用于科技文章，其原因可能是没有适当的规范动词能够代替或由于作者个人的爱好，如：

deal with（处理）；cut off（切断）；cool off（冷却）；

shut down（关闭）；run out of（消耗完）.

⑭ radioimmunoassay（RIA）放射免疫分析法，即利用抗体来检测微量物质（抗原）的方法。

一已知量的标记抗原物质和抗体加到试液中。标记和未标记（待测）抗原相互竞争性地和抗体作用，测定与抗体结合的标记抗原的量，待测抗原的量愈多，形成的标记抗原-抗体结合物就愈少。

Comprehension

1. Define the term 'plant cell biotechnology'. (p. 245)

2. What were the major difficulties impeding the development of plant cell cultures during 1950s? (p. 246)

3. What are the most salient features of the plant-derived products? (p. 247~248)

4. What is meant by the 'silent' genes? (p. 249)

5. State briefly how to start a plant culture. (p. 249~250)

6. What parameters are discussed in Section 9.2.2 Growth regimes? (p. 251~253)

7. What are the similar and dissimilar points regarding growth between cultured plants and microorganisms? (p. 253~254)

8. Enumerate the critical characteristics of plant cells with respect to mass growth. (p. 254)

9. Does conventional bioreacter be suitable for cultivating plant cells? If not, what modifications are needed? (p. 254~255)

10. What are the two main problems involved in the operation of a plant cell cultivation? (p. 255~256)

11. Why either a two-stage system or immobilized cells or fluidized bed at 'zero' growth conditions are commonly used for plant cell cultures aiming at secondary metabolites? (p. 256)

12. How could the gene manipulation techniques be possibly used in plant cell culture technology in two different ways, depending on the nature of the desirable product? (p. 260)

Vocabulary

Give another word or phrase to replace these words or phrases as they are used in the text:

prospect (246/37); prevailing (249/7); contemplate (249/17); outgrow (246/35); across (250/25); respective (253/20); explore (253/35); quote (254/7); dispense with (255/8); head space (255/20); bathing (256/39); exceedingly (259/37).

Word usage

1. Write sentences to bring out the difference between the following pairs of words:
rival (245/22), compete; encompass (245/24), involve (245/25); speculate (249/12), infer; specialized (253/16), special; appraise (257/21), estimate.

2. Make sentences with the following words or phrases:
play a significant part (245/9); make use of (245/11); in consequence (246/18); amenable to (250/36); in much the same way as (250/40); on the whole (255/15); envisage (256/8).

Sentence analysis and translation

First analyse the following sentences as in ch. 1，Note① and then translate into Chinese：

1. The sentences from line 31，page 246 to line 1，page 247；During the period 1940～ 1960……in vanishingly low concentrations.
2. The beginning of the section 9.2.1，from line 26 to 36 on page 249.
3. Section 9.5 Conclusion on page 260

Writing

The following is the Chinese translation of introductory part of a paper entitled "Monoclonal Antibody Purification of Trichoderma reesei EGI" published in Applied Biochemistry and Biotechnology，1990. Try to retranslate into English.

引言

近 30 年来，人们对 Trichoderma reesei 的纤维素酶系统的工业应用有浓厚兴趣，对该酶系统进行了广泛的研究。此真菌分解纤维素已证实是纤维二糖水解酶（CBH），内切葡聚糖酶（EG）和 β-葡糖苷酶的作用。这些酶协同作用能有效地分解纤维素成为可利用的基质。目前纤维素酶有多种用途，包括从食品调味品到有机原料的生产。

虽然纤维素酶对可再生资源（如木质纤维素）的利用前景很好，但应用时必须降低酶的生产成本。要达到这个目的，关键是需详细了解在纤维素转化中的协同作用。为了研究这个问题，对纯化的纤维素酶各组分（即 CBH I，CBH II，EG I 和 EG II），必须拥有毫克到克的数量。由于这四种酶的理化性能很相似，它们的分离和纯化相当困难。过去对纤维素酶系统的各别组分的纯化，一般要经过好几个步骤，如凝胶过滤、离子交换和制备型等电聚焦等。虽然能得到表观上高纯度的酶，但这种多步骤纯化可能会对蛋白质的构象和活性有害。因此经过较少的步骤获得纯化的纤维素酶和最终比较它们的活性是有益的。

自从 Kohler 和 Milstein 发表了关于 B-淋巴细胞杂交瘤的生产的里程碑式的文章以来，单克隆抗体获得多方面的应用。从复杂混合物中分离一种蛋白质，利用单克隆抗体进行亲和纯化，证明是很有效的。在本文中我们叙述了利用单克隆抗体纯化 T. reesei 的内切葡聚糖酶的主要组分 EG I 所取得的进展。

生词　Trichoderma 木霉菌属；纤维二糖水解酶 Cellobiohydrolase；内切葡聚糖酶 endoglucanase；协同作用 synergism；原料 feedstock；制备型等电聚焦 preparative isoelectric focusing；构象 configuration；里程碑 landmark.

Optional writing exercises

1. 没有近代蛋白质纯化技术的发展，新近生物工程引人注目的进展是不可能的。

   （引人注目的——dramatic。用虚拟语态过去时）

2. 外周膜蛋白一旦分离后，就和可溶性蛋白质相似，并能按此处理。

   （外周膜蛋白——peripheral membrane protein；处理——handle。用词组 as such。）

3. 记录光密度的降低直至它不再变化为止。

   （不再变化——level off。用过去时。）

4. 配制一系列不同浓度的牛血清蛋白在 20mL，pH＝7.0，0.01M Tris 缓冲液中的溶液，分别置于 50mL 烧瓶中。

   （牛血清蛋白——Bovine serum protein；烧瓶——flask）

5. 产物在冷却后置于玻璃细孔漏斗中，分别以己烷（200mL），甲苯（100mL），乙醇，水，1MHCl 和 0.3mol/LNaOH 洗涤至无氯离子，然后用水洗至中性，50℃真空干燥过夜，得到 9.1g 树脂。

   （玻璃细孔漏斗——sintered glass filter；己烷——hexane；甲苯——toluene。用过去时）

6. 钠盐要比游离酸易溶于水。

   （游离酸——free acid。注意连词 than 后的词序。）

7. 大颗粒使传质阻力大大增加，这是由于吸附质需要扩散到位于多孔结构深处的吸附位点上。

   （传质阻力——mass-transfer resistance；吸附质——adsorbate；位点——site。用现在时）

8. 最适 pH 向碱性方向移动超过 1 个 pH 单位。

9. 为了写一篇文章，我需要您提供尽可能多的数据。（用现在时）

10. 多肽链是柔性的，但不具有环绕所有键都能自由旋转那样的柔性。

    （柔性的——flexible；键——bond。用虚拟语态现在时）

11. 含胰蛋白酶和胰凝乳蛋白酶各 100mg/L 的酶溶液（在 50mMTris 中，pH＝8，10mMCa^{2+}），用蠕动泵以 25mL/min 的流速输送到一个容器中。

    （胰蛋白酶——trypsin；胰凝乳蛋白酶——chymotrypsin；蠕动泵——peristaltic pump）．

12. 可以利用 pH 和离子强度两者的改变，或者单独或者两者同时改变。

    （离子强度——ionic strength。用被动语态现在时）

附录 1 常用前缀、后缀和构词成分

a- 不，非
    aseptic 无菌的；apolar 非极性的

ab- 脱离，离开
    abnormal 反常的；abuse 滥用

-able（-ible） 可能的
    practicable 可行的，responsible 负责的

-ability （构成名词）能力
    acceptability 可接受性；permeability 渗透性

-age （构成名词）表示动作过程、量
    spillage 溢出；percentage 百分比

-al 1. 接在名词后形成形容词
    personal 个人的；exceptional 例外的
    2. 接在动词后形成名词
    arrival 到达；refusal 拒绝

an- 不，非
    anaerobic 厌氧的；analgesic 止痛的

-ant 动作者
    inactivant 失活剂；bioprotectant 生物保护剂

anti- 反对，对抗
    antibiotic 抗生素；antibody 抗体

aut(o)- 自己的，自动的
    autotrophic 自养的；autonomous 自发的

cent(i)- 一百的，百分之一的
    century 世纪；centimeter 厘米

-cide 杀害，消灭
    suicide 自杀；bactericide 杀菌剂

co- 一起，共同
    cooperate 合作；coincide 重合

con-(col-,com-,cor-) 连同，一起
    concentrate 集中；combine 结合
    correlation 相关；collaborate 协作

contra- 反对，相反
    contrast 对照；contrary 相反的

counter- 反，逆
    counter-circulation 逆向循环

cryo- 寒冷，冷冻

cryopreservation 冷冻保藏

de- 否定，除去，离开，降低，脱
    debug 排除故障；deceleration 降速；
    degeneration 退化；
    deoxyribonucleic acid 脱氧核糖核酸

di- 二，二倍，二重
    diploid 二倍体；dimer 二聚体
    divinylbenzene 二乙烯苯

dia- 横穿
    diameter 直径；dialysis 透析

dis- 否定，分离
    disintegration 破碎；disagree 不同意；
    dissemination 散播

en-(em-) 使成为，置于……中
    enable 能够；encode 编码；embed 包埋
    entrainment 夹带；encompass 包含

-(e)ry 场所；一类事物
    bakery 面包房；circuitry 电路系统
    perfumery 香料（总称）；poultry 家禽（总称）

e(x)- （构成动词）向外；超出；完全，彻底
    explant 外植体；elongate 拉长；
    evaluate 评价

ex(o)- 外，在外，产生
    exothermic 放热的；exergonic 放能的

extra- 超出
    extracellular 胞外的

-fold 倍
    twofold 两倍

-(i)fy 接名词或形容词后构成动词
    solidify 固化；simplify 简化

-gram 图形；记录的东西
    chromatogram 色谱图；polarograph 极谱图

-graphy 描绘、记录的方式、学科
    chromatography 色层分离法；
    autoradiography 放射自显影术

hemi- 半
    hemicellulase 半纤维素酶

heter(o)-　异，杂，异种
　　heterogeneous　异质的，不均一的；hetero-
　　trophic　异养的
hom(o)-　相同
　　homogeneous　同质的，均一的；homologous 同
　　源的
hydr(o)-　水，液体，氢
　　hydrocarbon　烃；hydrocolloid　水胶体
hyper-　超出，过度
　　hyperfiltration　反渗透；hypertension　高血压
in-(il-,im-,ir-)不，无；在内，入内
　　insoluble　不能溶解的；insuperable　不能克服
　　的
　　impermeable　不能渗透的；illegal　非法的；
　　irregular　不规则的；imbibe　吸入
infra-　下面，内部
　　infrastructure　基础结构；infrared　红外线的
inter-　相互，在……之间
　　interact　相互作用；intergeneric　属间的；
　　inter-particle　颗粒间的
intra-　在内，向内
　　intraspecific　种内的；intra-particle　颗粒内
　　的；intravenous　进入静脉的
-ish　略带一点的
　　greyish　浅灰色的
-ist　……的实行者，……专业人员（专家）
　　scientist　科学家；geneticist　遗传学家
-ize (-ise)　使成为
　　atomize　雾化；oxidize　使氧化
-less　无，不，不能
　　stainless　不锈的
-like　如……样的
　　sponge-like　海绵状的
-(o)logy(-ological,形容词)学科
　　biology　生物学；technology　技术（学），工艺
　　学；
　　toxicological　毒理学的
macro-　大的，宏观的
　　macromolecule　大分子；macroporous　大孔的
-ment　在动词后构成名词
　　development　发展；entrainment　夹带
-meter　计，表
　　spectrometer　分光计；viscometer　粘度计
-metric　测量的

gravimetric　（测定）重量的；volumetric（测
　　定）体积的；potentiometric（测量）电位的
micro-　微，微小的
　　microscope　显微镜；microcarrier　微载体
mono-　一，单，单一
　　monoclonal　单克隆的；monolayer　单层
multi-　多，多方面
　　multistage　多级
neur(o)-　神经
　　neural　神经的；neurotoxin　神经毒素
non-　非，无，不
　　non-Newtonian fluid　非牛顿型流体
　　non-aqueous solution　非水溶液
over-　在上面，超过
　　overshooting　过调节；overview　简明概述
-ory　1. 构成形容词
　　　transitory　短暂的；respiratory　呼吸的
　　2. 构成名词，表示"场所"
　　　depository　储藏所
-ous　构成形容词
　　extraneous　外来的；rigorous　严格的
-philic　亲……的
　　lipophilic　亲脂性的；hydrophilic　亲水的
-phobic　疏……的
　　hydrophobic　疏水的
poly-　多，聚
　　polysaccharide　多糖；polystyrene　聚苯乙烯
post-　后
　　post-transcriptional modification　转录后修饰
　　作用；post-exponential growth phase　后对数
　　生长期
pre-　前，在前
　　premature　过早的；precursor　前体；
　　premise　前提
-proof　耐……的
　　flame-proof　耐火的；explosion-proof　防爆的
proto-　原始，初
　　prototype　原型；protoplast　原生质体
pseud(o)-　假的
　　pseudo-plastic fluid　假塑性流体
re-　再，重新，反复
　　recirculation　循环；reversion　回复
retro-　后，向后，回复
　　retrovirus　逆转录病毒

self- 自身的

    self-fertilization 自体受精

semi- 半，部分

    semi-permeable membrane 半透膜；semi-synthetic 半合成的

sub- 下面，次于，近于

    subcellular 亚细胞的；subunit 亚基；subdivide 再分；substratum 底层

super- 上，上面，超，超级

    superior 上面的；supernatant 上清液的

syn-(sym-) 共同，合

    synchronize 同步；symbiosis 共生现象 synergistic 协同作用的

techn(o)- 技术，工艺

    technology 技术（学），工艺学；technique 技术

therm(o)- 热

    thermistor 热敏电阻；thermometer 温度计

-tion (-ation，-ition，-sion) 构成名词

    instrumentation 仪表化；trypsinization 胰蛋白酶消化作用；adhesion 粘着；

competition 竞争

trans- 横穿，通过，转移

    transformation 转化；transcribe 转录；transposen 转位子

tri- 三，三次，三级

    triplet 三联体；triangle 三角形

ultra- 超，极端，过分

    ultrasonic 超声波；ultracentrifugation 超离心

un- 不，相反，除去

    unfold 展开

under- 下面，低于，不足

    undergraduate 大学本科生；underpin 加固……的基础

uni- 单，一，同一

    uninucleate 单核的；unique 独一无二的

up- 向上，在上

    upstream 上游；upright 直立的

-wise 接名词或形容词后构成副词

    batchwise 分批地；likewise 同样地

附录 2 常用化学、化工、生物前缀、后缀和构词成分

aceto- 乙酰
    acetolactate 乙酰乳酸
    acetyl 乙酰（基）
    acetyl phosphate 乙酰磷酸
acyl- 酰基
    acyltransferase 转酰基酶
aden(o)- 腺
    adenovirus 腺病毒
aer(o)- 空气的
    aerobic 需氧的；aeration 通气
agro- 土壤；农业
    agrochemical 农用化学品；agronomical 农艺学的
-aldehyde 醛
    glutaraldehyde 戊二醛
amidino- 脒基
    amidinotransferase 转脒基酶
-amine 胺
    methylamine 甲胺
amino- 氨基
    aminoacylase 氨基酰化酶
amylo- 淀粉的
    amyloglucosidase 淀粉葡萄糖苷酶
-ane 烷
    methane 甲烷
-ase 酶
    urease 脲酶
-ate 盐，酯；表示涉及动作的对象、产物
    sulphate 硫酸盐；glycerate 甘油酸酯（盐）
    eluate 洗脱液；dialyzate 透析液
bio- 生物的
    biology 生物学；bioreactor 生物反应器
bromo- 溴的
    5-bromouracil 5-溴尿嘧啶
carb(o)- 碳的
    carbodiimide 碳二亚胺；carbohydrate 碳水化合物

carboxy(l) 羧基
    carboxy methylcellulose 羧甲基纤维素
carcin(o)- 癌
    carcinogen 致癌物
cardio- 心脏
    cardiotonic 强心的
chlor(o) 氯；绿
    chloramphenicol 氯霉素；chloroplast 叶绿体
chrom (o) - (chromat (o) -) 颜色
    chromatid 染色单体；chromosome 染色体
    chromatography 色谱法
-cide 杀，杀灭剂
    amoebicide 抗阿米巴药
-cyte 细胞
    leucocyte 白细胞
cyto- 细胞
    cytochrome 细胞色素；cytomegalovirus 巨细胞病毒
deoxy- 脱氧
    deoxycytosine 脱氧胞嘧啶
electr(o)- 电
    electrodialysis 电渗析
end(o)- 内
    endergonic 吸能的；endospore 内生孢子
enol 烯醇
    phosphoenolpyruvate 磷酸烯醇丙酮酸
-ene 烯
    ethylene 乙烯
enter(o)- 肠
    enterobacteria 肠细菌
epi- 表；变化
    epichlorohydrin 表氯醇；epimerase 差向异构酶
erythr(o)- 红，赤
    erythrose 赤藓糖；erythromycin 红霉素
    erythrocyte 红细胞
eu- 真正

eukaryote　真核生物

ferri-　高铁

　　ferricytochrome　高铁细胞色素

ferro-　亚铁

　　ferrocytochrome　亚铁细胞色素

formyl-　甲酰

　　formyltetrahydrofolate　甲酰四氢叶酸

-gen (-genic, -genous 形容词) 原，产生

　　glycogen　糖原；carcinogen　致癌物；
　　carcinogenic　致癌的；exogenous　外源的

glyc(o)-　糖

　　glycoprotein　糖蛋白

hem(o,a)-,haem(o,a)-,haemat(o)-　血的

　　hemoglobin　血红蛋白；haemagglutinin　血凝
　　素；haem　血红素

hepat(o)-　肝的

　　hepatitis　肝炎

hydroxy(l)-　羟基

　　hydroxyapatite　羟磷灰石；hydroxylase　羟化
　　酶

hypo-　低，(过) 少

　　sodium hypochlorite　次氯酸钠

-ic anhydride　酸酐

　　maleic anhydride　马来酐

-ide (构成名词) 化合物

　　sodium chloride　氯化钠

-imine　亚胺

　　ethyleneimine　哌嗪

imino-　亚胺基

　　iminodiacetic acid　亚胺基二乙酸

immuno-　免疫

　　immunogenic　致免疫的；immunoassay　免疫
　　分析

iso-　同，等，异

　　isomer　同分异构体；isomerase　异构酶

-itis　炎，发炎

　　hepatitis　肝炎；encephalitis　脑炎

kary(o)-　核，细胞核

　　karyology　胞核学

keto-　酮基

　　ketohexulose　酮己酮糖

leuco-　白，无色

　　leucocyte　白细胞

-lactone　内酯

β-propiolactone　β-丙醇酸内酯

lipo-　脂

　　lipoprotein　脂蛋白；lipoxygenase　脂氧合酶

lympho-　淋巴

　　lymphocyte　淋巴细胞

-lysis　分解作用，过程

　　glycolysis　糖醇解作用；hydrolysis　水解作
　　用；analysis　分析

-lytic (形容词，分解的)，-lyze (-lise) (动词，
　　分解)，-lysate (名词，分解液) hydrolytic 水解的；

hydrolyze　水解；hydro-lysate　水解液

megal(o)-　巨大

　　cytomegalovirus　巨细胞病毒

mercapto-　巯基

　　β-mercaptoethylamine　β-巯基乙胺

meso-　内消旋；中 (间)

　　meso inositol　内消旋肌醇；mesophilic　嗜温
　　的

meth-　甲基

　　methacrylate　甲基丙烯酸酯

methyl　甲基

　　methyltroph　甲基营养菌

-mycete　霉菌

　　streptomycete　链霉菌

-mycin　霉素，菌素

　　mitomycin　丝裂霉素；actinomycin　放线菌素

myco-　真菌

　　mycolytic　溶真菌的；mycotoxin　真菌毒素

nitro-　硝基

　　nitrofuran　硝基呋喃

nucle(o)-　核

　　nucleoside　核苷；nucleophilic　亲核的

-oid　类似物

　　carotenoid　类胡萝卜素；steroid　类固醇

-ol　醇

　　butanol　丁醇；inositol　肌醇

oligo-　寡

　　oligosaccharide　寡糖，低聚糖

-oma　瘤

　　myeloma　骨髓瘤；hybridoma　杂交瘤

onco-　肿瘤

　　oncogene　致癌基因

-one　酮

　　phenoxazinone　吩噁嗪酮

-ose 糖
  glucose 葡萄糖；ribose 核糖
-oside 糖苷
  galactoside 半乳糖苷；cardiac glycoside 强心苷
oxalo- 草酰，乙二酸-酰基
  oxalo acetate 草酰乙酸
oxy- 氧；羟基
  deoxyguanosine 脱氧鸟苷；oxytetracycline 土霉素
  oxyproline 羟脯氨酸
path(o)- 病
  pathogen 病原菌
peri- 周，周围
  perimeter 周长；periplasmic space 周质间隙
per- 过
  peroxisome 过氧化质体
phenyl 苯基
  phenylalanine 苯丙氨酸
-phoresis 移动
  electrophoresis 电泳
phospho- 磷酸基
  phosphofructokinase 磷酸果糖激酶
phosphoryl- 磷酰基
  phosphorylation 磷酸化作用
plasm(o)- 原生质，血浆
  plasmolemma 质膜
-plasm 血浆，原生质
  protoplasm 原生质
-plast 体，粒，团
  chloroplast 叶绿体；protoplast 原生质体
poly- 多，聚
  polysaccharide 多糖
pro- 原，前

prokaryote 原核生物；prostate 前列腺
pseud(o)- 假，拟
  pseudoplastic 假塑性的
pyro- 焦
  pyrophosphorylase 焦磷酸化酶
quasi- 类似，准
  quasi-homogeneous 准均匀的
radio- 辐射，放射
  autoradiography 放射自显影
rib(o)- 核糖
  ribosome 核糖体
-sis 构成名词，表示作用，过程
  mutagenesis 诱变作用；mitosis 有丝分裂；meiosis 减数分裂
-some 体
  chromosome 染色体；ribosome 核糖体
-stat 稳定装置
  chemostat 恒化器
thi(o)- 硫
  thiamine 硫胺素
thym(o)- 胸腺
  thymosin 胸腺素
toti- 全，全部，整个
  totipotency 全能性
-troph ……营养生物，……营养型(-trophic 构成形容词)
  methanotroph 甲烷营养菌；autotroph 自养生物；autotrophic 自养的
uro- 尿
  urokinase 尿激酶
vinyl 乙烯基
  polyvinylchloride 聚氯乙烯

附录3 语法、句型、词和词组的用法索引

附录 4　总词汇表

amylase n. 淀粉酶 104/17

amyloglucosidase n. 淀粉葡萄糖苷酶 144/25

amytal n. 阿米妥 32/22

an array of 大量 65/29

anabolic a. 合成代谢的 1/19

anaerobic a. 厌氧的 16/24

analgesic a. 止痛的 248/8

anchorage-independent cell 非贴壁依赖性细胞
232/15

ancillary a. 附属的，辅助的 112/37，235/3

anhydride n. 酐 17/17

annealing n. 退火 83/8

annulus n. 环隙 204/7

anthraquinone n. 蒽醌 258/3

antibiotic n. 抗生素 1/14

anticholinergic a.（或 n.）抗胆碱能的（药物）
248/13

antifertility a. 抗生育的 248/29

antigenity n. 抗原性 148/25

antihypertensive a.（或 n.）抗高血压的（药
物） 248/13

anti-inflammatory a.（或 n.）消炎的（药物） 248/
26

antileukaemic a.（或 n.）抗白血病的（药物） 248/
13

antimalarial a. 抗疟疾的 248/8

antimutator gene n. 减变基因 70/12

antimycin n. 抗霉素 32/23

antiquity n. 古代 128/20

antisera n. 抗血清 78/14

apart from 除……之外 38/28

apolar a. 非极性的 182/18

appraise vt. 评价 257/21

appreciate vt. 意识到 1/30

arachnid n. 蛛形纲动物 259/30

arginine n. 精氨酸 39/18

aroma n. 香味 258/25

array n. 大量，（排列整齐的）一批 245/3

arrhythmic a. 心率不齐的 257/30

artefact n. 赝物 66/8

as opposed to 与……不同；与……相反 18/17

ascites fluid 腹水 228/9

Ascomycetes n. 子囊菌纲 72/2

asparaginase n. 天冬酰氨酶 5/15，104/18

aspartase n. 天（门）冬氨酸酶 156/25

aspartate n. 天（门）冬氨酸盐（酯） 23/36

aspect ratio 高径比 113/19

assimilate n. 同化 23/39

assortement n. 分组 71/5

asymmetric membrane 不对称膜 179/28

atomize vt. 雾化 188/11

atropine n. 阿托品，颠茄碱 248/20

Attar of roses 玫瑰油 245/13

attemporator n. 温度调节器 114/6

autonomous a. 自发的，自主的 82/1

autoradiography n. 放射自显影 89/2

autotrophic a. 自养的 250/20

auxin n. 植物生长素，植物激素 252/40

Babylonian n. 巴比伦人 2/24

back-up n. 候补者 235/38

bacteria n. 细菌 1/6

baffle n. 挡板 115/11

baker's yeast 面包酵母 3/23

baking n. 烘，烤（面包） 2/22

balanced growth 平衡生长 108/15

ball mill 球磨机 175/30

barley n. 大麦 118/31

Basidiomycetes n. 担子菌纲 71/2

be subject to 应服从的；受制于……的 19/2，
120/3

beneficiation n. 选矿，富集 105/9

benzoquinone n. 苯醌 258/26

beverage n. 饮料 104/3

bile salt 胆汁盐 159/2

Bingham plastic 平汉塑性流体 202/28

biomass n. 生物体，菌体 1/11

blend n. 混合物 245/14

blunt end 钝端，平头 84/5

bn. n. 十亿 1/30

bob n. 浮子 204/4

borosilicate n. 硼硅玻璃 233/18

boryl n. 硼基 186/25

bowl n. 转筒 179/16

breeding n. 育种 65/6

breeding system 繁殖系统 71/18

brewing n. 酿酒 2/22

bromelain n. 菠萝蛋白酶 143/18

bromouracil n. 溴尿嘧啶 70/2

mosaic   n. 花斑病   73/16

mould   n. 霉菌   18/23

mounting   n. 座架   181/25

move on   继续前进   249/23

much the same   几乎相同的   250/40

mumps   n. （用作单或复）流行性腮腺炎   228/22

mushroom   n. 蘑菇   2/33

mutagen   n. 诱变剂   50/20

mutagenesis   n. 诱变作用，引起诱变   65/6

mutant   n. 突变体   50/17

mutase   n. 变位酶   36/13

mutation   n. 突变   4/28

mutator gene   增变基因   70/11

mutator strain   增变菌株   70/13

mycolytic   a. 溶真菌的   75/20

mycoplasma   n. 支原体   232/5

mycorrhizal   a. 菌根的   105/33

mycotoxin   n. 真菌毒素   148/24

myeloma   n. 骨髓瘤   78/19

NAD$^+$ (=nicotinamide adenine dinucleotide)
烟酰胺腺嘌呤二核苷酸；辅酶 I   19/5

NADH   还原型烟酰胺腺嘌呤二核苷酸；还原型
辅酶 I   19/5

NADP$^+$ (= nicotinamide adenine dinucleotide
phosphate)   烟酰胺腺嘌呤二核苷酸磷酸；辅
酶 II   19/33

NADPH   还原型烟酰胺腺嘌呤二核苷酸磷酸；
还原型辅酶 II   19/33

naphthoquinone   n. 萘醌   258/21

narcotic   n. 麻醉药，致幻毒品   257/37

neural   a. 神经的   228/5

neurotoxin   n. 神经毒素   259/29

Newcastle disease   新城病（指鸡的病毒性肺炎
及脑脊髓炎）在英国城市 Newcastle upon Type
首次发现。   228/26

Newtonian fluid   牛顿流体   202/27

Nichrome   n. 镍铬合金（原为商标名）   214/28

nicotine   n. 烟碱，尼古丁   258/11

nicotinic acid   烟酸，尼克酸   251/36

nitrofuran   n. 硝基呋喃   70/3

nitrogen mustard   氮介子气   70/3

none the less   还是，仍然   246/22

notorious   a. 著名的   246/30

NTP (normal temperature and pressure)   标准
温度和压力（0℃和 101.325kPa）   199/35

nucleic acid   核酸   16/13

nucleotide   n. 核苷酸   39/2

nystatin   n. 制霉菌素   250/7

oat flour   燕麦粉   118/32

objectionable   a. 令人不愉快的   65/18

obligatory   a. 必要的   179/3, 250/28

obscure   vt. 使变暗，遮蔽   90/39

obsolete   a. 废弃的   205/33

occlusion   n. 吸留，包藏   155/17

oestrogenic   a. 雌激素的   149/2

offering   n. 上市的股票   91/14

off-line   离线   120/33

offset   n. 残留误差   197/23

offspring   n. 后代   70/20

oleaginous   a. 含油的，油质的   238/7

oncogene   n. 致癌基因   232/17

on-line   在线   120/33

onset   n. 开始   196/10

ontjom   n. 发酵花生饼   128/9

onwards   adv. 向前   253/10

open loop control   开环控制   198/19

operator gene   操纵基因   42/4

operon   n. 操纵子   42/12

opiate   n. 鸦片制剂，麻醉剂，镇静剂   258/25

opium poppy   罂粟   248/9

osmotic shock   渗透压冲击   176/16

ostensibly   adv. 表面上地   231/27

out of all proportion to   与……相较大得不相称
2/41

out of favour   不受欢迎   217/16

outbreeding   n. 远交，远系繁殖   71/18

outgrowth   n. 长出物   67/15

override   vt. 使无效   74/12

overshooting   n. 过调节   199/21

overt   a. 明显的   72/10

overview   n. 简明概述（综述）   5/27，229/24

oxaloacetate   n. 草酰乙酸   23/36

oxalosuccinate   n. 草酰琥珀酸盐（酯）   23/23

oxidant   n. 氧化剂   24/2

oxidative phosphorylation   氧化磷酸化   24/4

oxidoreductase   n. 氧化还原酶   33/20

oxoglutarate   n. 酮戊二酸   23/33

oxygen transfer coefficient   氧传递系数   116/8

oxygenase　n. 氧合酶　28/6

oxytetracycline　n. 土霉素　104/16

painkiller　n. 止痛药　257/35

palindromic sequence　回文序列　84/30

pancreatic　a. 胰的　144/1

pantothenate　n. 泛酸　22/38

papain　n. 木瓜蛋白酶　143/18

parallel-flow extraction　顺流萃取　177/29

paramagnetic　a. 顺磁的　121/36，213/8

parasexual cycle　准性循环　67/15

parasitic　a. 寄生虫的　78/39

paucity　n. 量少　157/33

pectate　n. 果胶酸盐　151/16

pectinase　n. 果胶酶　104/18

penicillin acylase　青霉素酰化酶　144/43

penicillin amidase　青霉素酰化酶　156/24

penicillinase　n. 青霉素酶　144/45

pentose　n. 戊糖　19/31

per annum（拉）　adv. 每年　228/28

per se　（拉丁文）本身　151/29，236/16

percolate　v. 渗滤　160/29，234/30

perforate　vt. 穿孔　174/6

perfume　n. 香水　104/22，245/12

perfumery　n. 香料（总称）　105/7

perfumery　n. 香料制造厂　259/15

periwinkle　n. 长春花　257/27

peroxisome　n. 过氧化物酶体　40/2

perpetuate　vt. 使永久存在　24/8

pest　n. 有害的动、植物　245/30

pesticide　n. 杀虫剂　7/7

pharmacology　n. 药理学　248/14

pharmamedia　n. 药用培养基　118/33

phenotype　n. 表型　68/4

phenotypic　a. 表型的　68/4

phenoxozinone　n. 吩噁嗪酮　147/26

phenyl glycine　苯基甘氨酸　154/5

phenylalanine　苯丙氨酸　39/6，185/30

phosphodiesterase　n. 磷酸二酯酶　44/4

phosphoenolpyruvate　n. 磷酸烯醇丙酮酸　19/22

phosphofructokinase　n. 磷酸果糖激酶　19/27

phosphogluconate dehydrogenase　磷酸葡糖酸脱氢酶　20/36

phosphoglycerate kinase　磷酸甘油酸激酶　19/29

phosphoglycerol kinase　磷酸甘油激酶　33/3

phosphoglyceromutase　n. 磷酸甘油酸变位酶　19/29

phosphoketolase　n. 磷酸酮醇酶　21/38

phosphoroclastic split　磷酸裂解反应　36/26

phosphorylation　n. 磷酸化作用　17/28

pickle　n. 腌菜　104/4

pilocarpine　n. 毛果芸香碱（一种眼科缩瞳药）　248/36

plantation　n. 种植园　245/21

plaque　n. 噬菌斑，空斑　81/8

plasma cell　浆细胞　78/10

plasmalemma　n. 质膜，细胞膜　252/26

plasminogen activator　血纤维蛋白溶酶原激活素　229/23

plot　n. 图表　215/38

pneumatic　a. 气体的，气动的　120/21，187/25

pneumatic conveyor dryer　气流干燥机　187/34

pneumatically　adv. 气动地　205/3

polarographic　a. 极谱（法）的　206/33

polarographic probe　极谱型探头　121/30

polio virus　脊髓灰质炎病毒　228/4

polyacrylamide　n. 聚丙烯酰胺　151/6

polycarbonate　n. 聚碳酸酯　234/8

polyketide　n. 聚酮化合物　39/14

polyoma　n. 多瘤　73/15

polysaccharide　n. 多糖　3/25

polystyrene　n. 聚苯乙烯　234/8

polyvinylchloride　n. 聚氯乙烯　151/14

porosity　n. 空隙度　182/9

porphyrin　n. 卟啉　23/35

positive effector　n. 正效应物　24/20

post-transcriptional modification　转录后修饰作用　44/26

potent　a. 有力的　44/6

potentiate　vt. 使加强效力　238/5

potentiometric　a. 测量电压的　211/6

potion　n. 药水　248/5

poultry　n.（总称）家禽　228/26

precedent　n. 先例　256/1

preclude　n. 防止　77/25

precursor　n. 前体　19/7

predator　n. 捕食动物　229/18

premature　a. 过早的　206/39

premise　n. 前提　8/1

附录5 主要参考书目

1 周志培，冯文池编著．英汉语比较与科技翻译．上海：华东理工大学出版社，1995

2 张道真编著．实用英语语法．第二次修订本．北京：商务印书馆，1979

3 戴炜华，陈文雄编著．科技英语的特点和应用．上海：上海外语教育出版社，1984

4 孙婉嬿编著．科技英语写作语型．北京：中国标准出版社，1992

5 天津大学化工、精仪系外语教研组编．科技英语阅读手册．北京：石油化学工业出版社，1975

6 科技英语问题解答，北京：商务印书馆，1979

7 雷馨编．英语分类句型．北京：商务印书馆，1979

8 苏志尧，莫惠敏主编．科技英语构词成分词典．广州：华南理工大学出版社，1993

9 Herbert，A. J.，The Structure of Technical English，Longmans，1965

10 Flynn，J. and Glaser，J.，Writer's Handbook，Macmillan Publishing company，1984

11 Murphy，M. J.，Basic Writing in English for Science & Technology，Graham Brash (Pte) Ltd.，Singapore. 1983

12 The ACS Style Guide，A Manual for Authors and Editors，Dodd，J. S. (ed.)，American chemical Society. Washington，DC，1986

13 Crews，F.，The Random House Handbook，Sixth edition，McGraw-Hill，1992

14 Marius，R. and Wiener，H. S.，The McGraw-Hill College Handbook，McGraw-Hill，1985

15 陆谷孙主编．英汉大辞典．上海：上海译文出版社，1993

16 牛津现代高级英汉双解词典．第三版．伦敦：牛津大学出版社，1984

17 饶宗颐．朗文当代英汉双解词典．第一版．北京：现代出版社，1988

18 The American Heritage Dictionary of the English Language，Morris，W. (ed.)，Houghton Mifflin Company，Boston，1980

19 Webster's New Collegiate Dictionary，G. & C. Merriam Company，Springfield，Massachusetts，U. S. A. 1981

20 Reader's Digest Universal Dictionary，1988

21 英汉生物学词汇．第二版．北京：科学出版社，1997

22 金冬雁 黎孟枫编订．英汉分子生物学与生物工程词汇．北京：科学出版社，1996

23 王二力等编．英汉生物工程词典．上海：上海科学技术文献出版社，1993

24 英汉生物化学词典．北京：科学出版社，1983

25 英汉医学辞典．上海：上海科学技术出版社，1984

26 王祖农主编．微生物学词典．北京：科学出版社，1990

27 英汉化学化工词汇．第三版．北京：科学出版社，1982

28 日英汉化学化工词汇．北京：化学工业出版社，1985

29 The Language of Biotechnology，A Dictionary of Terms，Second edition，Walker，J. M. and Cox. M. American Chemical Society，Washington，DC，1995

30 Dictionary of Microbiology and Moleculor Biology，Second edition，Singleton，P. and Sainsbury，D. John Wiley & Sons，1987

31 Dictionary of Biochemistry and Molecular Biology，Second edition，Stenesh，J.，John Wiley & Sons，1989

32 The Filamentous Fungi，vol. 4，Smith，J，E. et al (eds.)，London，Arnold，1983

33 Fiechter，A.，Batch and Continual Culture of Microbial Plant and Animal Cells. In：Biotechnology，vol. 1，Rehm H. -J. and Reed G. (eds.) Microbial Fundamentals，p. 453～503. Weiheim，Chemie，1981

内 容 提 要

《生物工程/生物技术 专业英语》是根据《大学英语专业阅读阶段教学基本要求（试行）》而编写的，本书可供理工科院校生物工程专业、生物技术专业及相关专业学生使用，也可作为生物工程技术人员学习英语或其他科技人员了解生物工程的入门参考书。

本书共分 9 章，约 10 万词，内容选自两本著名的生物工程科普书，系统性强，覆盖生物工程的主要领域，包括：微生物生长和代谢的生物化学，诱变育种，基因重组，发酵，酶和固定化细胞技术，产品回收，检测仪表，动、植物细胞培养等。

本书力求将英语与专业紧密结合，通过专业阅读提高英语基础及其应用能力。本书的特色在于：1. 对专业内容给出科普性质的注释以帮助阅读理解；2. 结合课文给出注释或以习题形式介绍科技英语中常用的或易混淆的语法、词与词组的用法、句型等；3. 附有详尽的词汇表并注有音标；4. 习题量多，包括释义、辨义、造句、翻译和写作等，翻译习题取自课文，写作习题取自专业文献，重点在专业论文或摘要的常用表示方法。